GW01513953

"*Reconceptualising the Learning Crisis in Africa* is essential reading for anyone involved in educational policy and basic education. It had me nodding in agreement from start to finish. Africa is suffering from a learning crisis and educational deficit, so argue many experts, not least the World Bank. This is where Kwame Akyeampong and Sean Higgins enter the stage in this insightful and provocative book that offers an alternative to the technocratic models that, quite frankly, have not worked. The authors challenge the discourse of crisis that undergirds the analyses of the failures in the provision of education, and the solutions offered to deal with them. Learning is truncated from cultural realities and treated as a problem requiring technical solutions. Using successful examples of Accelerated Learning Programmes (ALPs) in Ghana, Liberia, and Ethiopia, countries where key barriers to education such as extreme poverty, conflict and inter-generational marginalization are pressing, they show how engaging with learning environments and including families and communities in learning strategies creates enjoyable learning experiences, builds confidence and leads to sustainable successful learning outcomes. This is not a work of fiction, yet I could not put it down as it engendered hope that there are tried and tested models that enhance learning for the marginalised not as a cliché, but a reality".
Akosua Adomako Ampofo, *Professor of African and Gender Studies, Institute of African Studies, University of Ghana and recent president of the African Studies Association, Africa*

"*Reconceptualising the Learning Crisis in Africa* offers a bold and timely reimagining of education on the continent. Moving beyond narrow metrics and deficit narratives, the authors advocate for approaches that center African values, community agency, and local knowledge. Through compelling case studies, this book demonstrates how culturally relevant education can unlock the potential of learners and reshape policies. An essential read for anyone committed to equitable and sustainable educational reform in Africa".
George Kronnisanyon Werner, *a highly experienced public sector leader, previously Minister for Education in Liberia who serves on the Expert Resource Group at the Harvard Ministerial Leadership Forum*

"This outstanding book offers a much-needed critique of the prevailing learning crisis discourse and its deficit framings of African learners and teachers. Akyeampong and Higgins show how pedagogical interventions driven by external agendas have ignored the lived realities and true capacities of teachers, and the centrality of issues such as language of instruction. In contrast, selected accelerated learning programmes, presented as contemporary case studies here, have drawn on some learner-centred traditions while generating more situated, contextualised and holistic practices.

The book is rich in theory, including an in-depth account of *Ubuntu* as a framing for pedagogy. It thus celebrates children's agentic roles not only in their own lives and learning but in their interdependent communities".

Michele Schweisfurth, *Professor of Comparative and International Education, University of Glasgow, UK*

"In their path-breaking work entitled *Reconceptualising the Learning Crisis in Africa: Multi-dimensional Pedagogies of Accelerated Learning Programmes,* Kwame Akyeampong and Sean Higgins provide a window on the importance of learning and quality of education when these issues are at the top of the UN agenda. These are not only policy matters of governments and agencies, but also issues that affect nearly all people at the ground level in Africa. How are children going to succeed in life, in their dreams and over the generations to come? The authors initially set the stage with an overview of African education, and its problems and opportunities over recent decades since Independence. They build on the unique concept of *Ubuntu,* based on the African notion of interdependence. Further, based on many years of applied research, the authors describe lessons from multiple Accelerated Learning Programmes that are aimed at improving rural African children's learning through appropriate pedagogies, better teacher training and, especially, the infusing of cultural values into local educational systems. In this volume, we find a refreshing and promising perspective toward re-envisioning of African education policy that replaces older post-colonial images of schools that fail with innovative effective pedagogical approaches to children's learning needs, and a much brighter future for all".

Daniel A. Wagner, *Professor of Education and UNESCO Chair in Learning and Literacy, University of Pennsylvania, USA*

"Kwame Akyeampong and Sean Higgins underscore the fundamental truth about the global learning crisis: Children everywhere are capable of learning remarkable amounts in a short period of time when they are met with rich, immersive, holistic learning pedagogies. Accelerated learning done right, unlocks their potential proving that the binding constraint is not the child but the quality of the education they receive. Such education programs are not merely a means to plug gaps left by mainstream systems. Done right, they can be so much more. These programs can serve as a true foundry for forging uniquely African pedagogical approaches, capable of delivering transformative learning not just to children at the margins, but also those in the mainstream. In this book, the authors do the vital work of centring accelerated learning programs as community-based crucibles of educational innovation".

Caitlin Baron, *CEO of the Luminos Fund, an international education non-profit organisation dedicated to providing a second chance education for out-of-school children*

Reconceptualising the Learning Crisis in Africa

This book offers a powerful, post-colonial rejection of the so-called global 'learning crisis' that depends upon deficit models of the experiences, knowledges, identities and relationships of African children, eroding their agency and dignity and undermining their learning opportunities and potential.

Three case studies of three accelerated learning programmes (ALPs) for out-of-school and lower-achieving children in Ethiopia, Liberia and Ghana illustrate multi-dimensional models that re-envision the purposes and pedagogies of basic education, reconnect with the lived experiences of African children and teachers and promote the role of communities in improving children's learning. Drawing on diverse social theory, the chapters reveal the use of children's funds of identity and knowledge, a material engagement with their natural environment, and highlight the transformative use of local languages. This book ultimately proves that a holistic approach to learning, based on the relational and community-rooted African philosophy of *Ubuntu*, produces vital personal and academic benefits for African children.

This book will be of great interest to academics, researchers and postgraduate students in the fields of international and comparative education, postcolonial studies, African education, education policy and transformative pedagogy. It will also appeal to development strategists and NGOs working with the Education for All agenda.

Kwame Akyeampong is Professor of International Education and Development at the Open University's Centre for the Study of Global Development (CSGD), UK.

Sean Higgins is Lecturer in Education and International Development, Institute of Education, University College London.

Education, Poverty and International Development Series
Series Editors Madeleine Arnot
Faculty of Education, University of Cambridge, UK

This series of research-based monographs and edited collections which was set up in collaboration with the late Professor Christopher Colclough contributes to global debates about how to achieve education for all. A major set of questions faced by national governments and education providers concerns how the contributions made by education to reducing global poverty, encouraging greater social stability and equity, and ensuring the development of individual capability and wellbeing can be strengthened. Focusing on the contributions that research can make to these global agendas, this series aims to provide new knowledge and new perspectives on the relationships between education, poverty and international development. It offers alternative theoretical and methodological frameworks for the study of developing-country education systems, in the context of national cultures and ambitious global agendas. It aims to identify the key policy challenges associated with addressing social inequalities, uneven social and economic development, and the opportunities to promote democratic and effective educational change in the name of social justice.

The series brings together researchers from the fields of anthropology, economics, development studies, educational studies, politics, international relations and sociology. It includes work by some of the most distinguished writers in the fields of education and development, along with new authors working on important empirical projects. The series contributes significant insights on the linkages between education, the economy, communities, and society, based on interdisciplinary, international and national studies.

Selected volumes include critical syntheses of existing research and policy, work using innovative research methodologies, and in-depth evaluations of major policy developments. Some studies will address topics relevant to poverty alleviation, national and international policy-making and aid, while others will be anthropological or sociological investigations of how education functions within local communities, for households living in poverty or for particular socially marginalised groups. The authors explore a diverse range of themes from the challenges associated with providing quality teacher, professional and entrepreneurial education, to those associated with promoting gender equality, reducing gender violence, understanding the impact of poverty on constructions of childhood, or assessing the impact of learner-centred school pedagogies. They offer sharp, critical studies that are intended to have a strategic influence on the thinking of academics, researchers and policy-makers.

Education, Poverty and Global Goals for Gender Equality
How People Make Policy Happen
Elaine Unterhalter and Amy North

Reforming Education and Challenging Inequalities in Southern Contexts
Research and Policy in International Development
Edited by Pauline Rose, Madeleine Arnot, Roger Jeffery, Nidhi Singal

Mothers and Schooling
Poverty, Gender and Educational Decision-making in Rural Kenya
Fibian Lukalo

The Politics of English Language Education and Social Inequality
Global Pressures, National Priorities and Schooling in India
Maya Kalyanpur, Padmini Bhuyan Boruah, Sarina Chugani Molina and Sunaina Shenoy

Decolonising Education in Islamic West Africa
Secular Erasure, School Preference and Social Inequality
Anneke Newman

Reconceptualising the Learning Crisis in Africa
Multi-dimensional Pedagogies of Accelerated Learning Programmes
Kwame Akyeampong and Sean Higgins

Related Titles

Educational Research Practice in Southern Contexts
Recentring, Reframing and Reimagining Methodological Canons
Edited by Sharlene Swartz, Nidhi Singal and Madeleine Arnot

For more information on the series, please visit https://www.routledge.com/Education-Poverty-and-International-Development/book-series/EPID

Reconceptualising the Learning Crisis in Africa

Multi-dimensional Pedagogies of Accelerated Learning Programmes

Kwame Akyeampong and Sean Higgins

LONDON AND NEW YORK

First published 2025
by Routledge
4 Park Square, Milton Park, Abingdon, Oxon, OX14 4RN

and by Routledge
605 Third Avenue, New York, NY 10158

Routledge is an imprint of the Taylor & Francis Group, an informa business

© 2025 Kwame Akyeampong and Sean Higgins

The right of Kwame Akyeampong and Sean Higgins to be identified as authors of this work has been asserted in accordance with sections 77 and 78 of the Copyright, Designs and Patents Act 1988.

All rights reserved. No part of this book may be reprinted or reproduced or utilised in any form or by any electronic, mechanical, or other means, now known or hereafter invented, including photocopying and recording, or in any information storage or retrieval system, without permission in writing from the publishers.

Trademark notice: Product or corporate names may be trademarks or registered trademarks, and are used only for identification and explanation without intent to infringe.

British Library Cataloguing-in-Publication Data
A catalogue record for this book is available from the British Library

Library of Congress Cataloging-in-Publication Data
Names: Akyeampong, Kwame, author. | Higgins, Sean, 1960– author.
Title: Reconceptualising the learning crisis in Africa: multi-dimensional pedagogies of accelerated learning programmes / Kwame Akyeampong and Sean Higgins.
Other titles: Education, poverty, and international development series.
Description: New York: Routledge, 2025. |
Series: Education, poverty and international development series |
Includes bibliographical references and index. |
Identifiers: LCCN 2024058015 (print) | LCCN 2024058016 (ebook) | ISBN 9781032028477 (hardback) | ISBN 9781032028484 (paperback) | ISBN 9781003185482 (ebook)
Subjects: LCSH: Education—Africa, Sub-Saharan. | Education and state—Africa, Sub-Saharan. | Postcolonialism. | Crisis management. | LCGFT: Case studies.
Classification: LCC LA1501 .A53 2025 (print) | LCC LA1501 (ebook) | DDC 370.967—dc23/eng/20250204
LC record available at https://lccn.loc.gov/2024058015
LC ebook record available at https://lccn.loc.gov/2024058016

ISBN: 978-1-032-02847-7 (hbk)
ISBN: 978-1-032-02848-4 (pbk)
ISBN: 978-1-003-18548-2 (ebk)

DOI: 10.4324/9781003185482

Typeset in Galliard Pro
by codeMantra

For Kwame, to the memory of his father, Kofi Akyeampong who inspired him to love learning, and mother, Evelyn Brown Akyeampong for her sacrifices to support his pursuit of education.

For Sean, to the loving memory of his mother, Brideen Deirdre Higgins and grandmother, Helen Winifred Towey, from whom he initially learnt a belief in the transformative power and potential of education, however challenging the circumstances.

Figure 0.1 In Ghana, Sankofa is a proverbial bird that stands for retrieving valuable indigenous or local knowledge from the past for the future.

Contents

Acknowledgements — xiv
List of Abbreviations — xvi
List of Figures — xvii
List of Tables — xviii
List of Images — xix
List of Permissions — xxi

Prologue: A Message from the Authors — 1

1 The Global 'Learning Crisis': Analysis, Critique and Re-envisioning — 4
  Our Critique of the 'Learning Crisis' Narrative 5
  Re-envisioning the 'Learning Crisis' through Accelerated Learning Programmes (ALPs) 11
  Illuminating ALPs through Social Theory 14
  Re-envisioning the 'Learning Crisis' through Diverse Evidence 17
  The Organisation of Chapters 19

PART I
Rethinking the Learning Challenge in Sub-Saharan Africa — 29

2 The Production of the 'Poor Child' as Deficit — 31
  Making the Connection: Poverty Alleviation and Educational Provision 32
  Historicising Deficit Framings of the 'Poor Child' 40
  The Contemporary Production of a Decontextualised 'Poor Child' 47
  Redemptive Interventions and the Loss/Absence of Children's Agency 51
  The Implications for Rethinking the 'Learning Crisis' 52

3 Language, Learning and Children's Identities — 62
The Language of Instruction in the 'Learning Crisis' 62
Silences in Global Educational Policy 65
Language of Instruction Policies and Teachers' Pedagogical Choices 68
Children's negative experiences of learning 70
Lessons for the 'Learning Crisis' 73

4 The Deficit Characterisation of the African Teacher — 80
Oral Culture and Learner-centred Instruction in the African Context 84
Imperfect Measurements and Symbols of Teaching Quality 85
De-professionalisation through Structured Lesson Plans (SLPs) 88
The Limits of Accountability Regimes and Practices 90
Deficit Framings of Teachers and Restrictions on Teacher Education Reforms 91
Conclusion 95

5 Beyond Deficit Framings: A Multi-dimensional Approach — 99
A Multi-dimensional Framing of Poverty and Children's Agency 99
Teachers as Multi-dimensional Agents 118
Reframing the 'Learning Crisis' 120

PART II
What Accelerated Learning Programmes Teach Us — 131

6 Recognising Children's Funds of Knowledge in Complementary Basic Education (CBE), Northern Ghana — 133
Funds of Knowledge and Funds of Identity 134
Complementary Basic Education in Ghana in Northern Ghana 137
Data Gathering: A Funds of Knowledge Approach 140
The Embedded Funds of Knowledge in CBE 142
Children's Funds of Identity 157
Lessons for the 'Learning Crisis' 161

7 Improving Learning Outcomes to Enable Transition: Speed Schools in Ethiopia — 169
A Post-humanist Approach to Children's Learning 170

Speed Schools in Ethiopia 172
Using Post-humanism to Understand Children's Experiences
  of Learning in Speed Schools 173
Learning to Teach as a Speed School Teacher 185
Improving Learning Outcomes and Transition 188
Lessons for the 'Learning Crisis' 200

8 Engaging Parents, Extended Families and Communities:
   Second Chance Programmes in Conflict-affected Liberia   205
   Rethinking Community Engagement: Vulnerability and
     Resistance 206
   Conflict, Education and 'Liberal Peace Building' in
     Liberia 210
   The Second Chance Programme and Accelerated Learning
     in Liberia 214
   Listening to the Experiences of Parental Engagement Groups
     (PEGs) 216
   Vulnerability and Resistance in PEGs 217
   Lessons for the 'Learning Crisis' 232

9 Accelerated Learning and the Power of African Values   242
   Centring Ubuntu in Education and Development 242
   Ubuntu, Learning and the Dignity of the African Child 245
   The Implications for Pedagogical Practices 247
   Conclusions: Accelerated Learning Programmes and
     Ubuntu 255

10 Beyond the 'Learning Crisis': The Implications for Policy
   to Improve Basic Education in Sub-Saharan Africa   261
   Towards an Afrocentric Policy Response 262
   A Renewed Postcolonial Agenda for EFA 266

Index   271

Acknowledgements

We want to thank all those colleagues and friends who have contributed to the journey of reflection, solidarity and thinking that has resulted in this book. But first, our deepest appreciation to Madeleine Arnot in the Faculty of Education at the University of Cambridge who, as Series Editor, offered exceptional support and guidance, engaging carefully and critically with our arguments in multiple readings and re-readings of the manuscript and maintaining faith in us.

We would also like to thank all those involved in the process of textual preparation, in particular, to Margaret Okole for her painstaking and scrupulous editing and also to Anna Nicolau and Drishya Yeo for careful work on references.

We have been inspired by conversations with colleagues at the Centre for International Education, University of Sussex whose commitment to the power of education to challenge social injustices has animated the book's concerns. We would like to thank especially Marcos Delprato, Ricardo Sabates, John Pryor, Jo Westbrook, Sarah Humphreys and Benjamin Zeitlyn who contributed to the studies in Ethiopia.

Similarly, our thanks to the diverse cohorts of students, including many from sub-Saharan Africa, who took the Masters in International Education and Development at the University of Sussex. Our discussions with them during lively seminar sessions on the failings of educational policy in the region were enormously generative, galvanising our commitment to rethinking and re-envisioning the status quo.

Writing this book has been a work of emotional as well as intellectual labour. Kwame would like to thank his wife, Betty, and children, Susan and Nana Kwame, for their constant encouragement to get the book done! Sean would like to recognise the love and support of his brothers, Patrick and Michael, both lifelong teachers, whose encouragement and understanding have been a source of great strength.

Thanks also to Tony Somerset and Keith Lewin for their kindness, encouragement and sharing of knowledges gleaned over many years working in the field of international education and development in diverse contexts.

Finally, this book draws on thinking and research emergent from our partnerships with local researchers in Ghana, Liberia and Ethiopia built over several years. In particular, we would like to extend our deep appreciation to Justice Agyei-Quartey, Latifa Seidu, Ernest Nniakyire, Fatawu Karandey Amidu, Abdul Wahid Alhassan, Vivien Delle, Josephine Tengan, David Haruna, Imoro Mubarak and Confidence Kpoh, Emmanuel Baapent and Elijah Yaw Danso in Ghana. Thanks also to Abba Karnga Jr, Alphanso Menyon, H. Kulu Blanyon, Clara P. Merchant, Joe Thomas and Joanna N. D. Welwean in Liberia and to Asmelash Haile Tsegay, Abinet Mensite, Rahel Abraham, Solomon Wolde, Teketel Adane, Tesfaye Semela, Selam Getachew and Yohannes Amado in Ethiopia.

Abbreviations

AEWG	Accelerated Education Working Group
ALP	Accelerated Learning Programme
BRICS	Brazil, Russia, India, China, South Africa
CBE	Complementary Basic Education
DFID	Department for International Development
EFA	Education for All
FCDO	The Foreign Commonwealth and Development Office
FGD	Focus Group Discussion
FLN	Foundational Literacy and Numeracy
GILLBT	Ghanaian Institute of Linguistics, Literacy and Bible Translation
INEE	Inter-Agency Network for Education in Emergencies
INGO	International Non-Government Organisation
MDGs	Millennium Development Goals
OECD	Organisation for Economic Co-Operation and Development
OOSC	Out-of-school child/children
PEG	Parental Engagement Group
SDGs	Sustainable Development Goals
SLP	Scripted Lesson Plan
SS	Speed School
SSA	Sub-Saharan Africa
TRC	Truth and Reconciliation Commission
UIS	UNESCO Institute of Statistics
UNDP	United Nations Development Programme
UNESCO	United Nations Educational, Scientific and Cultural Organization
UNICEF	United Nations International Children's Emergency Fund

Figures

0.1	In Ghana, Sankofa is a proverbial bird that stands for retrieving valuable indigenous or local knowledge from the past for the future	ix
2.1	Front Cover, Global Education Monitoring Report, UNESCO, 2010, Paris	48
5.1	A multi-dimensional framing of poverty (adapted from Lister, 2021, 10)	100
6.1	Children's funds of knowledge in CBE	162
7.1	Cumulative change in score for literacy test	190
7.2	Cumulative change in score for numeracy test	192
7.3	Repetition by wealth for Speed School students	193
7.4	Learning scores distributions based on IRT (2PL)	194
7.5	In attendance performance: Terciles of learning score distributions by school type for those currently attending	197
7.6	Drop out performance - Terciles learning score distributions by school type for those who had dropout	198

Tables

6.1	Supply and demand factors affecting educational provision and enrolment in Northern Ghana	139
6.2	Data gathering on the use of funds of knowledge in CBE provision	140
6.3	Facilitators' use of the 'funds of knowledge' approach	152
6.4	How CBE classes connect with life outside the classroom	158
7.1	Descriptive statistics for children's school history	189
7.2	Primary completion by wealth and gender	193
7.3	Percentage of correct answers	196
7.4	Percentage of correct answers by primary completion	196
7.5	OLS estimates for percentage of correct answers	199

Images

6.1	Productive trees	145
6.2	Fishing	146
6.3	Domestic animals	147
6.4	Grandfather	148
6.5	Cleaning up	149
6.6	Numeracy lesson using local pebbles	153
6.7	Facilitator taking CBE children around their local environment as part of a lesson on health and sanitation	155
6.8	Facilitator pointing out cow dung and explaining the dangers of spreading disease through flies	156
7.1	A Speed School classroom with walls and roof space covered with learning materials made with coloured paper, including the alphabet in English and Amharic	174
7.2	Children arranging coloured pebbles for their number work	175
7.3	Wall showing alphabets, words and musical instruments providing visually stimulating learning environment	175
7.4	Locally made wood board with carved letters	176
7.5	Children at work surrounded by rich display of letters, words, diagrams and pots made from local clay	176
7.6	A girl using numbered pebbles to count, a skill which she is demonstrating to her peers and rest of the class	178
7.7	Children using plastic bottle tops to create number signs and letters thereby doing addition together	178
7.8	Children using plastic bottle tops assisted by their teacher to carry out addition sums on a mini blackboard	179
7.9	Children in a group gathering around a mini blackboard learning how to write Amharic letters	179
7.10	Children in a group gathering around a mini blackboard learning how to write using the English alphabet	180
7.11	Children dramatising the process of greeting each other	181
7.12	Children proudly sharing their drawings of people greeting each other on coloured card	182

xx *Images*

7.13	Children organising cards with words and phrases on them linked to greeting someone	182
8.1	Parents and extended family members watching the facilitator and children	218
8.2	Children responding enthusiastically to a question from the facilitator	219
8.3	A girl demonstrating understanding of sounds and words	220
8.4	Parents, extended families and community elders watching and listening to children reading	221
8.5	A girl demonstrating her learning to the PEG	223
8.6	A bar of soap produced by a PEG	228

Permissions

Figure 5.1	Adapted from Material and non-Material Wheel of Poverty, Figure 0.2 in Lister (2021, 105)
Figures 7.1–7.2	Printed with permission from Geneva Global Inc. Speed School Programme Impact Report. 2012. University of Sussex, Centre for International Education, UK. Pages, 14 & 20
Figures 7.3–7.6	Printed with permission from Geneva Global Inc. Speed School Programme: Ethiopia. Tracking the Progress of Speed School Students: 2011–2017. Research Report: March 2018. Pages 24, 27, 28, & 30
Table 7.1	Printed with permission from Geneva Global Inc. Evaluation of Speed School Programme Baseline Report. University of Sussex, Centre for International Education, UK. Page 19
Tables 7.2–7.5	Printed from with permission from Geneva Global Inc. & Luminos Fund. "Speed School Programme: Ethiopia. Tracking the Progress of Speed School Students: 2011–2017. Research Report: March 2018. Pages 23, 27, 28, & 32
Image 2.1	UNESCO 2010 Reaching the Marginalised. EFA Global Monitoring Report Cover photo. Downloaded with permission from UNESCO
Images 7.1–7.10	Photographs used with permission from Luminos Fund
Images 7.11, 7.12 & 13	Taken by Sean Higgins and Kwame Akyeampong
Images 5.1–5.5	Photographs taken by Abdul Wahid Alhassan for the research
Images 6.1–6.5	Printed with permission from authors of CBE textbooks
Images 6.6–6.8	Photographs taken by Abdul Wahid Alhassan, reproduced with kind permission

Prologue: A Message from the Authors

This book is the result of our collaboration, conversations and companionship over several years as researchers and educators in the academic field of international education and development and also as teachers in contexts of poverty and hardship in sub-Saharan Africa (SSA). Our shared dissatisfaction with the narrative of the 'learning crisis' and its framing of children and their learning in SSA more broadly emerged from several intersecting 'concerns'.

First, in teaching and researching global responses of policymakers and development aid agencies to the 'learning crisis', we were struck by the inadequacy of the wholly negative framings of children in the global South, particularly in SSA, considered as a problem to be solved. Our own experiences with communities, children and teachers had created a discomfort with this narrative and the research that sustains it. In fact, the closer we looked at children's lived realities coming face to face with their circumstances of poverty and hardship, the more we became dissatisfied with the solutions.

Sean spent many years living and teaching in conflict-affected Sierra Leone, as well as teaching in schools in challenging areas of South London, where he encountered multiple dimensions of children's lives in all their complexity, richness and potential. Kwame spent many years of teaching and working with teachers in rural schools in Ghana where he witnessed their struggles, creativity and resilience. His engagement with global development organisations, international NGOs and ministries of education in many African countries saw him witness how interventions and policy reforms promised much but delivered little in terms of producing an education system that offered hope to millions of marginalised African children. Our awareness of the grounded experience of the micro-realities of African children, their teachers and the communities heightened our sense that policymakers were remote and disconnected from them.

We felt that those contriving the notion of the 'learning crisis' were engaged in oversimplification of the problems and their solutions, especially as it pertained to SSA. Our sense was that this was the unacknowledged tragedy affecting the prospects of millions of African children, teachers and their communities and that the solutions being offered gave little hope of transforming their lives, because they were seen as helpless and a problem to be fixed

DOI: 10.4324/9781003185482-1

through projects and programmes. This has created a growing industry in education interventions of fixing the 'poor' child, sidelining the 'incompetent' teacher and 'empowering' the community or parent.

Yet, we also began to feel a sense of hope that resulted from working on accelerated learning programmes (ALPs) that seem to take school dropouts and turn them into successful learners. In researching ALPs, we saw how they opened a window into a very different paradigm of educational provision that sought to recognise, respect and affirm African children's agency, resulting in a more democratic learning environment and producing positive outcomes.

Both our concern with the narrative of deficit and hope in the possibilities of ALPs led us to embrace a wider range of scholarship, including theory, empirical research and educational activism across disciplines in order to understand more deeply the potential of ALPs to offer an alternative vision of learning and successful education in the African context.

We realised that in order to understand why basic education in Africa is failing many of its children, we needed to look into fields of enquiry entirely missing in the field of education and development and bring into our analysis and response new voices, new disciplinary insights, new ways of envisaging education, new connections between insights and knowledges from within and outside the education and development literature. Consequently, this has been a long epistemic journey of discovery, connecting theory with practice, overcoming siloisations and straddling disciplinary divisions that split off education from other areas of social science. The journey of this book has therefore also been a research journey for us, connecting our insights as practitioners with ever-widening intellectual horizons to make sense of them. Theory and evidence are unsatisfactory or even useless if they cannot link to practice, just as practice needs theory to strengthen its claim to impact; neither can be isolated if we are to imagine a vision of successful education in SSA.

While always oriented to grassroots realities, we wanted to draw on academic insights and concepts to illuminate, explain and further understanding. We have therefore tried to bring the insights of theorists and practitioners closer together and speak with humility and openness to each other. Both are co-constitutive in the production of knowledge for promoting a better vision of education for the African child. Both are necessary to rethink today's global educational challenges of exclusions and inequities.

Writing this book has been a protracted experience. Writing and thinking together have been fitted in around the relentless, gruelling expectations and workload of the Academy. Yet, in all of this, we managed to maintain our conversations that enabled us to consider and reconsider our emerging arguments and interrogate our own and others' assumptions. They enlivened and energised us. For us, this journey of reflexivity was as important as the product. Many conversations took place during field trips. Writing the book has been a creative and transformational journey for both of us.

For us this is an unfinished conversation and the issues raised by the book continue and have been exacerbated by accelerating global inequalities, climate change and the aftermath of Covid, all affecting those already suffering socio-economic precarity most. We hope that this book will build momentum amongst all those dissatisfied with the learning crisis narrative and seek other more transformative ways of responding to educational marginalisation. We offer this book as something that may open further conversations, collaborations and directions on new research for all interested in addressing the needs of children experiencing educational marginalisation in Africa, but we also do not underestimate what needs to be done. This is a start rather than a finishing point, then, but one that hopefully reorients and reframes how we think about and respond to the learning needs of millions of African children.

1 The Global 'Learning Crisis'
Analysis, Critique and Re-envisioning

In the current preoccupation about a 'global learning crisis', Africa takes centre stage. This is evidenced in the numerous policy statements and pronouncements of major institutions, donors and international aid agencies operating in the global field of education and development (World Bank, 2018; UNICEF, 2021). The World Bank's (2018) report *Learning to Realise Education's Promise* offers the most influential iteration. The epistemic authority of the World Bank in agenda-setting within global educational discourse (Verger et al., 2014; Zapp, 2017) has contributed to the wide circulation of this report as a way of characterising, diagnosing and responding to educational marginalisation in sub-Saharan Africa (SSA). Indeed, the notion of 'crisis' has arguably become the 'dominant discourse of contemporary educational development' (Sriprakash et al., 2020, 676), producing a consensus that forecloses alternative framings of current global educational challenges.

The 'crisis of learning' is particularly associated with the recognition that millions of children are out-of-school globally (UIS, 2018, 2022). In 2022, the UIS and UNICEF (2022, 2) indicated that, out of the total of 244 million out-of-school in 2021, there were 67 million children of primary school age (about 6–11 years). Exclusion from access to education is most concentrated in SSA that has the largest out-of-school population and is apparently the only region where this population is growing (UIS and UNICEF, 2022, 4). Gender disparities were also more marked here than in other regions. Thus, in SSA, the out-of-school rate for girls in 2022 was 4.2% higher than the boys' rate, although it was 3.1% higher in Eastern and Southeast Asia (UNICEF, 2022, 5).

The progress made since 1999 to reduce the out-of-school rate at primary level by increasing school enrolments has stalled (Yasunaga, 2014, 13; Amani, 2021). Children in school receiving basic education have been found to have very poor literacy and numeracy outcomes, being unable to read even a sentence after five years of schooling (UNICEF, 2020; World Bank, 2018). In many policy reports and scholarly articles, underskilled and undermotivated, teachers are deemed lazy, seemingly unable to manage active learning experiences for their pupils (Robertson, 2012; Bruns et al., 2011).

Families and communities are said to be unable to appreciate the value of learning or to send their children to school (World Bank, 2018, 64). Each of these failures has a disproportionate effect on the experiences and opportunities of girls (Unterhalter and North, 2011; Crossouard and Dunne, 2021). Together, they are taken as symptomatic of a failure of current education provision in Africa to enable experiences of sustained and successful learning for children living in highly precarious, often conflict-affected contexts in which educational marginalisation intersects with extreme socio-economic hardship. The learning crisis is also represented as 'a moral crisis', in so far as its existence constitutes a global social injustice; "the children whom society is failing are the ones who most need a good education to succeed in life" (World Bank, 2018, xi).

Of particular relevance to the concerns of this book is that the current 'crisis' underscores the failure of the international development community to deliver on the goal of Education for All (EFA), enshrined as far back as 1990 at the Jomtien Conference (Buchert, 1995). That goal has since received various iterations in a series of reports and policy statements (UNESCO, 2005, 2014). These have been notable for their recognition of the inability to achieve targets for extending educational access and for a pattern of resetting deadlines for their realisation. Hence, in 2000, the target for achieving universal inclusive education was reset to 2015 in the Millennium Development Goals (MDGs) at the World Education Forum (Torres, 2001) and, in the most recent iteration in 2015, they were reset again, this time to 2030 in the Sustainable Development Goals (SDGs) (Bergman et al., 2018; Boeren, 2019). From a longer-term perspective, the current 'crisis' throws into relief a failure to deliver on the universal right to free basic education, decreed by the UN in 1948 (UN, 1948, 26).

The 'learning crisis' is almost synonymous with the under-achievement of marginalised children from poor or disadvantaged backgrounds. The damaging impact of educational marginalisation and under-achievement on the lives of children and their families has been brought into stark relief by the impact of Covid-19 and the resulting closure of schools and lack of access to learning for millions of children in Africa (Angrist et al., 2021). Not surprisingly, learning loss has proved most pronounced and difficult to mitigate in children from families with a prior tenuous relationship with formal schooling. The global educational emergency resulting from the pandemic has thus exacerbated a pre-existing crisis of provision and equity.

Our Critique of the 'Learning Crisis' Narrative

This book does not dispute that there is a 'crisis of learning' or 'a learning crisis'. Nor does it dispute the fact that the crisis represents an ethical failure to achieve global educational justice. Nor that there is an urgent need to do better, if only to avoid a further re-scheduling of goals to achieve EFA. However, this book challenges both the analysis of the failures of educational provision and the solutions currently being offered.

First, in this book, we challenge the discourse of crisis that rests on a narrow and reductive framing of what learning actually is and how it can be improved. Many scholars (for example, Croft, 2002; Barrett, 2007; Altinyelken, 2012; Alexander, 2015) have recognised that learning is a situated sociocultural process that is embedded in particular environments, with implications for the identity, well-being and agency of learners, their families and the wider community. This is to say that learning is strongly expansive, encompassing more than what happens in the confines of the classroom, is relational and achieves meaning through a recognition of who the learner is and their social environment. The persistent focus predominantly on literacy and numeracy as global yardsticks for defining and assessing learning has stripped it of its situated sociocultural context and process, resulting in a narrow vision of learning and what it means to improve it. This results in a highly reductive and instrumentalist view, narrowly conflating learning with cognitive achievement only, defined by measurable reading and numeracy outcomes.

Learning is therefore bracketed off, as a technical matter, from the contexts, relationships and lived experiences of children, their families and communities which are its pre-conditions and within which it acquires meaning and purpose. It is conceived in a narrow and reductive way, detached from its sociality in intersecting networks between, on the one hand, parents, guardians, extended families and their children and, on the other, teachers and educational officials (Humphreys et al., 2015; Ginsburg, 2012). Bypassed also is a framing of learning as an embodied, relational activity that takes place in a particular material context. This truncated view of a multi-dimensional activity ignores the contribution of learning experiences to the development of wider personal and inter-personal socio-emotional skills. It also fails to recognise the impact of those experiences on children's sense of identity and self-belief – what Klees et al. (2019, 5) call the "sense of agency that comes from mastery". In this book, we go a step further by arguing that this narrow and reductive framing of learning is actually a hindrance to improving learning even in relation to this framing. In other words, to secure improvements in basic literacy and numeracy skills, one has to embrace an expansive view and leverage it so as to achieve meaningful and sustainable learning.

The current framing of learning and the learning crisis also leads to policy responses that are narrow, piecemeal and incapable of addressing the root problem. As Sriprakash et al. (2020) have noted, the framing of learning within the narrative of crisis conceives learning as an activity operating in a social and cultural vacuum, ungrounded in the lived experiences of learners and their communities. Excluded from consideration are expansive models of learning as a potentially transformative activity, first through empowering learners and their families and communities not only to 'read the word' but to 'read the world', in the tradition of critical pedagogy (Klees et al., 2019, 8; Freire, 1970), and second by helping learners build their capabilities (Walker, 2012) that are relevant to their navigation of challenging contexts of hardship and deprivation. Moreover, the individualised and individualising emphasis on children's inadequate learning outcomes displaces attention from the impact of long-standing structural processes such as the imposition of Structural Adjustment Programmes in the global South which have undermined educational provision by reducing state investments and in which the World Bank has been directly implicated (Heidhues and Obare, 2011). Sriprakash et al. (2020, 683) are therefore right to argue that the discourse of the learning crisis 'obfuscates its own politics'. As a result, the international community and, in particular, the World Bank avoid being held responsible for generating the infrastructural failures to invest in schools, teachers and resources that have arguably contributed to creating the pre-conditions for the crisis of learning provision that they are so keen to highlight (Novelli and Selenica, 2021, 6). Analytical attention to the causes and components of 'crisis' is displaced from such pivotal historical and structural issues onto the figure of the individual under-achieving child, as measured by a generic indicator of learning. These are significant erasures that distort analysis of current learning challenges as well as the possibilities to re-envision solutions for communities whose educational marginalisation frequently intersects with multiple forms of disempowerment: socio-economic, political, cultural and linguistic.

Second, moving on from the narrow view of the experiences of learning, we critique the equally reductive view presented of pedagogical processes in the African context. Hence, in the 2018 World Bank report, the pre-conditions for successful learning are identified in a functionalist language of 'inputs' and 'outputs'. Critiquing this approach in understanding what is meant by 'quality' in educational provision, Alexander (2015, 251) notes that the inputs refer to indicators such as:

> pupil/teacher ratio, balance of male and female teachers, balance of trained and untrained teachers, expenditure per pupil as a percentage of GDP, net enrolment ratio, adult literacy rate, survival rate to grade 5.

The associated outputs refer to measurable outcomes in numeracy and literacy, as noted earlier. This focus on 'inputs' and 'outputs' glosses over the situated and highly contextualised nature of pedagogical processes, involving 'both the act of teaching and the ideas, values and knowledge and evidence that shape and justify it' (Alexander, 2015, 4). As Klees et al. (2019, 3) noted, the reduction of pedagogical processes to a functionalist rationality of inputs and outputs crucially 'ignores what happens in between'. So "learning is understood as a largely technical activity to be managed by skilled people available primarily in the world's richest countries" (605–606) with the global North privileged as the locus of expertise and insight. Erasing the grounded complexities of pedagogical processes on which the quality of learning depends, the narrative of crisis promoted by the World Bank repeats what Alexander has noted is a larger problem with the EFA global policy agenda – in other words, pedagogy or 'what in teaching and learning really matters' is ignored. This fundamental erasure is important because of how it informs policy actions that consequently do little to tackle the root causes of unproductive and alienating learning but instead perpetuate the 'crisis' narrative.

This second challenge to the construction of the 'learning crisis' notes the absence of critical attention given to the curriculum on offer within different formal state education systems, or to any interrogation of the underlying epistemic logics that determine its content and language of instruction (Trudell, 2007; Brock-Utne, 2014; Gerrard et al., 2022). Indeed, formal schools in many low-income countries push many disadvantaged children out-of-school for many different reasons, for example: their fixed school calendar and long hours, absent teachers, irrelevant and culturally unresponsive curriculum, poor teaching methods, use of corporal punishment, lack of accountability and the use of an unfamiliar language as the medium of instruction (Lewin and Akyeampong, 2009).

Our third challenge to the explanations for the global learning crisis points to its implicit pathologising of communities in SSA who are navigating educational marginalisation. Silova (2018) observes that 'the conceptual framing of the learning challenge ... – anchored in the idea of a 'learning crisis' in the 'developing world' – openly evokes dichotomous thinking characteristic of the logic of colonialism'. This binarism plays out in the portrayal of crisis-affected communities as dogged by an 'endless loop of poverty, corruption and backwardness, while portraying Western countries as examples to emulate' (2018, x). The discourse of crisis thus repeats a neo-colonialist logic in which outside agents and interventions purport to offer redemptive treatment for communities in SSA. This results in a top-down and paternalistic approach that blames disadvantaged communities for lack of educational aspiration, positioning them as problematic, lacking in agency and hence passive.

An under-estimation of the significance of not having any meaningful engagement with communities who experience educational marginalisation in SSA shapes the various logics that have been identified in the development practices and programmes of global aid agencies (Lewis, 2020; Verger et al., 2012; Novelli, 2016). These are embedded in 'problem–solving' approaches (Cox, 1996) that reduce complex educational challenges to problems that invite speedy, short-term solutions without sufficient consideration of the underlying conditions that structure the exercise of agency by those facing socio-economic precarity (of which educational exclusion is but one component). These logics are also evident in the tokenistic rhetorics around partnership, empowerment and participation (Vavrus and Seghers, 2010) that end up 'ventriloquising the poor' (Cornwall and Fujita, 2012, 1751). Paradoxically, whilst digital forms of communication have been used by international aid agencies to strengthen the contribution of socio-economically marginalised communities to policy-making and programming, studies suggest that, in fact, such communities tend to reproduce pre-existing inequalities and exclusions. The evidence suggests they do little to retrieve their voices and experiences in shaping more locally responsive policies and programmes (Chouliaraki and Georgiou, 2022).

Finally, the epistemic base of several analyses of the learning crisis is strikingly narrow. It depends largely on graphs and charts representing national and comparative data on enrolment and retention rates. These are useful in conveying achievements and progress in relation to the EFA goals and targets. This use of global quantitative data is aligned with a 'macro-social perspective' that often dominates development discourses (Dunne and Ananga, 2013). What is missing are the subjective voices, perceptions, experiences and knowledges of children, their families and communities about their expectations and aspirations for educational provision in contexts of precarity (UNICEF and UNESCO, 2015, 14). The result is to homogenise, as one undifferentiated group, the out-of-school children or the low-achieving children in poor communities who have a tenuous engagement with formal education. As Alexander (2015, 256) comments that "while numbers offer headlines and dramatic immediacy", he asks "are the classroom processes and outcomes that are truly transformative for our children adequately captured in such data?"

Awareness of this problem is particularly important if we are to develop a deeper understanding of the conditions that produce such numbers and how to achieve better results. The dominance of macro-level statistics and the silencing the experiences and voices of indigenous communities are thus symptomatic of an epistemological gap in which "the preferred evidence is top down. It reflects the world, the preoccupations, the priorities and experiences of policymakers, rather than those of teachers and children' (2015, 255).

Whilst the analysis of the construction of 'learning' in the discourse of 'crisis' thus falls short in so many ways, so too do the recommended solutions. A good example of this can be found in the World Bank 2018 report that prioritises a need to assess learning more effectively in order to address educational marginalisation. It points out: "To take learning seriously, start by measuring it" (World Bank, 2018, 58) – instead of encouraging a stance that says that to take learning seriously, we must start with an expanded view of learning and the pedagogies that promote learning and make it equally important to recognise who the learners are and how learning connects with their socio-cultural realities and values. Such assessment-driven solutions have been critiqued as little more than a continuation of policies and programmes that have manifestly failed over the past 20 years (Klees et al., 2012;2019). What has been termed the almost 'feverish' concern to collect data in order to measure learning outcomes (Sriprakash et al., 2020, 683) repurposes for the global South those approaches to raising standards developed in the global North which have already been widely critiqued for reducing teaching and learning to 'numbers on test scores' (Taubman, 2010, ix; see also Benavot and Smith, 2020).

The promotion of Western-derived assessment practices as the panacea for the global learning crisis is a further example of colonial logics at work in the analysis of the 'learning crisis' in SSA. Recommended as a solution is the mobilisation of the insights of brain science to enhance learning through drawing on 'promising evidence-based approaches' (World Bank, 2018, 68). Again, this uncritical endorsement of a 'technoscientific solution' (Sriprakash et al.,

2020, 686) privileges knowledges recently developed in the West over the perspectives and lived experiences of poor communities in Africa.

These limitations together with the solutions presented raise some fundamental questions:

1. How can we better understand the educational needs of children from poor communities who have experienced long-term marginalisation?
2. What pedagogical processes and curriculum provision are best able to re-engage them?
3. How can education provision better valorise, recognise and connect with the pre-existing resources, knowledges and agency which children, along with their families, bring to learning?
4. How can education provision for the poor avoid top-down and neo-colonial logics or framings and become more responsive to contexts and communities?

Whilst these questions are about learning and pedagogical processes, they also intersect with ontological issues – the nature of being, the social realities and the lived, embodied experiences of communities experiencing socio-economic hardship. Such processes are cultural. They reference the forms of meaning-making and social practices that matter to communities who have been marginalised in education provision. They are also epistemological. There is a difference between the knowledges that are privileged and those ignored or downgraded in current analyses of, and prescriptions to address, the identified learning challenges. This invites us to pay far more attention to issues that go well beyond what happens in the school classroom, the ways in which learning and pedagogical processes are viewed. We need to remind ourselves that learning and pedagogy should not be understood in narrowly 'educationist' terms (Robertson and Dale, 2008), as practices whose parameters start and finish in the formal school classroom. Rather, education provision and orientations to learning need to be understood as inseparable from and interconnected with living and being, demanding inter-disciplinary responses that draw on diverse insights, knowledges and voices. The questions we are raising are at the heart of this book's goal to rethink and re-envision the learning challenge especially in relation to basic and primary schooling which is the main focus of the crisis discourse.

So, rather than a narrow and overly technical view of learning and pedagogy, we stress its situated and intersectional nature. Rather than pathologise the poor, children and communities who are targeted in educational interventions, we recognise and value their agency and knowledges in contexts of massive hardship and precarity. Rather than adopt a problem-solving approach that seeks panaceas for the learning crisis, we interrogate and address the underlying structuring constraints that produce and sustain educational marginalisation. Rather than stay with a narrow evidential base in seeking solutions, we include the voices of children, their teachers and families. Challenging the underlying logics at work in the analysis of crisis and the prescriptions offered. Silova (2018, 1) argues that "it's not a learning crisis, it's an international development crisis" that calls for a fundamental re-evaluation of the principles of engagement, which may result in "different and far more radical interventions". Such a re-evaluation is possible if we look at the accelerated learning programmes (ALPs) developed in Africa, which offer an alternative modality of educational provision, a re-envisioning as it were of the learning crisis.

Re-envisioning the 'Learning Crisis' through Accelerated Learning Programmes (ALPs)

The way this book seeks to reconceptualise the 'learning crisis' and re-envision solutions is by focusing, in particular, on the responses to children of primary school or basic schooling age (7–14 years) who are experiencing educational marginalisation. It does so by drawing on the emerging insights from the successes of the non-formal so-called *Accelerated Learning Programmes* (ALPs) that have targeted children who have dropped out of primary school early because of their experiences of poor-quality education or who never attended formal school as a result of poverty, conflict and crisis. This is the very group whose truncated learning trajectories are at the heart of the global learning crisis. We draw on in-depth empirical case studies of the curriculum, pedagogical processes and impacts of these ALPs on children and their families, extended families and communities, in Northern Ghana, Ethiopia and Liberia, country contexts in which key barriers to education such as extreme poverty, conflict and inter-generational marginalisation (UNICEF and UNESCO, 2015) are prevalent and pressing. Our aim is to consider the lessons learnt from such programmes, and whether and if so, how ALPs' curriculum, pedagogical processes and approaches to providing education for marginalised communities and their children offer new ways of envisioning and responding to the learning challenge that avoid the shortcomings of the current analysis and prescriptions outlined above. We consider whether such programmes can furnish policy and programmatic responses that do better than reproduce the status quo.

Accelerated learning programmes come under a variety of names, including speed schools, second chance, community schools, bridging programmes, alternative basic education and complementary basic education or joyful learning. They have been implemented by a range of international and national development organisations, usually working in partnerships with state education systems. These include UNICEF, UNESCO, the World Bank, the Foreign and Commonwealth Development Office (previously DFID), the Norwegian Refugee Council as well as national NGOs such as the Bangladesh Rural Advancement Community (Rose, 2009; Longden, 2013; Fitzpatrick, 2020; Shah and Choo, 2020). They have been operationalised in diverse contexts to reach out-of-school children in contexts of extreme poverty, conflict and long-standing inter-generational educational marginalisation. These include

Afghanistan, Bangladesh, Columbia, Ethiopia, Guinea, Liberia, Mali, Malawi, Nigeria, Northern Ghana, Pakistan and Rwanda.[1]

Various studies suggest that ALPs in a range of contexts in SSA are successful in enabling this marginalised group to compensate in a short space of time for their lack of prior learning, and to develop the knowledges, skills and attitudes to make a sustained and successful transition into formal schooling.[2] ALPs are described as:

> flexible, age-appropriate programme, run in an accelerated timeframe, which aims to provide access to education for disadvantaged, over-age, out of school children and youth. This may include those who missed out on their education due to poverty, marginalisation, conflict and crisis.
> (Boisvert et al., 2017, 7)

Whilst mobilised in diverse contexts of educational marginality, and varying in size and scope, ALPs are usually characterised by:

- a condensed, simplified, locally relevant and flexible curriculum focusing on content directly relevant to children's lives;
- a supportive and friendly learning environment that builds the confidence and self-esteem of all learners;
- activities that encourage critical reflection, peer talk and collaborative learning;
- instruction in children's mother tongue;
- flexible scheduling of learning in afternoons, to accommodate the expectation that children may need to contribute to the economic survival of families, including family farming or household duties, or to fit in with the nomadic or pastoral lifestyles of their parents;
- participatory and experiential teaching approaches;
- recruitment of teachers – known as 'facilitators' from local communities who are aware of the daily lives of children and their families who navigate circumstances of extreme hardship and who share a common cultural and linguistic background;
- an absence of corporal punishment, and continuity with the same teacher, to help foster a friendly, supportive learning environment;
- the training of facilitators to eschew a view of teaching as the transmission of knowledge and conceive their roles as facilitating collaborative learning for the development of cognitive and other personal and social skills;
- regular consultations with children's families and extended families about their learning and the school schedule (UNESCO, 2014, 85) and
- relatively small classes of around 25 pupils.

In all of these ways, ALPs strikingly contrast with mainstream schooling in terms of their structure, organisation of teaching and learning and their responsiveness to the perspectives of disadvantaged communities (Randall et al.,

2020). Far from constructing such children or their communities as problems to be solved, at the core of the curriculum and pedagogies of accelerated education programmes is an attempt to connect with, and recognise as positive resources for learning, their situated knowledges, cultural identities, daily realities, hopes and fears.

ALPs have been recognised as providing a unique and critical role in addressing EFA goals – particularly for 'disadvantaged and underserved populations' (DeStefano et al., 2007, 1). They have been celebrated for their success in addressing educational exclusion through innovative curriculum and pedagogical approaches (Mfum-Mensah, 2017). The EFA Global Monitoring Report for Teaching and Learning (UNESCO, 2014, 282), for example, recognised that "where schools fail to deliver quality education and children are dropping out early, second chance accelerated learning programmes enable the disadvantaged to catch up". Hence, they are "an important way of accelerating children's progress and raising achievement for disadvantaged groups". As such they have been celebrated as 'crucibles of educational innovation' (UNICEF and UNESCO, 2015, 73). Their impacts on learning outcomes of the children they target are reportedly "superior to those achieved in government schools and achieved in shorter periods of time" (UNESCO, 2014, 282). ALPs are also associated with impressive levels of attendance, as well as strong learning outcomes and successful transition into formal primary education for girls as well as boys (Luminos Fund, 2018a, 2021, 2022; Akyeampong et al., 2018; University of Sussex, 2018; IDinsight, 2023).

The Findings from the Global Initiative on Out-of-School Children (UNICEF and UNESCO, 2015, 41) even argued that ALPs have a 'key' role to play in "fixing the broken promise of education for all" by providing a "pathway back to regular schooling" and avoiding a "business as usual approach". Likewise, the Luminos Fund (2018b, 2) suggested that Second Chance programmes were instrumental in "unlocking the light in every child" through providing an "experience of joyful learning" that would enable those children previously unable to access formal education provision to transition into mainstream schools

Policymakers' interest in accelerated learning modalities has also been catalysed by recognition that state education systems, on their own, are unable to meet ambitious international development agendas to achieve universal inclusive primary education (Yasunaga, 2014). The recent development by the Inter-Agency Network for Education in Emergencies (INEE) website of a resource for Accelerated Learning[3] and the formation of the Accelerated Education Working Group (AEWG)[4] demonstrates the increasing prominence of accelerated learning within the global institutional architecture of education and development. Pressure on education systems to find ways of compensating for learning losses experienced by children during school closures as a result of the impact of Covid-19 has also catalysed interest in the relevance of these programmes to addressing current educational challenges (Hoadley, 2020). And yet, despite such extraordinary levels of recognition, the experience of

ALPs has not been used to challenge or reenvisage the global learning crisis or reconceptualise the solutions. The World Bank strikingly refers to its own studies when framing and seeking solutions to the learning crisis (Klees, 2012). As Mitchell (2019, 1) found, the World Bank's observational instrument to promote inclusive education in the region represented 'minimal engagement with evidence from classrooms in sub-Saharan Africa'.

In this book, we intend to explain and illuminate the strengths and impacts of ALPs, to see what they can teach us about learning, about local conditions for effective learning and about the social conditions of learning in a range of African settings. We draw on in-depth empirical case studies of programmes operating in three ALPs in SSA that address the very high numbers of out-of-school children in Northern Ghana, Ethiopia and Liberia. These diverse country and cultural contexts typify the existence of apparently insurmountable barriers to children accessing and engaging with education provision. Our aim is to centralise, through case studies, the all too frequently unheard voices of children, their families and extended families, teachers and communities experiencing educational marginalisation. We also draw on the evaluative evidence of the pedagogic strategies being used that was collected by us and others over many years and in many projects.

Illuminating ALPs through Social Theory

Despite the burgeoning interest in ALPs' potential effectiveness for addressing educational marginalisation, there has been little attempt to synthesise the lessons to be learned from their distinctive curriculum, pedagogical approach or their impact on children and families suffering intergenerational exclusion from formal schooling. The recent work of the INEE AEWG has been exemplary in collating recent evidence from evaluations, reviews and other studies of ALPs globally (Shah and Choo, 2020), as well as developing the principles for effective practice and monitoring and evaluation toolkits (see https://inee.org/network-spaces/aewg). This has greatly strengthened the evidence base for understanding the impact of ALPs. However, there remains a lack of analytical and critical literature that explores and explains the effectiveness of ALPs and, in particular, which draws on social theory to understand their educational significance and impact. Farrell and Hartwell (2008) pointed out over a decade ago "the underlying reasons why such programmes work as well as they do from a pedagogical or learning theory point of view remains a mystery, leaving much that is not fully understood" (36). Arguably, this remains true today.

That this 'mystery' remains is due in part to the nature of the evidence base over the past decade or so. With notable exceptions (Shah, 2015; Boisvert et al., 2017) such as the publications of the AEWG (Shah and Choo, 2020; Sekaggya-Bagarukayo and Oddy, 2022), claims about the success of ALPs have tended to rely on discrete, largely descriptive evaluations of individual programmes by implementing agencies (Rose, 2009) with only anecdotal references to their benefits to individual children (Rose, 2009; Luminos Fund, 2021). Hence, ALPs have been celebrated as offering "joyful learning" (Luminos Fund, 2021, 7) to "those shut out of education by crisis, poverty or discrimination". The numbers of out-of-school children reached, or the number of words they are able to read, have also supported claims for their transformative impact (Luminos Fund, 2021, 2022) in addressing educational marginalisation.

Such celebratory rhetoric serves as a useful advocacy tool to gain the support of donors and policymakers. Yet in pointing to symptoms of success, such as good transition rates into formal schools and pupils' development of literacy and numeracy skills in a short space of time, they also demonstrate what Tikly (2015, 238) has termed the "hegemonic status of empiricism" and an "objectivist" view of learning. In other words, they align with the dominance of a 'what works' agenda in the institutional architecture of education and development post-2015 (Tikly, 2015, 237). This refers to a reductive framing of the impact of educational interventions as producing effects or learning outcomes, in a mechanistic way, narrowly focusing on cognitive development of individual students as the sole measure and means of understanding their success. A 'what works' approach therefore privileges immediately demonstrable impacts over deeper critical reflection on the children's situated learning experience.

Paradoxically, however, the celebration of 'what works' when applied to ALPs may also limit understanding. As Tikly (2015, 237) has noted:

> while the concept of learning has been placed at the heart of the education strategy and at the heart of current debates about the post 2015 education and development agenda, and while governments and donors are in the process of investing millions of dollars in research programmes aimed at finding out what works in raising learning outcomes for disadvantaged learners in low and middle income countries, the philosophical and methodological assumptions underlying much of the current discourse including what learning is (the ontology of learning) and how we come to know what learning is (the epistemology of learning) are rarely made explicit.

As a crucial field of educational research and practice, therefore, evaluations of ALPs and their impact and significance remain "evidence hungry, theory light" (Paulson, 2019, 33). By theory, we mean, following Anyon, (2008, 3), "an architecture of ideas – a coherent structure of inter-related concepts – whose contemplation and application helps us to understand and explain discursive and social phenomena". The case studies in this book therefore draw on diverse alternative theorisations of learning and the social world. These are invaluable as different concepts/conceptual frames help elicit and explain the impact of ALPs and understand their significance in addressing inter-generational educational marginalisation in contexts of conflict and extreme poverty. For example, we draw upon: (a) the concept of *funds of knowledge* (Hogg, 2012) that spotlights the knowledges and experiences that children bring into school but which are often forgotten when they are there; (b) *post-humanist theorisations* of the child and learning as conceptualised by Karen Murris (2016) and others who highlight how children's material environments matter in producing engaging learning experiences and (c) Butler's framing of the agency of communities experiencing precarity, including educational marginalisation, through the concepts of *'vulnerability and resistance'* (Butler et al., 2016). This conceptualisation help critique the association of such communities with passivity and lack of agency. Each theory highlights a different dimension of social and educational practice that can explain the impact and significance of ALPs. Each, in Biesta et al.'s (2011) words, promises to deepen understanding by "making things visible or intelligible that are not immediately observable" (227).

At the same time, the insights from the application of these Western theoretical perspectives are situated alongside an appreciation of how the values of the African ethical and social philosophy of *Ubuntu* (Le Grange, 2012, 2018) have shaped African ALPs. By bringing African ALPs into dialogue with diverse conceptual tools from different knowledge traditions, we offer a pluralistic use of theory that is aligned with the decolonising approach to knowledge production envisaged by de Sousa Santos (2007) who argued for a form of *global cognitive justice* that values the explanatory power of an 'ecology of knowledges'. Drawing on *Ubuntu* as an overarching way of understanding the significance of ALPs for African children, our analysis of responses to educational marginality aligns with the decolonising imperative to centre southern theory and non-Eurocentric knowledges in social analysis (Connell, 2020).

When used to understand ALPs, all these theoretical perspectives, in different ways, are especially useful in "making the familiar strange" (Biesta et al., 2011, 226). We are able to ask what exactly is it that produces the "light bulb moment" in children? What generates "joyful learning"? How and why are ALPs 'crucibles of educational innovation" (UNICEF and UNESCO, 2015, 73)? What warrants their reputation as having a "pivotal role to play in fixing the broken promise of education for all" (ibid)? Given a currently under-theorised knowledge base, therefore, this book's eclectic use of theory (Bhambra, 2014: Jackson and Mazzei, 2022) and its capacity to help us to 'think otherwise' (Jackson and Mazzei, 2013, 269) is especially apposite to probe and answer these questions.

Finally, as Maclure (2010, 277) recognises "the value of theory… lies in its power to get in the way; to offend and interrupt… to block the production of the bleeding obvious and open up new possibilities for thinking and doing". This form of disruption is precisely what is needed in the context of the epistemic power of international aid organisations to dominate global education agendas with authoritative, often doctrinaire framings of problems and solutions such as the notion of the 'learning crisis' that appear to defy problematisation or critique (Kothari, 2005).

Theory into practice

Biesta argues that there is a tendency "amongst educationists and policymakers to see theory as largely irrelevant to the daily lives of learners and teachers and the practices of teaching and learning" (Biesta et al., 2011, 226; see also Ball, 2001). This results in "unhelpful dichotomies of theory versus practice, the theoretical versus the empirical, or theoretical versus useful" (Biesta et al., 2011, 226). Such viewpoints can then lead to professional and epistemological siloisations between policymakers and researchers, between those professionals working on the ground to address educational marginalisation and those defining key global educational agendas – for whom the complexities opened up by theorised analysis do not lend themselves to simplistic policy solutions (Novelli et al., 2014, 18).

This book seeks to go beyond those silos. Whilst drawing on theory, then, we hope that its contents and readability will appeal to a range of audiences, including practitioners and professionals operating within educationally marginalised communities, national governments and international aid agencies, as well as policymakers, researchers and the hybrid academic practitioner. We seek therefore to complement the pragmatic aspirations of the AEWG in the INEE to strengthen the evidence base for all professionals working to address the learning challenges in SSA in order to improve the quality of ALPs now and in the future. What distinguishes our goals from the Group's is less a concern to standardise or synthesise knowledge about ALPs (Shah and Choo, 2020) but to provide theoretically informed interrogation of what we know about their successes. Hence, this book provides a variegated, epistemically diverse framing of their significance in making learning accessible and enjoyable for a marginalised and too little-heard demographic.

Re-envisioning the 'Learning Crisis' through Diverse Evidence

Combining visual and verbal forms of evidence in explanation of ALPs, the multifaceted data base for the case studies in this book recognises children's engagement in learning as an embodied, linguistic, emotional, inter-personal, situated and ongoing social activity.

The in-depth case studies of three ALPs draw on interviews with children, their families, communities and teachers, amplifying the voices of stakeholders too often ignored in the framing of global educational policy. They also draw on textbooks and instructional materials, photographs and lesson observations to evoke the learning environments and processes of ALPs. Data also extends beyond discrete snapshots of ALPs through the use of longitudinal studies that have followed children who experienced these programmes into transition schools to assess their longer-term impact. Moreover, qualitative data illuminating the meanings attaching to ALPs for all those affected by such programmes is complemented in our case studies by quantitative data on the learning outcomes achieved by children over time.

Bringing these diverse evidential sources together to explain the strengths of ALPs also enables the analysis in this book to connect insights into children's subjective experiences of learning with evidence of its realisation in concrete and specific learning outcomes in relation to literacy and numeracy gains. Too often, the current academic evidence base tends to concentrate on either one or the other, missing the opportunities to deepen and diversify explanation of their impacts through making mixed-methods connections. Methodologically, therefore, this book's marshalling of a range of forms of evidence about ALPs reflects our commitment to re-injecting careful attention to the processes of learning through which they maximise the opportunities for marginalised children whilst at the same time painstakingly tracking their impact on measurable learning outcomes – and most importantly, connecting both within a situated, rigorous and holistic narrative of their experience of learning.

Recognising that understanding children's educational experiences in contexts of marginalisation is an inter-disciplinary endeavour, this book brings into dialogue research from diverse fields of enquiry including anthropology, ethnography, the cultural political economy of education, childhood, poverty and development studies and applied linguistics. It marshals recent research as well as findings generated over the past 20 years to enhance and enrich the arguments, thus repurposing valuable and relevant knowledge ignored within the selective, self-referential and presentist knowledge base that purports to explain and respond to the 'learning crisis' (Hickling Hudson and Klees, 2012; Mitchell, 2019). Indeed, that so much relevant research over the past 20 years and longer into children's lives in Africa as well as transformative learning and pedagogical practices has been ignored by policymakers is itself a crisis of knowledge exchange that undermines effective responses to educational marginalisation.

Widening the evidence base is also an important goal of this book in order to avoid what has been termed 'educationism' (Robertson and Dale, 2008, 8). This is a tendency in educational analysis to 'disciplinary parochialism', or the restriction of educational explanation and analysis to "approaches that come within the field" (Robertson and Dale, 2008, 8). This precludes drawing on the insights of other disciplines into the range social, cultural and economic influences that shape and constrain how learning is framed, understood and experienced in and outside formal learning environments. A multi-disciplinary approach provides intellectual resources through which to problematise taken-for-granted assumptions about children, learning, and responses to educational marginalisation, and to imagine other possibilities. Given our critiques of the narrative of the 'learning crisis' for its decontextualised and technocratic approach, this rootedness of educational explanation in multiple sources of knowledge underpins our goal to reconceptualise the 'learning crisis' in SSA.

A timely moment

The imperative for a radical re-envisioning of educational provision for the millions of out-of-school children globally comes at a timely moment. Roy (2020, 3) has noted how "historically, pandemics have forced humans to break with the past and imagine their world anew", such that the recent experience of Covid-19 may be understood as a "portal, a gateway between one world and the next". The resulting massive loss of learning experienced by children globally, exacerbating pre-existing inequities, has yet again spotlighted the fundamental micro-level issue of who engages in learning, how and with what benefits. At the macro-level of global policy-making and agenda-setting, Novelli (2023, 2) has recently highlighted the collapse of the geopolitical power relationships on which the field and practice of development and the global agendas of the MDGs and SDGs and, in particular EFAs, were based. This is due to the shift away from a 'uni-polar' US-led Western hegemony represented by a 'resurgent China, an expanding BRICS alliance, and clear evidence of increased assertion of policy autonomy emerging from Latin America, the Middle East, and Asia'. This new 'multi-polar world' invites an 'openness to recognise – and respect – plurality of thought, culture, identity and polity' in the 'interests of the marginalised global majority' (2023, 2). Finally, that SDG 4 is already failing massively in its promise to achieve universal basic primary EFA – a goal that may not be realised until the end of this century (Klees, 2024) rather than the projected date of 2030 – indicates an urgent need for a fundamental paradigm change in framings of and responses to educational marginalisation. The current conjuncture therefore presents an unprecedented opportunity for us to rethink how the 'learning crisis' of millions of out-of-school children can be addressed in basic and primary education provision (Cohen et al., 2021). And in doing so to learn from what ALPs can teach us.

The Organisation of Chapters

In Part 1 (Chapters 2–5), we set out in detail the ways in which the learning challenge in SSA needs to be and can be rethought. Chapter 2 takes forward the critique offered in Chapter 1 by providing a rigorous and multifaceted analysis of the various ways in which African children who experience poverty are produced and positioned in deficit terms. The chapter starts by challenging the utopian and triumphalist rhetoric of poverty alleviation through education, noting its limited understanding both of poverty and also of learning. Through a historicising approach, it demonstrates how deficit constructions of African children are deeply embedded in a range of agendas that have shaped the field and practice of education and development since the Second World War. This chapter concludes by clarifying the limitations of educational responses to marginalisation and the need to draw on a multi-dimensional approach to the lived experiences of 'poor children'.

Chapter 3 turns to the often overlooked but fundamental issue of the language of instruction in basic education. It demonstrates how this also positions children in deficit terms by devaluing the often rich linguistic resources they have developed in their communities. The negative implications for teacher's pedagogical choices are highlighted as well as children's negative emotional experiences of learning that result, including their alienation, fear, shame, lack of confidence and withdrawal from learning processes resulting from linguistic and epistemic exclusion. We also show how these negative effects are gendered, thwarting opportunities for engagement by girls.

Chapter 4 discusses ways in which basic education teachers in SSA are often characterised in deficit terms as their commitment to improving learning is often called into question. The chapter starts by reviewing arguments and evidence that present the African basic education teacher as lacking the subject knowledge, pedagogical and general teaching skills necessary for improving student learning outcomes. This chapter discusses how quantitative measurements and symbols of teacher capabilities and teaching quality erode their freedoms and usher in interventions that deepen the deficit characterisation of the African teacher. It argues for teacher education reforms to focus much attention on re-thinking its curriculum to produce reflexive practitioners with a deep sense of their professional identity as agentic practitioners.

Chapter 5 concludes Part 1 by offering an alternative to deficit framings of African children by outlining an alternative, multi-dimensional approach that recognises diverse dimensions of their lived experiences. This chapter draws on a range of ethnographic and anthropological studies that illuminate children's viewpoints, perspectives and feelings; their contributions to household survival; informal learning and knowledge building through social practices and play, social positioning in friendship groups family networks and communities, as well as the temporalities and spatialities of their lives, and fundamentally the linguistic agency they bring to learning. The consequences of this reorientation for teacher education are also addressed.

In Part 2, Chapters 6–8 draw on case studies of ALPs in diverse African contexts to demonstrate how they exemplify an alternative modality of education provision with important lessons for rethinking the deficit assumptions about poor children and communities within the learning crisis narrative with implications for pedagogical practices, curriculum content and community engagement. In particular, each of the case studies concretely demonstrates the multi-dimensional approach outlined in Chapter 5.

Chapter 6 presents the first case study of an ALP in Northern Ghana, complementary basic education (CBE). It draws on the theory of children's *funds of knowledge* and *funds of identity* to show how in its curriculum content and instructional materials Complementary Basic Education (CBE) repositions African children outside of deficit framings. This chapter shows how children's funds of knowledge are embedded in various dimensions of CBE provision, starting from the preparation of instructional materials by linguists with local community-based knowledge. They are integral to the pedagogical strategies of facilitators, the engagement of communities in curriculum development and in turn are recognised by children attending as features of CBE that enhance their confidence, sense of efficacy and pleasure in learning. The resulting learning outcomes, as measured by longitudinal studies, are also very impressive, evincing the success of CBE in re-engaging learners to complete basic education in a challenging context of educational marginalisation. Drawing on data gathered over several years that sought to listen to children, their families and extended kinship networks, as well as facilitators, the evidence base attests to this book's concern to listen to grassroots voices usually ignored in top-down framings of the learning crisis.

Chapter 7 shows how an ALP in Ethiopia leverages objects and materials from children's physical environments to activate collaborative and engaging forms of meaningful learning. Such approaches achieve not only improved cognitive learning outcomes, as our data shows, but also provides an enjoyable experience of learning, promoting confidence in learning to enable successful transition to government schools. This chapter shows how this approach is based on a fundamental rethinking of the ontology of human exceptionalism. It discusses how Speed School teachers operationalise the Speed School pedagogy in ways which demonstrate how their teaching builds on a post-humanistic approach to children's learning and their agency. This indicates that children who experienced Speed Schools successfully transitioned into government schools and continued to achieve impressive learning outcomes.

Chapter 8 provides another angle on the success of ALPs in contexts of inter-generational educational exclusion by showing how the Second Chance programme in the challenging context of rural, conflict-affected Liberia, avoids framings of socio-economically marginalised communities as passive, problematic and lacking in agency. This chapter applies Butler's analytical lens to illuminate the significance of the programme's Parental Engagement Groups showing how these meetings provide a space for the celebration of learning as a social event, for the cultivation of joy and hope. This offers opportunities for challenging patriarchal norms that undermine girls' engagement with learning, for creating peace promoting and inclusive democratic spaces of discussion and for developing practical strategies in response to poverty, food insecurity and malnutrition. It also contributes to national peace promotion through youth activism.

Chapter 9 extends our understanding of the significance of ALPs by showing their deep cultural responsiveness in the African context. Drawing on the empirical evidence from the case studies, it demonstrates how various dimensions of their educational provision are aligned with the ontological and ethical concerns of the distinctively African value system of 'Ubuntu'. Hence ALPs, through their curriculum and pedagogical approaches, install the dignity, agency and relationality of the African child as fundamental underlying imperatives. This takes the argument beyond a technical 'what works' approach to show the grounded-ness and therefore the effectiveness of ALPs within a post-colonial lens that privileges rather than ignores indigenous culture as part of an African-led educational renaissance.

In Chapter 10, we conclude by highlighting the practical lessons for policymakers and practitioners to effect a fundamental rethink of the learning crisis drawing on the successes and strengths of ALPs in addressing educational marginalisation in SSA. We argue that the locus of the learning crisis does not lie in African children or teachers or communities but rather in the failure of global education policy to address key aspects of educational provision, in particular curriculum content, pedagogical strategies and community engagement. Global education policy fundamentally represents an uncritical reproduction of long-standing deficit assumptions that exacerbate and reproduce educational marginalisation. Herein is the moral crisis and the global social injustice that urgently demand a radical reappraisal of the paradigm through which learning challenges in Africa are understood.

Notes

1 See, for instance, studies by Miller et al. (2002), DeStefano et al. (2005, 2007), Farrell and Hartwell (2008), Rose (2009), Casely-Hayford and Hartwell (2013), Yasanuga (2014), Shah (2015), Menendez et al. (2016), Bano (2018), Shinohara (2021), Egbujuo (2022), Kan et al. (2022), Sekaggya-Bagarukayo and Oddy (2022) and Taka (2023).
2 The notion of 'best practice' has been similarly critiqued for its decontextualisation of pedagogical practices; see Schweisfurth and Elliott (2019).
3 https://inee.org/collections/accelerated-education
4 https://inee.org/network-spaces/aewg

References

Akyeampong, K., Carter, E., Higgins, S., Rose, P., and Sabates, R., 2018. *Understanding complementary basic education in Ghana: investigation of the experiences and achievements of children after transitioning into public schools*. Report for DFID Ghana Office (November 2018). REAL Centre, University of Cambridge.

Alexander, R., 2015. 'Teaching and learning for all? The quality imperative revisited'. In R. Alexander (ed.), *Routledge handbook of international education and development*. Routledge, pp. 138–152.

Altinyelken, H.K., 2012. 'A converging pedagogy in the developing world? Insights from Uganda and Turkey'. In H.K. Altinyelken (ed.), *Global education policy and international development: new agendas, issues and policies*. Bloomsbury Publishing, pp. 201–221.

Amani, J., 2021. 'Access to and participation in basic education in Tanzania: a decade of key achievements and challenges'. *SN Social Sciences*, 1(9): 239.

Angrist, N., de Barros, A., Bhula, R., Chakera, S., Cummiskey, C., DeStefano, J., Floretta, J., Kaffenberger, M., Piper, B., and Stern, J., 2021. 'Building back better to avert a learning catastrophe: estimating learning loss from COVID-19 school shutdowns in Africa and facilitating short-term and long-term learning recovery'. *International Journal of Educational Development*, 84: 102397.

Anyon, J., 2008. *Theory and educational research: toward critical social explanation*. Routledge.

Ball, S.J., 2001. '"You've been NERFed!" Dumbing down the academy: national educational research forum: "A national strategy? Consultation paper": a brief and bilious response'. *Journal of Education Policy*, 16(3): 265–268.

Bano, M., 2018. 'Barriers to primary completion and transition in Northern Nigeria: evidence from a non-formal schooling intervention'. *Compare: A Journal of Comparative and International Education*, 50: 107–122.

Barrett, A.M., 2007. 'Beyond the polarisation of pedagogy: models of classroom practice in Tanzanian primary schools'. *Comparative Education*, 43(2): 273–294.

Benavot, A., and Smith, W.C., 2020. 'Reshaping quality and equity: global learning metrics as a ready-made solution to a manufactured crisis'. In A. Benavot and W.C. Smith (eds.), *Grading goal four*. Brill, pp. 238–261.

Bergman, Z., Bergman, M.M., Fernandes, K., Grossrieder, D., and Schneider, L., 2018. 'The contribution of UNESCO chairs toward achieving the UN sustainable development goals'. *Sustainability*, 10(12): 4471.

Bhambra, G.K., 2014. *Connected sociologies*. Bloomsbury Academic.
Biesta, G., Allan, J., and Edwards, R., 2011. 'The theory question in research capacity building in education: towards an agenda for research and practice'. *British Journal of Educational Studies*, 59(3): 225–239.
Boeren, E., 2019. 'Understanding Sustainable Development Goal (SDG) 4 on "quality education" from micro, meso and macro perspectives'. *International Review of Education*, 65: 277–294.
Boisvert, K., Flemming, J., and Shah, R., 2017. 'AEWG guide to the accelerated education principles'. INEE Network Spaces, https://inee.org/network-spaces/aewg
Brock-Utne, B., 2014. 'Language of instruction in Africa: the most important and least appreciated issue'. *International Journal of Educational Development in Africa*, 1(1): 4–18.
Bruns, B., Filmer, D., and Patrinos, H.A., 2011. *Making schools work: new evidence on accountability reforms*. World Bank Publications.
Buchert, L., 1995. 'The concept of education for all: what has happened after Jomtien?' *International Review of Education/Internationale Zeitschrift für Erziehungswissenschaft/Revue Internationale de l'Education*, 41(6): 537–549.
Butler, J., Gambetti, Z., and Sabsay, L. eds., 2016. *Vulnerability in resistance*. Duke University Press.
Casely-Hayford, L., and Hartwell, A., 2013. 'Reaching the underserved with complementary education: lessons from Ghana's state and non-state sectors'. In L. Casely-Hayford and A. Hartwell (eds.), *Achieving education for all through public–private partnerships?* Routledge, pp. 55–67.
Chouliaraki, L., and Georgiou, M., 2022. *The digital border: migration, technology, power* (Vol. 44). NYU Press.
Cohen, E., Willemsen, L.W., Shah, R., Vavrus, F., Nkhoma, N.M., Anderson, S., Srivastava, P., and Dryden-Peterson, S., 2021. 'Deconstructing and reconstructing comparative and international education in light of the COVID-19 emergency: imagining the field anew'. *Comparative Education Review*, 65(2): 356–374.
Connell, R., 2020. *Southern theory: the global dynamics of knowledge in social science*. Routledge.
Cornwall, A., and Fujita, M., 2012. 'Ventriloquising "the Poor"? Of voices, choices and the politics of "participatory" knowledge production'. *Third World Quarterly*, 33(9): 1751–1765.
Cox, R., 1996. *Approaches to world order*. Cambridge University Press.
Croft, A., 2002. 'Singing under a tree: does oral culture help lower primary teachers be learner-centred?'. *International Journal of Educational Development*, 22(3–4): 321–337.
Crossouard, B., and Dunne, M., 2021. *Gender and education in postcolonial contexts*. In *Oxford research encyclopaedia of education*, Oxford University Press, pp. 1–23. https://doi.org/10.1093/acrefore/9780190264093.013.1583
de Sousa Santos, B., 2007. 'Beyond abyssal thinking: from global lines to ecologies of knowledges'. *Review (Fernand Braudel Center)*, 30(1): 45–89.
DeStefano, J., Hartwell, A., Schuh Moore, A., and Benbow, J., 2005. *Meeting EFA: cost-effectiveness of complementary approaches*. Education Quality Improvement Program, 2, Washington.
DeStefano, J., Schuh Moore, A., Balwanz, D., and Hartwell, A., 2007. *Reaching the underserved: complementary models of effective schooling*. Academy for Educational Development.

Dunne, M., and Ananga, E.D., 2013. 'Dropping out: identity conflict in and out of school in Ghana'. *International Journal of Educational Development*, 33(2): 196–205.

Egbujuo, C.J., 2022. *Opportunities and challenges to support out-of-school children and youth through accelerated education programmes*. University of Auckland and Accelerated Education Working Group (AEWG), Auckland, New Zealand, pp. 1–49.

Farrell, J.P., and Hartwell, A., 2008. *Planning for successful alternative schooling: a possible route to education for all*. Research Papers, International Institute for Educational Planning (IIEP), UNESCO, Paris.

Fitzpatrick, R., 2020. *Enablers and barriers to the successful delivery of accelerated learning programmes*. Education Development Trust London.

Freire, P., 1970. *Pedagogy of the oppressed*. Herder and Herder.

Gerrard, J., Sriprakash, A., and Rudolph, S., 2022. 'Education and racial capitalism'. *Race, Ethnicity and Education*, 25(3): 425–442.

Ginsburg, M., 2012. 'Teachers as learners: a missing focus in "learning for all"'. In S. Klees, J. Samoff, and N. Stromquist (eds.), *The World Bank and education*. Brill, pp. 83–93.

Heidhues, F., and Obare, G.A., 2011. 'Lessons from structural adjustment programmes and their effects in Africa'. *Quarterly Journal of International Agriculture*, 50(1): 55–64.

Hoadley, U., 2020. *Schools in the time of COVID-19: impacts of the pandemic on curriculum*. Resep non-economic working paper, Stellenbosch University. [Accessed 09.04.2021]. https://resep.sun.ac.za/wp-content/uploads/2020/11/COVID-CURRICULUM-WORKING-PAPER.pdf

Hogg, L., 2012. 'Funds of knowledge: an examination of theoretical frameworks'. *New Zealand Annual Review of Education*, 21: 47–76.

Humphreys, S., Moses, D., Kaibo, J., and Dunne, M., 2015. 'Counted in and being out: fluctuations in primary school and classroom attendance in northern Nigeria'. *International Journal of Educational Development*, 44: 134–143.

IDinsight, 2023. 'Luminos programme impact evaluation: randomised controlled trial of an accelerated learning programme for out of school children in Liberia'. https://www.idinsight.org/publication/luminos-program-impact-evaluation

Jackson, A.Y., and Mazzei, L.A., 2013. 'Plugging one text into another: thinking with theory in qualitative research'. *Qualitative Inquiry*, 19(4): 261–271.

Jackson, A.Y., and Mazzei, L.A., 2022. *Thinking with theory in qualitative research*. Routledge.

Kan, S., Fahez, M., and Valenza, M., 2022. *Foundational literacy and numeracy in rural Afghanistan: findings from a baseline learning assessment of accelerated learning centres*. UNICEF Office of Research, Innocenti UNICEF Afghanistan Country Office.

Klees, S.J., 2012. 'Ideological premises and ideological conclusions'. In S.J. Klees, J. Samoff, and N.P. Stromquist (eds.), *The World Bank and education*. Brill, pp. 49–65.

Klees, S.J., 2024. 'Why SDG4 and the other SDGs are failing and what needs to be done'. *International Journal of Educational Development*, 104: 102946.

Klees, S.J., Samoff, J., and Stromquist, N.P. eds., 2012. *The World Bank and education: critiques and alternatives* (Vol. 14). Springer Science and Business Media.

Klees, S.J., Stromquist, N.P., Samoff, J., and Vally, S., 2019. 'The 2018 world development report on education: a critical analysis'. *Development and Change*, 50(2): 603–620.

Kothari, U., 2005. 'Authority and expertise: the professionalisation of international development and the ordering of dissent'. *Antipode*, 37(3): 425–446.

Le Grange, L., 2012. 'Ubuntu, ukama and the healing of nature, self and society'. *Educational Philosophy and Theory*, 44(2): 56–67.
Le Grange, L., 2018. 'The notion of Ubuntu and the (Post) Humanist condition'. In L. Le Grange (ed.), *Indigenous philosophies of education around the world*. Routledge, pp. 40–60.
Lewin, K.M., and Akyeampong, K., 2009. 'Education in sub-Saharan Africa: researching access, transitions and equity'. *Comparative Education*, 45(2): 143–150.
Lewis, D., Kanji, N. and Themudo, N.S., 2020. *Non-governmental organizations and development*. Routledge.
Longden, K., 2013. *Accelerated learning programmes: what can we learn from them about curriculum reform?* Background paper for EFA Global Monitoring Report, p. 14.
Luminos Fund, 2018a. *Annual report*. Available at: https://luminosfund.org/wp-content/uploads/2021/10/Luminos_Annual_Report_2018_spreads.pdf (luminosfund.org) [Accessed: 23.02.2024].
Luminos Fund, 2018b. *Unlocking the light in every child*. Available at: https://luminosfund.org/wp-content/uploads/2018/07/Luminos-Summary-of-Sussex-Longitudinal-Study-Findings.pdf.
Luminos Fund, 2021. *Annual report*. Available at: https://luminosfund.org/wp-content/uploads/2022/07/Luminos-Fund-2021-Annual-Report.pdf [Accessed: 23.02.2024].
Luminos Fund, 2022. *2021–2022 endline evaluation report*. https://luminosfund.org/wp-content/uploads/2023/01/Liberia-2021-22-Endline-Evaluation-Report_Luminos-Fund.pdf
MacLure, M., 2010. 'The offence of theory'. *Journal of Education Policy*, 25(2): 277–286.
Menendez, A.S., Ramesh, A., Baxter, P., and North, L., 2016. *Accelerated education programs in crisis and conflict*. The Pearson Institute. [Accessed 09.09.2020] https://thepearsoninstitute.org/sites/default/files/2017-02/36.%20Menendez_Accelerated%20Education%20Programs_1.pdf.
Mfum-Mensah, O., 2017. *Education, social progress, and marginalised children in sub-Saharan Africa: historical antecedents and contemporary challenges*. Lexington Books.
Mitchell, R., 2019. *Student organisation as a facet of teaching quality in sub-Saharan Africa: evidence to inform the World Bank's Teach observation instrument*. UKFIET.
Murris, K., 2016. *The Posthuman child: educational transformation through philosophy with picture books*. Routledge.
Novelli, M., 2023. 'Historicising the geopolitics of education and the SDGs: from Western hegemony to a multi-polar world'. *International Journal of Educational Development*, 103: 1–3.
Novelli, M., Higgins, S., Ugur, M., and Valiente, O., 2014. 'The political economy of education systems in conflict-affected contexts: a rigorous literature review'. *GOV.UK*, https://www.gov.uk/government/publications/the-political-economy-of-education-systems-in-conflict-contexts.
Novelli, M., 2016. 'Capital, inequality and education in conflict-affected contexts'. *British Journal of Sociology of Education*, 37(6): 848–860.
Novelli, M., and Selenica, E., 2021. 'The political economy of education systems in conflict-affected contexts in a changed world order: a narrative literature review'. *UNIBO*, https://cris.unibo.it/handle/11585/919043.

Paulson, J., 2019. 'Evidence hungry, theory light: education and conflict, SDG16, and aspirations for peace and justice'. *Education and Conflict Review*, 2: 33–37.

Randall, J., O'Donnell, F., and Botha, S., 2020. 'Accelerated learning programs for out-of-school girls: the impact on student achievement and traditional school enrolment'. *FIRE: Forum for International Research in Education*, 6(2): 1–23.

Robertson, S.L., 2012. 'Placing teachers in global governance agendas'. *Comparative Education Review*, 56(4): 584–607.

Robertson, S., and Dale, R., 2008. 'Researching education in a globalising era: beyond methodological nationalism, methodological statism, methodological educationism and spatial fetishism'. In S. Robertson and R. Dale (ed.), *The production of educational knowledge in the global era*. Brill, pp. 17–32.

Rose, P., 2009. 'NGO provision of basic education: alternative or complementary service delivery to support access to the excluded?' *Compare*, 39(2): 219–233.

Roy, A., 2020. 'The pandemic is a portal'. *Financial Times*, 3 April. https://www.ft.com/content/10d8f5e8-74eb-11ea-95fe-fcd274e920ca.

Schweisfurth, M. and Elliot, J., 2019. 'Comparative education [Guest Editors]'. *Comparative Education*, 55(1): 1–8.

Sekaggya-Bagarukayo, D., and Oddy, J., 2022. *Opportunities and challenges to support out-of-school children and youth through accelerated learning programmes: case Study of Uganda*. University of Auckland and Accelerated Education Working Group (AEWG).

Shah, R., 2015. *Norwegian refugee council's accelerated education responses: a meta-evaluation*. NRC.

Shah, R., and Choo, W., 2020. *Accelerated education evidence review: strengthening the evidence base for accelerated education*. Accelerated Education Working Group (AEWG), UNHCR.

Shinohara, T., 2021. 'Complementary basic education programmes for out-of-school children in Bangladesh, Ghana and Ethiopia: a comparative overview'. In T. Shinohara (ed.), *Education and development*, Sevhage Publishers, Nigeria, pp. 71–93, https://sevhage.wordpress.com.

Silova, I., 2018. 'It's not a learning crisis, it's an international development crisis! A decolonial critique'. *Worlds of Education*. https://www.ei-ie.org/en/item/22332:wdr2018-reality-check-13-its-not-a-learning-crisis-its-an-international-development-crisis-a-decolonial-critique-by-iveta-silova

Sriprakash, A., Tikly, L., and Walker, S., 2020. 'The erasures of racism in education and international development: re-reading the "global learning crisis"'. *Compare: A Journal of Comparative and International Education*, 50(5): 676–692.

Taka, M., 2023. 'When education in emergencies fails: learners' motivations for a second chance education in post-conflict Rwanda'. *Compare: A Journal of Comparative and International Education*, 53(2): 217–234.

Taubman, P.M., 2010. *Teaching by numbers: deconstructing the discourse of standards and accountability in education*. Routledge.

Tikly, L., 2015. 'What works, for whom, and in what circumstances? Towards a critical realist understanding of learning in international and comparative education'. *International Journal of Educational Development*, 40: 237–249.

Torres, R.M., 2001. 'What happened at the world education forum?' *Adult Education and Development*, 56: 45–68.

Trudell, B., 2007. 'Local community perspectives and language of education in sub-Saharan African communities'. *International Journal of Educational Development*, 27(5): 552–563.

UIS (UNESCO Institute of Statistics), 2018. *One in five children, adolescents and youth is out of school.* UIS Fact Sheet No. 48, UIS/FS/2018/ED/48.

UIS (UNESCO Institute of Statistics) and UNICEF, 2022. *Factsheet 62 Policy Paper 48 New Estimation confirms out of school population is growing in sub-Saharan Africa.* https://unesdoc.unesco.org/ark:/48223/pf0000382577

UN General Assembly, 1948. Universal declaration of human rights. Available at: https://www.un.org/en/about-us/universal-declaration-of-human-rights

UNESCO, 2005. *Education for all; the quality imperative.* Education for All Global Monitoring Report.

UNESCO, 2014. *Teaching and learning: achieving quality for all.* Education for All Global Monitoring Report.

UNICEF, 2021. *The state of the global education crisis: a path to recovery: A joint UNESCO, UNICEF and WORLD BANK report..* Available at: https://www.unicef.org/reports/state-global-education-crisis.

UNICEF, and UNESCO, 2015. *Fixing the broken promise of education for all: findings from the global initiative on out-of-school children.* UNICEF.

University of Sussex, 2018. *A longitudinal study of out of school education in Ethiopia.* Luminos Fund.

Unterhalter, E., and North, A., 2011. 'Girls' schooling, gender equity, and the global education and development agenda: conceptual disconnections, political struggles, and the difficulties of practice'. *Feminist Formations*, 23(3): 1–22.

Vavrus, F. and Seghers, M., 2010. 'Critical discourse analysis in comparative education: a discursive study of "partnership" in Tanzania's poverty reduction policies'. *Comparative Education Review*, 54(1): 77–103.

Verger, A., Edwards Jr, D.B., and Altinyelken, H.K., 2014. 'Learning from all? The World Bank, aid agencies and the construction of hegemony in education for development'. *Comparative Education*, 50(4): 381–399.

Verger, A., Novelli, M. and Altinyelken, H.K., 2012. 'Global education policy and international development: An introductory framework'. In A. Verger, M. Novelli, and H.K. Altinyelken (eds.), *Global education policy and international development: New agendas, issues and policies.* Bloomsbury, pp. 3–32.

Walker, M., 2012. 'A capital or capabilities education narrative in a world of staggering inequalities?'. *International Journal of Educational Development*, 32(3): 384–393.

World Bank, 2018. *World Development Report 2018: learning to realise education's promise.* The World Bank.

Yasunaga, M., 2014. 'Non-formal education as a means to meet learning needs of out-of-school children and adolescents'. In *Background paper prepared for fixing the broken promise of education for all: findings from the global initiative on out-of school children.* UNESCO Institute for Statistics, Montreal.

Zapp, M., 2017. 'The World Bank and education: governing (through) knowledge'. *International Journal of Educational Development*, 53: 1–11.

Part I
Rethinking the Learning Challenge in Sub-Saharan Africa

2 The Production of the 'Poor Child' as Deficit

In this chapter, we take forward the issues raised in the critiques of the framings and assumptions of the 'global learning crisis' we discussed in Chapter 1. We show in more detail the ways in which these issues are so embedded in historical and contemporary deficit thinking about the child living in poverty that no account is taken of children's capacities, cultures or the communities in which they live. The effect of initiatives such as Education for All arguably is that these agendas do not offer them education in any meaningful sense. The education offered is largely irrelevant to reducing children's poverty. The construction of the 'poor child' (Hopkins and Sriprakash, 2015)[1] and of 'poor' communities experiencing educational marginalisation forecloses alternative approaches to pedagogical practices, community engagement and the content and goals of learning and cannot provide an expansive view of educational provision that may be better tailored to their needs and lived experiences.

Our approach is different. Our starting point is an interrogation of the connection between poverty alleviation and educational provision through hegemonic global agendas in the field and practice of education and development. These agendas defy critique in their claims to certainty. Yet, as we show below, there are underlying assumptions about poverty and education, which underscore their framing of both and the resulting failure to achieve Education For All (EFA's) triumphalist promises. We show how, whilst purportedly a response to current learning challenges in sub-Saharan Africa, the responses of diverse international aid agencies to the 'learning crisis' carry the legacy of long-standing framings of 'poor children' and the 'poor' as a demographic in this region. These framings are mediated through development, humanitarian and colonialist discourses and practices that frame poverty in narrowly materialistic terms as shortfalls in income and economic capital. Similarly, we highlight a failure to recognise the gendered experiences of poverty faced by girls in poverty alleviation schemes that purport to empower them whilst, in effect, diminishing their lives and agency. The characterisations of 'poor children' installed at the heart of development activities are Western-centric stereotypes and context-blind notions establishing a particular child subject as a global ideal and norm. We argue that the consequent partial social imaginaries of 'poor children' result in a narrow framing of the parameters and scope of educational interventions.

DOI: 10.4324/9781003185482-4

In the final section, we show how this deficit model of the child living in poverty is now assumed by international aid agencies that are committed to improving children's chances of an education and thus of helping reduce poverty in the long run in their country. We unpack the way the six agencies which are, at the time of writing, highly influential in shaping education and development practices in sub-Saharan Africa represent 'poor children' and their development needs, both in words and images. Our reading of such representations indicates a convergence across diverse development institutions about the framing of the 'poor child' that focuses only on what these children and their communities lack. Overall, through critiquing and historicising the taken-for-granted assumptions that underpin framings of the 'learning crisis', we encourage the field of international and comparative education, including education scholars and policymakers, to rethink the ways in which educational provision is linked to poverty alleviation and to re-envision responses that draw on a multi-dimensional approach to understanding the lived experience of 'poor children'. We describe this approach in detail in Chapter 5.

The following discussion mobilises anthropological and ethnographic studies of the lives of the poor. It focuses, for example on the ways in which children experience poverty, drawing upon the sociology and cultural politics of childhood, studies of poverty alleviation strategies in social policy and critical approaches within the field of research into education and development. Mobilising diverse epistemic resources to illuminate the role of education for 'poor children' counters a tendency towards disciplinary siloisation. As noted by Nieuwenhuys (2013, 6), many childhood studies are notable for the "compartmentalisation of different fields of intervention". We therefore, bring into play the insights gained from studies of the micro-level experiences of 'poor children' and contrast them with the assumptions of macro-level policy and programming that mobilise education for this demographic. In doing so, we interrupt, interrogate and rethink policymakers' conceptualisation of the 'learning crisis'. The current self-referential skewing of the evidence base by the World Bank's publications privileges narrowly economistic accounts of the purpose and value of educational provision (Klees, 2012; Ravallion, 2016a,b). Widening the epistemic base to understand children's experiences of learning is therefore an underlying methodological commitment in this book.

Making the Connection: Poverty Alleviation and Educational Provision

The promise that education provision may enable children, their families and communities to escape the intergenerational transmission of poverty has long been an uncontested leitmotiv of global social development policy and practice.[2] As noted by Bessel (2017, 145):

among key international agencies of quite different ideological perspectives, including UNDP, UNICEF, UNESCO and the World Bank, education is represented as a pathway out of poverty both for individuals, potentially their families and for nations.

This promise has been most recently reiterated in the vision for global social transformation outlined in the UN Sustainable Development Goals (SDGs) (Sachs, 2012; Sayed and Moriarty, 2020). As stated in SDG 1, providing inclusive, equitable quality education for all (a target in SDG 4) is considered a pivotal contribution to achieving the overarching aim to 'eradicate extreme poverty by 2030 for all people everywhere' (Kamruzzaman, 2016, 87). This highlights the fact that more than "700 million people or 10 per cent of the world population, still live in extreme poverty today, struggling to fulfil the most basic needs like health, education, and access to water and sanitation, to name but a few". SDG 4 declares that "education enables upward socio-economic mobility and is key to escaping poverty".[3]

The link between education and reducing poverty also forms part of the SDGs' agenda to address global inequality and injustice through the interdependence of its separate goals (Wulff, 2020). So, SDG 1 and SDG 4 resonate with SDG 10 that aims to "reduce inequality within and between countries" (Wulff, 2020, 8). Such aspirations tie education into what is widely framed not only as an economic but also a moral and social justice imperative of global social policy (Pemberton, 2016; Gaisbauer et al., 2016; Roelen, 2017). As Lister (2021, 1) notes, "poverty as a material reality disfigures and constrains the lives of millions of women, men and children". The following statement in the report of the UIS and UNICEF (2015, 7 quoted in Datzberger, 2018, 3) captures this halo effect which is associated with the impact of educational provision in global policy rhetoric:

> Education represents the hopes, dreams and aspirations of children, families, communities and nations around the world – the most reliable route out of poverty and a critical pathway towards healthier, more productive citizens and stronger societies.

The pivotal role of education in reducing poverty in developing countries has been promoted by the World Bank in particular. Yunus (2022) notes that 'poverty' emerged as one of the 'top priorities' of the World Bank's development programmes in the 1990s even as education began to be circulated as critical for improving growth rates and reducing poverty. Education thus forms a key component in the Poverty Reduction Strategy Papers produced by the World Bank and the IMF from 1999 (Bonal and Tarabini-Castellani, 2009; Tarabini and Jacovkis, 2012). By influencing the agendas of diverse international aid agencies (Mason, 2012, 496), these publications have been characterised as establishing a *hegemonic link* between education provision and poverty alleviation within global development policy (Tarabini and Jacovkis, 2012, 507, 515).

In addition, in what has become known as the 'girling of development' (Hayhurst, 2011, 523; see also Khoja-Moolji, 2015, 87), or the 'girl powering of development' (Koffman and Gill, 2013, 86 in Khoja-Moolji, 2015), the emancipatory promise of education is deemed especially relevant for girls experiencing precarity. They constitute the most educationally marginalised demographic (Paddison, 2017). In sub-Saharan Africa for every 100 boys of primary school age, there are 123 girls who are not in education (UIS, 2018; UNESCO, 2020; Crossouard and Dunne, 2021). Hence, Khoja-Moolji writes of a 'global consensus' that educating girls is 'a commonsensical solution to poverty' (2015, 87). This has resulted in what some scholars consider are inflated and unrealistic claims for the developmental benefits of providing education. Hence:

> it is assumed that if girls in the global south can obtain schooling, they will marry at a later age, delay childrearing, participate in the wage based economy, take good care of their children and families and ultimately bring their nations out of abject poverty and violence.
>
> (2015, 88)

The challenges of alleviating poverty through education have been much sharpened by unprecedented global developments, in particular the ongoing and converging impacts of the Covid-19 pandemic and climate change. Whilst the pandemic has been global in its reach, it has affected the rich and the impoverished differently, in effect intensifying global and national inequalities (Stiglitz, 2021; Wulff, 2020). Meanwhile, the environmental degradation and people's vulnerability to natural disasters resulting from global warming have severely affected the already fragile ecosystems and hence the chances of household survival of the poor in developing countries.

Interruptions to learning provision because of the pandemic have also exacerbated the challenge of achieving quality education for all. A report on progress towards achieving the SDGs notes that "Covid-19 has cast a shadow on an already dire picture of learning outcomes" worsening a pre-existing 'crisis in learning' (UN, 2022, 34). According to this 2022 update:

> an estimated 147 million children missed more than half of their in-person instruction over the past two years.
>
> (UN, 2022)

The report recognised that "school closures have had worrisome consequences for children's learning and wellbeing, particularly for girls and those who are disadvantaged, including children with disabilities, rural dwellers and ethnic minorities" (UN, 2022, 34). In particular they have deepened disparities in learning and access to education between high- and low-income households, worsening already entrenched inequalities in engagement with education provision (UN, 2022, 11). Hence, "children living in rural areas and in the poorest households are consistently more disadvantaged in terms of educational participation" (UN, 2022, 11). The long-term impact of closures means that '24 million learners may never return to school' (UN, 2022, 11). Also, the gendered impact of Covid-19 on the livelihood opportunities of women and girls and the intensified demand for unpaid care work in low-income households have had direct and indirect consequences for girls' opportunities to access formal education (Kabeer et al., 2021), exacerbating their pre-existing marginalisation.

Narrow framings of poverty

The role of education in poverty alleviation therefore has never been more pressing or more challenging. However, the approach of the World Bank and other leading international development agencies has been extensively critiqued (Klees, 2008; Mason, 2012; Dyer, 2012, 2013; Connell, 2013). Both the way that poverty and education are understood and, in turn, how the intersection between education and alleviating poverty is framed in the triumphalist rhetoric of global policy have become matters of concern. For instance, Bray et al. (2020, 1) note a lack of specificity about what exactly is meant by poverty. Hence, "The Sustainable Development Goals require countries to halve poverty in all its dimensions by 2020 but the dimensions are nowhere specified" (2020, 1) Moreover, the top-down approach of international aid agencies bypasses the United Nation's aspiration that "policy should be informed by the meaningful participation of persons living in poverty" (2020, 1).

Of particular relevance are critiques of the World Bank's use of economic indicators such as household income to define poverty, resulting in a reductive and 'technocratic' discourse (Tarabini and Jacovkis, 2012, 508). Linking poverty alleviation narrowly to macro-economic growth, the experience of poverty is reduced to only material deprivation (Caillods and Hallak, 2004, 27; Tarabini and Jacovkis, 2012). Such an approach ignores the social, cultural and political dimensions of poverty. Thus, Caillods and Hallak (2004), in their review of the World Bank's Poverty Reduction Strategy Papers, argue that "an approach dominated by economic analysis fails to capture the many dimensions of poverty while a multi-disciplinary approach can deepen our understanding of the lives of the poor" (28). Arguing for a wider understanding of the experience of poverty, these authors argue that:

> direct consultations with poor people have revealed that vulnerability, physical and social isolation, insecurity, lack of self-respect, lack of access to information, a distrust of state institutions, and powerlessness can be seen as [being as] detrimental to the poor as a low income.
> (Caillods and Hallak, 2004, 28)

In other words, what is bypassed in dominant framings are the varied experiences and exposure to asymmetrical power relationships of the demographics characterised as experiencing poverty.

Scholars have highlighted a need to consult with the poor about how they understand and experience their situation, and also to be careful to avoid using adult-centric and homogenising framings that fail to differentiate children's experiences of poverty from those of adults (see for example: Boyden, 2003; Bourdillon and Boyden, 2011; Boyden et al., 2019). Twenty years ago, Feeny and Boyden (2004, 1) recognised that:

> the rhetorical commitment to 'putting children first' has not always been translated faithfully into practice, and the research base still suffers from an overall tendency to prioritise adult perspectives that often bear little resemblance to the actual experience of the child and may even serve to obscure the real dimensions of their poverty further.

Hence, they caution that:

> Many of the conclusions drawn around child poverty are the result of generalised statistics or simplistic theoretical assumptions riven with cultural and conceptual biases. There is still far too little understanding of how a child experiences poverty, what impoverishment means to them, or how their perceptions/priorities interact with those of local communities and the agendas of international aid agencies.
> (Feeny and Boyden, 2004, 1)

Phiri and Abebe (2016) added that "dominant approaches within academia and international policy fail to reflect the diversity and complexity of the lived experiences of children living in poverty" (378), with implications for how educational provision is framed.

Empirical studies that seek to retrieve children's distinctive experiences of poverty in order to establish new frontiers in the fight against child poverty in Africa' (Roelen et al., 2019) suggest that this adult-centricity and narrowly economistic approach continues in poverty alleviation strategies (Crivello et al., 2009; Phiri and Abebe, 2016; Roelen et al., 2019). Ngutuku (2019, 26) noted, "child poverty goes beyond income deprivation ... is multi-dimensional and affects children differently from adults". Hence, "there is a need for an approach that focuses on finer textures of children's experiences beyond deprivation and the dominant categories of poor and vulnerable children" (2019, 27). Also, more child-centric understandings of the experience of poverty can draw attention to its highly gendered impact, overlooked within a field that has remained largely 'gender blind' (Esquivel and Sweetman, 2016; Kabeer et al., 2021). Lack of understanding of the distinctive needs of girls (and boys) undermines the tailoring of education provision that is required to realise the lofty ambition of alleviating poverty.

Narrow framings of learning

The framings of education provision by the World Bank and other development agencies have also been subjected to trenchant critiques. As noted in Chapter 1, easily measurable indicators, such as enrolment rates of 'poor children' in formal education, dominate in macro-social global policy at the expense of understanding children's experiences of learning and the pedagogical processes and curriculum content that may best promote them (Unterhalter, 2020; Alexander, 2015; Barrett, 2011). The narrow focus on measuring the development of cognitive skills in the global framing of educational priorities (Benavot and Smith, 2020) also ignores the importance of children's wider social and emotional development. Foreclosed in such framings of the solution to educational marginalisation is an expansive conception of educational provision that addresses childrens' well-being and identity as well as the possibility of contributing to social transformation for them as well as their families and communities.

Attempting to 'measure the unmeasurable' (Unterhalter, 2020) with a reliance on quantitative indicators prevents attention being given to the subjectivities of marginalised learners in their engagement with learning opportunities. In contrast, Humphreys et al. (2015, 135) usefully distinguish between (a) access as enrolment, (b) access as sustained attendance (sustained access), (c) access to the classroom, once in school, and (c) access to the curriculum, with pupils engaged in 'meaningful learning. Yet, all these elements are often elided together in the reduction of children's experiences of learning to a statistical synthesis. The situated and contingent experiences of children who suffer educational marginalisation because of poverty are obscured by quantitative indicators that ignore the 'myriad out of school factors that can draw children into school or push them out even within the same day' (Humphreys et.al., 2015, 134). Moreover, the use of an operational proxy of primary school attendance to measure educational deprivation (Dyer, 2012, 259) implicitly conflates learning only with formal schooling, not recognising the multiple other contexts within which children learn.

As a result, the framing of education and poverty alleviation strategies can generate narrow educational priorities, and also foreclose deep attention to teaching approaches and curriculum content. The effect is to limit opportunities to align them with a holistic and context-responsive understanding of children's needs and their situated lived experiences. The study of Poverty Alleviation Strategies by Caillods and Hallak (2004, 75) noted that:

> there is no innovative teaching/learning reform proposed.... that could be regarded as having been designed to address the specific needs of the poor, while at the same time seeking quality improvement, relevance and meeting the target of integrating them in the development process.

The framing of appropriate teaching and learning processes without recognising children's experiences of poverty is arguably symptomatic of what Schweisfurth (2015, 261) terms a "lack of critical engagement with pedagogy at the international level". Hence, the 'policy space' of educational provision for the poor has been filled with 'ready-made' prescriptions that deny the 'contingent' nature of pedagogy. This is apparent in the widespread support by international aid organisations, including the World Bank, donor agencies and NGOs, for what, paradoxically, are termed 'learner-centred' or 'child-centred' approaches to teaching and learning. *Learner-centred pedagogy* has become a 'globally travelling prescription for improvements to teaching and learning, even a panacea' (Schweisfurth, 2015, 259). Yet, Altinyelken (2018, 209) has warned of the dangers of a "converging pedagogy in the global south" that ignores the context-responsive nature of teaching and learning. For Tikly (2004), the dissemination of this pedagogy in low-income contexts amounts to a form of 'cultural imperialism'.

Hence, empirical studies that have shown how decades of poverty alleviation strategies have failed to result in practical improvements in the lives of the poor (Craig and Porter, 2003; Balagopalan, 2019, 2022; Boyden et al., 2021). UIS and UNICEF (2015) reported that, over the past two decades, long-standing patterns of educational inequality and exclusion have largely been reproduced and the most marginalised communities have seen little progress. In 2018, Datzberger's study of poverty alleviation strategies in Uganda with the salutary title, *Why Education is not helping the Poor* concluded that "progress in poverty alleviation is not only stagnant but the role of education therein can be described as 'modest' at best" (2018, 124). She explained that "current strategies to reduce poverty revolve around a strong assimilation-based development agenda": (2018, 124) fail to mobilise education such that it addresses and transforms the structural roots of poverty and the daily lived experiences of those living in poverty or to recognise their agency to "make their own decisions about their futures and lives" (2018, 127).

That "agreements like EFA, the Millennium Development Goals and the SDGs have made hardly a dent in global marginalisation and suffering" (Klees, 2020, 23) underscores the utopianism of the repeated promotion of education as transformative for those experiencing poverty. As Wulff (2020, 1) pointed out, the aims of the SDGs to address educational marginalisation in the service of poverty alleviation have to be set against a background of the failures of previous EFA goals. Thus "the promise of education for all in September 2015" was reaffirmed 'for the third time in three decades" (Wulff, 2020, 1). Ansell et al. (2020) add that the triumphalist rhetoric assuming a direct causal link between education provision and poverty alleviation is less and less compelling in "remote rural areas whose populations are surplus to the requirements of the global economy" (17). In effect, achieving employment in well-rewarded economic activity as a result of education is "unattainable by most" (17) in communities whose environment is rendered hostile by climate change or who are displaced from their land by global corporations. In such contexts, the repeated promise that education will transform the lives of 'poor children' arguably amounts to an "abuse of aspiration" (Ansell et al., 2020, 18).

Problematising the framings of poverty and education and highlighting a persistent gap between rhetoric and reality, these diverse critiques suggest the need to keep a critical distance from the triumphalism of current equations of education provision with poverty alleviation, and in so doing, rethink and re-envision how education and, in particular, pedagogical strategies and the curriculum can be better tailored to meeting the needs of children and communities who experience poverty. Yet, as noted by Mason (2012, 494), "questions about the connections between education development policies and the alleviation of poverty are among the most intractable in the field" (2012, 494). In this context, Lister (2021) notes that responses to poverty in social policy "are shaped by the conceptualisation, definition and measurement of poverty, together with the explanations implicit in them" (11). Similarly, Cornwall and Fujita (2012) point to the fact that 'the poor' "is not a category of analysis that many people living in poverty would claim for themselves... rather it is a label used to designate others" (1756). Significantly, policy responses are predicated upon 'social imaginaries' (Taylor, 2004; Sum and Jessop, 2015, 16) or assumptions about the lived experiences and sociality of those labelled poor which inform and justify such assumptions. Sum and Jessop draw attention to the partiality and simplification of all such social imaginaries that directs attention to 'some aspects of the world out of countless possibilities'.

As noted in Chapter 1, these issues raise a fundamental ontological question: how are the social realities of 'poor children' construed? (Kromidas, 2019). They also raise epistemological questions, such as whose knowledges count and whose do not count in understanding the lived experience of poverty? What is foregrounded, and rendered visible and what is excluded or invisible as a result? And what are the implications for defining and tailoring educational provision through appropriate pedagogies and curriculum? Such questions invite a historicised interrogation of the social imaginaries underpinning education and poverty alleviation strategies which scrutinises the historical conditions in which particular conceptions of poverty and policy responses emerged. They also invite examining the power relationships operative in promoting conceptions of education and poverty. As Lister (2021) noted, poverty is a highly contested and multi-valent concept and "in general it is the understandings held by more powerful groups rather than by those who experience poverty, that are reflected in the dominant conceptualisations" (2021, 5).

In the next section, we address these questions through a historical analysis of diverse but complementary agendas in development policies and practices that have shaped how 'poor children' are construed and that converge in producing the 'poor child'. These historical determinants shaping contemporary global education policy are often forgotten in the tendency to a narrow 'presentism' (Hartog, 2016) that characterises framings of this demographic in the 'learning crisis' narrative. As Lister noted:

> there is no single concept of poverty that stands outside of history and culture ... it is a construction of different societies' that carries 'implicit explanations.
>
> (2021, 4)

Historicising Deficit Framings of the 'Poor Child'

Our starting point in deconstructing the notion of the 'poor child' is Arturo Escobar (2011)'s recognition that, after the Second World War, negative views of the poor became basic to the development practices of international aid agencies, including the World Bank. These views were based on a one-dimensional characterisation of the poor as lacking material wealth. The 'poor' were constructed as a demographic defined by their failure to meet an annual per capita income measure (Sachs 1990, 9) and therefore in need of 'scrutiny and regulation' by Western nations through the mobilisation of professional 'expert knowledge' (Escobar, 2011, 45). Sachs (1990) captures the artificiality of this designation by pointing out that "the construction of two thirds of the world as poor after 1945 resulted from the statistical application of the annual per capita income measure" (9). Hence, "almost by fiat, two thirds of the world's peoples were transformed into poor subjects". Consequently, "poverty became an organising concept and the object of a new problematisation" (Escobar, 2011, 24) within the practices and interventions of international development agencies. This generated framings that located such demographics in stereotypical negative terms. So, within the priorities of the emergent field of development:

> ... societies of the Third World were no longer seen as diverse and incomparable possibilities of human living arrangements but were rather placed on a single progressive track judged more or less advanced according to the criteria of western industrial nations.
> (Sachs, 2008, 2)

> A failure to valorise the culture and lifestyles of those designated poor was thus constitutive of the 'archaeology' of the 'development idea'
> (Sachs, 2008, 2).

Of relevance is the narrow framing of poverty itself on which damaging assumptions about the experiences of the poor were predicated. As noted by Escobar (2011, 24):

> the essential trait of the Third World was its poverty, and that the solution was economic growth and development, material advancement achieved through capital investment, became self-evident, necessary and universal truths.

Yet, the equation of poverty solely with household income "has little resonance in most of Africa". In particular, it omits a situated and relational understanding of the positionality of the 'poor child'. As noted by Phiri and Abebe (2016, 379/380) children's:

> resourcefulness in contributing to household survival through income-generating labour is overshadowed because it is assumed that they are dependent on adults and that income is only generated by adults.

This underscores the relational dynamics missing in the statistical representation of household income. However, the economistic framing of poverty underpins various international agendas that prefer to use a human capital approach to children.

Children as potential economic capital

The framing of 'poor children' as in need of developing economic capital through education by organisations such as the World Bank aligns directly with the tenets of *human capital theory*. This is a highly influential discourse shaping the goals and justifications for development interventions and, in particular, the provision of education for poverty alleviation by donor agencies, international aid organisations and financial institutions, especially the World Bank.[4] A central premise is that investment in education is a key driver of economic growth (Schultz, 1961, 3) and has major economic benefits. Hence, "education may be seen as a form of capital along with land and labour" (Resnik, 2006, 181). In other words, education is seen as an investment in individual skills that make one productive and employable (Klees, 2020, 11). Its key purpose is to contribute to developing children's economic capital to enable them to compete in an economic marketplace. Promoted as a form of 'neutral and scientific knowledge,' human capital theory appeals to policymakers because it enables investment in education to be justified in "quantitative and predictive terms" (Resnik, 2006, 174). This has produced what has been termed an *education – economic growth black box*, amounting to a form of 'global educational culture' (Resnik, 2006, 173). Hence, policymakers' blindness to other ways of conceptualising the goals of education provision for poverty alleviation that go beyond intended impacts on macro-economic and (questionable) rates of returns from education.

Within the logics of human capital theory, children experiencing poverty are framed in negative terms. Resnik (2006) notes that they are understood to lack the ability to contribute to the national 'stock of human capital' (171), thus needing education interventions targeting a narrow range of skills, literacy and numeracy in compensation (Klees et al., 2019, 607) that would prepare them to be able to compete in the global market economy (Brown et al., 2010). The wording of SDG 4 that states that "many students are not fully prepared to participate in a highly complex global economy", reiterates this narrowly economistic educational agenda (Sayed and Moriarty, 2020, 198). For Carnoy (1974), such a framing of learning serves to "colonise children's minds in developed and underdeveloped countries so as to contribute to capitalist accumulation" (quoted in Resnik, 2006, 176).

For Wheelahan et al. (2022), the reduction of education to the development of cognitive competencies linked to human capital development is also symptomatic of a 'skills fetish' in which skills become separated from 'embodied agents on the one hand and from social relations on the other' (476), producing an 'impoverished view of human beings and learning' (476). Hence, the construction of 'poor children' only as potential carriers of economic capital erases their location within challenging circumstances of precarity, implicitly devaluing their 'positive' agency as social actors navigating such contexts and, in doing so building knowledges, skills and other capitals outside of those connected to the imperatives of global capitalism (Wheelahan et al., 2022). In other words, the other forms of capital that children bring to learning – cultural, linguistic, social – forged in their daily lived experiences are erased from this picture.

In framing 'intellectual formation' only as a 'mode of economic capital' (Marginson, 2019, 2), a human capital approach thereby excludes the possibility that education provision might connect with the other many dimensions of children's lives and the creativity and resourcefulness that they may develop in navigating challenging circumstances. Such assumptions underpin the narrow framing of education provision as a matter of developing cognitive skills understood in isolation from children's wider identity and agency noted in Chapter 1. As Sayed and Moriarty (2020, 199) note, "a utilitarian imperative that reduces quality to literacy and numeracy, limits the ability of education to unlock a child's (or an adult's) full potential". Missing in this one-dimensional view is an expansive vision of education to contribute in a transformative and holistic way to the lives of 'poor children' (Ansell et al., 2020; Abebe and Biswas, 2021; Balagopalan, 2008, 2019, 2022).

Children as agents of modernisation

The devaluation of the contexts and cultures of 'poor children' and their communities is also aligned with what has been termed *modernisation theory* that has been similarly influential in shaping the policy advice and prescriptions of international organisations and Western governments (Bull and Bøås, 2012; Ntini, 2016). Modernisation theory stresses not only the economic backwardness but also the cultural backwardness of societies deemed poor (Rostow, 1960; Inkeles and Smith, 1974). Hence, the goals of development, and in turn education, were to produce 'modern' individuals where modernity is associated with possessing the skills required to contribute to the economic wealth of nations. This framed the role of education as engineering a progressive disconnection from traditional cultural values and practices in the interest of social progress, so as to enable less developed countries to catch up with their more developed counterparts. Education was therefore the 'key that unlocks the door to modernisation' (Harbison and Myers, 1964, 3).

This vision of the purpose of education problematises the indigenous lifestyles and culture of the poor within a highly ethnocentric Western approach. Indeed, the non-Western culture of poor communities was a "residual variable, to disappear with the advance of modernisation" (Escobar, 2011, 44). The paternalist and pathologising approach of the modernisation agenda is aligned with the neo-colonialist *'mission civilisatrice'* that similarly devalued local knowledges and experiences, seeking national behaviour change through Western-style formal education for select, elite groups. The poor became subjects of a classificatory system that distinguished between the civilised and the uncivilised (Tikly, 2004).

Construing the global poor in these ways problematises their lives and lifestyles as a homogenous demographic. Bonal and Zancajo (2018, 20);[5] noted the continuing influence of this approach in the World Bank's Poverty Reduction Strategy Papers. These assume a 'culture of deprivation' (2018, 20) that critiques the decision-making processes of households experiencing poverty and assumes an inability to make optimal choices to invest in their children's education. They thus ignore the difficult choices households have to make on an everyday basis in contexts of extreme hardship.

Gendered experiences of poverty: the production of girls as deficit

The multiple ways in which African children experiencing poverty are produced in deficit terms take on a distinctive register in relation to girls. As noted earlier, they are a key target of development agendas promoting the role of education in poverty alleviation. Considered to be a homogenous demographic, girls are constructed as 'anti-poverty agents' (Dogra, 2011, 340) and 'ideal subjects of development' (Switzer et al., 2016, 33), investment in whom will solve multiple development challenges. Yet, whilst hailing the agency of 'poor girls' as an 'answer to everything' (Unterhalter, 2023, 145), such framings have been critiqued for a failure to recognise the complexity of their lived experiences and the highly gendered challenges and constraints they face in navigating contexts of precarity (Monkman and Hoffman, 2013; Kabeer, 2015; Khoja-Moolji, 2017).

International aid organisations, NGOs, the World Bank and large corporations have framed investing in adolescent girls as a form of 'smart economics' (Chant and Sweetman, 2012) that will strengthen macro-economic development at national and global levels[6] A case in point is the 'girl effect' initiative of the Nike Foundation (Chant and Sweetman, 2012, 520; Koffman and Gill, 2013) whose promotional materials argue that strengthening 'girl power' in the global South is the best way to lift the developing world out of poverty' and a form of 'smarter economics' (Educate Girls, n.d.). Girls are consequently instrumentalised as entrepreneurial subjects whose poverty amelioration is associated with their receipt of waged labour and their participation as consumers in the market economy (Monkman and Hoffman, 2013). This amounts to a highly reductive understanding of their lives in circumstances of precarity that works to essentialise the girl subject in the global South as an 'untapped resource' (Calkin, 2015, 655) – a demographic dividend within the logics of neoliberal capitalism. As Dogra (2011, 339) comments: such messages project a neoliberal logic of good economic sense where women can act as a fundamental source of growth that can power our economies.

By 'responsibilising' individual girls, this projection displaces attention from the oppressive social norms and power relationships they face as gendered subjects, and the social, economic and political restrictions at local, national and global levels that contribute to their distinctive experiences of poverty (Khoja-Moolji, 2015, 53). Moreover, the association of their escape from poverty with their transition into waged labour is highly decontextualised, given the reliance of the majority of the rural poor in Africa on subsistence agriculture for economic survival (Crossouard and Dunne, 2021, 9).

Smart economics approaches also carry a hierarchical binary between girlhood in the Western world and girls who are experiencing poverty in the global South. The latter are deemed lacking, inadequate and in need of redemptive interventions (Khoja-Moolji, 2015) to enable them to acquire the 'girl power' displayed by their counterparts in the global North. This framing of 'poor girls' repeats the iconic image of the 'poor, powerless and pregnant' Third World Woman (Dogra, 2011, 333; Tiainen, 2023) who is 'traditional, needy and deserving' in contrast to Western Women who are construed as 'educated, modern and have the freedom to make their own decisions' (Dogra, 2011, 336). Such projections ignore girls' contributions to the reproductive work of families in unpaid domestic labour (Hoskyns and Rai, 2007; Rai et al., 2019). Hence, Khoja-Moolji (2015, 104) argues that:

> eembedded in these narratives is a devaluation of reproductive work that women and girls often perform in the household such as cleaning, cooking, caring for siblings and children.

Smart economics, whilst aggrandising girls' agency as the catalyst of social transformation, effectively diminishes their lives in treating them as 'untapped human capital' (Khoja-Moolji, 2015, 104). Chant and Sweetman (2012, 524) capture this contradictory positioning in asking whether such an approach amounts to 'fixing women or fixing the world?'

Such framings of the 'poor girl' in the global South are symptomatic of a wider gender blindness in poverty alleviation strategies (Kabeer, 1996; Whitehead and Lockwood, 1999; Prügl, 2017) of international aid agencies. Kabeer (1996, 11) observed how they are "premised on the concept of a male actor and male-centred notions of well being", ignoring the distinctive female experiences of poverty. Hence, the equation of poverty with household income fails to interrogate or recognise "how equitably household income is distributed amongst family members and the extent to which gender inequalities in basic needs fulfillment are a feature of this distribution" (Kabeer, 1996, 12). The focus on a static view of poverty as material needs deprivation ignores the relational nature of the experience of poverty which is shaped by the operation of gender norms and power relationships within and between households and which "set the parameters within which all women make or do not make choices regardless of household income" (Kabeer, 1996, 19). Hence, critics highlight girls' 'empowerment' as a 'journey not a destination' (Kabeer, 1996; Eyben et al., 2008; Cornwall and Edwards, 2010, 6). The concept of a journey would encourage an ongoing process of shifting the power relationships that thwart girls' horizons of action and possibility, rather than supporting a process that is understood in individualising terms as the outcome of girls' 'rational autonomous action' (Crossouard and Dunne, 2021, 13). Hence, Cornwall and Edwards (2010, 6) warn that meaningful empowerment happens when "individuals and organised groups are able to imagine their world differently and to realise that vision by changing the relations of power that have been keeping them in poverty".

Klees et al. (2019, 614) concur with this argument, pointing out whilst the World Bank Report signals the lack of gender parity between boys and girls in enrolment, access and outcomes as symptomatic of the learning crisis, it only provides a 'superficial set of solutions'. As many scholars have noted,[7] reliance on educational data tracking created according to binary sex differences ignores the social/institutional processes and operation of norms, within and outside of schooling, that constrain girls' opportunities. The effect is to reduce gender to an 'outcome' (Dunne, 2019, 49) rather than a product of particular, highly localised social and cultural contexts. Unterhalter (2023, 149) describes this as a 'techno-rationalist approach' in which gender is considered as a 'noun' and gender equality reduced to counting numbers, rather than being located as emergent from social relations and behaviours. Also missing from such desocialised framings of gender is the intersection of gendered experiences with other forms of exclusion rooted in ethnicity, religion and language.

The World Bank's diagnosis of the gender dimensions of the 'learning crisis' also ignores the significance of the 'opportunity structures' and intergenerational dynamics and expectations that shape girls' gendered experiences of poverty outside of school and which determine how they respond to the opportunity of formal educational provision (Devine et al., 2023, 1). Devine et al.'s study, for example, reveals how gendered experiences of schooling intersect with girls' out-of-school lives in rural communities in northern Sierra Leone that are experiencing abject poverty. They conclude that "it is their [girls'] social positioning in the community that has a significant influence on children's capacity to engage with schooling" (Devine et al., 2023). By framing gender in binary terms, and focusing on girls only, the vision of gender parity does not have a relational understanding of the production of gender. It needs to include boys' and men's attitudes and behaviours if it is to form part of a truly transformative agenda for gender justice (Cornwall and Rivas, 2015). The World Bank's education strategy's diagnosis of gender inequalities in education precisely repeats such exclusions and thus reifies the complex lives of girls in circumstances of poverty (Stromquist, 2012). Allied to its concerns for educational interventions to regulate girls' fertility and reproductive rights, such responses appear to represent a 'technology of global governance' rather than a 'path to gender equality' (Vaughan and Longlands, 2023, 282). They make invisible and thus fail to challenge or undo the oppressive gender regimes operative in school processes, pedagogical practices and learning environments that reproduce and exacerbate their social and educational marginality (Dunne, 2007; 2009; Humphreys et al., 2015; Bhana et al., 2011). This includes the pervasive lower expectations of girls' performance (Dunne, 2009, 6).

Such distorted projections about girls experiencing poverty and the limited understandings of the social, relational and power-laden nature of their gendered experiences therefore undermine the power of education provision to contribute to the transformatory goals promised. Education provision has a pivotal role to play through the micro-social experiences for boys and girls created by its pedagogical processes and relationships, curriculum content, learning environments and participatory forms of community engagement that privilege the agency, voices and experiences of women (Stromquist, 2020). Education can also form part of an inter-sectoral approach that addresses wider socio-economic structures and patriarchal norms and processes (Maclure and Denov, 2009).

The cultural politics of the 'poor child': a case of idealisation

If human capital and modernisation agendas have helped shape the production of the poor as 'lacking' and therefore as targets of intervention, they have also produced what has been termed the 'cultural politics of the poor child' (Hopkins and Sriprakash, 2015). Scholars working at the intersection of childhood studies and development discourses and practices have highlighted the universalisation of an ethnocentric and Westernised notion of childhood by international development agencies intervening in post-colonial country contexts in the global South (Hanson and Nieuwenhuys, 2013; Liebel, 2020). As noted by Hopkins and Sriprakash (2015, 3):

> the poor child at the centre of development activity is often measured against and reformed towards an idealised, globalised and normalised child subject.

Likewise, Nieuwenhuys (2009) notes that "development agencies have decided that the highest possible goal for non-western childhood is the emulation of a kind of childhood that the west has set up as a golden standard" (148).

Of particular relevance is the resulting normative framing of childhood as a distinctive component of a linear trajectory to adulthood (Dunne and Humphreys, 2022, 4; Nieuwenhuys, 1998; Burman, 2008). This sets up a binary between the innocent and dependent child and the rational, autonomous, responsibilised adult (Burman, 2008, 2010; Bourdillon et al., 2010, 10), conceiving childhood as a progression from the former to the latter. Hopkins and Sriprakash (2015, 9) suggest that this constructs the child as an immanent adult and 'sets up childhood as a space of deficit, pinning the hopes for the child on the future adult subject'. Yet as Dunne and Humphreys (2022, 4) argue, this generates a:

> universalised linear chronology that defines age related life stages, which underpins many of the international development goals and associated

campaigns, does not necessarily map onto the culturally specific experiences of people in different societies.

The universalisation of Western framings of childhood diminishes and pathologises alternative trajectories that defy such norms amounting to a 'politics of contempt' (Niewenhuys, 1998, 267).

This normative framing foregrounds childhood innocence, excluding therefore the lived experiences of many children living in contexts of poverty in sub-Saharan Africa who contribute to household survival and also exercise responsibility and resourcefulness, developing skills and knowledges in doing so (Prout, 2011). Feeney and Boyden (2004, 10) note that such framings invite a "rescue and rehabilitation response with adults in the driving seat".

Taking a moment, with these critiques in mind, to consider key international education reports is valuable. Our textual analysis of the work of UNESCO, UNICEF and other international agencies' reports on poverty and education offers vivid illustrations of the points raised so far.

The Contemporary Production of a Decontextualised 'Poor Child'

The cover page of the UNESCO Global Monitoring Report (UNESCO, 2010) shows a small girl (Figure 2.1). She sits alone and listless in front of a closed wooden door. She appears to be frowning. Her eyes look out sadly as if enlisting sympathy and concern. There is no indication of where she is, her relationships with others, her community context or physical environment. The title, *Reaching the Marginalised*, superimposed on the image in bold white letters, suggests that this girl is representative of the educationally marginalised demographic who needs to be reached. The logos of the organisations supporting the report's authorship and publication, UNESCO and Oxford University Press, are also included.

In this report on educational marginalisation, poverty looms large. "Being born into poverty is one of the strongest factors leading to marginalisation in education" (10). The urgency of the need to address poverty is recognised: "with poverty rising, unemployment growing and remittances diminishing, many poor and vulnerable households are having to cut back on education spending or withdraw their children from school" (1). It notes that "many children are failing to master basic literacy and numeracy skills". These are cited as examples of their 'learning poverty', a concept that suggests how their poverty extends into the quality and nature of their educational experiences. Various policy solutions are proffered as part of the 'inclusive-education triangle' (11). These include increasing accessibility/affordability for excluded groups; improving the availability of well-qualified teachers in schools facing greatest deprivation; and, measures to increase entitlements and opportunities, including legal provisions, social protection programmes such as cash transfers and redistributive public spending (11). UNESCO's analysis is supported with

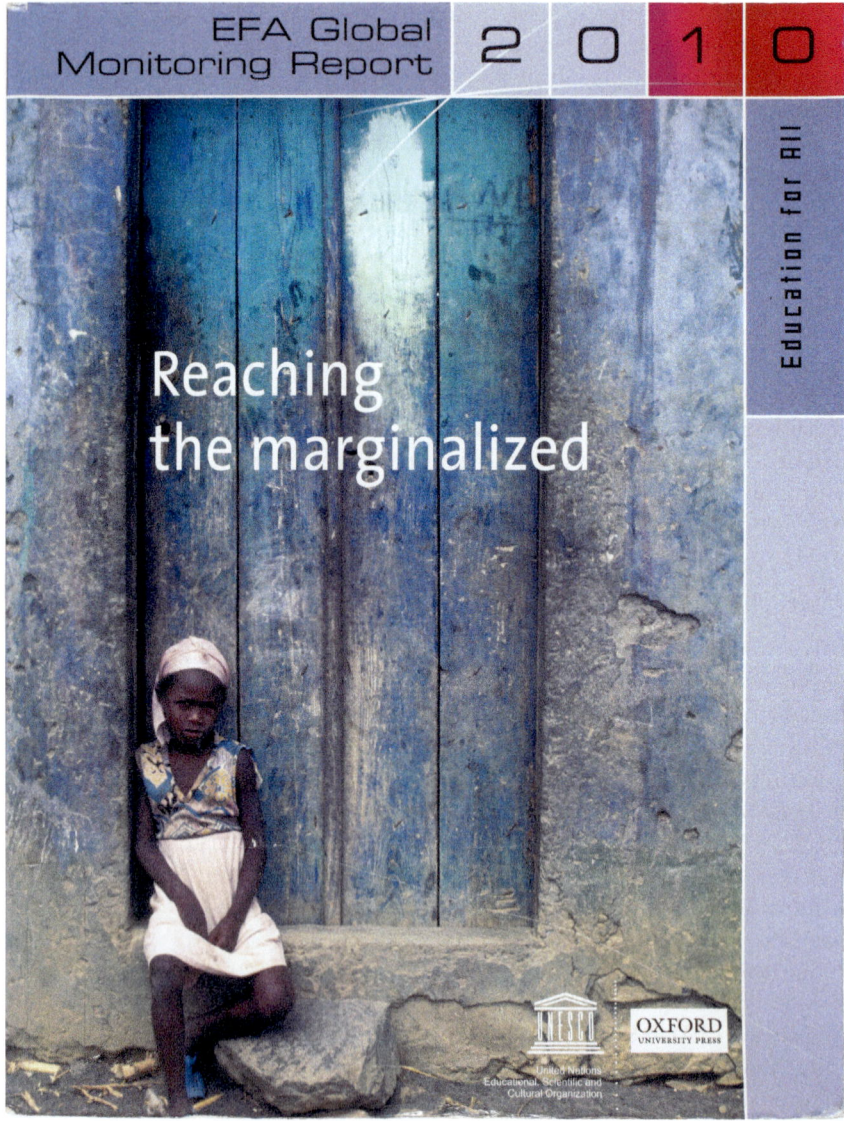

Figure 2.1 Front Cover, Global Education Monitoring Report, UNESCO, 2010, Paris.

a dizzying array of tables, charts, graphs providing statistical cross-country comparisons of numbers of children out of school, correlations between school enrolment and wealth inequalities across nations, dropout rates as well as references to reports from the World Bank, UNESCO, African Development Bank and the OECD.

Meanwhile, the suggestion of the title page, with its evocative image of an isolated girl, is that we might learn here about the perspectives of 'poor children' and their families, but it remains unrealised. This image repeats the representations of Third World women and girls discussed earlier in this chapter as wholly passive, lacking in agency and in need of 'empowerment'. 'Reaching' the marginalised appears to mean simply putting into practice policy solutions developed outside the contexts of these children's lives. Despite the wealth of references and data provided, the agency of the poor girls and boys who are the subjects of this report is not recognised. Lacking context, we are invited to respond to children who experience poverty only as objects of pity and concern rather than as located within households navigating daily precarity; or as themselves knowledgeable and able to speak. What is missing in the representation of this demographic is any valorisation of these children's prior agency in navigating experiences of precarity, the learning that this may have generated and, in turn, the possibility that education provision may intersect with their daily lived experiences. Children's active role in what has been termed 'life making' (Tadiar, 2022) in contexts of hardship is entirely occluded as well as its implications for tailoring education provision to their distinctive needs and context.

The same mix of victimhood, helplessness, erasure of agency and lived experience and a skewing of power and authority to external agencies are apparent in the representation of 'poor children' by the Global Initiative on Out-of-School Children (UIS and UNICEF, 2015). Their report, *Fixing the Broken Promise of Education for All*, shares the findings of the Global Initiative to address the educational needs of 'out-of-school children'.

The cover of this report shows a picture of a boy emerging from a tunnel, carrying what could be a pickaxe and wearing a miner's helmet with torchlight beaming. This boy is evidently a child labourer involved in mining somewhere in the world. The boy looks sadly out at the reader, as if enlisting sympathy. The title of the publication is in a box obscuring the boy's body, and the logos of aid organisations associated with the project include those of UNESCO, UIS and UNICEF, who produced the report. This image and the report's commentary, which includes statistics on household poverty aligned with school enrolment figures, suggest that a key reason for children either remaining out-of-school or dropping out before completing primary education is the practice of child labour, thwarting the promise of Education for All. The locus of agency within this analysis of educational marginalisation is granted to the apparent 'fixers', the international aid organisations in their attempts to abolish child labour and promote school enrolment for 'poor children'.

Presenting child labour and formal schooling as incompatible, the report does not contextualise how child labour occurs and is usually expected within poor households. Nor, within the binary suggested between child labour and formal education, is there any attempt to nuance a wholly negative understanding of the former. Recent research that stresses its benefits in enabling children to exercise agency within precarious circumstances and to learn and develop cognitive and social skills is ignored. This results in an implicit judgemental assessment of the livelihood practices and lifestyles of households navigating precarity. As noted by Balagopalan (2019),

> *Fixing the Broken Promise* is invested in measuring the child's risk of dropping out of school and less interested in the complexities that mark this subaltern child's continued investments in wage labor while attending school.
>
> (234)

Despite ignoring their voices and experiences and locating agency in international actors rather than in children and their communities, such reports are prescriptive about what precise learning needs they have. Thus, the World Bank report *Poverty and Shared Prosperity, Reversals of Fortune* (World Bank, 2020) provides an analysis of the impact of Covid-19 in accelerating global economic inequality. It explains that "between 88 and 115 million people could fall back into extreme poverty as a result of the pandemic" (v). The report recognises that "people who are poor and vulnerable are already bearing the brunt of the crisis". However, of particular relevance is the significance it gives to this problem and its implications for how the educational needs of children experiencing poverty are understood. Thus, the "crisis risks large human capital losses among people who are already disadvantaged, making it harder for countries to return to inclusive growth even after acute shocks recede" (8). These human capital losses will affect poor and rural children in particular, because of their inability to attend school. The characterisation of the learning challenges faced by 'poor children' echoes the wording of SDG 4 that states that "many students are not fully prepared to participate in a highly complex global economy". In this account, 'poor children' are again framed as targets for the development of human capital, which is needed to enhance their contribution to national and global economic competitiveness and macro-economic stability. However, children's appropriation to an economistic agenda for development constructs them as inadequate and in need of the compensatory impact of education, narrowly construed only as addressing their lack of economic capital.

As noted in Chapter 1, the representation of 'poor children' in the World Bank's recent publication *Learning to Realise Education's Promise* (2018) foregrounds such lack or what they cannot do. In its characterisation of the global learning crisis are anecdotes about such children's failures in literacy and numeracy – for example their failure to understand 'The name of the dog is Puppy', and pointing out that 'in rural India, just under three-quarters of students in grade 3 could not solve a two-digit subtraction' (2018, 3). Notably missing in this report's stark and unequivocal representation of educational failure is any attempt to valorise the context-specific social agency being exercised by these children outside of the technical and decontextualised exercise of reading words in a short text or solving a numerical problem.

Evaluated according to an external standard of best educational global practice (Furuta, 2022, 228), such children are represented only by their cognitive failure. As Klees et al. (2019) argued, the global assessment regime promoted as the answer to the so-called 'learning crisis' reduces students in impoverished contexts to "objects of observation, not subjects whose agency is central" (606). Bypassed is the possibility that these children may have developed mathematical literacy through their daily activities supporting household survival through petty trading in the informal economy, or that they may be highly communicative and expressive in their mother tongue languages.

Perhaps, the quintessential representation of 'the poor child' in the field of education and development is that of the category of those designated 'out-of-school'. Here, the very term suggests a state of inadequacy through a failure to engage in formal schooling. This essentially privileges the experience of formal schooling within a stark binary between formal school and the experiences of children outside of its parameters. This mode of classification epitomises the tendency of the 'macro social perspective on development' (Dunne and Ananga, 2013, 196) to foreground national-level statistics for cross-country comparison. These in effect homogenise and objectify those experiencing educational marginality rather than engaging with their subjective experiences in localised contexts. Hence, 'the paucity of the truncated and uni-dimensional description' of 'drop out' (Dunne and Ananga, 2013, 197).

Redemptive Interventions and the Loss/Absence of Children's Agency

For Balagopalan (2014, 12), the framings of 'poor children' analysed in this chapter amount to a "pathological reading of children's lives in the non-west". By locating such negative framings of children in the socio-economic and cultural agendas used in development practices in the global South, her analysis confirms Katz's (2008) observation that the figure of the child is a "site of accumulation, commodification and desire – in whose name much is done" (5). Educational interventions resulting from these assumptions are narrowly framed and privilege cognitive learning outcomes over other dimensions of educational provision that might address their needs holistically. As Lister (2021:34) noted, the privileging of only material definitions "can encourage a myopic, technocratic approach that, in its preoccupation with measuring poverty's extent (and sometimes depth) overlooks how it is experienced and understood".

The visual representations discussed show the silent and suffering faces of 'poor children' in need of compassion and redemptive interventions from agents and agencies outside of their context are designed to elicit what Fassin (2011) has termed the production of 'humanitarian reason' in their viewers. This is a cultural practice associated with representations of children and adults who experience poverty or precarity in social media, and especially in fundraising appeals by charitable organisations (Burman, 1994; Chouliaraki, 2013).

In particular, such practice refers to a 'moral economy' that encourages a desire to remedy their 'suffering' through an appeal to 'moral sentiments or emotions' in a 'secular imaginary of communion and redemption' (Fassin, 2011, xii). However, whilst apparently benign and compelling, Fassin draws attention to the asymmetrical power relationships that inform these representations, such that their production is by those 'external to the situation' within an 'unequal engagement' with 'no possible reciprocity'. These may then result in regulatory responses that aim to "manage populations and individuals, faced with situations of inequality, contexts of violence and experiences of suffering" (Fassin, 2011, xii). Girls, in particular, are the targets of such approaches, leading Khoja-Moolji (2020, 65) to characterise the 'contemporary politics of humanitarianism' around gender as a form of 'death by benevolence'.

Whilst eliciting paternalistic feelings, these framings "have done little to portray the full picture of the lives of children" (Hewitt, 1992, cited in Panter-Brick, 2000, in Abebe, 2008, 27) in sub-Saharan Africa. As Burman (1994, 29) has observed, images of black southern children used in fundraising appeals repeatedly "connote qualities of dependence and powerlessness". Indeed, global media portrayals of African children stereotypically as "passive victims" align with what has been termed the 'discourse of Afro-pessimism' (Abebe and Ofosu-Kusi, 2016, 303). Such representations of African childhood rarely attend to "how children thrive despite these adversities", conflating them with stereotypes of Africa as the "dark continent lacking the technological, economic and political circumstances of the 'developed' world" (Twum Danso Imoh, 2016, 455). A key characteristic of deficit thinking is that the poor are treated as "passive objects for attention, whether benign or malevolent" (Piachaud, 1987, 161). This approach amounts to a lack of respect and recognition that is fundamentally dehumanising (Sennett, 2003; McCrudden, 2013).

The Implications for Rethinking the 'Learning Crisis'

The dominance of deficit framings in policy approaches to the education of children living in poverty and, in particular, ethnic minority students in the global North, has been widely critiqued (Valencia, 2012, xii; Wrigley, 2013). Their reproduction within the discourses and practices of international development in sub-Saharan Africa and its implications for shaping the logics of responses to educational marginalisation have received less attention (Nxumalo and Brown, 2020; Valencia, 2012, 2019). Yet, this chapter has shown how deeply embedded deficit framings of 'poor children' are in the 'knowledge network' (Read, 2019) of international education and development that promotes the notion of the 'learning crisis'. The similarities between representations across international aid agencies illustrate that 'trend towards uniformity and convergence in thinking' of contemporary education policy discourse, and also that relating to education and poverty reduction (Mason, 2012, 494; see Ball, 2012, 12). This produces a form of 'common sense' regarding the way development challenges are framed and the solutions prescribed within the global educational policy field (Lingard and Rawolle, 2011, 490; Verger et al., 2018). The representations of poor children we described above are presented as certain and unquestionable (Monkman and Hoffman, 2013, 63), testifying to the pervasive 'power of policy discourse' to (mis)frame both problems and solutions.

The notion of the 'learning crisis' is thus predicated on deficit assumptions of African children that call out for radical critique and re-envisioning. Lister characterises this approach as a form of othering which 'condemns the poor for what they do or looks down on them for the qualities they are considered to lack' (2021, 90). Such a framing "divests them of their social and cultural identities by diminishing them to their stereotyped characteristics and by casting them as silent objects" (Lister, 2021, 92). In the field of educational thought and practice, a deficit approach is associated with forms of educational provision that see 'poor children' as 'lacking across a range of developmental, cultural, linguistic and individual domains' (Nxumalo and Brown, 2019, 1), thus erasing the individual, cultural and developmental abilities and desire for learning amongst children and their families from the curriculum (Nxumalo and Brown, 2019, 4). The truncation of African children's subjectivity extends to the narrow emotional range they are granted, in visual and verbal representations that emphasise either their despair and sadness or their joyful appreciation of the interventions of international actors. They are also individualised and de-socialised – either represented as isolated and outside of any relational or spatial contexts or evoked as statistics for inter-national comparison.

The erasure of children's voices and experiences and those of their communities also constitutes an epistemic imbalance in the politics of knowledge production at work in these framings. The representation of these children as passive and problematic beneficiaries of the actions of external agencies typifies asymmetrical power relationships between the poor and 'dominant groups' (Sayer, 2005, 90/92) by whom they are characterised and scrutinised. For Ryan (1971), these processes of othering and judgementalism of an already marginalised demographic function to blame the victim, constituting in itself a form of social injustice and oppression (Frost and Hoggett, 2008). This raises the question of how such framings can fit within a rhetoric of education and poverty alleviation associated with aspirations to equity and social justice.

In the next chapter, we continue our critique of the deficit assumptions about children in the 'learning crisis' narrative by showing how this extends to their languages.

Notes

1 Sriprakash (2012) examines provision for the rural poor and the "poor chid" in India; see also Sriprakash (2015).
2 See studies by Bonal and Tarabini-Castellani (2009), Bonal and Zancajo (2018, 21), Sayed and Moriarty (2020), Yunus (2022).
3 https://unstats.un.org/sdgs/report/2019/goal-04.

4 See studies by Resnik (2006), Tikly (2011, 5), Mason (2012, 496), Tarabini and Jacovkis (2012, 510), Novelli (2016).
5 See also Bonal and Tarabini-Castellani (2009, 9).
6 See, for example: Hoskyns and Rai (2007), Plan International (2009), Chant and Sweetman (2012), Hickel (2014), Khoja-Moolji (2015), Moeller (2018).
7 Durrani and Halai (2020), Crossouard and Dunne (2021), Unterhalter (2023).

References

Abebe, T., 2008. 'Trapped between disparate worlds? The livelihoods, socialisation and school contexts of rural children in Ethiopia'. *Childhoods Today*, 2(1): 1–29.

Abebe, T., and Biswas, T., 2021. 'Rights in education: outlines for a decolonial, childist re-imagination of the future – commentary to Ansell and colleagues'. *Fennia: International Journal of Geography*, 199(1): 118–128.

Abebe, T., and Ofosu-Kusi, Y., 2016. 'Beyond pluralising African childhoods: introduction'. *Childhood*, 23(3): 303–316.

Alexander, R., 2015. 'Teaching and learning for all? The quality imperative revisited'. In R. Alexander (ed.), *Routledge handbook of international education and development*. Routledge, pp. 138–152.

Altinyelken, H.K., 2018. 'A converging pedagogy in the global South? Insights from Uganda and Turkey'. In H.K. Altinyelken (ed.), *Global education policy and international development: new agendas, issues and policies*. Bloomsbury Publishing, p. 209.

Ansell, N., Froerer, P., Huijsmans, R., Dungey, C., and Dost, A., 2020. 'Educating "surplus population": uses and abuses of aspiration in the rural peripheries of a globalising world'. *Fennia: International Journal of Geography*, 198(1–2): 17–38.

Balagopalan, S., 2008. 'Memories of tomorrow: children, labor and the panacea of formal schooling'. *Journal of the History of Childhood and Youth*, 1(2): 267–285.

Balagopalan, S., 2014. *Inhabiting 'childhood': children, labour and schooling in postcolonial India* (1st edn). Palgrave Macmillan.

Balagopalan, S., 2019. '"After school and during vacations": on labor and schooling in the post colony'. *Children's Geographies*, 17(2): 231–245.

Balagopalan, S., 2022. 'The politics of deferral: denaturalising the "economic value" of children's labor in India'. *Current Sociology*, 70(4): 496–512.

Ball, S.J., 2012. *Global Education Inc.: new policy networks and the neoliberal imaginary*. Routledge.

Barrett, A.M., 2011. 'A millennium learning goal for education post-2015: a question of outcomes or processes'. *Comparative Education*, 47(1): 119–133.

Benavot, A., and Smith, W.C., 2020. 'Reshaping quality and equity: global learning metrics as a ready-made solution to a manufactured crisis'. In A. Benavot and W.C. Smith (eds.), *Grading goal four*. Brill, pp. 238–261.

Bessel, S., 2017. 'Education, school, and learning: dominant perspectives'. In T. Abebe, and J. Waters (eds.), *Laboring and learning, geographies of children and young people* (Vol. 10). Springer, pp. 131–155.

Bhana, D., Nzimakwe, T., and Nzimakwe, P., 2011. 'Gender in the early years: boys and girls in an African working class primary school'. *International Journal of Educational Development*, 31(5): 443–448.

Bonal, X., and Tarabini-Castellani, A., 2009. 'Global solutions for global poverty?: The World Bank education policy and the anti-poverty agenda'. In M. Simons, M. Olssen, and M.A. Peters (eds.), *Re-reading education policies*. Sense Publishers, pp. 96–111.

Bonal, X., and Zancajo, A., 2018. 'Demand rationalities in contexts of poverty: do the Poor respond to market incentives in the same way?' *International Journal of Educational Development*, 59: 20–27.
Bourdillon, M., and Boyden, J. eds., 2011. *Childhood poverty: multidisciplinary approaches*. Springer.
Bourdillon, M., Levison, D., Myers, W., and White, B., 2010. *Rights and wrongs of children's work*. Rutgers University Press.
Boyden, J., 2003. 'Children under fire: challenging assumptions about children's resilience'. *Children, Youth and Environments*, 13(1): 1–29.
Boyden, J., Dawes, A., Dornan, P., and Tredoux, C., 2019. *Tracing the consequences of child poverty*. Policy Press.
Boyden, J., Porter, C., and Zharkevich, I., 2021. 'Balancing school and work with new opportunities: changes in children's gendered time use in Ethiopia (2006–2013)'. *Children's Geographies*, 19(1): 74–87.
Bray, R., de Laat, M., Godinot, X., Ugarte, A., and Walker, R., 2020. 'Realising poverty in all its dimensions: a six-country participatory study'. *World Development*, 134:1–10.
Brown, P., Lauder, H., and Ashton, D., 2010. *The global auction: the broken promises of education, jobs, and incomes* (1st edn). Oxford University Press.
Bull, B., and Bøås, M., 2012. 'Between ruptures and continuity: modernisation, dependency and the evolution of development theory'. *Forum for Development Studies*, 39(3): 319–336.
Burman, E., 1994. 'Poor children: charity appeals and ideologies of childhood'. *Changes: Journal of Psychology and Psychotherapy*, 12: 29–36.
Burman, E., 2008. *Developments: child, image, nation* (1st edn). Routledge.
Burman, E., 2010. 'Un/thinking children in development'. In E. Burman (ed.), *Childhoods: a handbook*. Peter Lang, pp. 9–26.
Caillods, F., and Hallak, J., 2004. *Education and PRSPs: a review of experiences*. UNESCO, IIPE.
Calkin, S., 2015. 'Post-feminist spectatorship and the girl effect: "Go ahead, really imagine her"'. *Third World Quarterly*, 36(4): 654–669.
Carnoy, M., 1974. *Education as cultural imperialism*. David McKay Company.
Chant, S., and Sweetman, C., 2012. 'Fixing women or fixing the world? "Smart economics", efficiency approaches, and gender equality in development'. *Gender and Development*, 20(3): 517–529.
Chouliaraki, L., 2013. *The ironic spectator: solidarity in the age of post-humanitarianism*. John Wiley and Sons.
Connell, R., 2013. 'The neoliberal cascade and education: an essay on the market agenda and its consequences'. *Critical Studies in Education*, 54(2): 99–112.
Cornwall, A. and Edwards, J., 2010. 'Introduction: negotiating empowerment'. *Ids Bulletin*, 41(2): 1–9.
Cornwall, A., and Fujita, M., 2012. 'Ventriloquising "the Poor"? Of voices, choices and the politics of "participatory" knowledge production'. *Third World Quarterly*, 33(9): 1751–1765.
Cornwall, A., and Rivas, A.M., 2015. 'From "gender equality" and "women's empowerment" to global justice: reclaiming a transformative agenda for gender and development'. *Third World Quarterly*, 36(2): 396–415.
Craig, D., and Porter, D., 2003. 'Poverty reduction strategy papers: a new convergence'. *World Development*, 31(1): 53–69.

Crivello, G., Camfield, L., and Woodhead, M., 2009. 'How can children tell us about their wellbeing? Exploring the potential of participatory research approaches within young lives'. *Social Indicators Research*, 90: 51–72.

Crossouard, B., & Dunne, M., 2021. Gender and education in postcolonial contexts (Version 1). University of Sussex. https://hdl.handle.net/10779/uos.23480609.v1 Published in Oxford Research Encyclopedia of Education Link to external publisher version https://doi.org/10.1093/acrefore/9780190264093.013.1583

Datzberger, S., 2018. 'Why education is not helping the poor: findings from Uganda'. *World Development*, 110: 124–139.

Devine, D., Samonova, E., Bolotta, G., Sugrue, C., Sloan, S., Symonds, J., Capistrano, D., and Crean, M., 2023. 'Gendering childhood (s) and engagement with schooling in rural Sierra Leone'. *Compare: A Journal of Comparative and International Education*, 53(1): 19–36.

Dogra, N., 2011. 'The mixed metaphor of 'Third World Woman': gendered representations by international development NGOs'. *Third World Quarterly*, 32(2): 333–348.

Dunne, M., 2007. 'Gender, sexuality and schooling: everyday life in junior secondary schools in Botswana and Ghana'. *International Journal of Educational Development*, 27(5): 499–511.

Dunne, M., 2009. 'Gender as an entry point for addressing social exclusion and multiple disparities in education'. In *UNGEI Global Advisory Committee Technical Meeting* (Vol. 2). United Nations Girls Initiative.

Dunne, M., 2019. 'Gender docility: the power of technology and technologies of power in low-income countries'. In A. Chronaki (ed.), *Mathematics, technologies, education: the gender perspective*. Thessaly University Press, pp. 45–56.

Dunne, M., and Ananga, E.D., 2013. 'Dropping out: identity conflict in and out of school in Ghana'. *International Journal of Educational Development*, 33(2): 196–205.

Dunne, M., and Humphreys, S., 2022. 'The edu-workscape: re-conceptualising the relationship between work and education in rural children's lives in Sub-Saharan Africa'. *World Development Perspectives*, 27: 100–443.

Durrani, N., and Halai, A., 2020. 'Gender equality, education, and development: tensions between global, national, and local policy discourses in postcolonial contexts'. In A. Wulff (ed.), *Grading goal four: tensions, threats and opportunities in the sustainable development goal on quality education*. Brill.

Dyer, C., 2012. 'Formal education and pastoralism in western India: inclusion, or adverse incorporation?' *Compare: A Journal of Comparative and International Education*, 42(2): 259–281.

Dyer, C., 2013. 'Educating the poorest and ideas of poverty'. *International Journal of Educational Development*, 33(3): 221–224.

Educate Girls, n.d. *Smarter economics: investing in girls*. https://www.educategirls.ngo/pdf/GirlEffect_Smarter-Economics-Investing-in-Girls.pdf.

Escobar, A., 2011. *Encountering development: the making and unmaking of the third world* (Vol. 1). Princeton University Press.

Esquivel, V., and Sweetman, C., 2016. 'Gender and the sustainable development goals'. *Gender and Development*, 24(1): 1–8.

Eyben, R., Kabeer, N., and Cornwall, A., 2008. *Conceptualising empowerment and the implications for pro poor growth*. DAC Poverty Network by the Institute of Development Studies, Brighton.

Fassin, D., 2011. *Humanitarian reason: a moral history of the present*. University of California Press.

Feeny, T., and Boyden, J., 2004. *Acting in adversity: rethinking the causes, experiences and effects of child poverty in contemporary literature*. Literature and Thought on Children and Poverty, Children and poverty series working paper, 116. Queen Elizabeth House University of Oxford QEH Working Paper Series – QEHWPS.

Frost, L., and Hoggett, P., 2008. 'Human agency and social suffering'. *Critical Social Policy*, 28(4): 438–460.

Furuta, J., 2022. 'The rationalisation of "Education for All": the worldwide rise of national assessments, 1960–2011'. *Comparative Education Review*, 66(2): 228–252.

Gaisbauer, H.P., Schweiger, G., and Sedmak, C., 2016. *Ethical issues in poverty alleviation*. Springer Publishing.

Hanson, K., and Nieuwenhuys, O. eds., 2013. *Reconceptualising children's rights in international development: living rights, social justice, translations*. Cambridge University Press.

Harbison, F.H., and Myers, C.A., 1964. *Education, manpower, and economic growth*. McGraw Hill.

Hartog, F., 2016. *Regimes of historicity: presentism and experiences of time*. Columbia University Press.

Hayhurst, L.M., 2011. 'Corporatising sport, gender and development: postcolonial IR feminisms, transnational private governance and global corporate social engagement'. *Third World Quarterly*, 32(3): 531–549.

Hewitt, T. (1992): 'Children, abandonment and public action'. In M. Wuyts, M. Mackintoshb, and T. Hewitt (eds), *Development, policy and public action*. Oxford University Press, pp. 39–58.

Hickel, J., 2014. 'The "girl effect": liberalism, empowerment and the contradictions of development'. *Third World Quarterly*, 35(8): 1355–1373.

Hopkins, L., and Sriprakash, A. eds., 2015. *The 'poor child': the cultural politics of education, development and childhood*. Routledge.

Hoskyns, C., and Rai, S.M., 2007. 'Recasting the global political economy: counting women's unpaid work'. *New Political Economy*, 12(3): 297–317.

Humphreys, S., Moses, D., Kaibo, J., and Dunne, M., 2015. 'Counted in and being out: fluctuations in primary school and classroom attendance in northern Nigeria'. *International Journal of Educational Development*, 44: 134–143.

Inkeles, A., and Smith, D.H., 1974. *Becoming modern: individual change in six developing countries*. Harvard University Press.

Kabeer, N., 1996. 'Agency, well-being and inequality: reflections on the gender dimensions of poverty'. *IDS Bulletin*, 27(1): 11–21.

Kabeer, N., 2015. 'Gender, poverty, and inequality: a brief history of feminist contributions in the field of international development'. *Gender and Development*, 23(2): 189–205.

Kabeer, N., Razavi, S., and van der Meulen Rodgers, Y., 2021. 'Feminist economic perspectives on the COVID-19 pandemic'. *Feminist Economics*, 27(1–2): 1–29.

Kamruzzaman, P., 2016. 'A critical note on poverty eradication target of sustainable development goals'. *European Journal of Sustainable Development*, 5(2): 87–87.

Katz, C., 2008. 'Cultural geographies lecture: childhood as spectacle: relays of anxiety and the reconfiguration of the child'. *Cultural Geographies*, 15(1): 5–17.

Khoja-Moolji, S., 2015. 'Suturing together girls and education: an investigation into the social (re) production of girls' education as a hegemonic ideology'. *Diaspora, Indigenous, and Minority Education*, 9(2): 87–107.

Khoja-Moolji, S., 2017. '"Empowered girls" in neoliberal times: Malala as the effect of heterogeneous discourses'. In J. Louth and M. Potter (eds.), *Edges of identity*. University of Chester, pp. 18–52.

Khoja-Moolji, S., 2020. 'Death by benevolence: third world girls and the contemporary politics of humanitarianism'. *Feminist Theory*, 21(1): 65–90.

Klees, S.J., 2008. 'A quarter century of neoliberal thinking in education: Misleading analyses and failed policies'. *Globalisation, Societies and Education*, 6(4): 311–348.

Klees, S.J. 2012. 'World Bank and education: ideological premises and ideological conclusions'. In S.J. Klees (ed.), *The World Bank and education critiques and alternatives*. Sense, pp. 49–65.

Klees, S.J., 2020. 'Beyond neoliberalism: reflections on capitalism and education'. *Policy Futures in Education*, 18(1): 9–29.

Klees, S.J., Stromquist, N.P., Samoff, J., and Vally, S., 2019. 'The 2018 world development report on education: a critical analysis'. *Development and Change*, 50(2): 603–620.

Koffman, O., and Gill, R., 2013. '"The revolution will be led by a 12-year-old girl": girl power and global biopolitics'. *Feminist Review*, 105(1): 83–102.

Kromidas, M., 2019. 'Towards the human, after the child of man: seeing the child differently in teacher education'. *Curriculum Inquiry*, 49(1): 65–89.

Liebel, M. 2020. *Decolonising childhoods: from exclusion to dignity*. Policy Press.

Lingard, B., and Rawolle, S., 2011. 'New scalar politics: implications for education policy'. *Comparative Education*, 47(4): 489–502.

Lister, R., 2021. *Poverty*. John Wiley and Sons.

Maclure, R., and Denov, M., 2009. 'Reconstruction versus transformation: post-war education and the struggle for gender equity in Sierra Leone'. *International Journal of Educational Development*, 29(6): 612–620.

Marginson, S., 2019. 'Limitations of human capital theory'. *Studies in Higher Education*, 44(2): 287–301.

Mason, M., 2012. 'Education, policy and poverty reduction'. *International Journal of Educational Development*, 32(4): 494–498.

McCrudden, C., 2013. 'In pursuit of human dignity: an introduction to current debates'. In *Understanding Human Dignity, Proceedings of the British Academy*. Oxford University Press.

Moeller, K. 2018. *The gender effect: capitalism, feminism, and the corporate politics of development*. University of California Press.

Monkman, K., and Hoffman, L., 2013. 'Girls' education: the power of policy discourse'. *Theory and Research in Education*, 11(1): 63–84.

Ngutuku, E., 2019. 'Beyond categories: rhizomatic experiences of child poverty and vulnerability in Kenya'. In E. Ngutuku (ed.), *Putting children first: new frontiers in the fight against child poverty in Africa*. Ibidem Press Stuttgart, p. 25.

Nieuwenhuys, O., 1998. 'Global childhood and the politics of contempt'. *Alternatives*, 23(3): 267–289.

Nieuwenhuys, O., 2009. 'Is there an Indian childhood?' *Childhood*, 16(2): 147–153.

Nieuwenhuys, O., 2013. 'Theorizing childhood (s): why we need postcolonial perspectives'. *Childhood*, 20(1): 3–8.

Novelli, M., 2016. 'Capital, inequality and education in conflict-affected contexts'. *British Journal of Sociology of Education*, 37(6): 848–860.

Ntini, E., 2016. 'Today's world: can modernisation theory still explain it convincingly?' *Journal of Sociology and Social Anthropology*, 7(1): 56–67.

Nxumalo, F., and Brown, C.P. eds., 2019. *Disrupting and countering deficits in early childhood education*. Fact Sheet No 48, UIS/FS/2018/ED/48. UIS, Montreal.

Nxumalo, F. and Brown, C.P. eds., 2020. *Disrupting and countering deficits in early childhood education*. Routledge.

Paddison, L., 2017. 'Educating girls: the key to tackling global poverty'. *Guardian*. https://www.theguardian.com/opportunity-international-roundtables/2017/oct/04/global-poverty-child-marriage-education-girls

Panter-Brick C., 2000. 'Nobody's children? A reconsideration of child abandonment'. In C. Panter-Brick and M.T. Smith (eds.), (eds.), *Abandoned children*. Cambridge University Press, pp. 1–27.

Pemberton, S.A., 2016. *Harmful societies: understanding social harm*. Policy Press.

Phiri, D.T., and Abebe, T., 2016. 'Suffering and thriving: children's perspectives and interpretations of poverty and well-being in rural Zambia'. *Childhood*, 23(3): 378–393.

Piachaud, D., 1987. 'Problems in the definition and measurement of poverty'. *Journal of Social Policy*, 16(2): 147–164.

Plan International, 2009. *The state of the world's girls 2009: girls in the global economy: adding it all up*. Available at: https://plan-international.org/publications/the-state-of-the-worlds-girls-2009-girls-in-the-global-economy/ [Accessed: 22.04.2024].

Prout, A., 2011. 'Taking a step away from modernity: reconsidering the new sociology of childhood'. *Global Studies of Childhood*, 1(1): 4–14.

Prügl, E., 2017. 'Neoliberalism with a feminist face: crafting a new hegemony at the World Bank'. *Feminist Economics*, 23(1): 30–53.

Rai, S.M., Brown, B.D., and Ruwanpura, K.N., 2019. 'SDG 8: Decent work and economic growth–A gendered analysis'. *World Development*, 113: 368–380.

Ravallion, M., 2016a. 'Are the world's poorest being left behind?' *Journal of Economic Growth*, 21: 139–164.

Ravallion, M., 2016b. 'The World Bank: why it is still needed and why it still disappoints'. *Journal of Economic Perspectives*, 30(1): 77–94.

Read, R., 2019. 'Knowledge counts: influential actors in the education for all global monitoring report knowledge network'. *International Journal of Educational Development*, 64: 96–105.

Resnik, J., 2006. 'International organisations, the "education–economic growth" black box, and the development of world education culture'. *Comparative Education Review*, 50(2): 173–195.

Roelen, K., 2017. *Shame, poverty and social protection*. IDS Working Paper 489, IDS, Brighton.

Roelen, K., Morgan, R., Tafere, Y., Odunayo Akinyemi, J., Akomolafe, O., Araya, M., Bantebya-Kyomuhendo, G., Chase, E., Coast, E., Conklin, S., and Devereux, S., 2019. *Putting children first: new frontiers in the fight against child poverty in Africa (CROP international poverty studies)*. Columbia University Press.

Rostow, W.W. 1960. *The stages of economic growth: a non-communist manifesto*. Cambridge University Press.

Ryan, W., 1971. *Blaming the victim*. Pantheon.

Sachs W., 1990. 'The archaelogy of the development idea'. *Interculture*, 23(4): 1–37.

Sachs, W., 2008. *The archaeology of the development idea*. Earthcare Books.

Sachs, J.D., 2012. 'From millennium development goals to sustainable development goals'. *The Lancet*, 379(9832): 2206–2211.

Sayed, Y., and Moriarty, K., 2020. 'SDG 4 and the "education quality turn": prospects, possibilities, and problems'. In A. Wulff (ed.), *Grading goal four: tensions, threats and opportunities in the sustainable development goal on quality education*. Brill, pp. 194–213.

Schultz, T.W., 1961. 'Investment in human capital'. *The American Economic Review*, 51(1): 1–17.

Schweisfurth, M., 2015. 'Learner-centred pedagogy: towards a post-2015 agenda for teaching and learning'. *International Journal of Educational Development*, 40: 259–266.

Sennett, R., 2003. *Respect in a world of inequality*. WW Norton and Company.

Sriprakash, A., 2012. *Pedagogies for development: the politics and practice of child-centred education in India*. Springer.

Sriprakash, A., 2015. 'Modernity and multiple childhoods: interrogating the education of the rural poor in global India'. In A. Sriprakash and L. Hopkins (Eds.), *The 'poor child'*. Routledge, pp. 151–167.

Stiglitz, J., 2021. 'Lessons from COVID-19 and Trump for theory and policy'. *Journal of Policy Modelling*, 43(4): 749–760.

Stromquist, N.P., 2012. 'The gender dimension in the World Bank's education strategy: assertions in need of a theory'. In *The World Bank and education*. Brill, pp. 159–172.

Stromquist, N.P., 2020. 'Girls and women in the educational system: the curricular challenge'. *Prospects*, 49(1): 47–50.

Sum, N., and Jessop, B., 2015. *Towards a cultural political economy: putting culture in its place in political economy*. Edward Elgar Publishing.

Switzer, H., Bent, E., and Endsley, C.L., 2016. 'Precarious politics and girl effects: exploring the limits of the girl gone global'. *Feminist Formations*, 28(1): 33–59.

Tadiar, N.X., 2022. *Remaindered life*. Duke University Press.

Tiainen, R., 2023. 'The spectacle of a third world girl: colonial imagery in Plan International Finland's campaign'. *International Education*, 46(5): 745–763.

Tarabini, A., and Jacovkis, J., 2012. 'The poverty reduction strategy papers: an analysis of a hegemonic link between education and poverty'. *International Journal of Educational Development*, 32(4): 507–516.

Taylor, C., 2004. *Modern social imaginaries*. Duke University Press.

Tikly, L., 2004. 'Education and the new imperialism'. *Comparative Education*, 40(2): 173–198.

Tikly, L., 2011. 'Towards a framework for researching the quality of education in low-income countries'. *Comparative Education*, 47(1): 1–23.

Twum-Danso Imoh, A., 2016. 'From the singular to the plural: exploring diversities in contemporary childhoods in sub-Saharan Africa'. *Childhood*, 23(3): 55–468.

UIS, 2018. 'One in five children, adolescents and youth is out of school'. https://uis.unesco.org/sites/default/files/documents/fs48-one-five-children-adolescents-youth-out-school-2018-en.pdf

UIS, and UNICEF, 2015. *Fixing the broken promise of education for all: findings from the global initiative on out-of-school children*. Montreal. http://dx.doi.org/10.15220/978-92-9189-161-0-en

UNESCO, 2010. *EFA global monitoring report: reaching the marginalised*. Oxford University Press.

UNESCO, 2020. *Her education: our future: the latest facts on gender equality in United Nations*. UNESCO.

United Nations (UN), 2022. *The sustainable development goals report*. United Nations.

Unterhalter, E. ed., 2020. *Measuring the unmeasurable in education*. Routledge.

Unterhalter, E., 2023. 'An answer to everything? Four framings of girls' schooling and gender equality in education'. *Comparative Education*, 59(2): 145–168.

Valencia, R.R. ed., 2012. *The evolution of deficit thinking: educational thought and practice*. Routledge.

Valencia, R.R., 2019. *International deficit thinking: educational thought and practice*. Routledge.

Vaughan, R.P., and Longlands, H., 2023. 'A technology of global governance or the path to gender equality? Reflections on the role of indicators and targets for girls' education'. *Comparative Education*, 59(2): 282–304.

Verger, A., Altinyelken, H.K., and Novelli, M., 2018. *Global education policy and international development: new agendas, issues and policies*. Continuum.

Wheelahan, L., Moodie, G., and Doughney, J., 2022. 'Challenging the skills fetish'. *British Journal of Sociology of Education*, 43(3): 475–494.

Whitehead, A., and Lockwood, M., 1999. 'Gendering poverty: a review of six World Bank African poverty assessments'. *Development and Change*, 30(3): 525–555.

World Bank, 2018. *Learning: to realize education's promise*. World Bank Group.

World Bank, 2018. *World development report 2018: learning to realize education's promise*. The World Bank.

World Bank, 2020. *Poverty and shared prosperity 2020: reversals of fortune*. The World Bank.

Wrigley, T., 2013. 'Class and culture: sources of confusion in educational sociology'. *Journal for Critical Education Policy Studies*, 11(1): 1–40.

Wulff, A. ed., 2020. *Grading goal four: tensions, threats, and opportunities in the sustainable development goal on quality education*. Brill.

Yunus, R., 2022. '"Labour class" children in Indian classrooms: theorising urban poverty and schooling'. *British Journal of Sociology of Education*, 43(1): 104–119.

3 Language, Learning and Children's Identities

The previous chapters have highlighted the need to reconceptualise the learning challenge by first re-envisioning poor children who suffer educational marginalisation as resourceful, agentic, knowledgeable and second as active participants in the daily struggles of their communities. Both of these imply the need to develop innovative curricular and pedagogical strategies that recognise such children in this way. In this chapter, we take as a starting point something which has notably been ignored in framings of the contemporary 'learning crisis' – the fundamental question of the language or languages in which children in Africa are expected to learn.

We interrogate and unpack various dimensions of the international and national failure to address this fundamental learning need. Here too is a story of a deficit positioning of children in which the rich linguistic resources they bring to learning are denied in their early engagement with education provision.

We first highlight the complex, multi-scalar nature of debate about the language of instruction to be used in schools, implicating actors and agendas at global, national and local levels. We consider the location of this issue in a long history of contestation, contradiction and compromise in which the learning experiences of children have largely taken second place or been ignored. We then draw on micro-studies of children's experiences of learning across a range of African contexts to show how current language of instruction policies systematically undermine their ability to learn effectively and to enjoy the process of learning.

The Language of Instruction in the 'Learning Crisis'

Research evidence over the past 50 years has consistently demonstrated the educational value of an extended (up to six years) period of learning in a child's local language or the languages that are most widely spoken in their homes and communities (Cummins, 1996; Alidou and Brock-Utne, 2011; Benson, 2016; Mose and Kaschula, 2019). This research has underscored the enormous benefits to children for their cognitive development, by, for example, (a) increasing their ability to learn other languages including English, (b) securing the foundations for their subsequent learning by building literacy

DOI: 10.4324/9781003185482-5

and numeracy skills, (c) increasing their motivation to engage in meaningful and relevant learning and therefore to remain in school and (d) enlisting the support of their families and communities, even though poor, to engage with formal education.

These educational rationales have long been promoted as normative legal goals in the mandates of international development agencies[1] In a 1953 report, *The Use of Vernacular Languages in Education*, UNESCO declared that:

> it is axiomatic that the best medium for teaching a child is his [sic] mother tongue. Psychologically, it is the system of meaningful signs that in his mind works automatically for expression and understanding. Sociologically, it is a means of identification among the members of the community to which he belongs. Educationally, he learns more quickly through it than through an unfamiliar linguistic medium.
> (UNESCO, 1953, 11)

Yet, according to the World Bank, in 2021, over 6 million children were being educated in a language that they did not understand. The UNESCO Global Initiative on *Out-of-School Children* in 2015 had already concluded that "too many children are sidelined by education that is delivered in a language they neither speak nor understand" (7). Such a systemic failure in appropriate educational provision is most prevalent in regions where societal multilingualism is greatest, such as in sub-Saharan Africa (UNESCO, 2016a) and where the dominant language of instruction is an ex-colonial language, such as English, French or Portuguese. Not surprisingly such linguistic exclusion and the resulting educational marginalisation are recognised as key factors in stalling the realisation of the Sustainable Development Goals (SDGs) in education (Ingutia, 2020).

In many contexts of sub-Saharan Africa, this linguistic pattern is a result of education policies that devalue the languages in which African children communicate in their daily lives. Yet, such languages are described as the "rich resources represented by African multilingualism and multiculturalism" (Benson, 2018, 218) that they bring to the classroom. Education policy in many African countries usually allows some learning in mother tongues but only for a short period of time (such as two or three years), if at all. The African child then transitions into an English-only (or French) medium of instruction in upper basic education. This approach has been described as 'early exit' or 'subtractive' (Benson, 2005).

These policies have deep troubling consequences. African children's home languages are trivialised as preparation for immersion in an ex-colonial language, rather than valued for their potential in facilitating meaningful and engaging learning opportunities (Adejunmobi, 2004; Cummins, 2007). This results in what has been termed systemic forms of *epistemic exclusion* (Kiramba, 2018, 291; Trudell, 2016a; Kuchah et al., 2022). Children are unable to access the curriculum content in the international language offered in secondary schooling – they have to switch into a new medium of instruction when their levels of proficiency are too low for them to use the language effectively for learning (Alidou et al., 2006; Afitska et al., 2013; Desai, 2016). Nor has the child developed sufficient proficiency in their home language to transfer knowledge and skills to promote learning. These linguistic conditions of learning for the majority of children in sub-Saharan Africa have, in effect, set them up to fail (UNESCO, 2016a). This is a situation that Ngugi wa Thiong'o has characterised as nothing less than the 'normalisation of the absurd' (Thiong'o, 1986, 2 quoted in Westbrook et al., 2022, 856). The title of the policy paper by UNESCO (2016) captures this absurdity well – "If you don't understand how can you learn?"

Language of instruction policies and practices has been critiqued using a range of perspectives. They have been challenged, for example as:

- vehicles for sustaining racist teaching approaches (Sriprakash et al., 2020);
- examples of Afro-pessimism (Mbembe, 2001);
- a recolonisation of the African mind (Sefa Dei et al., 2022);
- a denial of children's rights (UNESCO, 2003) and the rights of ethnic minorities (Watson, 2007);
- a threat to the survival of the languages, knowledges and identities of indigenous communities (Nakagawa and Kouritzin, 2021; Phyvak and De Costa, 2021).

At the same time, re-envisioning the language of instruction has been construed as an issue of social justice, a vehicle for addressing educational inequality, expanding opportunity and realising children's rights (Dutcher, 2001; Tikly, 2016; Milligan and Tikly, 2016)[2] and a key component of decolonising imperative to recentre 'silenced voices from the global south' (Docrat, 2022, 252).

In this chapter, we draw on all these approaches. However, its overarching goal is to return attention to what is notably absent in framings of the learning crisis – the micro-level educational experiences of children and the impact of current language-of-instruction policies and practices in optimising or constraining their agency as learners. Erasing attention to these issues arguably misrepresents and consequently misdiagnoses what is at stake.

One of the vital aspects at the core of the World Bank's characterisation of the learning crisis and debates about what the language of instruction policy should be is the use of evidence about children's deficient English skills. The findings from a cross-national reading test that tested children's ability to describe the name of a dog as a puppy is taken to be symptomatic of a learning crisis that is leaving millions of children illiterate when they leave primary school (Klees et al., 2019). Shoehorning children's learning outcomes for English literacy into one homogenising account of a language crisis, the World Bank's (2018) diagnosis of educational under-achievement is significant for what is left out – particularly, the variegated and complex linguistic realities and related learning challenges and opportunities of African children.

By seeking to establish levels of children's proficiency in English only and by attaching great significance to this test, the World Bank reproduced, without critique, the Anglo-normative assumptions of language of instruction policies that have failed many learners throughout sub-Saharan Africa. Moreover, the use of a contrived sentence as the metric through which to evaluate all children's literacy skills amounts to what Klees et al. (2019) argue is "no more than a technical exercise of reading words in a short text without grounding them in lived experience" (8). Detaching language proficiency from the situated agency of learners, the metric to measure literacy demonstrates an approach to learning as a 'largely technical activity' (2019, 3). That these children could express their knowledge about dogs and their environment in other languages is ignored within this testing regime.

In the narrative of the learning crisis, children in sub-Saharan Africa are represented as linguistically deficient – as problems to be solved rather than linguistically resourceful, and as children whose languages and the knowledges they contain can be harnessed for their learning. Writing about children's linguistic repertoire in Kenya, Bunyi (2008b, 6) signals that:

> indigenous communities are multi-ethnic, and children learn their mother language first, then through early social relations, they acquire other languages that are spoken by the children from one or more ethnic groups…English as a medium of instruction may not be the students' second language.

The World Bank's analysis in effect distracts attention from the linguistic failures at primary and secondary school levels in teaching not just English, but also home languages and other international languages, some of which are likely to have produced the test result and which account for massive educational under-achievement across Africa. It is to these 'silences' that we now turn.

Silences in Global Educational Policy

The World Bank's failure to address the key role of the language of instruction in shaping or constraining children's experiences of learning is the latest iteration of a longstanding silence within the field of development education and development (Pinnock, 2009; Bamgbose, 2014; Milligan et al., 2020). For example, the report of the Association for the Development of Education in Africa (ADEA) (Alidou et al., 2006, 27) argued that 'the language factor' is "practically totally absent from mainstream development discourse". Its study of donor policies, practices and investment priorities in support of education found a failure to consider linguistic exclusion and its impact on educational opportunity. The persistent invisibility of the issue in global education and development agendas also prompted Brock-Utne (2014, 4) to comment that the 'language of instruction' is "the most important and least appreciated issue" amongst donors to education in Africa. Likewise, Tikly (2016) has observed that "it is alarming that language in education policy is so often at the periphery of global debates about the quality of education" (408). Hence, the ambitious global agendas to expand educational opportunity through Education For All and the SDGs appear utopian since they fail to address exclusionary linguistic processes.[3] There is a paradox in the imperative to promote 'learner-centred' teaching, yet failing to attend to the linguistic environments that often thwart that very aspiration. In all such ambitions for the promise of education, the language of instruction is repeatedly the 'missing link' (Pinnock, 2009).

Contemporary framings of the learning crisis reflect a longstanding disjunction between, on the one hand, research insights into what language teaching is best for children's learning and, on the other hand, international development agendas and practices that aim to address educational marginalisation. Despite recent shifts to evidence-based policy-making (Littoz-Monnet, 2017, 1), the significance of the language of instruction "as the key to communication and understanding in the classroom" (Benson, 2005, 2) remains a blind spot. Erling et al. (2021, 4) rightly recognise that:

> with the weight of... evidence in mind it is difficult to understand why there has not been wider recognition of the importance of language and multilingual education approaches in achieving quality education in SSA and why the struggle to implement indigenous language in education policies endures.

Below we rehearse some of the arguments about the importance of language education and the implications for learning of the ways in which the learning crisis discourse has addressed or ignored that importance and African government responses to the language dilemmas they face.

Resistance to change

We need to recognise that the silence on language of instruction issues within the educational agendas of international development agencies co-exists with the resistance to change of stakeholders at national and local levels. Diverse political, social and economic agendas militate against recognition of the pedagogical benefits of using children's home languages for learning. Hence, some African governments face a tension between concerns to promote national unity and patriotism through a monolingual education policy and the valorisation of local languages and indigenous cultures and identities (Sefa Dei, 2005; García, 2009a, 2009b; Arnot et al., 2018). African government responses have veered from allowing local languages for an overly short period of time in initial basic education, to using colonial languages as the only languages of instruction throughout schooling. The oscillating priorities of language of instruction policies can be seen, for example, in Ghana, Tanzania and Uganda (Tollefson and Tsui, 2014; Tikly, 2016).

Economistic approaches to national development have privileged English as the language best able to secure citizens' participation in a competitive global marketplace (Nakagawa and Kouritzin, 2021). Keen to preserve their social, economic and political power, national elites invariably tend to favour the hegemony of English (Bunyi, 2008a; Opoku-Amankwa, 2009; Bennell, 2021; Erling et al., 2021, ix). Western publishing companies are also reluctant to publish instructional materials in mother tongue languages, given their investment in the lucrative production of English-language textbooks (Brock-Utne, 2001, 121; Bunyi, 2008b, 35; Edwards and Ngwaru, 2012). Parents frequently resist the use of local languages, preferring English because of its associations with success in the labour market and its cultural prestige as the language of international communication (Trudell, 2005; 2016b). The result is that decisions on the language of instruction are skewed to block what should be of central significance, their impact on children's ability to learn. As Adamson (2021, 188) has pointed out:

> one of the limitations of existing debates about language of instruction is that those on different sides of the argument are focused on different goals for language. This results in the narrowing of the lens through which the issue of language-in education is viewed, and in evidence being side-lined or ignored that clearly demonstrates that the use of an unfamiliar medium of instruction has negative effects on learning.

The language of instruction is also a field of contestation shaped by what have been described as 'myths' (Brock-Utne, 2014, 14). For example, there are myths that:

- There are too many African languages to enable mother tongue instruction (Prah, 2005, 9);
- African languages cannot function as vehicles for the expression of difficult concepts (Kioko et al., 2014, 3);
- The cost of instructional materials in home languages will be prohibitive.
- Immersion in English language-only instruction will enable swifter acquisition of fluency;
- Learning in home languages will undermine learning in English;
- Recognition of African languages in post-colonial country contexts will threaten national unity.

Obanya (1999) concludes that "most of the arguments against the promotion of African languages in education are neither linguistic nor pedagogic but belong rather to the realm of a genuine fear of the unknown" (98). As a result, since the 1980s, "the question of language of instruction in sub-Saharan Africa has been generating a lot of heat but very little light" (Erling et al., 2021, ix). These debates not only have implications for national language policies but also for the pedagogical logics used in the classroom and consequently for children's experiences of learning. It is to these we now turn our attention.

Language of Instruction Policies and Teachers' Pedagogical Choices

There are "taken for granted beliefs, values and cultural frames that continually circulate in society informing the ways in which language is conceptualised and represented as well as how it is used" (McKinney, 2016, 19). Language assumptions shape "what counts in formal schooling, language curricula and everyday practices in schools and classrooms of both teachers and students", They are "central in shaping whose language resources count in formal schooling, which languages are chosen as languages of instruction and how language is taught" (19).

Referring to the South African context, McKinney explains that "the dominant approach to language in schooling is not to see language as a resource or to recognise the often complex linguistic repertoires which individuals bring with them to school" (42). Hence, the question arises: "How is it possible that the most valuable resource a child brings to formal schooling, their language, can be consistently recast as a problem?" (161). Deficit views of children's languages carry deficit views of their communities, signalling the social and cultural inferiority of the culture and people whose mother tongue is denied. This reproduces the neo-colonialist hierarchy according to which the language of the colonising powers (whether English, French, Spanish or Dutch) was deemed superior, civilised and civilising (Adejunmobi, 2004). For Brock-Utne (2002), despite the aspirations for Education for All in global development agendas, the pervasive afterlife of such assumptions in current educational provision for children constitutes nothing less than a "recolonisation of the African mind" (1). The dominant medium of instruction therefore forecloses any possibility of leveraging "languages of instruction for African emancipation" (Brock-Utne and Hopson, 2005). African children are consequently obliged to "continue in the shadows of colonialism" (Adzahlie-Mensah and Dunne, 2018, 44).

Various pedagogical practices follow that undermine opportunities for meaningful learning, as teachers face children who are unable to understand the language they are required to teach in. Studies of classrooms in sub-Saharan Africa have highlighted the pervasiveness of 'safe talk' (Chick, 1996; Erling et al., 2021) in the dominant language. This consists of teachers cueing and eliciting chorus responses from children in which they repeat the limited words and phrases they have grasped in the dominant language they are unfamiliar with (Adamson, 2022, 1). This form of contrived participation saves children embarrassment at providing incorrect answers. Yet, their repetition of learned phrases only disguises their lack of comprehension and a reluctance to speak. Teachers are also understandably reluctant to create any opportunities for children to draw on their often rich linguistic repertoire of home languages to support learning. As a Kigali teacher cited in the 2014 *Education for All Global Monitoring Report* eloquently explains:

> There remains no doubt that the main barrier to basic education is the forced use of English as medium of instruction. ... [It] not only impedes learning for the children but is also a major challenge for Rwanda's

teachers. Without adequate knowledge in English, teachers are unable to interact with the students, and the result is a strict chalk-and-talk structure.

(UNESCO, 2014, 297)

Opoku-Amankwa (2009) cites the predicament of a boy, Amakpor, in Northern Ghana who is 'multilingual'. In addition to Ewe, his mother tongue, he also speaks Twi, the local language of the area, and Ga fluently, languages he has learned from socialisation with friends and elders in his community without any formal instruction. His language usage on a daily basis is characterised by "translation, code mixing and switching, and repetition of words, expressions, and sentences between his peers and member of his community" (130). Yet, "the language learning and communicative practices in the classroom contrast sharply with what obtains in the community". Within the English-only language policy of his primary school, he is one of many pupils "who are classified as weak students mainly because they are unable to express their thoughts and ideas in English, the official language for teaching" (130). This is a salutary example of how deficit categorisations of children emerge directly, and misleadingly, from language of instruction policies. In some classroom contexts, authoritarian pedagogies intersect with disciplinary regimes in which speaking local languages results in humiliating punishments (Brock-Utne, 2007, 493).

These limited and limiting forms of teacher-pupil interaction undermine opportunities for the exploratory talk that is a pre-condition for meaningful learning, whether amongst children or between teachers and children (Alexander, 2008). McKinney's (2016) report on a science lesson on matter, conducted in English rather than in the home language isiXhosa for a class of nine- to ten-year-old in a township school of the Western Cape, South Africa is important. She noted that the "children are robbed of the opportunity of dialogic engagement and meaning making and thus robbed of the opportunity to grapple conceptually with the object of study" (59). A study of restrictive language policy and practices in Kenya (Kiramba and Oloo, 2019) found that it was grounded in 'monoglossic orientations', not surprisingly drawing attention to children's 'untapped communicative resources' (171) that could be leveraged to promote their learning, but which are erased because of their inhibitions.

Scholars have highlighted the obduracy of monolingual ideologies within language of instruction policies in sub-Saharan Africa even though the silencing of pupils' languages leads to silencing of the knowledges and experiences they embody and express (Makalela, 2015; Erling et al., 2021, 7; Milligan and Adamson, 2022). The disjunction these policies create between school and home experiences brackets off children's language use at home and their informal learning from the pedagogical processes they experience in school. Such narrow framings of language learning discourage pedagogical strategies that connect curriculum content with children's lived experiences and knowledges to ensure relevance and to scaffold new knowledge (Kerfoot and Simon-Vandenbergen, 2015). Children's 'funds of knowledge' (Moll et al., 2006) are erased as resources on which to create meaningful and engaging learning experiences. Opoku-Amankwa (2009, 130) describing pedagogical practices in a primary school in Ghana points out that "the multiethnic community in which the children attending Tomso primary live offers opportunities and cultural resources which are valuable assets for language learning and learning in general, but which are often totally ignored in formal literacy learning". Devaluing their languages and knowledges in favour of monolingualism means that such pedagogical strategies deny children the opportunity to 'take up positions as legitimate learners and knowers' (McKinney, 2016, 31).

Teachers, regulated by national language of instruction policies, therefore collude unintentionally in what amounts to a systemic denial of access to knowledge at the very core of educational provision (Kerfoot and Simon-Vandenbergen, 2015). The results are massive levels of under-achievement, dropping out-of-school and disengagement from learning, with the poorest children the most affected (Dutcher, 2001; UNESCO, 2016, 1, 3; Clegg, 2019; Erling et al., 2021). Linguistic exclusions thus intersect with educational disadvantage arising from poverty. As noted by Brock-Utne (2001, 120),

> in the crucial early grades when children are trying to acquire basic literacy as well as to adjust to the demands of the school setting, not speaking the language of instruction can make the difference between succeeding and failing in school, between remaining in school and dropping out. Monolingual language of instruction policies therefore reproduce and exacerbate educational and social inequalities.

Children's negative experiences of learning

The linguistic exclusion experienced by children can produce deeply alienating experiences of learning. Theorists of the role of language in learning have shown how our identity is constituted in and through our language usage. Hence, "language is the place where our sense of ourselves, our subjectivity is constructed" (Weedon, 1997, 21 quoted in Norton, 2013, 4). The language of instruction is therefore by no means a wholly linguistic issue. It is inextricable from children's sense of who they are, how they relate and in turn how they have learned and what they know in the particular contexts of their lives outside as well as inside formal learning environments. Language therefore has a fundamental ontological significance as its usage is constitutive of social identity (Gee, 1992, 2007). By excluding children's languages, monolingual education policies and the pedagogical and curriculum approaches that result devalue their lives and lived experiences. In doing so, they thwart opportunities to draw on their familiar communicative practices to facilitate learning and thereby to build their identity as learners. The resulting experience of alienation is evoked in the ADEA report *Optimising Learning and Education in Africa: The Language Factor* (Alidou et al., 2006, 7) when it reports how:

> children or adults are empowered when their first language is used. Conversely, when the mother tongue is not used, they are made to feel awkward, inferior, and stupid. Their culture is denigrated, and the children are scared, confused, and traumatized. This has long-term effects.

Such negative experiences of learning are of particular significance given the highly contingent relationship to the opportunities of formal educational provision invariably experienced by children designated as 'out-of-school'. It is not surprising then that Obanya (1980, 88, quoted in Brock-Utne, 2005) observed that:

> it has always been felt by African educationists that the African child's major learning problem is linguistic. Instruction is given in a language that is not normally used in his [sic] immediate environment, a language which neither the learner nor the teacher understands and uses well enough.
>
> (173)

Yet, the socio-emotional impacts of language of instruction policies are "rarely discussed in the language in education literature in Sub-Saharan Africa" (Adamson, 2022, 3). Of particular relevance to the concerns of this book are recent ethnographic studies that have spotlighted the consequences that undermine children's affective orientation to engage in learning when an unfamiliar language is used as a medium of instruction. For example, Nigerian educator Okonkwo reports:

> There is little doubt that the systematic but frequently ignored differences between the language and culture of the school and the language and culture of the learner's community have often resulted in educational programmes with only marginal success at teaching anything except self-deprecation.
>
> (Okonkwo, 1983, 377; quoted in Benson, 2002, 304)

Children in diverse African contexts are invited to perceive themselves, for example, as 'dumb' (Brock-Utne and Hopson, 2005); 'nobodies' (Adzahlie-Mensah, 2014, xiii); 'slow learners' (Opoku-Amankwa, 2009, 4) and 'mute, empty vessel(s)' (Adzahlie-Mensah and Dunne, 2018, 56) or unable to fulfil the linguistic criteria for 'being a good student' or "*soma kwa bidi* [a kiswhali phrase for studying hard in Tanzania] and thus blaming themselves for failure and 'personal weakness'" (Adamson, 2022, 14). A study of primary school classrooms in rural Kumasi in Ghana showed how "the use of English – an unfamiliar language – creates anxiety among students and stalls effective classroom participation" (Opoku-Amankwa, 2009, 121). Such experiences amount to systemic 'inferiorisation' (Opoku-Amankwa, 2009, 44) or 'stupidification' (Brock-Utne, 2007, 487). Metaphors of 'sinking and drowning' or 'torture' evoke the existential angst generated for millions of children by the linguistic conditions of their learning (Benson, 2002, 4; Kioko et al., 2014, 3; Milligan et al., 2020, 116). Fear accompanies anxiety as children anticipate shame and embarrassment at potential exposure to weak English and negative reactions from peers and teachers.[4] Adamson's study of student experiences in an English medium secondary school in Tanzania quotes a student who commented that:

> a person is afraid most of the time… a person can have their answer and they go to say it but they fail, they tremble. They are not confident with their answer because they do not believe in themselves'.
>
> (2022, 6)

Likewise, a study of a primary school in Senegal (Speciale, 2020) found that children were drawn into a 'cycle of shame' by teachers' enforcement of the school's official language practices (teaching in French) in which any word spoken in the home languages met with punishment and ostracism. Such feelings paralyse participation, reducing children to silence, passivity, frustration and disengagement, in what has been described as nothing less than an experience of 'torture to the child' (Kioko et al., 2014, 3). Such alienating experiences of learning lead directly to lower levels of attainment and higher dropout rates.

Linguistic and epistemic exclusion intersecting with socio-emotional alienation is a gendered process, impacting girls even more than boys. In a recent policy paper on language and girls' education, Milligan and Adamson (2022) conclude that:

> low proficiency in the language of instruction is consistently associated with girls' poor attendance, lower learning outcomes, lower transition rates and higher risk of drop out from schooling'.
>
> (5)

Girls are less likely than boys to be exposed to the ex-colonial language of instruction, given that their lives are more likely to be restricted to the home and family where the local language is spoken (UNESCO, 2003, 16). Learning in an unfamiliar language therefore compounds the challenges that girls already experience in accessing educational provision. A study of girls' interactions with each other and their teachers in an English medium basic education in Rwanda found that "reluctance to speak in class and respond to teacher's question, combined with lack of confidence as evidenced through body language, deprived girls from participating in spontaneous classroom talk" (Kuchah et al., 2022, 1).

Milligan and Adamson (2022) found that girls' apprehensiveness about attending school in a language they are not familiar with exacerbates pre-existing challenges that deter them from engagement in formal education, such as household responsibilities, lack of family support and the distance of the school from home. This finding suggests that the absence of attention to language of instruction issues in SDG goal 4's aspiration to achieve gender equality and empowerment represents a lamentable failure to appreciate its significance in contributing to educational inequalities and gender injustice more broadly (Benson, 2016, 3). There is an urgent need to put language of instruction on the girls' education agenda as a priority 'if we are to enable all girls to access and progress in quality, equitable education' (Milligan and Adamson, 2022, 4).

Lessons for the 'Learning Crisis'

Commenting on how monolingual language policies depress school achievement in Africa, Clegg concluded that "instead of giving them [disadvantaged learners] extra help, we make schooling harder for them than for most children in the world" (2019, 89). Children already experiencing a highly contingent relationship with formal schooling experience frustration, alienation and loss of confidence in the process of navigating learning environments that belittle or erase the languages and knowledges they bring. As we have seen, the language of instruction currently acts as a mechanism of marginalisation and exclusion in sub-Saharan Africa. This is the crisis that needs to be addressed, through the 'centralising' of the language of instruction rather than by neglecting its significance and impact (Clegg, 2021).

This chapter has demonstrated how language of instruction policies and their pedagogical consequences systematically produce deficit and alienating experiences of learning for children. The impacts on the cognitive development of children are well known. The studies discussed have widened the analysis to spotlight their socio-emotional impact and the resulting damage to African children's sense of efficacy as learners. As a result, the limited levels of school achievement in sub-Saharan Africa can be seen to be directly attributable to the language policies and the linguistic conditions for learning, which constitute a major barrier to enjoyable as well as meaningful learning (Erling et al., 2021). For Heugh (2009, 108) their "design guarantees educational failure". Yet, the possibilities of building children's fragile momentum for learning by using their linguistic resources to embed meaningful and engaging teaching approaches have not been canvassed. Essentially, the system as it now stands reproduces and exacerbates educational marginalisation for children who are targeted by the 'learning crisis'. It creates alienation, anxiety and exclusion at the very moment of initial engagement or re-engagement with educational provision. The result is nothing less than a systemic educational tragedy affecting many African countries and their children. This failure to address the issues and the evidence about the language of instruction meaningfully at the level of international aid organisations or national governments is of considerable concern. Given the constitutive role of language in learning, the invitation to 'Realise Education's Promise' (World Bank, 2018) without attention to the language of instruction amounts to a contradiction in terms.

In the next chapter, we demonstrate how not only children and communities but also their teachers in sub-Saharan Africa are framed in deficit terms within a discourse of Afro-pessimism that similarly underestimates their knowledges and agency, voices and experiences.

Notes

1 For example, in the International Convention on the Rights of the Child (1989), UNESCO (2003, 2006, 2014a, 2014b, 2015, 2016).
2 See also for the Indian context, Kalyanpur et al. (2022).
3 See Romaine (2013), Vuzo (2018), Milligan et al. (2020), Bennell (2021), van Pinxteren (2022), Ulmer et al. (2023).
4 See Rea-Dickens and Yu (2013), Madonsela (2015), Mokibelo (2016), William and Ndabakurane (2017), Sibomana (2022).

References

Adamson, L., 2021. 'Language of instruction: a question of disconnected capabilities'. *Comparative Education*, 57(2): 187–205.

Adamson, L., 2022. 'Fear and shame: students' experiences in English-medium secondary classrooms in Tanzania'. *Journal of Multilingual and Multicultural Development*, 45(8): 3275–3290.

Adejunmobi, M., 2004. 'Vernacular palaver: imaginations of the local and non-native languages in West Africa'. *Multilingual Matters*, 9.

Adzahlie-Mensah, V., 2013. Being "Nobodies"; school regimes and student identities in Ghana. Unpublished PhD thesis, University of Sussex.

Adzahlie-Mensah, V., and Dunne, M., 2018. 'Continuing in the shadows of colonialism: the educational experiences of the African Child in Ghana'. *Perspectives in Education*, 36(2): 44–60.

Afitska, O., Ankomah, Y., Clegg, J., Kiliku, P., Osei-Amankwah, L., and Rubagumya, C., 2013. 'Dilemmas of language choice in education in Tanzania and Ghana'. In L. Tikly, and A.M. Barrett (eds.), *Education quality and social justice in the global south: challenges for policy, practice, and research*. Routledge, pp. 154–167.

Alexander, R., 2008. 'Culture, dialogue and learning: notes on an emerging pedagogy'. In N. Mercer and S. Hodgkinson (eds.), *Exploring talk in school*. Sage, 91–114.

Alidou, H., Boly, A., Brock-Utne, B., Diallo, Y.S., Heugh, K., and Wolff, H.E., 2006. *Optimizing learning and education in Africa: the language factor*. ADEA.

Alidou, H., and Brock-Utne, B., 2011. 'Teaching practices – teaching in a familiar language'. In A. Ouane and C. Glanz (eds.), *Optimising learning, education and publishing in Africa: the language factor. A review and analysis of theory and practice in mother-tongue and bilingual education in sub-Saharan Africa*. UIL and ADEA, pp. 159–186.

Arnot, M., Casely-Hayford, L., and Yeboah, T., 2018. 'Post-colonial dilemmas in the construction of Ghanaian citizenship education: national unity, human rights and social inequalities'. *International Journal of Educational Development*, 61: 117–126.

Bamgbose, A., 2014. 'The language factor in development goals'. *Journal of Multilingual and Multicultural Development*, 35(7): 646–657.

Bennell, P., 2021. 'The political economy of attaining Universal Primary Education in sub-Saharan Africa: social class reproduction, educational distancing and job competition'. *International Journal of Educational Development*, 80: 102303.

Benson, C.J., 2002. 'Real and potential benefits of bilingual programmes in developing countries'. *International Journal of Bilingual Education and Bilingualism*, 5(6): 303–317.

Benson, C., 2005. *The importance of mother tongue-based schooling for educational quality*. Commissioned study for EFA Global Monitoring Report, 24.

Benson, C., 2016. *Addressing language of instruction issues in education: recommendations for documenting progress*. Background paper commissioned by UNESCO for the Global Education Monitoring Report 2016. Paris: UNESCO. Available at: https://unesdoc.unesco.org/images/0024/002455/245575E.pdf [Accessed: 21.07.2023].

Benson, C., 2018. 'Celebrating the rich resources represented by African multilingualism and multiculturalism in education: discussant paper'. *Current Issues in Language Planning*, 19(2): 218–225.

Brock-Utne, B., 2001. 'Education for all – In whose language?' *Oxford Review of Education*, 27(1): 115–134.

Brock-Utne, B., 2002. *Whose education for all?: The recolonization of the African mind*. Routledge.

Brock-Utne, B., 2005. Language-in-education policies and practices in Africa with a special focus on Tanzania and South Africa—Insights from research in progress. In Z. Joseph, K. Freeman, M. Geo-JaJa, M. Suzanne, R. Val and R. Zajda (eds.), *International handbook on globalisation, education and policy research: global pedagogies and policies*. Springer Netherlands, pp. 549–565.

Brock-Utne, B., 2007. 'Learning through a familiar language versus learning through a foreign language: a look into some secondary school classrooms in Tanzania'. *International Journal of Educational Development*, 27(5): 487–498.

Brock-Utne, B., 2014. 'Language of instruction in Africa: the most important and least appreciated issue'. *International Journal of Educational Development in Africa*, 1(1): 4–18.

Brock-Utne, B., and Hopson, R.K., 2005. 'Introduction: educational language contexts and issues in postcolonial Africa'. In B. Brock-Utne and R. Hopson (eds.), *Languages of instruction for African emancipation: focus on postcolonial contexts and considerations*, Dar es Salaam.

Bunyi, G. 2008a. 'Constructing elites in Kenya: implications for classroom language practices in Africa'. In M. Stephen (ed.), *Encyclopedia of language and education*. Springer, pp. 899–909.

Bunyi, G.W., 2008b. 'The place of African indigenous knowledge and languages in education for development: the case of Kenya'. In G.W. Bunyi (ed.), *New directions in African education: challenges and possibilities*. University of Calgary Press, pp. 15–39.

Chick, J.K., 1996. 'Safe-talk: Collusion in apartheid education'. In H. Coleman (ed.), *Society and the language classroom*. Cambridge University Press, p. 2139.

Clegg, J., 2019. 'How English depresses school achievement in Africa'. *ELT Journal*, 73(1): 89–91.

Clegg, J., 2021. 'Multilingual learning in Anglophone Sub-Saharan Africa: how to help children use all their languages to learn'. In J. Clegg (ed.), *Multilingual learning and language supportive pedagogies in sub-Saharan Africa*. Routledge pp. 144–169.

Cummins, J., 1996. *Negotiating identities: education for empowerment in a diverse society*. California Association of Bilingual Education.

Cummins, J., 2007. 'Rethinking monolingual instructional strategies in multilingual classrooms'. *Canadian Journal of Applied Linguistics*, 10(2): 221–240.

Desai, Z., 2016. 'Learning through the medium of English in multilingual South Africa: enabling or disabling learners from low income contexts?' *Comparative Education*, 52(3): 343–358.

Docrat, Z., 2022. 'Decolonising multilingualism in Africa: recentering silenced voices from the global south', *South African Journal of African Languages*, 42(2): 252–253.

Dutcher, N., 2001. *Expanding educational opportunity in linguistically diverse societies*. Center for Applied Linguistics.

Edwards, V., and Ngwaru, J.M., 2012. 'African language books for children: issues for authors'. *Language, Culture and Curriculum*, 25(2): 123–138.

Erling, E.J., Clegg, J., Rubagumya, C.M., and Reilly, C. eds., 2021. *Multilingual learning and language supportive pedagogies in Sub-Saharan Africa*. Routledge.

Erling, E.J., Safford, K., and Tugli, F.M., 2021. 'Classroom talk in Ghanaian upper primary schools: understanding English-only, teacher-dominant practices'. In E.J. Erling, J. Clegg, C.M. Rubagumya, and C. Reilly (eds.), *Multilingual learning and language supportive pedagogies in Sub-Saharan Africa*. Routledge, pp. 79–97.

García, O., 2009a. Education, multilingualism and translanguaging in the 21st century. In *Social justice through multilingual education*. Multilingual Matters, pp. 143, 158.

García, O. 2009b. *Bilingual education in the 21st century: a global perspective*. Wiley-Blackwell.

Gee, J.P., 1992. *The social mind: language, ideology, and social practice*. Bergin and Garvey.

Gee, J.P., 2007. 'Self-fashioning and shape-shifting: Language, identity, and social class'. In D.E. Alvermann, K.A. Hinchman, D.W. Moore III, D.W. Moore, S.F. Phelps, and D.R. Waff (eds.), *Reconceptualizing the literacies in adolescents' lives*. Routledge, pp. 197–218.

Glewwe, P., Kremer, M., and Moulin, S., 2009. 'Many children left behind? Textbooks and test scores in Kenya'. *American Economic Journal: Applied Economics*, 1(1): 112–135.

Heugh, K., 2009. *Literacy and bi/multilingual education in Africa: Recovering collective memory and expertise* (Doctoral dissertation, Multilingual Matters).

Ingutia, R., 2020. 'Does marginalisation in education stall the progress of sustainable development goals?' *Education 3–13*, 48(5): 495–511.

Kerfoot, C., and Simon-Vandenbergen, A.M., 2015. 'Language in epistemic access: mobilising multilingualism and literacy development for more equitable education in South Africa'. *Language and Education*, 29(3): 177–185.

Kioko, A.N., Ndung'u, R.W., Njoroge, M.C., and Mutiga, J., 2014. 'Mother tongue and education in Africa: publicising the reality'. *Multilingual Education*, 4(1): 11.

Kiramba, L.K., 2018. 'Language ideologies and epistemic exclusion'. *Language and Education*, 32(4): 291–312.

Kiramba, L.K., and Oloo, J.A., 2019. 'Untapped communicative resources in multilingual classroom settings: possible alternatives'. *Southern African Linguistics and Applied Language Studies*, 37(2): 171–187.

Klees, S.J., Stromquist, N.P., Samoff, J., and Vally, S., 2019. 'The 2018 world development report on education: a critical analysis'. *Development and Change*, 50(2): 603–620.

Kuchah, K., Adamson, L., Dorimana, A., Uwizeyemariya, A., Uworwabayeho, A., and Milligan, L.O., 2022. 'Silence and silencing in the classroom: Rwandan girls' epistemic exclusion in English medium basic education'. *Journal of Multilingual and Multicultural Development*, 45(10): 4301–4315.

Littoz-Monnet, A. ed., 2017. *The politics of expertise in international organizations: how international bureaucracies produce and mobilize knowledge*. Taylor and Francis.

Madonsela, S., 2015. 'Language anxiety caused by the single mode of instruction in multilingual classrooms: the case of African language learners'. *Africa Education Review*, 12(3): 447–459.

Makalela, L., 2015. 'Moving out of linguistic boxes: the effects of translanguaging strategies for multilingual classrooms'. *Language and Education*, 29(3): 200–217.

Mbembe, A., 2001. *On the postcolony*. University of California Press.

McKinney, C., 2016. *Language and power in post-colonial schooling: ideologies in practice*. Routledge.

Milligan, L.O. and Adamson, L., 2022. *Girls education and language of instruction: an extended policy brief*. Institute for Policy Research.

Milligan, L.O., Desai, Z., and Benson, C., 2020. 'A critical exploration of how language-of-instruction choices affect educational equity'. In L.O. Milligan, Z. Desai, and C. Benson (eds.), *Grading goal four: tensions, threats and opportunities in the sustainable development goal on quality education*. Brill/Sense.

Milligan, L.O., and Tikly, L., 2016. 'English as a medium of instruction in postcolonial contexts: issues of quality, equity and social justice'. *Comparative Education*, 52(3): 277–280.

Mokibelo, E., 2016. 'Transition from Setswana to English: a policy dilemma'. *Journal of Language Teaching and Research*, 7(4): 665–674.

Moll, L., Amanti, C., Neff, D. and Gonzalez, N., 2006. 'Funds of knowledge for teaching: using a qualitative approach to connect homes and classrooms'. In L. Moll, C. Amanti, D. Neff, and N. Gonzalez (eds.), *Funds of knowledge*. Routledge, pp. 71–87.

Mose, P.N., and Kaschula, R.H., 2019. 'Developing mother tongues as academic languages in primary schools in Kenya: exploring extent and indispensability'. *Journal of Language, Identity and Education*, 18(5): 329–342.

Nakagawa, S., and Kouritzin, S., 2021. 'Identities of resignation: threats to indigenous languages from neoliberal linguistic and educational practices'. *Journal of Language, Identity and Education*, 20(5): 296–310.

Norton, B., 2013. *Identity and language learning: extending the conversation*. Multilingual Matters.

Obanya, P., 1980. Research on alternative teaching in Africa. In E.A. Yoloye and J. Flechsig (eds.), (eds), *Educational research for development*. Deutsche Stiftung für Internationale Entwicklung, pp. 67–112.

Obanya, P., 1999. 'Popular fallacies on the use of African languages in education'. *Social Dynamics*, 25(1): 81–100.

Opoku-Amankwa, K., 2009. 'English-only language-in-education policy in multilingual classrooms in Ghana'. *Language, Culture and Curriculum*, 22(2): 121–135.

Phyak, P., and De Costa, P.I., 2021. 'Decolonial struggles in Indigenous language education in neoliberal times: identities, ideologies, and activism'. *Journal of Language, Identity and Education*, 20(5): 291–295.

Pinnock, H., 2009. *Language and education: the missing link. How the language used in school threatens the achievement of education for all*. CfBT Education Trust.

Prah, K.K., 2005. 'Languages of instruction for education, development and African emancipation'. In B. Brock-Utne and R. Hopson (eds.), *Languages of instruction for African emancipation: focus on postcolonial contexts and considerations*. Dar es Salaam.

Rea-Dickens, P., and Yu, G., 2013. 'English medium instruction and examining in Zanzibar: ambitions, pipe dreams and realities'. In C. Benson and K. Kosonen (eds.), *Language issues in comparative education: inclusive teaching and learning in non-dominant languages and cultures*. Sense Publishers, pp. 189–207.

Romaine, S., 2013. 'Keeping the promise of the millennium development goals: why language matters'. *Applied Linguistics Review*, 4(1): 1–21.

Sefa Dei, G.J., 2005. 'Social difference and the politics of schooling in Africa: a Ghanaian case study'. *Compare*, 35(3): 227–245.

Sefa Dei, G.J.S., Karanja, W., Erger, G., Dei, G.J.S., Karanja, W., and Erger, G., 2022. 'Responding to the epistemic challenge–a decolonial project'. In G.J.S. Sefa Dei, W. Karanja, G. Erger, G.J.S. Dei, W. Karanja, and G. Erger (eds.), *Elders' cultural knowledges and the question of black/African indigeneity in education*, Springer, Critical Studies of Education Series, pp. 79–111.

Speciale, T., 2020. 'A cycle of shame: how shaming perpetuates language inequalities in Dakar, Senegal'. In J.A. Windle, D.D. Jesus, and L. Bartlett (eds.), *The dynamics of language and inequality in education: social and symbolic boundaries in the global south*. Multilingual Matters.

Sriprakash, A., Tikly, L., and Walker, S., 2020. 'The erasures of racism in education and international development: re-reading the "global learning crisis"'. *Compare: A Journal of Comparative and International Education*, 50(5): 676–692.

Tikly, L. 2016. 'Language-in-education policy in low-income, postcolonial contexts: towards a social justice approach'. *Comparative Education*, 52(3): 408–425.

Tollefson, J.W., and Tsui, A.B., 2014. 'Language diversity and language policy in educational access and equity'. *Review of Research in Education*, 38(1): 189–214.

Trudell, B., 2005. 'Language choice, education and community identity'. *International Journal of Educational Development*, 25(3): 237–251.

Trudell, B., 2016a. *The impact of language policy and practice on children's learning: evidence from eastern and Southern Africa*. UNICEF.

Trudell, B., 2016b. 'Language choice and education quality in Eastern and Southern Africa: a review'. *Comparative Education*, 52(3): 281–293.

Ulmer, N., Divine, N., and Wydra, K., 2023. 'Lost in translation? Tanzanian students' views on sustainability and language, and the implications for the pledge to leave no one behind'. *International Journal of Sustainability in Higher Education*, 24(7): 1381–1397.

UNESCO, 1953. *The use of vernacular languages in education*. Available at: https://www.tolerancia.org/upimages/Manifiestos/unesco_1953_english.pdf [Accessed: 19.05.2024].

UNESCO, 2003. *Education in a multilingual world*. UNESCO Education Position Paper. Paris: UNESCO. https://unesdoc.unesco.org/ark:/48223/pf0000129728

UNESCO, 2014. EFA global monitoring report Teaching and Learning Achieving Quality for all, United Nations Educational, Scientific and Cultural Organization 7, Place de Fontenoy, 75352 Paris 07 SP, France.

UNESCO, 2016a. *If you don't understand, how can you learn?* Policy Paper 24 of Global Education Monitoring Report, Paris: UNESCO. Available at: https://unesdoc.unesco.org/ark:/48223/pf0000243713 [Accessed: 21.07.2023].

UNESCO, 2016b. *Every child should have a textbook.* Global Education Monitoring Report Policy Paper 23.

Van Pinxteren, B., 2022. 'Language of instruction in education in Africa: how new questions help generate new answers'. *International Journal of Educational Development,* 88: 102–524.

Vuzo, M., 2018. 'Towards achieving the sustainable development goals: revisiting language of instruction in Tanzanian secondary schools'. *International Review of Education,* 64: 803–822.

Watson, K., 2007. 'Language, education and ethnicity: whose rights will prevail in an age of globalisation?' *International Journal of Educational Development,* 27(3): 252–265.

Westbrook, J., Baleeta, M., Dyer, C., and Islei, A., 2022. 'Re-imagining a synchronous linguistic landscape of public and school uses of Runyoro-Rutooro and Runyankore-Rukiga in early childhood education in Western Uganda'. *Journal of Multilingual and Multicultural Development,* 44(9): 846–859.

William, F., and Ndabakurane, J., 2017. 'Language Supportive Teaching and Textbooks (LSTT) for bilingual classrooms: mathematics teaching and learning in Tanzania'. *African Journal of Teacher Education,* 6(1): 96–118.

World Bank, 2018. *Learning to realise education's promise.* World Bank Group.

World Bank, 2021. *Loud and clear: effective language of instruction policies for learning.* Available at: https://documents1.worldbank.org/curated/en/517851626203470278/pdf/Loud-and-Clear-Effective-Language-of-Instruction-Policies-For-Learning.pdf [Accessed: 21.07.2023].

4 The Deficit Characterisation of the African Teacher

A distinguishing feature of the 'learning crisis' narrative is the mobilisation of a discourse of derision against teachers, especially in sub-Saharan Africa. Not only is their commitment often called into question, but their deficiencies are also presented as affecting students' progress in learning "and in turn placing limits on their capacity to contribute to national economic development" (Robertson, 2012, 584). To illustrate, Robertson (2012, 591) notes that on the front cover of one of the World Bank's policy briefings on accountability (Bruns et al., 2011), there is a picture of a teacher who is asleep, sandals off, with outstretched legs. The specific context of this classroom is not identified but its lack of materials and resources, the absence even of a blackboard, as well as its poor physical infrastructure are typical of the bleak environments teachers face in Africa. That teachers are "the main culprits failing children and their learning in these settings is the message" (Robertson, 2012, 591). Their failure assumes greater significance when it is linked to teacher quality and economic development arguments (e.g., Hanushek, 2011) becoming a lens through which the World Bank and bilateral organisations assess the value and contribution of African education to economic growth. It is based on an argument that says competent or high-quality teachers have significant impact on improving student learning and, in turn, on economic growth (Hanushek, 2011; UNESCO, 2013/14). Poor-quality teachers in sub-Saharan Africa are therefore viewed as a threat to the development of its human resources for economic and social transformation.

The characteristics and performance of basic education teachers in sub-Sahara Africa have therefore assumed great importance in 'learning crisis' discourse. In particular, multilateral international organisations have questioned their abilities based on research on the causal links between teachers' knowledge base or pedagogical practices and student learning outcomes (Pesambili et al., 2022). Quantitative research has been used to identify and isolate the key teacher characteristics, behaviours, knowledge and practices responsible for improving student learning outcomes. This growing interest in multivariate quantitative research by policymakers:

> treats schools and teachers as bearers of variables (attitudes, qualifications, strong leadership, etc.) to be correlated with pupil outcomes,

DOI: 10.4324/9781003185482-6

measured on standardized tests. This gave an educational interpretation to the managerialist idea – derived from the muddled discourse of 'excellence' in corporate management – that there is always a 'best practice' that can be instituted and audited from above.

(Connell, 2009, 217)

In relation to the 'learning crisis', the search for some sort of 'best practice' to address cognitive gaps in children's foundational literacy and numeracy (FLN) skills has motivated research looking for certainty in terms of specific teacher characteristics, instructional behaviours and practices that can improve student learning outcomes. However, such research has led to a reductionist framing of teaching and teacher quality, ignoring its complexity and the importance of the sociocultural context in learning to become an effective teacher (Pesambili et al., 2022).

Research on which teacher characteristics improve learning outcomes has not produced reliable links (Hanushek, 2011, 467). After several decades of research seeking to correlate a wide variety of teacher characteristics with student learning outcomes, Kennedy (2010, 591) points out that "none has demonstrated very high correlations". Besides, the idea that one can objectively quantify either teacher characteristics or performance and link it directly to student learning outcomes has been questioned by some researchers who argue that "it is unfair to hold teachers as exclusively accountable for student learning, and that teacher motivation and cooperation might be adversely affected as a result" (Bramwell et al., 2014). The constant derision of teachers working in African basic education as largely incompetent whilst not taking account of the challenging educational environments in which they work, risks demoralising and demotivating them and arguably will prove counterproductive in the effort to improve student learning.

Emphasis on the lack of teacher competence lies behind calls for accountability and programmes to measure and monitor their performance (Robertson, 2012; Verger, 2021). But unlike this debate in the global North:

> the teacher accountability debate [in Global South countries] has a very different focus [and tone] … is more about controlling teacher attendance and whether unqualified teachers can teach better and more efficiently than regular teachers.
>
> (Verger, 2021, 800)

Teacher accountability policies increasingly stifle teacher professionalism and autonomy, allowing influential global development organisations and their actors to promote interventions that have the effect of deepening the de-professionalisation of teaching in sub-Saharan Africa (Robertson, 2012; Verger, 2021). It was noted that:

> teachers are now [more] visible in the form of attention being paid to teacher policies … they are notably invisible as individuals with desires and passions to make a difference in the lives of students'.
>
> (Robertson, 2012, 603)

Commenting on the emergence of this discourse of accountability, Robertson notes that:

> since early 2000, a growing number of global actors have gained greater control over the rules for classifying and framing the good teacher, legitimated by arguments such as the need to create more efficient education systems and competitive knowledge economies and to manage a crisis in the teaching profession.
>
> (2012, 589)

So, to improve teacher attendance in basic schools in sub-Saharan Africa, for example, measures have included the use of local monitoring and digital tools. In Gambia, the Ministry of Education working in partnership with the World Bank and a local technology company introduced a mobile phone platform as a 'promising initiative' to collect data on 'teacher absenteeism and tardiness' – "Head teachers [use] this platform to send data on key attendance indicators on a daily basis to a computer server which reduces the challenge of tracking and consolidation of data and makes the information available in real time" (4).[1] But as Bennell and Akyeampong (2007) point out, the problem lies deeper and reflects how over time teacher morale and commitment has been weakened by policies such as Education for All and economic conditions of the World Bank and International Monitory Fund's (IMF) structural adjustment programmes which have negatively impacted teachers' work and living conditions. Unless addressed, tracking teacher attendance will only produce short-term improvements. Although regular teacher attendance is important, it is insufficient for improving learning and student achievement if unaccompanied by pedagogical processes that can sustain impact (Guerrero et al., 2012).

Similarly, the research on teachers, teaching and teacher education has exerted "strong pressure for uniform measures that quantify teachers' work, knowledge, and performance ... [and made] it easy to lose a more nuanced perspective and, in particular, the voices and perspectives of teachers" (Paine and Zeichner, 2012, 577). Bengtsson et al. argue that "missing from current analyses of [teacher and] teaching quality are the perceptions and viewpoints of teachers themselves" (2020, 217). In the African context Kwame, and his co-researchers (Akyeampong et al., 2006) explored Ghanaian teachers' understandings of learning, teaching and assessment, in an attempt to dig deeper into teachers' understanding of their practice and give voice to their experiences of promoting effective learning. They found that, when invited to reflect deeply on their practice, teachers are able to articulate effective practice and attribute their successes to how it promotes meaningful learning. They argued that this:

> appears more promising than generalised, static descriptions of teacher quality captured usually through standardised surveys, where the situated context that gives rise to teaching attributes is relegated to the

> background. Teaching cultures are contextually bounded and complex, so understanding and producing insight into this culture require approaches that explore, in depth, teachers' *reasoning* about teaching, learning and assessment based on specific educational contexts and accounts of experience within them.
>
> (Akyeampong et al., 2006, 161)

If one looks beyond quantitative measures of teachers' competence to approaches that invite them to reflect on their experiences on what works to improve learning, teachers are able to "produce a more sophisticated account of teaching and learning and how they might go about actualising it" (171). Harnessing teacher's situated reflexivity using qualitative methods signifies their competence in ways that are often not visible using quantitative measures.

Unfortunately, the framing of African teachers' competence has narrowed to whether or not they can demonstrate prescriptive behaviours or teaching strategies considered essential to improve student learning. The recent World Bank-supported *Teach Observer Manual* is an example. It reduces "the complex social dynamics of teaching and learning ... to a set of directions that establish principles for quantifying practices" (Pesambili et al., 2022). Presented as an authoritative manual for describing and quantifying 'good teaching', it essentially erases teacher agency as exercised through reflective practice, the ecological classroom context that shapes their choices and the effect on their instructional outcomes. It is as if *all* teachers work in an ecological classroom vacuum or face the same classroom conditions and policy environment. Pesambili et al. (2022:6) argue that the:

> Teach observation tool provides a reductionist and technocratic view of teaching, benignly constructing teachers as unprofessional, with no autonomy to make their own judgements about what and how students should learn.

Alexander (2008, 271) claims that, "researchers have become adept at dissecting teaching but poor at reconstructing it". Tools that dissect teaching processes produce outcomes that miss critical elements that explain them because of many unaccounted contextual factors or conditions. The more difficult task that much research on teachers avoid is reconstructing an overall characterisation of teaching as a complex and multidimensional activity. Kennedy (2010:592) argues that a model of teaching that is based on a reduced set of teacher actions and characteristics:

> presume(s) that teaching practices follow directly from such enduring personal characteristics as credentials, knowledge, or perhaps dispositions and personality traits ... and presumes that those [student learning] outcomes are largely in teachers' hands and overlooks the role of the textbook, the physical space, and other resources.
>
> (592)

It is misleading, as Akyeampong et al. (2006) pointed out, to characterise teachers simply as incompetent especially when their practices are viewed through the lens of strict inspection regimes that place unrealistic demands and expectations. They argue that instead if one works "with the premise that teachers are potentially competent, but struggling to cope with difficult circumstances, [these practices] can instead be seen [as] a rational response to a burdensome and counterproductive system" (170). It is to these competences that we now turn.

Oral Culture and Learner-centred Instruction in the African Context

Croft (2002) studied practices of teachers in Malawian primary schools seeking explanations for the techniques they use. Her intention was to explore whether "learner-centred teaching in large classes with few resources might involve a largely oral teaching style, and the relationship of this teaching style to the strengths of local oral culture". (323). The oral culture in African societies presents a view on literacy that can also be taken to mean the idea of "knowing and doing ... as a practice of encountering and coming to be in the world" (Perry, 2024, 45). Children from a rich oral culture should therefore not be assumed to be 'illiterate' when they first encounter formal schooling. Perry argues that:

> literacy can be interpreted from all manner of practices and experiences – from dancing to making, from coding to playing – and with frameworks of literacy theory, analyses of these practices allow us to understand, articulate, justify, and build on these literacies for educational purposes.

As Croft points out in her research, before entering school, Malawian children are more familiar with listening, speaking and singing than reading and writing, and that teachers used singing to manage large classes whilst also maintaining a focus on learning that showed evidence of improved learning outcomes. The oral culture can therefore provide a powerful bridge between the listening, speaking and singing traditions that children are more familiar with than the more standardised forms of reading and writing. The Malawian teachers made use of their oral culture to produce what could be described as Afrocentric learner-centred instruction that took "account of the physical, socio-cultural and emotional context of their pupils" (333). Using songs in whole group learning settings is common in communal cultures and part of children's lived experience outside the formal school.

Viewed through a narrowly western conceptualisation of learner centred instruction, the practices revealed by Croft may be judged to be pedagogically unsound and unproductive. However, Croft argues that:

> learner-centred education means that teachers are likely to develop different teaching styles in different situations and that these styles will be

related to local conditions but not completely determined by them, because teachers make choices about the way they use available resources.

(335)

Ignoring the local conditions and context and how they influence teachers' instructional decisions can lead to simplistic judgements about their capabilities when, in reality, teachers might be experimenting to find appropriate solutions to formidable teaching challenges. Croft's decision not to use a Western conceptualisation of child-centred pedagogy to understand and interpret Malawian teachers' classroom practices avoids dismissing the oral culture and its importance and value in teaching large classes, common in many African schools. She was able to combine "observation(s) with talking to teachers to uncover their theories of learning and teaching, and then working with them to test [them]" (335). Her research is an example of how a deeper understanding of African teachers' practices can be accessed, tested and theorised. It is a reminder of why it is important to take a positive view of African classrooms as 'laboratories for innovative' practice'. Making teachers organise teaching using a Eurocentric conceptualisation of learner-centred instruction would show them as incompetent and reinforce the deficit characterisation of their practice. This truncates opportunities to experiment and find solutions that work under the many challenging educational settings basic education teachers in Africa face.

Imperfect Measurements and Symbols of Teaching Quality

Because many international assessments of African teachers' practices focus on using pre-determined standardised observation instruments without room to engage in critical dialogue with them on their reflections on practice (Pesambili et al., 2022), it is easy to misrepresent or misinterpret their practice and fail to recognise its potential in producing holistic and productive learning. Reducing the complex activity of teaching to quantifiable and decontextualised indicators without including qualitative insights from context, teacher reasoning and motives, misrepresents its inherent uncertainty and context-specificity. The result is to erase the multiple challenges teachers face leading to the construction of teaching as a relatively easy, unproblematic and mechanical practice that is far from the reality (Labaree, 2000).

At the same time, although Western education systems have a long history of researchers and policymakers advocating and experimenting with new models of teaching that challenge previous ideas and myths about effective teaching, the models of teaching imported into the African context are rarely subjected to similar experimentation and critique. What is presented as 'good' or 'effective' teaching often excludes a sociocultural analysis of pedagogical processes and the epistemological and ontological assumptions that underpin them and are unhelpful in understanding what good teaching looks like in the African context. Understanding African teacher's adaptive behaviours and how a broader conception of these as necessarily localised and effective in promoting learning is rarely given serious attention in the research on its teachers.

The consequences of limiting methodological approaches in the development context is that the weak subject knowledge of basic education teachers in Africa has been used to suggest the existence of a 'teaching crisis' and has been linked to the 'learning crisis' (Akyeampong, 2022b; Zuilkowski et al., 2022; Schweisfurth, 2023). Zuilkowski et al. (2022) point to studies in South Africa, Zambia and Nigeria that show evidence of teachers with weak subject knowledge, often as weak as the students they teach. We do not dispute that addressing this issue is important but making it a driver of teacher quality policy or prioritising it over pedagogical processes *overestimates* its contribution to effective teaching and learning. Yet, a teacher with good subject knowledge is likely to struggle to improve children's learning if that teacher is demotivated as a result of poor living and working conditions. In their research on teachers in sub-Saharan Africa and South Asia, Bennell and Akyeampong (2007:40) found that issues such as conflict, security, the policy environment and pay are conditions that teachers said lowered their motivation. They argued:

> teachers are not poorly motivated through self-perceived inadequacies in their capacities as teachers, [rather] ... many do struggle to cope in the classroom, which does adversely affect their levels of job satisfaction and morale.

The implications of teachers having a combination of lower educational qualification and weak subject knowledge are to be found in the characterisation of the teaching profession in low-income countries, particularly in sub-Saharan Africa (UNESCO, 2013/14). As proxy measures of teaching competency, these deepen the deficit characterisation of African teachers when this does not represent the totality of what they are able to achieve, especially with appropriate support. Global development organisations and their actors have used the outcomes of such measures to justify interventions such as structured pedagogy or structured lesson plans (SLPs) that diminish that potential. These proxy measures have *de facto* come to redefine what is legitimate pedagogical practice and are used to justify symbolic control over how the African basic education teacher should teach. As Robertson points out, a small group of global actors have:

> come to dominate the field of symbolic control over teachers and their work through reclassifying and reframing [their] pedagogic discourse, largely through data gathering and statistical tools aimed at representing, comparing, and ranking the national geographical distributions of the "good teacher".
>
> (2012, 592)

Defining what constitutes a 'good African teacher' through external normative constructions is not helpful especially when imposed. It misses important qualities that they bring to the teaching process, such as their *resourcefulness, creativity and resilience* – all qualities of a good teacher, which are critical especially when teaching marginalised and disadvantaged children in challenging or poorly resourced environments. Who is a good teacher is dependent particularly on conditions and support within the school system. As Akyeampong et al. (2006) argued, all teachers have potential to be good, provided the support to motivate improvement is there: good teachers evolve through a process of supportive supervision. Kennedy (2010) cautions that attributing teacher or teaching quality to their qualification status and other proxy measures also overlooks the importance of enhancing and maximising the collective competence of teachers to improve learning. The quality of education a child receives is determined not by a single teacher, but by the teaching quality they experience, and educational ethos promoted by the teaching culture, understood collectively rather than individualistically. As Connell (2009) points out, it:

> is often the group of teachers, and the institution they work in, that are effective or not effective. The task of improving teaching, accordingly, cannot be understood only as a matter of motivating or re-skilling individuals ... any definition of teacher quality ... that tends to impose a *single* model of excellence on the teaching workforce – whatever that model may be – is likely to be damaging to the education system as a whole.
>
> (223)

More importantly, it does little to 'achieve good education in the fullest and broadest sense of the term' (Biesta, 2015, 83).

If situational factors are important in producing effective teaching, so is the ability of teachers to make appropriate and intelligent decisions based on how they are *reasoning* and *interpreting* what is going on in their classrooms. The 1966 ILO/UNESCO recommendation concerning the status of teachers stressed that the teaching profession should orient towards giving teachers greater freedoms in determining instructional practice in their classrooms. It states:

> The teaching profession should enjoy academic freedom in the discharge of professional duties. Since teachers are particularly qualified to judge the teaching aids and methods most suitable for their pupils, they should be given the essential role in the *choice* and *adaptation* of teaching material, the *selection* of textbooks, and the *application* of teaching methods, within the framework of approved programmes, and with the assistance of the educational authorities.
>
> (VIII. 61) (ILO/UNESCO, 2008, 9) [*emphasis added*]

In Africa, however, we have seen a gradual erosion of teachers' freedom to exercise more control over their instructional choices and practice, and how to improve them. The characterisation of African teachers in strong deficit terms justifies this erosion, influencing the way in which pre- and in-service teacher education programmes are designed or reformed, with less emphasis on developing teachers' ability to make context-relevant instructional choices and to learn from the effect of their choices on student learning and to improve future practice. Instead, there is more focus on prioritising pre-determined teaching practices or implementing pre-packaged standardised instructional methods (Hook, 2023) over developing teachers' ability to make instructional decisions based on learning from their practice. This happens because of a basic mistrust in the ability of the African teacher to learn from practice and the perceived harm that allowing them to do so will inflict learning loss on children. This has created a performance culture in African classrooms that can best be described as 'controlled or compliant professionalism', making teachers more conservative and passive practitioners unlikely to view themselves as active agents able to 'contribute to the production and co-production of new knowledge about practice in order to improve it' (Sachs-Israel, 2016, 424 cited in Bengtsson et al., 2020, 219). We explore this further below.

De-professionalisation through Structured Lesson Plans (SLPs)

The de-professionalisation of teaching, which paradoxically is associated with the 'learning crisis', raises vital issues for education in sub-Saharan Africa, especially when one considers the marginalisation and vulnerability of children living in poverty. In this section, we discuss one of the ways in which the 'learning crisis' is being addressed – the promotion of SLPs, sometimes referred to as direct instruction (Shalem et al., 2016; Moussa et al., 2024), or structured pedagogy (Piper and Dubeck, 2024) that is increasingly becoming the tool for de-professionalising basic education teachers in Africa. The growing trend of SLPs as tools to tackle the 'learning crisis' is strongly linked to the quest to find a simple and quick solution to Africa's 'learning crisis' (Shalem, De Clercq, Steinberg et al., 2018; Moussa et al., 2023; Shalem, 2017). Advocates present it as a way to minimise learners' conceptual ambiguity through a prescribed style of instruction with a lot of teacher-directed prompts and modelling (Shalem et al., 2018, 7) to promote equity in learning (Narayanan et al., 2024) Yet, structured lesson plans (SLPs) are symbolic of the de-professionalisation of teaching as their deployment undermines the importance of developing teachers' professional autonomy, perpetuating instructional logics that frame African teachers' capacity in deficit terms and that and that in effect serve as a pretext to control their instructional behaviour.

Piper and Dubeck (2024) argue that *structured pedagogy* – which they define as an umbrella term for a continuum of practices from 'every word scripted for teachers' to a 'menu of suggested activities' – can make room for teachers to make adaptations to meet the needs of students. However, they cite research that suggests that when teachers do this, "the majority of the changes ... actually reduce the quality of teaching" (3). In other words, teachers actually lack the ability to make effective pedagogical choices. They add that this can be corrected with training but do not specify what type or form of training can make this possible. Current teacher education approaches that we discuss later in this chapter are not designed to start teachers off on a journey to become autonomous and agentic teachers and are unlikely to produce the 'correction' that Piper and Dubeck hope training might produce.

The framing of the exercise of teacher agency within structured or scripted pedagogy in essence problematises teacher's capacity to make pedagogical decisions *in situ*, moment by moment, as something to be guarded against and carefully regulated. A vital aspect of teachers' professional autonomy is to orient teaching and learning to the context and needs of the children they teach – yet, this is deemed dispensable. In the sub-Saharan African contexts of educational marginalisation where teachers face distinctive challenges rooted in impoverished communities with highly contingent relationships with formal schooling, such attempts to delimit teacher's autonomy are nothing less than counter-productive and disempowering. As Schon (2017) has made clear, teacher autonomy is an ongoing process of being a 'reflective practitioner', a professional who 'thinks in action'. This is an organic and often unpredictable process, essential to teacher agency in the challenging contexts of sub-Saharan Africa classrooms and is not reducible to being measured on a continuum.

Our focus is not primarily on the effectiveness or otherwise of SLPs that according to the global literature is somewhat mixed (see, Fitz and Nikolaidis, 2020) but on how it overshadows the importance of developing contextual teacher knowledge to promote the sorts of holistic and meaningful learning that we describe in Part 2. The SLP approach and its variations work against the very idea of life-long learning to become a more proficient practitioner in teaching, as it undervalues reflective and adaptive practice from the point when teachers begin their teaching careers. As Shalem et al. (2018, 6) argue, even if SLPs are implemented well, for example through the relatively flexible format of so-called *Educative Curriculum Materials* that require teachers to use flexibly the prescribed activities or materials, it would require more than knowing what to teach in a prescriptive and structured manner. Crucially, it would also require teachers who could recognise:

> distinctions between ways of explaining and representing specific content and knowing *how* to apply subject matter knowledge to learners of a specific age and cognitive level of development ... to combine their organised propositional knowledge of subject matter with educational considerations such as context, types of knowledge, learning misconceptions, styles of pedagogy, and assessment so as to enact the lesson plans effectively.
>
> (Shalem et al., 2016, 31), [*emphasis added*]

Advocates of structured pedagogies do not give this the attention we believe it deserves. What matters are teachers' practical knowledge and their understanding of context and classroom conditions including knowledge of the background characteristics of the children they teach. When Shalem and colleagues explored how SLPs s are used in a region in South Africa, they found that there are aspects of teacher knowledge that can be provided by SLPs through experiencing teaching as the application of pre-determined steps or routine practice. However, there are other "aspects which cannot be provided because the experience of teaching routines is not sufficient for acquiring that knowledge" (Shalem et al., 2016, 31). Although teachers can use SLPs to achieve good results (Moussa et al., 2024; Piper and Dubeck, 2024) and some may even find it helpful (Fitz and Nikolaidis, 2020), ultimately, SLPs do a great disservice to developing teachers' conceptual and practical knowledge of teaching and underestimate the importance of prior professional knowledge in learning to teach effectively (Shalem, 2017, 3–4). If SLPs are presented as the solution to the 'learning crisis' without a serious attempt to invite teachers, even novice ones, to *think* and *work* through how they might repurpose, reconstruct or re-envision them as part of how they learn to teach effectively, they will restrict teachers' growth and ability to become proficient practitioners who can help African children learn more effectively.

The Limits of Accountability Regimes and Practices

Another way in which SLPs are shaping the landscape of African schooling is through their central role in promoting low-fee private education and for-profit small management chains such as Bridge and Rising Academies (Hook, 2023). SLPs and their variants are an example of 'policy borrowing' from the global North (see Blumenreich and Falk, 2015) such that the entry of these chains into the schooling system in Africa (e.g., Liberia, Kenya) is legitimised. The claim is that SLPs are able to ensure a basic level of quality and equity in education (Klees, 2018; Hook, 2023; Narayanan et al., 2024). Bridge Academy schools in Liberia, according to Hook (2023:102), used standardised lessons and tablets to "send back teacher and student data in real time to field officers, who intervene to keep teachers on track", becoming therefore a device for controlling teachers' behaviour, treating them like factory workers and negating any sense of their agency.

Hook describes how teachers were told not to go off script – 'don't escape, don't add, whatever it is, you say it out' – producing a 'plantation-style education monologue' (101), ignoring the highly precarious working conditions under which teachers worked with no care for their living conditions. These instructions had a huge impact on their work as teachers (102).

MacGillivray et al.'s (2004) critique of a scripted reading programme in the US using terms drawing on neo-colonial theory is particularly insightful for understanding how it can impact teacher governance in the countries that embrace such programmes. They introduce three terms: *redefined*, *restricted* and *subsumed* to describe the identities and experiences of the teachers they studied. MacGillivray and colleagues "use the label *redefined* to refer to the condition by which the coloniser has recreated the identity of the colonised and maintains a system to limit their development" (2004, 133). *Restricted* refers to "being subject to a dominant group's authority and power, (in which) the less powerful group's possibilities for autonomy are narrowed": (134), and *subsumed* "refers to the condition in which the colonised believe they are dependent to some degree on the coloniser – a naturalisation process which erodes any capacity for critical thinking on the part of either the colonised or the coloniser" (134). Surveillance plays a key part in the sense that it:

> is framed as helpfulness, a desire by the coloniser to enable the colonised to function in the world as necessitated by specific rules and norms. In time, surveillance becomes a way to assure compliance".
> (MacGillivray et al., 2004, 133–134)

These framings, in our view, can be applied to the way in which bilateral and multilateral organisations and their actors introduce ideas or use in-service teacher education to promote hard or soft forms of SLPs. By "basing professional activity on scientific evidence about 'what works'" (Biesta, 2015, 82; Ede, 2006) in terms of improving student learning outcomes, these organisations 'recreate' the identity of who a 'good' or 'effective' teacher is, minus their agency and professionalism. SLPs are presented as tried and tested, leaving no or little room for their recontextualisation or reframing by teachers using knowledge and understanding of children's identity formation and their social context. SLPs, especially those who recommend keeping to the letter of the text, invite strong surveillance and bureaucratic control, treating teachers who deviate from them as incompetent or delinquent practitioners.

Deficit Framings of Teachers and Restrictions on Teacher Education Reforms

Reforms that advocate SLPs and Eurocentric instructional approaches such as student-centred pedagogy as *solutions* to the learning crisis in public basic schools in Africa, invariably, restrict the re-envisioning of teacher education especially pre-service teacher education. Pre-service teacher education has received far less attention as a site for deep reforms from global development organisations, their actors and national governments interested in addressing the 'learning crisis', than in-service teacher education. The latter has become a route for pushing through 'pedagogical innovations' baked in Western or non-African educational environments. These innovations are promoted as a fast response to the 'learning crisis' and driven by narratives about the urgent need to achieve the SDG 4 goal of quality education for all children by 2030. Reforming pre-service teacher education to address the learning challenge becomes a cost that might also delay achieving this goal. As Zuilkowski et al. (2022, 1) point out:

despite the central role of pre-service teacher education (PSTE) in promoting quality education, it has largely been left out of the significant investments made to improve foundational literacy and numeracy (FLN) in low- and middle-income countries (LMICs) over the past two decades… bilateral- and multilateral-funded interventions have instead tended to focus on in-service teacher training as a means of producing faster results at scale.

In-service teacher education has been used to fill gaps or address 'failings' in teachers practice and has become the site for quick fixes to the learning crisis without a commitment to the development of teacher professionalism. Teachers are reduced to factory workers and their value judged on how well they can use tools or prescribed methods to improve learning outcomes. The literature and research on African teachers are replete with narratives of their failings and not much about looking for and understanding the nature of their creative practice and how it produces learning that is sustainable in the African context. As Schon (1983) points out, teacher's expertise develops through their ability to understand teaching and learning problems and experimenting to find appropriate solutions or responses. Rarely are basic education teachers in Africa given the freedom to exercise and develop this ability. Pre-packaged pedagogical interventions such as SLPs send the message that this is not necessary and, in fact, make pre-service teacher education expensive and of limited value.

Yet, pre-service teacher education has an important role to play in changing the deficit view of teachers described above. It has failed to do so, partly because its curriculum is fashioned to produce teachers with limited understanding of what it means to grow to become self-directed and proficient practitioners. Also, its curriculum is designed not with a strong focus on promoting critical engagement and reflection on learning to teach and in-service teacher education lacks commitment to making critical dialogue, professional reasoning and creativity a fundamental goal of learning to teach (Akyeampong, 2003). An analysis of the pre-service teacher education curriculum in Africa shows that it does not place enough emphasis on developing teachers' ability to analyse, question and reimagine effective practice (Pryor et al., 2012). The curriculum, for example, does not draw on the embodied experiences of teachers, children and their communities to develop a professional identity capable of producing holistic learning. Instead, it is designed in search of a teacher who is either a 'technical practitioner', 'well-grounded academically' or an 'efficient instructor' (Lewin and Stuart, 2003) – framings of a professional identity that limits the development of teachers as reflexive and agentic practitioners. The curriculum gives little or no attention to how teachers can connect with and use sociocultural knowledges to develop innovative practices to reinstate their agency.

Sathorar and Geduld (2018) argue that teacher education in Africa has to decolonise its curriculum so that it opens up a space for alternatives tailored to African and localised approaches. A decolonised curriculum offers the opportunity to re-engage Afrocentric values of education in which local languages and children's identity are foregrounded, and the binary lines of teacher-student are blurred, and roles re-inscribed as shown in the ALP classrooms that we describe in Part 2. Such a decolonised and re-envisioned teacher education curriculum would create a more democratic classroom environment where children and teachers see a value in bringing their lived experiences and funds of knowledge into the pedagogical and learning process. It will mark a significant departure from a fundamental assumption underpinning pre-service teacher education programmes in Africa:

> [an] assumption that once teachers have acquired the 'legitimate' tools of the trade – which often means specific pedagogical knowledge and skills, they will …through practicum, be able to foster teaching as theoretically conceptualised in training …[upholding] … a decontextualised professional knowledge base of teaching… from which teachers' qualification status is derived and validated.
>
> (Akyeampong, 2002a, 10)

Teacher education in the sub-Saharan Africa context needs reform that values African classrooms and school environments as sites for generating good ideas and strategies for effective teaching, despite their well-known limitations. It has to resist a generalised view of the African classroom as an:

> educational disaster zone with the only hope of resuscitating it coming through innovations that have worked elsewhere and packaged almost in the same way as technical assistance is packaged and presented.
>
> (Akyeampong, 2002a, 11)

In the early 2000s, Kwame was involved in a multi-site teacher education research (MUSTER) project focused on four countries – Ghana, Lesotho, Malawi, South Africa and Trinidad & Tobago – which sought out the potential of classrooms in these countries. The MUSTER project explored how to change pre-service teacher education so as to improve the quality and supply of teachers. The Ghana case study revealed that many trainee teachers begin training with a positive mindset about what training can help them become and achieve in terms of improving children's learning. This belief fades quickly by the time they start their teaching career (Akyeampong, 2003) mainly because the curriculum fails to offer them experiences which develop their confidence and build upon their prior beliefs about their capabilities (Akyeampong and Lewin, 2002). Two years into their career, many had recognised the importance of "teach(ing) to the level of pupils i.e. that teachers need to tailor their lessons to pupils' level of understanding" (71), if children are to make progress in their learning – in order words, orient teach(ing) at the right level of the child. However, their training had not sensitised them nor prepared them to address this challenge. The MUSTER project concluded that teacher education programmes in Ghana, Lesotho and Malawi were out of touch with the concrete problems of teaching and learning that would have required developing teachers' critical thinking and professional reasoning capabilities to adequately address them (Lewin and Stuart, 2003). Pryor et al. (2012) reached a similar conclusion more than a decade later when they studied teacher education in Ghana, Mali, Senegal, Kenya, Uganda and Tanzania, arguing that the training was not a transformative experience – as the teachers it produced felt less not more confident in their ability to tackle gaps in children's FLN skills.

If teacher education in sub-Saharan Africa is to be transformational then, arguably, it needs a new identity that is built on the strong relational culture of African societies. As we discuss in Chapter 9, this means developing a vision of learning to teach based on the relational values of Ubuntu that respects mutually supportive peer learning involving the whole body and mind with all its emotions, senses and receptors and 'invok(ing) a sense of community' (Croft, 2002, 328) geared towards addressing learning gaps. The ALP case studies in Part 2 demonstrate how this produces agentic learners whose learning experiences are transformed and who consequently improve their FLN skills. Teachers would need training in how to assume a different role and identity in the classroom consistent with an Afrocentric pedagogy which preserves African values of learning and considers how to promote them. Evidence from the ALPs we describe in Part 2 suggests that, when teachers take on dialogic and critical educator roles, they are able to produce holistic learning and outcomes. They are inspired by the belief that every African child can learn and achieve the goals of education. But to do so requires foregrounding and validating their culture, values and funds of knowledge in the teaching and learning process. ALP teachers, as we shall see, create opportunities for children to draw on their rich linguistic repertoire of home languages and connect the content of lessons to their lived experiences for a deeper and meaningful learning experience. For teacher education in the African context, to produce teachers with similar abilities requires a shift from current teacher education curriculum practices and norms and:

> insights into the appropriate conceptual model that can change the way in which teachers have traditionally viewed their professional roles and responsibilities in the classroom.
> (Akyeampong, 2002a, 2)

Pryor et al. (2012) argued that for such a change to materialise, the curriculum of teacher education in Africa has to focus on mapping what actually happens in the everyday classroom to allow differences and dissonances to provoke trainees' responses that set them on a path to become reflexive and innovative practitioners. Unfortunately, African teacher's own narratives of successful teaching, which would be important in the mapping process, are largely missing in the research on its teachers. These could be used as case studies to produce insights into what is possible and become truly consequential in terms of how it changes the deficit narratives about the African teacher. Over two decades ago, Kwame pointed out that:

> simply locating a greater part of teacher education in school-based context by itself is not a panacea for addressing the issue of teacher quality, at least not until the curriculum that underpins it is structured to engender a high sense of professional agency.
> (Akyeampong, 2003, 13)

Unfortunately, the teacher education reforms in Africa assume that, if only trainees spend more time in classrooms, then better quality teachers will be produced. But *what* and *how* will they be learning are fundamental questions that need to be addressed first. Spending more time in schools learning to teach has to be about 'reflections on their practice', exploring what works or doesn't, drawing pedagogically on children's funds of knowledge that connects learning to their lived experiences and creating environments that make them agentic learners. In Chapters 6 and 7, we show how this has the added value of improving children's learning outcomes.

Conclusion

This chapter has focused on the way in which teachers and the teaching profession in sub-Saharan Africa context have been characterised in deficit terms, in much the same way as African children (see Chapter 2). The discourse of derision erases the exercise of professional agency by teachers, projecting a view of them as incapable and only able to address the 'learning crisis' if handed a script to follow and subjected to surveillance and control. This chapter has also indicated how teacher education is currently unable to prepare teachers to meet the learning needs of most children. Re-envisioning the so-called 'learning crisis' entails repositioning teachers outside of deficit and regulatory assumptions, thus reclaiming their pivotal role as agents of transformative learning by valorising their agency, knowledges and situated reflexivity on their practice and the children they teach.

Note

1 https://www.adeanet.org/en/system/files/resources/policy_brief_reducing_teacher_absenteeism.pdf.

References

Akyeampong, K., 2002a. 'Reconceptualising teacher education in the sub-Saharan African context'. *Journal of International Co-operation in Education*, 5(1): 11–30. http://sro.sussex.ac.uk/id/eprint/44/

Akyeampong, K., 2022b. 'Teaching at the bottom of the pyramid: teacher education in poor and marginalised communities'. In D. Wagner, N.M. Castillo, and S.G. Lewis (eds.), *Learning, marginalisation, and improving the quality of education in low-income countries*. Open Book Publishers, pp. 77–112.

Akyeampong, K., 2003. *Teacher training in Ghana: does it count? Multisite teacher education research project*. DFID.

Akyeampong, K., and Lewin, K., 2002. 'From student teachers to newly qualified teachers in Ghana: insights into becoming a teacher'. *International Journal of Education Development*, 22(3/4): 339–352.

Akyeampong, K., Pryor, J., and Ampiah, J.G., 2006. 'A vision of successful schooling: Ghanaian teachers' understandings of learning, teaching and assessment'. *Comparative Education*, 42(2): 155–176.

Alexander, R., 2008. *Essays on pedagogy*. Routledge.

Bengtsson, S., Kamanda, M., Ailwood, J., and Barakat, B., 2020. 'Teachers are more than 'supply': toward meaningful measurement of pedagogy and teachers in SDG4'. In A. Wulff (ed.), *Grading goal four: tensions, threats, and opportunities in the sustainable development goal on quality education*. Brill/Sense.

Bennell, P., and Akyeampong, K., 2007. *Teacher motivation in Sub-Sahara Africa and South Asia*. DFID.

Biesta, G., 2015. 'What is education for? On good education, teacher judgement, and educational professionalism'. *European Journal of Education*, 50(1): 75–87.

Blumenreich, M., and Falk, B., 2015. 'Research and teacher self-inquiry reawaken learning'. *Phi Delta Kappan*, 96(5): 47–51.

Bramwell, D., Anderson, S., and Mundy, K. (2014). *Teachers and teacher development: a rapid review of the literature*. Ontario Institute for Studies in Education.

Bruns, B., Filmer, D., and Patrinos, H.A., 2011. *Making schools work: new evidence on accountability reforms*. World Bank Publications.

Connell, R., 2009. Good teachers on dangerous ground: towards a new view of teacher quality and professionalism. *Critical Studies in Education*, 50(3): 213–229.

Croft, A. 2002. Singing under a tree: does oral culture help lower primary teachers be learner-centred? *International Journal of Educational Development*, 22: 321–337.

Ede, A., 2006. 'Scripted curriculum: is it a prescription for success?' *Childhood Education*, 83(1): 29–32.

Fitz, J.A., and Nikolaidis, J.A., 2020. 'A democratic critique of scripted curriculum'. *Journal of Curriculum Studies*, 52(2): 195–213.

Guerrero, G., Leon, J., Zapata, M., Sugimaru, C., and Cueto, S., 2012. *What works to improve teacher attendance in developing countries? A systematic review*. EPPI. Centre, Social Science Research Unit, Institute of Education, University of London. ISBN: 978-1-907345-39-5

Hanushek, E.A., 2011. 'The economic value of higher teacher quality'. *Economics of Education Review*, 30: 466–479.

Hook, T., 2023. 'Schooling as plantation: racial capitalism and plantation legacies in corporatized education reforms in Liberia'. *Comparative Education Review*, 67: 89–109. SI: Black Lives Matter and Global Struggles for Racial Justice in Education.

ILO/UNESCO, 2008. *The ILO/UNESCO recommendation concerning the status of teachers (1996) and the UNESCO recommendation concerning the status of higher education teaching personnel (1997)*. UNESCO and ILO.

Kennedy, M.M., 2010. 'Attribution error and the quest for teacher quality'. *Educational Researcher*, 39(8): 591–98.

Klees, S., 2018. 'Liberia's experiment with privatising education: a critical analysis of the RCT study'. *Compare: A Journal of Comparative and International Education*, 48(3): 471–482.

Labaree, D.F., 2000. 'On the nature of teaching and teacher education: difficult practices that look easy'. *Journal of Teacher Education*, 51(3): 163–235.

Lewin, K.M., and Stuart, J., 2003. *Researching teacher education: new perspectives on practice, performance and policy*. DFID.

MacGillivray, L., Ardell, A.L., Curwen, M.S., and Palma, J., 2004. 'Colonised teachers: examining the implementation of a scripted reading program'. *Teacher Education*, 15(2): 131–144.

Moussa, W., Louge, N., Pauwelyn, L., Contreras-Gomez, R., and Cao, Y., 2024. 'Should teachers stick to the script? Examining the effects of scripted lessons on student literacy in Madagascar'. *International Journal of Educational Research*, 124: 1–14.

Narayanan, M., Shields, A.L., and Delhagen, T.J., 2024. 'Autonomy in the spaces: teacher autonomy, scripted lessons, and the changing role of teachers. *Journal of Curriculum Studies*, 56(1): 17–34.

Paine, L., and Zeichner, K., 2012. 'The local and the global in reforming teaching and teacher education'. *Comparative Education Review*, 56(4): 569–583.

Perry, M., 2024. *Pluriversal literacies for sustainable futures – when words are not enough*. Routledge.

Pesambili, J.C., Sayed, J., and Stambach, A., 2022 'The World Bank's construction of teachers and their work: a critical analysis'. *International Journal of Educational Development*, 92: 1–8.

Piper, B., and Dubeck, M.M., 2024. Responding to the learning crisis: structured pedagogy in sub-Saharan Africa. *International Journal of Educational Development*, 109: 103095.

Pryor, J., Akyeampong, K., Westbrook, J., and Lussier, K. 2012 'Rethinking teacher preparation and professional development in Africa: an analysis of the curriculum of teacher education in the teaching of early reading and mathematics'. *The Curriculum Journal*, 23(4): 409–502.

Robertson, S.L., 2012. Placing teachers in global governance agendas. *Comparative Education Review*, 56(4): 584–607.

Sachs-Israel, M. 2016. 'The SDG 4-education 2030 agenda and its framework for action: the process of its development and first steps in taking it forward'. *Bildung und Erziehung*, 69(3): 269–290.

Sathorar, H., and Geduld, D., 2018. Towards decolonising teacher education: reimagining the relationship between theory and praxis. *South African Journal of Education*, 38(4): 1–12.

Schon, D. A., 1983. *The reflective practitioner: how professional think in action*. Basic Books.

Schon, D., 2017 *The reflective practitioner: how professionals think in action*. Routledge.

Schweisfurth, M., 2023. 'Disaster didacticism: pedagogical interventions and the "learning crisis"'. *International Journal of Educational Development*, 96: 102707.

Shalem, Y., 2017. 'Scripted lesson plans – What is visible and invisible in visible pedagogy?' In B. Barrett, U. Hoadley, and J. Morgan (eds.), *Knowledge, curriculum and equity: social realist perspectives*. Routledge.

Shalem, Y., De Clercq, F., Steinberg, C., and Koornhof, H., 2018. 'Teacher autonomy in times of standardised lesson plans: the case of a primary school language and mathematics intervention in South Africa'. *Journal of Educational Change*, 19, 205–222. https://doi.org/10.1007/s10833-018-9318-3

Shalem, Y., Steinberg, C., Koornhof, H., and De Clercq, F. 2016. 'What and how in scripted lesson plans: the case of the Gauteng primary language and mathematics strategy'. *Journal of Education*, 66: 13–36.

UNESCO, 2013/14. *Education for all global monitoring report: teaching and learning: Achieving quality for all.* UNESCO Publishing.

Verger, A., 2021. '"Teachers and the teaching profession in global education policy theory: a commentary": special section on teachers, teaching, and globalisation'. *Comparative Education Review*, 65(4): 790–806.

Zuilkowski, S.S., Sowa, P, Ralaingita, W., and Piper, B. 2022. 'Literature review on pre-service teacher education for primary-grade literacy and numeracy'. *Science of Teaching.* https://scienceofteaching.site/wp-content/uploads/2022/11/Literature-Review-on-Pre-service-Teacher-Education-for-Primary-Grade-Literacy-and-Numeracy.pdf.

5 Beyond Deficit Framings
A Multi-dimensional Approach

It is clear from our discussions in the previous chapters that a new, very different, framing of children's experiences of poverty is now needed to counteract the negative assumptions underneath the notion of a global 'learning crisis' in sub-Saharan Africa. It is arguably only by working with a *multi-dimensional experiential model* that the learning needs of children living in poverty can be adequately understood and supported through educational institutions.

Our starting point for such a task must be to diversify, nuance and most importantly valorise, as educationally significant, such children's active social and situated agency. This raises possibilities of orienting the scheduling, content and framings of education provision so that they recognise children's lived experiences, positive exercise of their agency and the knowledges, skills and resources they bring to learning as well as the challenges faced by their communities. In this chapter, we model such a multi-dimensional approach that draws upon what we already know about poor communities in sub-Saharan Africa and how young people experience them. We highlight a range of materialistic, subjective, relational, symbolic and gendered dimensions of children's lives as well as recognising the voices and experiences of the poor and of their children. Such an approach recuperates, if you like, an enlarged view of the child who is being taught. This chapter starts by outlining what a multi-dimensional framing of poverty and children's agency means. This is followed by an analysis of the various dimensions and contexts in which they exercise their agency. The chapter concludes by clarifying the implications of such a different model for rethinking the learning crisis narrative and re-envisioning educational responses.

A Multi-dimensional Framing of Poverty and Children's Agency

Narrowly economistic framings of poverty have been challenged by critics with alternative approaches (Roelen, 2017; Bray et al., 2020, 2). For example, in Figure 5.1, Lister (2021, 10) visualises a multi-dimensional approach to the complex experiences of poverty:

The hub of the wheel represents the core experiences of poverty – material deprivation and hardship, including 'lack of decent work', 'insufficient and

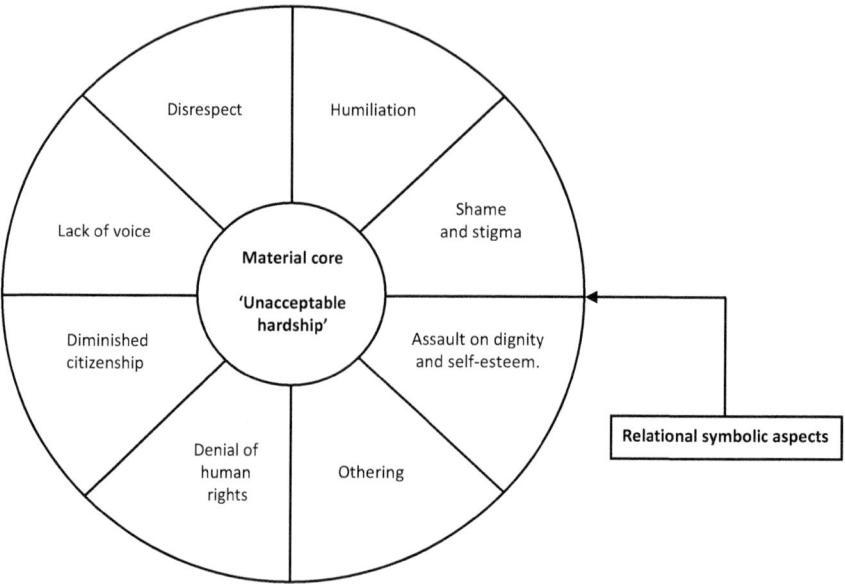

Figure 5.1 A multi-dimensional framing of poverty (adapted from Lister, 2021, 10).

insecure income' and 'material and social deprivation'. The rim represents the other dimensions with which these intersect, especially its relational and symbolic dimensions. The *relational dimension* recognises that poverty is 'constituted by social relationships' (Spicker, 2020, 6) and is experienced within social networks in particular places at particular times. The relational dimension recognises the personal or subjective and inter-personal aspects of the experience of the poor. This dimension may include the daily challenge of navigating deficit assumptions made about their lives, including their experience of disrespect and shame, loss of dignity and self-esteem; the denial of their human rights, diminished citizenship; and the voicelessness and powerlessness frequently felt by those experiencing poverty (Lister, 2021, 9). The *symbolic dimension* offers further insights into the relational aspect of poverty by highlighting the meanings attached to the experience of poverty and its implications for how those who experience this condition make sense of their daily lives, and their strategies for living, including their approaches to educational and health provision. These dimensions recognise that "the material and the social are interwoven in their everyday experience of poverty and social suffering" (Lister, 2021, 9).

A key challenge is to acknowledge that those who experience poverty are not only victims but also agentic in navigating and also 'resisting' their situation. Contemporary qualitative research recognises that "combatting child poverty.... calls for nuanced understandings of the complex realities that children face" (Roelen et al., 2019, 12).[1] For example, Bray et al. (2020, 8) in a six-country study identify the various 'hidden' dimensions of poverty that include 'material and social deprivation', the lived experience of 'disempowerment, suffering in mind and body' and 'struggle and resistance'. Navigating such determinants beyond their individual control, many were found to reject the label of victim – for 'they are not without agency'. Indeed, the suffering that participants insisted afflicted them in 'body, mind and heart' had a counterpart in "the struggle necessary to survive, even to thrive, in the most adverse of circumstances" (2020, 8). As Lister (2021, 205) comments, such struggles represent the:

> positive exercise of agency by people in poverty.... even despite their structurally disadvantaged position and the exercise of agency by more powerful actors.

Below we highlight some of the micro-level insights that such empirical studies offer about the lives of children, especially in rural poverty in the global South, particularly in sub-Saharan Africa. Given that the majority (almost three quarters) of the poorest people live and work in rural areas, this rural focus is particularly appropriate (Cremin and Nakabugo, 2012). Methodologically innovative and child-focused, these studies make visible those aspects of children's experiences of poverty that challenge the deficit assumptions of the 'learning crisis' and are of particular significance for reconceptualising education provision for this demographic. They include:

- children's viewpoints and perspectives;
- children's agency and contribution to household survival;
- children's informal learning and knowledge-building through social practices;
- children's play as a vehicle for learning;
- the temporalities and spatialities of children's lives;
- children's feelings;
- children's social positioning in friendship groups, family networks and communities and
- children's linguistic agency for learning.

Below, we address each of these aspects in turn.

Children's viewpoints and perspectives

The importance of 'listening carefully' to the voices of children is a key priority in studies of children's poverty (Mizen and Ofosu-Kusi, 2013; Hopkins, 2015, 11; Phiri and Abebe, 2016, 379; Ansell et al., 2020). This serves as a corrective to the absence of children's voices in programmes on child poverty, ensuring a child-centred perspective is used (Boyden, 2003; Ngutuku, 2019, 28). The importance of "recognising the agency of children and giving them the opportunity to define and express what poverty means to them" (Feeny and Boyden, 2003, 23) means that children are viewed as 'competent actors' (Redmond, 2009; 541) who have 'voices' on things essential for their lives. These studies argue for a methodological process to ensure listening to "children's own understandings of their experiences and situations" (Mizen and Ofosu-Kusi, 2010, 256).

Several insights are offered in such studies that challenge deficit constructions of the 'poor child' in education and poverty alleviation strategies. First, they indicate that children living in poverty are highly reflexive of the causes and the ways of moving out of the conditions of precarity they were experiencing (Boyden, 2013; Phiri and Abebe, 2016). There are a "myriad ways in which children interpret poverty" (Phiri and Abebe, 2016, 379). For instance, Boyden et al.'s (2003) study of children from Belarus, Bolivia, India, Kenya and Sierra Leone found that children expressed views on the role of the government in social protection, the need for improved employment prospects, the need for agricultural development and education opportunities in order to end persistent poverty.

Second, children are keen to represent themselves as more than just victims. Thus, in a study of Ethiopian children, Tafere (2012) notes that "the data from these children also indicate that children are not just victims of poverty… they are also agents of its alleviation" (22). And, "they have also demonstrated their agency and resilience, mainly by providing data about their lives and by making practical efforts to manage life in poverty" (22). For these children, not being listened to was itself experienced as a process of victimisation.

Third, the affective range of children's representations beyond the sole focus on despair and hopelessness and wholly adult-centred perspectives has been widened by empirical studies. Feeny and Boyden (2004, 3) found that "despite the severity of their situation, many children continue to hold positive attitudes and aspirations and are able to draw upon this morale as part of their coping strategies". These insights suggest that just as participatory consultations with adults experiencing poverty have generated a counter-narrative to the tropes of helplessness and hopelessness (Lister, 2021, 207), so too with children navigating poverty. In demonstrating how children 'attach meanings to their social and material contexts' (Phiri and Abebe, 2016, 378), they render the absence of children's voices in education and poverty alleviation policy and programming an astonishing erasure. It is no surprise that Tafere (2012, 59) argues "researchers and policy makers need to listen to children and use their data to act on poverty". This recommendation applies to the framing of educational priorities for 'poor children'.

Achieving this goal, however, needs to avoid the sometimes tokenistic and appropriative agenda to listen to 'student voice' in school contexts of the global North that would merely reproduce the exclusion 'poor children' in the global South already experience (Clark and Richards, 2017). Superficial attempts to listen to student voices hide the ongoing power relations within the pedagogical encounter. Including children's voices and viewpoints in formulating educational priorities would constitute a radical interruption to the largely exclusionary nature of decision-making processes in the Sustainable Development Goals (SDGs). As Rai et al. (2019, 2) point out, such inclusion in practice is:

> dominated by INGOs, multinational corporations and state actors… who are equipped with greater resources to influence the agenda compared to the marginalised sectors of society whose lives the SDGs aim to transform.

The global educational agenda to be 'with' rather than 'for' the marginalised (Sayed and Ahmed, 2015, 332) involves widening educational consultations to include the most marginalised demographic such as children living in poverty. This promises to achieve the emancipatory and democratic goals of participatory research approaches (Patrick, 2020, 251), thereby giving meaning to the imperative to 'child-centredness' in the rhetoric of international aid agencies.

Children's agency and contribution to household survival

Children's agency has been defined as 'the capacity to act' (Redmond, 2009, 544) within structuring conditions that shape and constrain that capacity. Insights into the situated agency of 'poor children' (and also youth) have benefited from a proliferation of nuanced qualitative, ethnographic studies, some longitudinal tracking the multiple ways in which they exercise agency when navigating contexts of poverty. Children in sub-Saharan Africa have been found to be involved in:

- claiming their right to work on the streets (Hanson and Nieuwenhuys, 2013);
- organising collectively to support each other in precarious circumstances (Liebel et al., 2012);
- drawing on the resources of friendship groups to survive conditions of hardship on the streets of Accra (Mizen and Ofosu-Kusi, 2010);
- advocating with national and international NGOs to explain and justify their involvement in child labour (Woodhead, 1999; Bourdillon et al., 2010, 9, 143);
- being 'extraordinary survivors' showing 'resilience and competency' as leaders or members of child-headed households in the face of adversity (Payne, 2012, 399);
- contributing to environmental conservation and sustainability (Smith, 2014, 28) and
- finding ways of contributing to their family's economic survival as they face the consequences of economic restructuring processes resulting from the inroads of extractive global capitalism on traditional livelihood strategies in their communities (Katz, 2004).

As Abebe and Ofosu-Kusi, (2016, 303) note, children's engagements in social, economic, cultural and political life contribute to the well-being and reproduction of their communities. Research has revealed how the exercise of agency by 'poor children' takes the form of work (e.g. Odonkor, 2007; Abebe, 2011; Jonah and Abebe, 2018; Boyden et al., 2021). Rural sub-Saharan Africa is estimated to have the largest number of young people involved in child labour (ILO and UNICEF, 2021). Work-related activities include collecting firewood and water, subsistence farming; hawking, electrical artisan jobs, bricklaying, and reproductive work within the household chores relating to home and family (Orkin, 2012; Kassa, 2016a,b; Dunne and Humphreys, 2022). This work by children is supported and sanctioned within their communities as a key part of their contribution to inter-generational relationships and survival (Kassa, 2016a,b). The diversity of their forms of work, in combinations depending on need and necessity, has been described as a 'wide portfolio of work activities' (Crossouard et al., 2022, 226) that is usually undertaken in the informal economy (Phiri and Abebe, 2016, 379/380). Such work enables the child's family to get food or to support themselves and pay for their schooling. Most work is part-time, seasonal and unpaid. It is gender differentiated, with boys being more likely to engage in farming and girls in domestic activities such as cleaning, cooking, care work and household management (Abebe, 2011; Pankhurst et al., 2016).

These child contributions to household survival and the informal economy rarely appear in narrowly economistic indicators of household wealth where it is assumed that income is only generated by adults. As Robertson and Dale (2015, 153) noted, it is important to avoid conflating the economy or the relations of production distribution and exchange with one model of global capitalism. Of particular relevance to the concerns of this book is the ignoring of the informal economies that shape and delimit children's lives. Erased in such partial framings is the unpaid domestic economy, largely managed by women and girls (Abebe, 2011; Crossouard et al., 2022). Consequently, children's resourcefulness in enabling their families and communities to navigate circumstances of precarity on a daily basis by earning income as well as by being involved in non-income generating activities (Maconachie et al., 2020, 2022) is ignored. Through such activities, children, both boys and girls, are actors who 'make valuable albeit overlooked economic contributions to household and society' (Robson, 2004, 193).

The lack of attention to the gendered dimensions of experiences of poverty that we discussed in Chapter 2 means that what is not taken into account are the contributions of girls (and to a lesser extent boys) as carers for the disabled, sick, young children and elder members of their families and networks (Robson et al., 2006; Woldehanna et al., 2008). For instance, research by Pande (2014) focuses on young carers aged 11–16 living in a slum settlement in Lucknow, India and unable to attend school because of their caring responsibilities. She describes how the children's perspectives and experiences remain largely unheard in studies of school truancy and absenteeism.

Hence, their involvement in what has been termed 'love labour' (Lynch, 2007; Lynch et al., 2016) is rendered invisible to policymakers. This is a form of non-commodifiable or wage-based form of labour involving the physical and mental as well as emotional work that is often essential to the daily survival of families experiencing long term poverty. Whilst the girls were aware that their responsibilities interrupted their education, they valued this work and at the same time aspired to return to school. Although it was demanding and prolonged, they recognised that they also developed capabilities, skills and knowledges in taking on care responsibilities. They pointed out that this labour encouraged them to reflect when planning each day to manage their responsibilities – thus acquiring a form of practical reason (Pande, 2014, 207). They valued engaging in forms of social interaction outside of their homes – listening, empathising and providing support for others – which they found rewarding. They developed friendships and developed pride and self-esteem in their awareness that they were contributing to their family's well-being as well as being respected within their wider communities (Pande, 2014, 233). When they, as well as their parents, were weighing up the benefits of doing this versus going to school, the latter was often associated with learning content that was irrelevant to their lives. Such considerations were important influences in their making a decision about future engagements with schooling. Here, the emotional, relational and community-oriented dimensions of children's lives are revealed as key factors in their exercise of agency, as are beliefs in the value of what young carers learned outside formal schooling. Too often, such determinations of children's engagement with formal schooling are missing in the conflation of education provision with the achievement of cognitive learning outcomes in literacy and numeracy.

Deficit approaches that frame education provision in decontextualised terms, such as capital building for 'poor children', bypass these sorts of skills, competencies and resourcefulness that children bring to their engagement with educational provision (Camfield et al., 2008, 8; Phiri and Abebe, 2016, 380). Studies of child labour have challenged wholly negative assessments of these forms of children's agency in anti-child labour campaigns by the ILO and UN organisations (Feeny and Boyden, 2004; Dunne and Humphreys, 2022, 2). Whilst acknowledging that child labour can sometimes be exploitative and detrimental to children's well-being, researchers have highlighted its potential benefits. As we have seen, children have been found to perceive their involvement in child labour or livelihood activities as a vehicle of their self-efficacy and self-esteem in contributing to household survival and navigating precarity (Bourdillon et al., 2010, 97; Maconachie et al., 2020, 2022). Feeny and Boyden (2004, 40) note, "in many cases, children make the decision to work themselves and look upon it very positively as a vehicle for self-actualisation, economic autonomy and responsibility" (see also Woodhead, 1999; Bourdillon et al., 2010, 38). Tafere (2012) found that children in Ethiopia took pride in their contributions to poverty reduction and that "all agreed that they needed to support their families by working" (150). This was part of their "struggle to sustain a positive identity and sense of self in the face of negative representations and shaming" (2012, 150). Zambian children in Phiri and Adebe's (2016) study understood that their work formed part of an inter-generational reciprocity between children and adults in the household (2016, 390) which meant, given the harsh realities, they all faced that children were both "suffering and thriving" (2016, 378). Their work contributed to improving household productivity.

That African children are expected to be involved in work by their families and communities problematises the universalisation of an ethnocentric conception of childhood that demarcates this phase of life as a time of innocence and lack of responsibility, one falling outside of the relational dynamics that shape their exercise of agency. The tendency to individualise 'poor children' as targets of educational interventions means that such intergenerational relational worlds as well as the opportunities they provide for their knowledge-building are missed (Bourdillon et al., 2010, 86, 95; Krauss, 2017, 548).

These insights highlight what is at stake in the dominant approaches to the learning crisis that ignore how such forms of embedded sociality are part of children's lived experiences. The result is that the possibilities that education may connect with and capitalise on them are not developed. As a consequence, the next section takes time to explore the knowledges that children glean from their exercise of their 'work' and that they may also bring to learning.

Children's informal learning and knowledge-building in social practices

The binary division between schooling and work separates the spaces of children's experiences in oppositional terms. This polarity constructs formal schooling as a 'benevolent site of learning' (Dunne and Humphreys, 2022, 1) and child labour as an 'obstacle to being there' as well as ignoring other forms of experiences that may contribute to learning. This stark demarcation of formal schooling from the wider lived experiences of children in sub-Saharan Africa is a legacy of colonial educational provision that privileged schools as sites of the transmission of western academic knowledge, erasing the relevance of local indigenous knowledges. Hence, those forms of knowledge developed outside of schooling through children's exercise of agency in their daily lives were and continue to be delegitimised and devalued, resulting in what Yeboah and Daniel (2019, 2) call a form of 'silent exclusion'. Treating children experiencing poverty as a *tabula rasa*, awaiting the development of human capital by outside agencies, reproduces such assumptions.

Yet, as we have seen children learn social skills and competencies and develop a range of knowledges from their experiences of contributing to their households' survival. Moreover, the household is deemed to be the primary site of learning in communities in sub-Saharan Africa (Yeboah and Daniel, 2019). Studies have shown how children work alongside adults in agricultural production and family subsistence farming, in domestic reproduction within households and in market trading (Robson, 2004, 193).

Such intergenerational 'situated' forms of knowledge acquisition by 'poor children' are rooted in their practical experience, imitation and team involvement (Serpell, 2018). Through such learning, children may develop entrepreneurial skills and become 'economically savvy' (Aitkin, 2001, 124). They may acquire numeracy, literacy and communication and advocacy skills, farming and food production skills and knowledge of their local natural environment (James and Prout, 1997; Balagopalan, 2008; Abebe and Bessel, 2011; Abebe and Ofosu-Kusi, 2016).

These forms of learning, as we have seen, are inter-connected with the family socialisation of children that contributes to their self-esteem, identity, sense of self-efficacy and sense of themselves as participating in a collective response to their material vulnerability (Boyden, 1994, 40; Woodhead, 1999; Tafere, 2012). They also strengthen familial relationships in the process (Bourdillon et al., 2010, 31). Katz's (2004) study of children growing up in the rural community of Howa in South Sudan revealed their acquisition of a rich body of environmental knowledges through their participation in a 'community of practice' (Lave and Wenger, 1991 quoted in Katz, 2004, 112) with their peers, older children and adults around them. Several modalities of learning emerged from their community's social practices and rituals. Hence:

> through direct oral instruction, stories, songs, riddles, demonstration, apprenticeship, and shared activities adults ensured that their rich and evolving store of knowledge about the environment was passed on as a routine part of everyday life.
>
> (Katz, 2004, 60)

Learning developed through such means "often seemed osmotic; a seemingly easy 'familiarising process' into the material social life around them" (Katz, 2004, 118). The result was that these children could recognise a wide range of plants, distinguish cultivated from unwanted plants, make judgements about the local micro-environment and vegetation appropriate for grazing animals, predict weather conditions and explain complex ecological processes affecting land use (Katz, 2004, 109–133). With similar import, albeit from a different continent, Banerjee et al.'s (2017, 1) study of children working as 'shopkeepers' in informal markets in Kolkata, West Bengal, reveals their 'untapped maths skills', developed through their experience in market transactions. Whilst rooted in social dynamics, the modes of learning that emerge from children's social practices and routines are also aligned with context specific, socio-cultural processes. They are part of the oral transmission of practical know-how across generations dating back to pre-colonial eras. As emergent and organic, this is a form of knowledge transmission frequently perceived by communities as a means of preserving their cultural heritage (Krauss, 2017; Yeboah and Daniel, 2021) and also an essential means of socio-economic survival, especially, but not wholly, in rural contexts of poverty.

Of particular significance is that children are proactive and strategic in relation to such knowledge-building opportunities, perceiving such knowledges as their exercise of agency to support family survival (Iglesias et al., 2022). Children's learning and living are thereby fused. Studies foreground these modes of learning as emergent from children's 'natural curiosity and motivation to emulate those who are more expert' (Lancy, 2010, 79), thus positioning 'parents as teachers'. For instance, a study of the intergenerational interactions of rural Zambian children aged 6–12 involved in farming activities, sibling care and domestic work showed how children spent much of their time "observing and eavesdropping on older members of their families, as well as siblings, cousins and friends" (Clemensen, 2016, 317). Learning in such cases emerges from 'intent community participation' that involves children "actively observing and listening in during ongoing community activities and contributing when ready" (Rogoff et al., 2015, 479). Within this modality of informal learning, children are "potential agents of social change, actively employing the information and conditions presented to them in creative ways" (Clemensen, 2016, 332).

Such informal processes of knowledge-building enable 'poor children' to develop a rich reservoir of 'cognitive and skills development' (Bourdillon et al., 2010, 95) aligned with, rather than separated from, their socialisation. These forms of knowledge-building have a pedagogical significance as examples of a relational, dynamic and "non-individualist notion of knowledge and learning" as 'everyone engages in producing and exchanging knowledge" (Katz, 2004, 110). Here, children act as co-producers of knowledge such that "the simple roles of teacher or learner are routinely exceeded" (Katz, 2004, 110).

These insights serve as a corrective to what Tikly (2011, 8) has noted is a process of atomising learners within some forms of learner-centred pedagogy promoted by international aid agencies that constructs disadvantaged children as "independent units isolated from the economic and social forces that influence what they bring to learning" (see also Burman, 2012). As noted in Chapter 1, de Sousa Santos (2015) argues that a key form of social justice is *cognitive justice* that seeks to ensure that knowledge systems outside of 'northern epistemologies' are recognised and valorised as parts of building an *ecology of knowledges*. In the case of children navigating poverty in sub-Saharan Africa, this would mean an epistemic shift in the content of curriculum and pedagogies that recognises them as already knowledge-rich and active learners, rather than as empty vessels awaiting capital formation and generic cognitive skills development.

Children's play as a vehicle for learning

This brings us to the next dimension of children's learning – that of play. By foregrounding the multi-dimensional quality of 'poor children's' experiences, ethnographic studies have illuminated and sought to restore the value of children's play, as a vehicle, not only of socialisation but also of learning.

Such approaches eschew another dichotomy, this time between work and play which is often assumed within ethnocentric ideals of childhood as a blissful period 'unencumbered by care and responsibility' (Bourdillon et al., 2010, 10). Within this framing, play is construed as an expression of childhood innocence, thus depriving it of any association with developing knowledge or exercising responsibility, and in particular distinguishing it from work or labour. According to Bourdillon et al., (2010. 10) there is a "need to avoid overly simple dichotomies between work and play" especially since "some work like guarding crops, grazing livestock, caring for infants or work on the streets can easily be combined with play".

Similarly, Katz's (2004, 2012) ethnographic research on children's play in rural contexts of South Sudan underscores the intersection between children's working and playing – pointing out that:

> ..in their work and play, 10 year old children learned, integrated, mastered and used many of the environmental skills and much of the knowledge fundamental to the agriculture, animal husbandry, forestry and resource use that dominated the economic life of Howa.
> (Katz, 2004, 62)

Of particular interest are her insights into how play served as a vehicle for children's meaning-making and knowledge-building through its significance as a 'mimetic' activity. Following Walter Benjamin's characterisation of mimesis, this faculty is associated not only with imitation, or the "ability to see resemblances and create similarities between things", but also with creative interpretation or "the flash of insight read off or made in the process that impels a moment of invention" (p. 98). Hence children used 'local debris, domestic waste, agricultural detritus, scraps, and dung' in order to play "vivid geo-dramatic' games of 'fields,' 'store,' and 'house,' wherein they created miniature landscapes which they animated by enacting the tasks and social relations associated with agriculture, commerce, and domestic life" (Katz, 2004, 47). Within these enactments children interpreted the social contexts that they drew on, creating "amazing, imaginary worlds of farming and economic and social exchange in which they had a place" (Katz, 2004, 47). Children were found to have:

> internalized, worked out, and expressed the economic relations they saw around them, but with a little bit of a tweak — a gesture toward utopia — no one went broke, everyone had at least some assets, the exchanges were relatively equal, often riotous and always exuberant.
> (Katz, 2011, 56

As a meaning-making, interpretative, imaginative and inventive activity, one in which children exercised judgements about their socio-economic contexts and their social worlds, this 'workful play' constituted a significant form of learning for these children. In particular, conceptualised as a form of 'world making', (Katz, 2011, 56) play catalysed their creativity in making sense of their contexts as well as simultaneously developing peer-group solidarity and socialisation.

Such elucidations of the value of play as a creative form of learning suggest that educational interventions aimed at children navigating poverty should pay greater attention to integrating this mode of informal learning into curriculum and pedagogical provision. Indeed, that children are already engaged in such forms of playful learning makes the case all the more compelling. These insights throw into sharp relief what is at stake and what is lost in constructing notions of a learning crisis that ignore the potential of children's lived experiences, even those which are deemed insignificant, as resources for learning.

The temporalities and spatialities of children's lives

The above considerations of the voices, knowledges and agency of so-called 'poor children' emphasise that their quotidian experiences are variegated and dynamic, enacted within multiple spaces and shaped by temporal rhythms and constraints. This underlines the one-dimensionality and essentialising nature of snapshots that seek to represent the totality of 'poor children' but occlude their location within socio-economic processes. These spatial and temporal features of their lives are aspects of multi-dimensionality but obscured in constructions that serve to reify the complex and processual nature of the lives of children. For instance, Crossouard et al.'s (2022) study of rural youth in southern Nigeria reports on the variegated spaces of their lives as they "simultaneously navigated schooling, farming, children's labour, low paid vocational work and family obligations..." (218). The spaces of the farm, the household, the local physical environment and formal schooling are all mutually constitutive of the experiences of children. They represent "interwoven and overlapping social arenas" (2022, 218). Dunne and Humphreys have usefully characterised these intersecting spaces of children's lives as the '*edu-workscape*' (2022, 1).

Multi-season research with 'poor children' has also revealed how their lives in poor rural contexts in Ethiopia, Nigeria and Zambia are shaped by work, seasonal cycles and changes that generate diverse agricultural conditions (Abebe, 2011, 2013; Humphreys et al., 2015; Phiri and Abebe, 2016). Certain periods of the year, such as the harvesting seasons, put greater pressure on families who then expect children to contribute to the household's productivity. Phiri and Abebe (2016) research highlights, for example, the importance for 'poor children' of synchronising the timings and scheduling of schooling with the temporal rhythms of their daily lives. The need for children to work on farms or household chores early in the morning or to support their families during market days puts pressure on their ability to attend school at the appropriate times. Also, school holidays do not usually coincide with the planting (June/July) and harvesting (October/November) periods at either end of the rainy season, when children's labour is most needed. When there is already poverty and educational marginalisation, this lack of fit undermines children's sustained presence in school.

Understanding 'poor children' holistically means taking into account spatial, temporal and contingent dimensions of their lives and adjusting the structuring and contents of educational provision. There is a need for educational provision to be flexible, accommodating these constitutive aspects of their existence through the timing and scheduling of schooling and the school day. In the Kenyan context, according to Muriithi (2015, 80), responsive timetabling and educational provision would demand:

> flexibility ... to allow for example school calendars to be synchronised with peak demands for family labour, such as harvesting seasons and to enable curricula that are socially, culturally and economically relevant to particular contexts.

Finally, ethnographers of the spatial and temporal dimensions of experiences of poverty in Africa (Cooper and Pratten, 2015) have highlighted the ongoing uncertainty that pervades daily existence in rural contexts. This existential predicament results from a range of material socio-economic factors, including endemic food insecurity, vulnerability to disease, death, the unreliability of all sources of income and, increasingly, environmental uncertainty induced by climate change and the likelihood of freak weather conditions. This experience of ongoing forms of precarity gives rise to an existential 'ethos of contingency' (Whyte and Siu, 2015, quoted in Cooper and Pratten, 2015, 5) characterised by constant anxiety about the future and a sense of unpredictability.

The uncertainty of the lives of 'poor children' underscores the rigidity associated with school disciplinary regimes in sub-Saharan African contexts. These include, for instance, expectations of wearing the school uniform, corporal punishment for lateness and authoritarian forms of discipline and regulation. Bringing such features of formal schooling into relation to the lives of 'poor children' underlines their inherent tension and conflict. Tailoring learning environments to the lived experiences of 'poor children' thus entails re-envisioning them to recognise and respond to the material and emotional challenges they have to navigate. However, the contingent nature of their daily existence, whilst causing suffering and hardship, can also be a productive and creative force (Cooper and Pratten, 2015). Experiencing uncertainty can generate hope, motivation for communal solidarity and reflexivity and actions towards the future. This brings into relief another important task for education provision, namely the need for educational provision to be responsive to the affective dimensions of children's lives to which we now turn.

Children's feelings

Without an awareness of the creative ways in which children negotiate the realities they face, representations of such children who are assumed to be affected by the 'learning crisis' in sub-Saharan Africa represent them either as sad and desperate and in need of interventions by international actors or as happy and joyful because of the interventions of those self-same actors. This produces 'poor children' within a very narrow affective register, underscoring their positioning within dominant agendas of education and development, either as passive victims or at the other extreme, grateful recipients.

In contrast, multi-dimensional studies of children's experiences of poverty highlight psycho-social and symbolic dimensions, and in particular the diverse range of emotions with which children respond to their situations. For example, Feeny and Boyden (2004, 2-3) argue that within an:

> unerring focus on the negative aspects of poverty ... no mention is made of the things that many poor children retain, such as resourcefulness, courage and – more often than adults – optimism.

This delimits their subjectivity, offering only a 'partial picture of the child'. Other studies have indicated the hope and optimism vested in the possibilities of social mobility (Boyden, 2013). Hence, Boyden's longitudinal study of formal education, social mobility and child migration in Ethiopia, Peru, India and Vietnam takes as its title the salutary words of children who vowed that "we're not going to suffer like this in the mud" (Boyden, 2013, 580). This evokes the spirit of hope and determination animating children's relationships and expectations on learning. Likewise, participatory consultations with poor children in the global North and South have shown that "despite the anxiety that poverty often engenders, the optimism of many children and the sheer joy of living come through" (Save the Children, 2001, 23 quoted in Feeny and Boyden, 2004, 14).

This is not to say that children's experiences of poverty in sub-Saharan Africa do not also generate a range of negative feelings. Walker et al. (2013 quoted in Lister, 2021, 114), in a cross-national study with adults and children experiencing poverty, found that in all contexts "shame was found to be associated with poverty ... variably leading to pretence, withdrawal, self-loathing, 'othering', despair". "Shame is a universal concomitant of poverty", constituting a *poverty-shame nexus* which causes individuals 'social and psychological pain'. Hence, as Redmond (2009, 544) notes, "it is not the poverty *per se* that hurts, but the social exclusion or the symbolism of poverty that accompanies it".

'Poor children' are likely to experience this nexus and the negative feelings resulting in relation to their anticipated and actual engagement with formal schooling. For instance, Feeny and Boyden (2004, 32) found that:

> poverty can be a source of stigma and shame for children all around the world. Much of the abuse may come from other children and peer groups, particularly in institutions such as schools, where the inability of poor children to conform physically, materially or intellectually often incites bullying.

Kyomuhendo et al.'s (2019) study of children and young people's poverty-related shame in Uganda and the UK argues that development practices and policies have tended to bypass the psychosocial impacts of poverty on children's well-being, in particular "ignoring the propensity of poverty to expose children to indignity" (Roelen et al., 2019, 67).

Lister adds that "clothing is a key signifier of poverty and represents a visible badge of shame and humiliation" (2021, 115). Studies of 'poor children' in sub-Saharan Africa found that embarrassment at not being dressed correctly or the anticipation of not being able to wear school uniforms were sources of daily anxiety and indeed shame (Phiri and Abebe, 2016). Such feelings alienated them from the prospect of engaging in formal schooling that was anticipated as a site of teasing and humiliation (Phiri and Abebe, 2016, 390). Tafere's (2012, 9) study of poor children in Ethiopia similarly found that they are easily identified in school because of their inability to afford uniforms and/or lack of school materials, and as a result felt 'side-lined'.

Highlighting the psycho-social dimension of material deprivation, these studies reveal how "poverty forces children to examine their self-perceptions and relationships with others" (Tafere, 2012, 12). This may result in experiences of humiliation that are "painfully injurious to identity, self-respect and self-esteem" (Lister, 2021, 115). In relation to education, in particular, they indicate how spaces of learning may play a role in generating shame through their rules and expectations, thus alienating the very group who stands to benefit most from sustained attendance. In this way, learning spaces structured around a particular set of expectations for school uniforms demonstrate that shame is a socially induced emotion, with "structural as well as individual components" (Walker et al., 2013, 217; see also Redmond, 2009, 544).

Empirical studies such as those which we have referred to have important implications for pedagogy and curriculum since they make visible and do not truncate the emotional lives of children experiencing poverty. The turn to 'affect' in the social sciences and within educational studies has underscored this key but too often neglected role of emotions in both motivating and demotivating learners (Mulcahy, 2019). Studies have tended to focus on the affective dimensions of children's engagement with formal schooling in the global North, focusing on Europe or the US (Roelen, 2017) rather than those living in the global South.

There is a need, then, to recognise rather than erase the spectrum of affective responses of children navigating contexts of poverty in sub-Saharan Africa. This means orchestrating learning environments that, on the one hand, do not reproduce the negative feelings of stigma children might experience yet, on the other hand, leverage and nurture the many positive emotions or dispositions to learning that they bring. This attention to the educational relevance of the affective registers of children experiencing poverty brings into relief the narrowness of a sole focus on the cognitive outcomes of individual children or the enhancement of economic capital as priorities for educational provision. The current systemic failure to adopt such approaches in the pedagogies and curriculum offered to 'poor children' reproduces and exacerbates their marginality.

Children's social positioning in friendship groups, family networks and communities

In bringing into visibility the voices, agency and knowledges of children living in poverty, as well as the affective, embodied, temporal, spatial and playful nature of their lived experiences, multi-dimensional approaches to poverty underscore the profoundly relational nature of their existence (Mosse, 2010; Jamieson and Milne, 2012; Punch and Tisdall, 2012). This brings to our understandings of children's lives a recognition that the material and psychosocial are 'interwoven' (Hooper et al., 2007, 18) in their everyday experience of poverty and social suffering (Lister, 2021, 9). These insights highlight the inadequacy of the binary between childhood and adulthood within Eurocentric framings underpinning approaches to the learning crisis and educational provision. Having observed children's navigation of intergenerational relationships and social expectations in rural and urban Ethiopia, Kassa (2016a,2016b) observed that the exercise of agency by children is never wholly located in the individual child as such but should always be understood within their 'social positioning', and in particular within the inter-generational relationships between children and their immediate and extended families and others. These are underpinned by a commitment to the values of inter-dependence and reciprocity between parents and children. Similarly, Phiri and Abebe's (2016) study, referred to earlier, of children's perspectives and interpretations of poverty and well-being in rural Zambia concluded that "boys and girls interpret poverty largely in social relational terms" (378), framing their experiences as aspects of their familial and inter-generational relationships. Such insights challenge individualistic framings of children and encourage us to recognise both children's social positioning and their daily navigation of complex inter-generational structures. The imperatives of individualisation embedded in education for poverty alleviation interventions (discussed in Chapter 2) all constitute a form of closure that excludes this key dimension of the ontological reality of children navigating poverty.

Recognition of the relational dimensions of children's experiences of poverty also points to the importance of community-wide engagement (Mfum-Mensah, 2017). This entails reframing communities experiencing precarity outside of deficit projections within a putative 'culture of deprivation' (see Chapter 2). Recent studies of consultations with families of children in Northern Ghana (Mfum-Mensah, 2017, 2009) underscore their benefits in enabling curriculum content to be tailored to the lives and challenges faced by children in their situated contexts, thus contextualising pedagogical practices. As one member of the local community commented:

> it was beneficial and a matter of common sense to approach curriculum development in this way in a context such as rural northern Ghana where

communities' socioeconomic, sociocultural and religious reasons influence parents' decision about whether a child goes to school or not.
(Mfum-Mensah, 2017, 159)

These social dynamics clearly have educational significance. For example, when the children in Phiri and Adebe's study eschewed the binary between schooling and their wider lives noted above, they refused such compartmentalisation, instead talking holistically about the multiple spaces in which they exercised agency, whether working in the household or farming, playing with their peers or taking the opportunities to engage with schooling when and if possible. In this way, they actively counter the "narratives of lack, deficit and failure" (Hopkins, 2015, 168) which are attributed to them.

Twum-Danso (2022) highlighted the reciprocal obligations that characterise such intergenerational relations in Ghana within social expectations of both duty and dependence (440). These expectations of "reciprocity, respect and responsibility" (Twum-Danso, 2009, 415) characterising child-adult relations are key dimensions of the ontological reality of children's lives – what Twum-Danso characterises as a culturally embedded "moral framework about personhood, reciprocity, relatedness and collectivism" (Twum-Danso, 2009, 415). Hence:

[a] failure to make these connections between children's lives in this context and the broader belief systems and their attendant moral frameworks that continue to underpin conceptualisations of childhood and intergenerational relationships results in depictions of African childhoods that are partial, limited and out of context.
(Twum-Danso, 2022, 439)

Children's linguistic agency for learning

All of these multi-dimensional aspects of children's exercise of agency rely on their use of the languages that they are familiar with as vehicles of communication and socialisation. Yet, as we discussed in Chapter 3, these fundamental expressions of their identity are ignored within pedagogical strategies constrained by monolingual language of instruction policies. If we are to reverse the deficit positioning of children within the narrative of the learning crisis, we need to valorise and reinstate children's linguistic agency for learning. This would mean celebrating rather than erasing the 'rich resources represented by African multilingualism' in education provision (Benson, 2018).

Teachers in sub-Saharan Africa already resort to illicit code switching or switching between African as well as ex-colonial or international languages, to achieve better communication and learning (Ferguson, 2003, 2009). This is an example of teacher creativity in adapting to the linguistic ecologies of their students and responding to their evident struggle to understand in English. One teacher quoted by Brock-Utne (2016, 36) explained her use of code switching to use isiXhosa, in a South African primary school in a black township. Rather using than the mandated English language only: "That is what I am supposed to do, but if I do that, the children do not understand anything. It would be like teaching dead stones".

Mother-tongue–based bilingual programmes in a range of African contexts[2] result from similar concerns about enabling understanding and improving cognitive outcomes and affective orientations to learning. As explained by UNESCO (2016, 3):

> mother tongue based bilingual education means starting with the learner's knowledge and experiences by developing reading, writing and thinking skills in the mother tongue or home language while teaching the second language or foreign language as a subject.

Mother-tongue–based education allows learners to transfer skills (linguistic, conceptual and cognitive) from the first language to the unfamiliar one (Cummins, 2007). Studies in Cameroon (Laitin et al., 2016), Kenya (Piper et al., 2016) and Uganda (Brunette et al., 2019), for example, have shown how the rates at which children learn to read are accelerated when they are taught in a language with which they are familiar.

Translanguaging and code-switching practices further diversify the language of instruction beyond one language by using students' entire language repertoire (as opposed to a shift between only two languages) as resources for learning.[3] Such pedagogical approaches are informed by an understanding of languages, whether local or international, not as discrete entities or 'linguistic boxes' (Makalela, 2015, 200), but rather as communicative resources which African children draw on as parts of a single unitary social system. This approach avoids false binaries that present the acquisition of home languages and English as an either – or – choice. Instead, both languages are recognised as parts of a single communicative continuum (Tikly, 2016, 416–420; Trudell, 2016b, 281). Leveraging rather than pathologising this communicative resource through mother-tongue–based pedagogies enables teachers to respond to the often rich linguistic repertoires African children bring to their learning. Benson (2005a, 254, 255) usefully summarises the benefits of bilingual instruction in a range of sub-Saharan African contexts:

- becoming literate in a familiar language;
- gaining access to communication and literacy skills in the L2 [second language];
- having a language and culture that are valued by formal institutions like the school;
- feeling good about the school and the teacher;
- being able and even encouraged to demonstrate what they know;
- participating in their own learning;

- having the courage to ask questions in class (students) or ask the teacher what is being done (parents);
- attending school and having an improved chance of succeeding (all children and especially girls) and
- not being taken advantage of (all children and especially girls).

Transforming the linguistic conditions for children's learning through recognising and valuing their languages therefore repositions children as knowers, bringing valuable linguistic and knowledge resources. This opens up the possibility for pedagogical choices that enhance rather than undermine their learning.

Studies in sub-Saharan classrooms also point to the benefits of learning of the *exploratory talk* made possible when children are encouraged to articulate their ideas without fear or anxiety (Nikièma, 2011; UNESCO, 2016, 3). For instance, Fafunwa (1989) recounts the benefits of the Ife Project in Nigeria that took place in the 1970s and that used Yoruba throughout six years of primary education. He suggested that this choice "makes it possible for the learner to give free rein to his [sic] thoughts and express the same in creative language, thus paving the way to meaningful education" (10). Rather than being despised or excluded, learners' linguistic resources can be used as tools for meaning-making (García and Wei, 2015) and as 'legitimate thinking tools' (Kiramba, 2018, 300). In a South African science classroom, Charamba (2023, 69) found that students were able "to engage in a practice of generating and creating scientific explanations in their own voice, resulting in better academic performance". Children are also able to draw on their funds of knowledge to support and scaffold learning through opportunities in exploratory talk to reference their lived experiences, including their homes, play activities and lives outside school. Jones and Mutumba's (2019, 217) study of mother-tongue–based instruction in a pre-school in South Central Uganda concluded that:

> the children were able to convert and activate their funds of knowledge and affirm, express and develop their identities in agentive ways that enabled them to fully inhabit and situate themselves comfortably, linguistically and culturally, within the educational context.

Brock-Utne's (2007, 497) description of the lively interactions between teacher and students in a Tanzanian classroom demonstrates how mother tongue instruction and exploratory talk also restore children's access to understanding the curriculum:

> The students bring their own experiences in when taught in Kiswahili. They challenge the teacher, and they are critical and lively. They pose many questions themselves, something that never happens when the class is taught in English. They also add to and build on each other's answers. There is a situation of give and take in the classroom where the

teaching is done through the medium of Kiswahili. The students bring their knowledge into the classroom and often know things the teachers do not know. In this way they teach the teacher as well as each other.

These findings give new meaning to the aspiration to produce active and participatory learners associated with 'learner-centredness', highlighting its essential linguistic pre-conditions.

Repositioning children as agentic and knowledgeable generates positive emotions towards learning (Bamgbose, 2005; Jones and Mutumba, 2019; Mose and Kaschula, 2019). Hence, more effective communication between teachers and pupils creates 'warmer, more comfortable learning environments' (Benson, 2002a, 310).

Highlighting the key contribution of mother-tongue–based schooling to addressing the distinctive challenges of girls' marginalisation, Benson (2005, 5) notes that:

> ..when learners can express their full range of knowledge in a language in which they are competent, and their backgrounds are valued and used as a basis for instruction, they develop higher self-esteem and greater self-confidence, as well as higher aspirations in schooling and in life.

The transformation of the emotional as well as intellectual interactions between teachers and pupils has important benefits to secure girls' participation (Milligan and Adamson, 2022, 7) given that the learning environment in which their language and lives are referenced results in less apprehension about attending school.

These findings all point to the way in which recognition of children's linguistic repertoires and the knowledges and lived experiences that they express results in a fundamental shift in the power relationships operating in processes of learning that position children in deficit terms. As Cummins (2000, 31) acknowledged, shifting the language of instruction to children's home languages leverages a transition from 'coercive to collaborative relations of power'. Hence:

> ..students' identities are affirmed, and academic achievement promoted when teachers express respect for the language and cultural knowledge that students bring to the classroom and when the instruction is focused on helping students generate new knowledge, create literature and act on social realities that affect their lives.
>
> (2000, 34)

Teachers as Multi-dimensional Agents

Just like the children we have discussed, teachers multi-dimensional experiences are a powerful resources for promoting effective learning but are silenced in their training. Their knowledges, experiences, feelings, languages, and exercise of agency within communities are key to connecting with children in the ecological space of the classroom. Many teachers in sub-Saharan Africa have deep experiences of poverty, deprivation, conflict (Bennell and Akyeampong, 2007) similar to what the children they teach might have experienced and are therefore not ignorant bystanders whose responsibility is simply to provide them with an education to lift them out of poverty. The ability to relate to children living in poverty is key to how teachers can transform their learning.

In a study which asked global 'best teachers' what qualities they found were key to their success in helping disadvantaged children learn and achieve their potential, the most highlighted qualities that Akyeampong et al. (2018, 34–35) found were (i) compassion and kindness; (ii) empathy and patience; and (iii) grit and perseverance. More importantly, such teachers pointed to their own knowledge and experiences of disadvantaged communities as helping them to build deep relationships with their students. 'Relatability' was key – a recognition that many teachers share common struggles and understand the social deprivation of the children they teach and that these can be used to build bonds of trust and a shared vision about the purpose of education. Yet, this relatability is rarely prized as a critical resource in the response to the 'learning crisis'. This connection is imperative for teachers if they are to be effective in helping children from disadvantaged backgrounds learn and succeed. As one teacher pointed out:

> …relatability is very critical. There is more respect offered to teachers [by their students] for being relatable than for being seen as an authority or an expert. The level of respect is about how much or how quickly students can connect and understand your point of view rather than what you know.
> (quoted in Akyeampong et al., 2018, 19)

Teachers are the product of the societies or communities in which they teach, the struggles, dreams, energies, grit and agency of children are not alien to them and for highly effective teachers are what inspires commitment to active engagement at the classroom level (Akyeampong et al., 2018). However, these qualities shared by both teachers and children are mostly occluded in the deficit framings of pre-service and in-service teacher training as discussed in Chapter 4. We would argue that teachers' training programmes need to align with a multi-dimensional approach if they are to re-envision what constitutes a successful education system that values children outside of deficit terms. Such programmes need to be re-purposed to recognise the expansive learning opportunities that benefit children living in poverty.

However, despite the research evidence presented above, the SDG 4 target that calls for an increased supply of qualified teachers (using help from international teacher training) has not included any call for the re-envisioning of teacher education. The drive to mass produce qualified teachers has meant using training designs and methods that can deliver this goal cheaply and quickly and has even led, it seems, to trained teachers not feeling confident in teaching to improve African children's Foundational Literacy and Numeracy skills (Pryor et al., 2012). Also, the push for more teachers has implications for who is selected for training. Many countries base their recruitment almost entirely on an applicant's prior academic qualifications with little use of interviews or other methods to explore applicants' multi-dimensional qualities. This can lead to a teacher cadre which is less diverse than the student body and which provides limited role models for some groups of students (Akyeampong et al., 2018, 37). Second, basing selection criteria strictly or solely on academic qualifications for entry to teacher education lowers the value of important multi-dimensional teacher qualities needed in the transformation of learning for African children. An interest in and empathy with children, commitment to the social justice goals of teaching, patience, compassion, creativity and adaptability are all qualities that are important in the selection for training (Akyeampong et al., 2018, 37).

Similarly, pre-service teacher education programmes in sub-Sahara Africa as currently designed have a restrictive view of the qualities needed for the African teacher. They fail to utilise the rich funds of knowledge, varied experiences of poverty and perspectives of teaching and learning reflecting their own journeys of schooling to frame the curriculum (see Chapter 4). Recognising that teachers' conception of themselves, their roles and identities are shaped by their own biographical experiences, in which their home environment, family and kinship networks and their own schooling experiences play a crucial part (Akyeampong and Stephens, 2002) needs factoring into the process of creating agentic teachers, capable and skilled at working in diverse challenging contexts.

If reforms and research on teacher education in Africa were to use this multi-dimensional view and relational perspective, they would produce teachers with a positive image of themselves and their ability to expand children's learning outside of deficit models. Even more significantly, unless this happens, the African teacher will continue themselves to be characterised in deficit terms, subjected to reforms and interventions that do little to make them change agents.

Reframing the 'Learning Crisis'

In this chapter, we addressed the critique we offered earlier of the deficit framings embedded in the contemporary global learning crisis. We have proposed a number of dimensions that need to be considered if those conceptualisations are to be reframed. The deeply embedded historical agendas and cultural politics shaping the development field and its practices discussed in Chapter 2 privileged a particular Eurocentric model of childhood and a narrowly economistic understanding of poverty which coalesce in a social imaginary of the poor, 'poor children' and their teachers in the global South as 'lacking'. Consequently, a narrow logic of educational intervention has privileged the development of cognitive skills, of economic capital and the redemptive agency of external actors. Such deficit framings individualise and decontextualise children living in poverty allowing them to become targets of intervention. This approach erases their positionality as social actors within communities, whose lives and lived experiences as we have shown involve diverse relational, affective, spatial and temporal dimensions, all of which have implications for curriculum and pedagogical responses.

In contrast, taking a multi-dimensional approach brings to the fore the lived experiences of children navigating contexts of poverty, opening up a more holistic understanding of their everyday lives. This is achieved through valorising their voices and languages, their reflexivity, their exercise of agency, their informal knowledge-building as well as the affective, temporal embodied, dynamics of their lived experiences. Here, children experiencing precarity are revealed as agentic and resourceful, already learners *in situ* in terms of a wealth of intergenerational expectations and relationships. These insights contribute to our overriding concern to reconceptualise the learning crisis in sub-Saharan Africa.

This reconceptualisation suggests that in relation to children experiencing poverty, the challenge is less one of needing to compensate for deficits in educationally marginalised children, but rather of how to strategise for and respond to their 'positive' agency in all its dimensions – voice, knowledges, feelings, nouse and know-how.

First, it points to the need for an expansive conceptualisation of education that may integrate and build on, rather than dismiss and/or erase, children's agency and the many knowledges and other resources they bring to learning. Second, reframing the learning crisis entails centralising the fundamental issue of language of instruction in addressing educational marginalisation. Third, it means eschewing what have been termed 'educationist approaches' that tend to dominate the global educational policy agenda. These are characterised by a problem-solving mission, focusing on educational issues as discrete problems to be solved through narrowly educational solutions (Robertson and Dale, 2020) rather than locating them in broader social and community-rooted contexts and challenges. Fourth, it means being more measured about the capacity of education interventions *alone* to eradicate poverty, as in the utopian promises of policy and programming rhetoric.

This alternative agenda means foregrounding the need for education to connect with multi-sector responses that address the intersecting forms of precarity experienced by the communities whose children suffer educational marginalisation. Such an approach reframes what is termed the learning challenge within processes that go beyond educational marginalisation to include addressing political economy and structural challenges of accessing health care and paid employment, obtaining land rights and forms and spaces of representation and confronting food insecurity and the impacts of climate change on their local environments. It would enable alignments and co-ordination between education and other sectors, effectively inviting greater connectivity between the implementation of the separate SDGs.

All these strategies are predicated on a commitment to reverse that process of 'othering' or objectification which Lister (2021, 122) has noted characterises global social policy addressing poverty and which this analysis has shown to be so pervasive in educational responses to poor children. In the case studies that follow in Part 2, we show how accelerated learning programmes in Ghana, Ethiopia and Liberia have taken up this challenge, and through their innovative educational provision for out-of-school children, have affirmed rather than belittled these children's lived experiences, their agency and that of their families and communities, thereby promoting enjoyable and successful learning such that they were motivated and able to continue onto, and to complete basic education.

Notes

1 See also Bourdillon and Boyden (2011), Phiri and Abebe (2016), Boyden et al. (2019).
2 See studies by: Fafunwa (1989), Lavoie (2008), Opoku-Amankwa (2009), Barrett and Bainton (2016), Clegg and Simpson (2016), Jones and Mutumba (2019), Benson (2000, 2002b, 2005, 2022), Bretuo (2021), Clegg (2021), Mkhize (2023).
3 See studies by: García (2009), Abiria et al. (2013), Mokgwathi and Webb (2013), Cenoz (2017), Banda (2018), Erling et al. (2021, 1), Chamberlain et al. (2022).

References

Abebe, T., 2011. 'Gendered work and schooling in rural Ethiopia: exploring working children's perspectives'. In *Not just a victim: the child as catalyst and witness of contemporary Africa*. Brill, pp. 147–171.

Abebe, T., 2013. *Childhood and local knowledge in Ethiopia: livelihoods, rights and intergenerational relationships*. Akademika forlag.

Abebe, T., and Bessell, S., 2011. 'Dominant discourses, debates and silences on child labour in Africa and Asia'. *Third World Quarterly*, 32(4): 765–786.

Abebe, T., and Ofosu-Kusi, Y., 2016. 'Beyond pluralizing African childhoods: introduction'. *Childhood*, 23(3): 303–316.

Abiria, D.M., Early, M., and Kendrick, M., 2013. 'Plurilingual pedagogical practices in a policy-constrained context: a Northern Ugandan case study'. *Tesol Quarterly*, 47(3): 567–590.

Aitken, S.C., 2001. 'Global crises of childhood: rights, justice and the unchildlike child'. *Area*, 33(2): 119–127.

Akyeampong, K., and Stephens, D. 2002. 'Exploring the backgrounds and shaping factors of beginning teachers in Ghana: towards greater contextualisation of teacher education'. *International Journal of Education Development*, 22(3/4): 261–274.

Akyeampong, K., Vegas, E., Wolfenden, F., Saldanha, K., Al-Attia, Haifa Dia, Wigdortz, B., Oduro, E., and Weinstein, J. 2018. *Qualities of effective teachers who teach disadvantaged students: insights from the Varkey Teacher Ambassador community*. Alliances – Varkey Foundation, Global Skills Forum & REAL, University of Cambridge.

Ansell, N., Froerer, P., Huijsmans, R., Dungey, C., and Arshima Champa Dost & Piti, 2020. 'Educating "surplus population": uses and abuses of aspiration in the rural peripheries of a globalising world'. *Fennia: International Journal of Geography*, 198(1-2): 17–38.

Balagopalan, S., 2008. 'Memories of tomorrow: children, labor, and the Panacea of formal schooling'. *Journal of the History of Childhood and Youth*, 1(2): 267–285.

Bamgbose, A., 2005. 'Mother tongue education: Lessons from the Yoruba experience'. In B. Brock-Utne and R.K. Hopson (eds.), *Languages of instruction for African emancipation: Focus on postcolonial contexts and considerations*. Casas Book Series, pp. 231–257.

Banda, F., 2018. 'Translanguaging and English/African language mother tongues as linguistic dispensation in teaching and learning in a black township school in Cape Town'. *Current Issues in Language Planning*, 19(2): 198–217.

Banerjee, A.V., Bhattacharjee, S., Chattopadhyay, R., and Ganimian, A.J., 2017. 'The untapped math skills of working children in India: evidence, possible explanations, and implications'. Unpublished manuscript.

Barrett, A.M., and Bainton, D., 2016. 'Re-interpreting relevant learning: an evaluative framework for secondary education in a global language'. *Comparative Education*, 52(3): 392–407.

Bennell, P. and Akyeampong, K., 2007. *Teacher motivation in sub-Saharan Africa and south Asia* (Vol. 71). DfID.

Benson, C.J., 2000. 'The primary bilingual education experiment in Mozambique, 1993 to 1997'. *International Journal of Bilingual Education and Bilingualism*, 3(3): 149–166.

Benson, C.J., 2002a. 'Real and potential benefits of bilingual programmes in developing countries'. *International Journal of Bilingual Education and Bilingualism*, 5(6): 303–317.

Benson, C., 2002b. 'Bilingual education in Africa: an exploration of encouraging connections between language and girls' schooling'. In *Education—A Way Out of Poverty: Research Presentations at the Poverty Conference 2001*. New Education Division Documents No. 12. Sida, Stockholm.

Benson, C., 2005a. *The importance of mother tongue-based schooling for educational quality*. Commissioned study for EFA Global Monitoring Report, 24.

Benson, C., 2005b. *Girls, educational equity and mother tongue-based teaching*. UNESCO Bangkok. Asia and Pacific Regional Bureau for Education, PO Box 967, Prakhanong Post Office, Bangkok 10110, Thailand.

Benson, C., 2018. 'Celebrating the rich resources represented by African multilingualism and multiculturalism in education: Discussant paper'. *Current Issues in Language Planning*, 19(2): 218–225.

Benson, C., 2022. 'An innovative "simultaneous" bilingual approach in Senegal: promoting interlinguistic transfer while contributing to policy change'. *International Journal of Bilingual Education and Bilingualism*, 25(4): 1399–1416.

Bourdillon, M., and Boyden, J. eds., 2011. *Childhood poverty: multidisciplinary approaches* (Palgrave Studies on Children and Development). Springer.

Bourdillon, M., Levison, D., Myers, W., and White, B., 2010. *Rights and wrongs of children's work* (Rutgers Series in Childhood Studies). Rutgers University Press.

Boyden, J., 1994. *The relationship between education and child work*. Innocenti Occasional Papers, Child rights series No. 9, UNICEF, Florence.

Boyden, J., 2003. 'Children under fire: challenging assumptions about children's resilience'. *Children, Youth and Environments*, 13(1): 1–29.

Boyden, J., 2013. '"We're not going to suffer like this in the mud": educational aspirations, social mobility and independent child migration among populations living in poverty'. *Compare: A Journal of Comparative and International Education*, 43(5): 580–600.

Boyden, J., Dawes, A., Dornan, P., and Tredoux, C., 2019. *Tracing the consequences of child poverty*. Policy Press.

Boyden, J., Eyeber, C., Feeny, T., and Scott, C., 2003. *Children and poverty: experiences and perceptions from Belarus, Bolivia, India, Kenya and Sierra Leone* (Children and Poverty Series). Christian Children's Fund.

Boyden, J., Porter, C., and Zharkevich, I., 2021. 'Balancing school and work with new opportunities: changes in children's gendered time use in Ethiopia (2006–2013)'. *Children's Geographies*, 19(1): 74–87.

Bray, R., de Laat, M., Godinot, X., Ugarte, A., and Walker, R., 2020. 'Realising poverty in all its dimensions: a six-country participatory study'. *World Development*, 134: 105025.

Bretuo, P., 2021. 'Using language to improve learning: teachers' and students' perspectives on the implementation of bilingual education in Ghana'. *Language, Culture and Curriculum*, 34(3): 257–272.

Brock-Utne, B., 2007. 'Learning through a familiar language versus learning through a foreign language: a look into some secondary school classrooms in Tanzania'. *International Journal of Educational Development*, 27(5): 487–498.

Brock-Utne, B., 2016. 'The ubuntu paradigm in curriculum work, language of instruction and assessment'. *International Review of Education*, 62: 29–44.

Brunette, T., Piper, B., Jordan, R., King, S., and Nabacwa, R., 2019. 'The impact of mother tongue reading instruction in twelve Ugandan languages and the role of language complexity, socioeconomic factors, and program implementation'. *Comparative Education Review*, 63(4): 591–612.

Burman, E., 2012. 'Deconstructing neoliberal childhood: towards a feminist antipsychological approach'. *Childhood*, 19(4): 423–438.

Camfield, L., Streuli, N., and Woodhead, M. 2008. 'Children's well-being in contexts of poverty: approaches to research, monitoring and participation'. *Young Lives*.

Cenoz, J., 2017. 'Translanguaging in school contexts: international perspectives'. *Journal of Language, Identity and Education*, 16(4): 193–198.

Chamberlain, L., Rodriguez-Leon, L., and Woodward, C., 2022. 'Disrupting language of instruction policy at a classroom level: oracy examples from South Africa and Zambia'. *Literacy*, 56(3): 264–274.

Charamba, E., 2023. 'Translanguaging as bona fide practice in a multilingual South African science classroom'. *International Review of Education*, 69(1): 31–50.

Clark, J., and Richards, S., 2017. 'The cherished conceits of research with children: does seeking the agentic voice of the child through participatory methods deliver what it promises?' In J. Clark and S. Richards (eds.), *Researching children and youth: methodological issues, strategies, and innovations*. Emerald, pp. 127–147.

Clegg, J., 2021. 'Multilingual learning in Anglophone Sub-Saharan Africa: how to help children use all their languages to learn'. In J. Clegg (ed.), *Multilingual learning and language supportive pedagogies in Sub-Saharan Africa*. Routledge, pp. 144–169.

Clegg, J., and Simpson, J., 2016. 'Improving the effectiveness of English as a medium of instruction in sub-Saharan Africa'. *Comparative Education*, 52(3), 359–374.

Clemensen, N., 2016. 'Exploring ambiguous realms: access, exposure and agency in the interactions of rural Zambian children'. *Childhood*, 23(3): 317–332.

Cooper, E., and Pratten, D., eds., 2015. *Ethnographies of uncertainty in Africa*. Springer.

Cremin, P., and Nakabugo, M.G., 2012. 'Education, development and poverty reduction: a literature critique'. *International Journal of Educational Development*, 32(4): 499–506.

Crossouard, B., Dunne, M., Szyp, C., Madu, T., and Teeken, B., 2022. 'Rural youth in Southern Nigeria: fractured lives and ambitious futures'. *Journal of Sociology*, 58(2): 218–235.

Cummins, J., 2000. *Language, power and pedagogy: bilingual children in the crossfire*. Multilingual Matters.

Cummins, J., 2007. 'Rethinking monolingual instructional strategies in multilingual classrooms'. *Canadian Journal of Applied Linguistics*, 10(2): 221–240.

de Sousa Santos, B., 2015. *Epistemologies of the south: justice against epistemicide*. Routledge.

Dunne, M., and Humphreys, S., 2022. 'The edu-workscape: re-conceptualising the relationship between work and education in rural children's lives in Sub-Saharan Africa'. *World Development Perspectives*, 27: 100–443.

Erling, E.J., Clegg, J., Rubagumya, C.M., and Reilly, C., eds., 2021. *Multilingual learning and language supportive pedagogies in Sub-Saharan Africa*. London: Routledge.

Fafunwa, A.B., 1989. *Education in mother tongue: the Ife primary education research project (1970–1978)*. Ibadan University Press. Available at: https://files.eric.ed.gov/fulltext/ED350120.pdf

Feeny, T., and Boyden, J., 2003. *Children and poverty: a review of contemporary literature and thought on children and poverty* (Children and Poverty series, part I). Christian Children's Fund. https://typeset.io/pdf/children-and-poverty-a-review-of-contemporary-literature-and-hmgms3fdep.pdf

Feeny, T., and Boyden, J., 2004. *Acting in adversity: rethinking the causes, experiences and effects of child poverty in contemporary literature*. QEH Working Paper Series, QEHWPS 116.

Ferguson, G., 2003. 'Classroom code-switching in post-colonial contexts: functions, attitudes and Politics'. *AILA Review*, 16: 38–51.

Ferguson, G., 2009. 'What next? Towards an agenda for classroom codeswitching research'. *International Journal of Bilingual Education and Bilingualism*, 12(2): 231–241.

García, O. 2009. *Bilingual education in the 21st century: a global perspective*. Wiley-Blackwell.

García, O., and Wei, L., 2015. 'Translanguaging, bilingualism, and bilingual education'. In *The handbook of bilingual and multilingual education*. John Wiley and Sons, pp. 223–240.

Hanson, K., and Nieuwenhuys, O., 2013. *Reconceptualizing children's rights in international development: living rights, social justice, translations*. Cambridge University Press.

Hooper, C., Gorin, S., Cabral, C., and Dyson, C., 2007. *Living with hardship 24/7*. Frank Buttle Trust.

Hopkins, L., 2015. 'Picturing education, poverty and childhood from the perspectives of yak herder children in Bhutan'. In L. Hopkins and A. Sriprakash (eds.), *The poor child*. Routledge, pp. 180–202.

Humphreys, S., Moses, D., Kaibo, J., and Dunne, M., 2015. 'Counted in and being out: Fluctuations in primary school and classroom attendance in northern Nigeria'. *International Journal of Educational Development*, 44: 134–143.

Iglesias, E., Esteban-Guitart, M., Puyaltó, C., and Montserrat, C., 2022. 'Fostering community socio-educational resilience in pandemic times: its concept, characteristics and prospects'. *Frontiers in Education*, 7: 1–9.

ILO, and UNICEF, 2021. *Child labour: global estimates 2020, trends and the way forward*. Available at: https://www.ilo.org/ipec/Informationresources/WCMS_797515/lang--en/index.htm [Accessed: 22/02/2024].

James, A., and Prout, A., 1997. *Constructing and reconstructing childhood: contemporary issues in the sociological study of childhood* (2nd edn). Routledge.

Jamieson, L., and Milne, S. 2012. 'Children and young people's relationships, relational processes and social change: reading across worlds'. *Children's Geographies*, 10(3): 265–278. https://doi.org/10.1080/14733285.2012.693377.

Jonah, O.T., and Abebe, T., 2018. 'Tensions and controversies regarding child labor in small-scale gold mining in Ghana'. *African Geographical Review*, 38(4): 361–373.

Jones, S., and Mutumba, S., 2019. 'Intersections of mother tongue-based instruction, funds of knowledge, identity, and social capital in a Ugandan pre-school classroom'. *Journal of Language, Identity and Education*, 18(4): 207–221.

Kassa, S.C., 2016a. 'Negotiating intergenerational relationships and social expectations in childhood in rural and urban Ethiopia'. *Childhood*, 23(3): 394–409.

Kassa, S.C., 2016b. 'Drawing family boundaries: children's perspectives on family relationships in rural and urban Ethiopia'. *Children and Society*, 31(3): 171–182.

Katz, C., 2004. *Growing up global: economic restructuring and children's everyday lives*. University of Minnesota Press.

Katz, C., 2011. 'Accumulation, excess, childhood: Toward a countertopography of risk and waste'. *Documents d'anàlisi geogràfica*, 57(1): 47–60.

Katz, C., 2012. 'Work and play: economic restructuring and children's everyday learning in rural Sudan'. In M. Bourdillon and G. Spittler (eds.), *African children at work: working and learning in growing up for life* (Vol. 52). Lit Verlag, p. 227

Kiramba, L.K., 2018. 'Language ideologies and epistemic exclusion'. *Language and Education*, 32(4): 291–312.

Krauss, A., 2017. 'Understanding child labour beyond the standard economic assumption of monetary poverty'. *Cambridge Journal of Economics*, 41(2): 545–574.

Kyomuhendo, G.B., Chase, E., and Kyoheirwe, F., 2019. 'Children and young people's experiences of managing poverty related shame in Uganda and the UK'. In G.B. Kyomuhendo, E. Chase, and F. Kyoheirwe (eds.), *Putting children first: New frontiers in the fight against child poverty in Africa*. Ibidem Press, p. 49.

Laitin, D., Ramachandran, R., and Walter, S., 2016. *Language of instruction and student learning: evidence from an experimental program in Cameroon*. Paper presented at the WIDER Development Conference on Human Capital and Growth, Helsinki, Finland. Available at: https://www.wider.unu.edu/ [Accessed: 21.07.2023].

Lancy, D.F., 2010. 'Learning "From nobody": the limited role of teaching in folk models of children's development'. *Childhood in the Past*, 3(1): 79–106.

Lavoie, C., 2008. '"Hey, teacher, speak black please": the educational effectiveness of bilingual education in Burkina Faso'. *International Journal of Bilingual Education and Bilingualism*, 11(6): 661–677.

Liebel, M., Hanson, K., and Nieuwenhuys, O., 2012. 'Do children have a right to work? Working children's movements in the struggle'. In M. Liebel (ed.), *Reconceptualizing*

children's rights in international development: living rights, social justice, translations.* Cambridge University Press, pp. 225–249.
Lister, R., 2021. *Poverty.* John Wiley and Sons.
Lynch, K., 2007. 'Love labour as a distinct and non-commodifiable form of care labour'. *Sociological Review,* 55(3): 550–570.
Lynch, K., Baker, J., Lyons, M., Feeley, M., Hanlon, N., Walsh, J., and Cantillon, S., 2016. *Affective equality: love, care and injustice.* Springer.
Maconachie, R., Howard, N., and Bock, R., 2020. *Theorising "Harm" in relation to children's work.* ACHA Working Paper No. 4. ACHA, IDS.
Maconachie, R., Howard, N., and Bock, R., 2022. 'Re-thinking "harm" in relation to children's work: a "situated", multi-disciplinary perspective'. *Oxford Development Studies,* 50(3): 259–271.
Makalela, L., 2015. 'Moving out of linguistic boxes: the effects of translanguaging strategies for multilingual classrooms'. *Language and Education,* 29(3): 200–217.
Mfum-Mensah, O., 2009. 'An exploratory study of the curriculum development process of a complementary education program for marginalized communities in Northern Ghana'. *Curriculum Inquiry,* 39(2): 343–367.
Mfum-Mensah, O., 2017. *Education, social progress, and marginalized children in sub-Saharan Africa: historical antecedents and contemporary challenges.* Lexington Books.
Milligan, L.O. and Adamson, L., 2022. *Girls education and language of instruction: an extended policy brief.* University of Bath. https://researchportal.bath.ac.uk/en/publications/girls-education-and-language-of-instruction-an-extended-policy-br
Mizen, P., and Ofosu-Kusi, Y., 2010. 'Unofficial truths and everyday insights: understanding voice in visual research with the children of Accra's urban poor'. *Visual Studies,* 25(3): 255–267.
Mizen, P., and Ofosu-Kusi, Y., 2013. 'Seeing and knowing? Street children's lifeworlds through the camera's lens'. In K. Hanson and O. Nieuwenhuys. (eds.), *Reconceptualizing children's rights in international development: living rights, social justice and translations.* Cambridge University Press, pp. 48–70.
Mkhize, D.N., 2023. 'Reconceptualising the notion of cross-linguistic transfer in multilingual spaces: a global south perspective from South Africa'. *Language Sciences,* 100: 101–573.
Mose, P.N., and Kaschula, R.H., 2019. 'Developing mother tongues as academic languages in primary schools in Kenya: exploring extent and indispensability'. *Journal of Language, Identity and Education,* 18(5): 329–342.
Mosse, D., 2010. 'A relational approach to durable poverty, inequality and power'. *Journal of Development Studies,* 46(7): 1156–1178.
Mulcahy, D., 2019. 'Pedagogic affect and its politics: learning to affect and be affected in education'. *Discourse: Studies in the Cultural Politics of Education,* 40(1): 93–108.
Muriithi, A.G., 2015. 'Child labour, schooling and the reconstruction of childhood: a case study from Kenya'. In A.G. Muriithi (ed.), *The poor child.* Routledge, pp. 77–95.
Ngutuku, E., 2019. 'Beyond categories: rhizomatic experiences of child poverty and vulnerability in Kenya'. In E. Ngutuku (ed.), *Putting children first: new frontiers in the fight against child poverty in Africa.* Ibidem Press, p. 25.
Nieuwenhuys, O., 2005. *Children's lifeworlds: gender, welfare and labour in the developing world.* Routledge.
Nikièma, N., 2011. 'A first-language-first multilingual model to meet the quality imperative in formal basic education in three "francophone" West African countries'. *International Review of Education,* 57: 599–616.

Odonkor, M., 2007. *Addressing child labour through education: a study of alternative/complementary initiatives in quality education delivery and their suitability for cocoa-farming communities.* International Cocoa Initiative (ICI).

Opoku-Amankwa, K., 2009. 'English-only language-in-education policy in multilingual classrooms in Ghana'. *Language, Culture and Curriculum*, 22(2): 121–135.

Orkin, K., 2012. 'Are work and schooling complementary or competitive for children in rural Ethiopia? A mixed-method study'. In J. Boyden and M. Bourdillon (eds.), *Childhood poverty: multidisciplinary approaches.* Palgrave Macmillan, UK, pp. 298–313.

Pande, M. 2014. *The impact of poverty on the lives and education of young carers in India* (University of Cambridge unpublished PhD Thesis).

Pankhurst, A., Crivello, G., and Tiumelissan, A., 2016. 'Children's work in family and community contexts: examples from young lives Ethiopia'. *DFiD*, https://www.gov.uk/research-for-development-outputs/young-lives-working-paper-147-childrens-work-in-family-and-community-contexts-examples-from-young-lives-ethiopia.

Patrick, R., 2020. 'Unsettling the anti-welfare common sense: the potential in participatory research with people living in poverty'. *Journal of Social Policy*, 49(2): 251–270.

Payne, R., 2012. '"Extraordinary survivors" or "ordinary lives"? Embracing "everyday agency" in social interventions with child-headed households in Zambia'. *Children's Geographies*, 10(4): 399–411.

Phiri, D.T., and Abebe, T., 2016. 'Suffering and thriving: children's perspectives and interpretations of poverty and well-being in rural Zambia'. *Childhood*, 23(3): 378–393.

Piper, B., Zuilkowski, S.S., and Ong'ele, S., 2016. 'Implementing mother tongue instruction in the real world: results from a medium-scale randomized controlled trial in Kenya'. *Comparative Education Review*, 60(4): 776–807.

Pryor, J., Akyeampong, K., Westbrook, J., and Lussier, K. 2012 'Rethinking teacher preparation and professional development in Africa: an analysis of the curriculum of teacher education in the teaching of early reading and mathematics'. *The Curriculum Journal*, 23(4): 409–502.

Punch, S., and Tisdall, E.K.M., 2012. 'Exploring children and young people's relationships across majority and minority worlds'. *Children's Geographies*, 10(3): 241–248.

Rai, S.M., Brown, B.D., and Ruwanpura, K.N., 2019. SDG 8: 'Decent work and economic growth: a gendered analysis'. *World Development*, 113: 368–380.

Redmond, G., 2009. 'Children as actors: how does the child perspectives literature treat agency in the context of poverty?' *Social Policy and Society*, 8(4): 541–550.

Robertson, S.L., and Dale, R., 2015. 'Towards a "critical cultural political economy" account of the globalising of education'. *Globalisation, Societies and Education*, 13(1): 149–170.

Robertson, S.L., and Dale, R., 2020. 'Towards a "critical cultural political economy" account of the globalising of education'. In S.L. Robertson and R. Dale (eds.), *Globalisation and education.* Routledge, pp. 104–125.

Robson, E., 2004. 'Children at work in rural northern Nigeria: patterns of age, space and gender'. *Journal of Rural Studies*, 20(2): 193–210.

Robson, E., Ansell, N., Huber, U.S., Gould, W.T., and van Blerk, L., 2006. 'Young caregivers in the context of the HIV/AIDS pandemic in sub-Saharan Africa'. *Population, Space and Place*, 12(2): 93–111.

Roelen, K., 2017. *Shame, poverty and social protection*. IDS Working Paper 489, Brighton: IDS.

Roelen, K., Morgan, R., Tafere, Y., Odunayo Akinyemi, J., Akomolafe, O., Araya, M., Bantebya-Kyomuhendo, G., Chase, E., Coast, E., Conklin, S., and Devereux, S.,

2019. *Putting children first: new frontiers in the fight against child poverty in Africa* (CROP International Poverty Studies). Ibidem Press.

Rogoff, B., Moore, L., Correa-Chávez, M., and Dexter, A.L., 2015. 'Children develop cultural repertoires through engaging in everyday routines and practices'. In B. Rogoff, L. Moore, M. Correa-Chávez, and A.L. Dexter (eds.), *Handbook of socialization: theory and research* (2nd edn). Guilford Press, pp. 472–498.

Save the Children UK, 2001. *Different places, same stories – children's views of poverty, north and south*. Save the Children UK.

Sayed, Y., and Ahmed, R. (2015). 'Education quality, and teaching and learning in the post-2015 education agenda'. *International Journal of Educational Development*, 40: 330–338.

Serpell, R., 2018. 'Grounding innovative promotion of literacy in local funds of knowledge'. *Papers in Education and Development*, 35: 1–13.

Smith, T.A., 2014. 'The student is not the fisherman: temporal displacement of young people's identities in Tanzania'. *Social Cultural Geography*, 15(7): 786–811.

Spicker, P., 2020. *The poverty of nations: a relational perspective*. Policy Press.

Tafere, Y., 2012. 'Children's experiences and perceptions of poverty in Ethiopia'. *Young Lives*.

Tikly, L., 2011. 'Towards a framework for researching the quality of education in low-income countries'. *Comparative Education*, 47(1): 1–23.

Tikly, L. 2016. 'Language-in-education policy in low-income, postcolonial contexts: towards a social justice approach'. *Comparative Education*, 52(3): 408–425.

Trudell, B., 2016b. 'Language choice and education quality in Eastern and Southern Africa: a review'. *Comparative Education*, 52(3): 281–293.

Twum-Danso, A., 2009. 'Reciprocity, respect and responsibility: the 3Rs underlying parent-child relationships in Ghana and the implications for children's rights'. *The International Journal of Children's Rights*, 17(3): 415–432.

Twum-Danso, A., 2022. 'Framing reciprocal obligations within intergenerational relations in Ghana through the lens of the mutuality of duty and dependence'. *Childhood*, 29(3): 439–454.

UNESCO, 2016. *If you don't understand, how can you learn?* Policy Paper 24 of Global Education Monitoring Report, UNESCO, Paris.. Available at: https://reliefweb.int/report/world/if-you-don-t-understand-how-can-you-learn. [Accessed: 21.07.2023].

Walker, R., Kyomuhendo, G.B., Chase, E., Choudhry, S., Gubrium, E.K., Nicola, J.Y., Lødemel, I., Matthew, L., Mwiine, A., Pellissery, S., and Ming, Y., 2013. 'Poverty in global perspective: is shame a common denominator?' *Journal of Social Policy*, 42(2): 215–233.

Whyte, S.R., and Siu, G.E., 2015. 'Contingency: interpersonal and historical dependencies in HIV care'. In S.R. Whyte and G.E. Siu (eds.), *Ethnographies of uncertainty in Africa*. Palgrave Macmillan UK, pp. 19–35.

Woldehanna, T., Jones, N., and Tefera, B., 2008. 'The invisibility of children's paid and unpaid work: implications for Ethiopia's national poverty reduction policy'. *Childhood*, 15(2): 177–201.

Woodhead, M. 1999. 'Combatting child labour: listen to what the children say'. *Childhood*, 6(1): 27–49.

Yeboah, S.A., and Daniel, M., 2019. '"Silent exclusion": transnational approaches to education and school participation in Ghana'. *Africa Today*, 66(2): 1–26.

Yeboah, S.A., and Daniel, M., 2021. 'Towards a sustainable NGO intervention on child protection: taking indigenous knowledge seriously'. *Development in Practice*, 31(2): 174–184.

Part II

What Accelerated Learning Programmes Teach Us

6 Recognising Children's Funds of Knowledge in Complementary Basic Education (CBE), Northern Ghana

Many studies of the reasons why children fail to access formal schooling draw attention to an irrelevant and alienating curriculum, in addition to their need to farm or contribute to household survival (Ohanu et al., 2021). Asking the question "Why do African schools have declining school attendance and rising dropout rates as well as increasing numbers of out-of-school children?", Ingutia (2020, 500) concludes that the school environment estranges children from learning because:

> The curriculum content in rural schools has minimal relevance to local realities including agriculture, it does not focus on processes and abilities of students to think and solve problems that are relevant to societal needs.

Likewise, in a study of barriers to ensuring inclusive educational environments in sub-Saharan Africa, Le Fanu (2013) noted that many children may be "physically present in school but still feel alienated". Hence, physical inclusion needs to be accompanied by 'curricular inclusion' (47) so that learning experiences "relate to the everyday experience of all children in the school". There is a pressing need, therefore, to "make schooling become a place that African children look forward to going" (Ingutia, 2020, 498). Reconfiguring the curriculum involves listening to children and their families. As Ingutia points out, "children... can contribute ideas to the kinds of school inputs and school curriculum that will boost retention in schools" (509).

This chapter demonstrates how complementary basic education (CBE), an accelerated learning programme (ALP) offered to out-of-school children in Northern Ghana, achieves precisely these goals. It does so through curriculum provision that puts back children's situated experiences and knowledges, as well as the languages with which they are familiar. These provide the basis for a meaningful and enjoyable form of learning that both engages and affirms their identity as learners whilst also producing positive learning outcomes. This chapter starts by outlining two useful concepts – *funds of knowledge* and *funds of identity* – which can help us understand and explain the significance of the CBE curriculum. Both concepts are a way of framing

DOI: 10.4324/9781003185482-9

learning to give value to the knowledges and experiences that children bring to their navigation of hardship. The two concepts were initially developed to highlight the knowledges that children of Mexican immigrants to the US brought to formal education provision, but which were not recognised by their teachers. We describe below how they have since been applied in other contexts of precarity and hardship, noting that children's household knowledges are in danger of being belittled and understood in deficit terms in ways that undermine their ability to engage and to learn.

In the second section, we describe CBE provision in Ghana generally, followed by an analysis of the distinctive challenges of educational marginalisation in Northern Ghana where this ALP was developed. Drawing on extensive data gathered over several years by Sean, Kwame and Ghanaian researchers, we show how CBE, through its curricular and pedagogical strategies, affirms children's agency by recognising and leveraging children's funds of knowledge and funds of identity. This enables them to develop the confidence to complete basic education. We conclude by drawing out the lessons for rethinking the assumptions of the 'learning crisis' narrative.[1]

Funds of Knowledge and Funds of Identity

First developed in the 1980s to challenge deficit notions of children of Mexican immigrants in the US (Gonzáles et al., 2006; Esteban-Guitart, 2023, xii), the concepts of funds of knowledge and funds of identity offer a means of rethinking education provision for constituencies of "less advantaged children" who "suffer historical and structural processes of exclusion, silence and injustice" (Esteban-Guitart, 2023, 2, 3).[2] The concept of 'funds of knowledge' has also been used by Kendrick and Kakuru (2012) to understand children's exercise of agency in child-headed households in Uganda especially their 'resourcefulness, competence and knowledges' in conditions of extreme adversity (397). As far as we are aware, neither concept has been applied to understand the success of ALPs in re-engaging out-of-school children in sub-Saharan Africa.

Whilst variously defined, the concept of *funds of knowledge* refers to the repositories of knowledge which children accumulate informally over time from their lived experiences, and which they bring with them into formal learning environments (Llopart and Esteban-Guitart, 2018). In its initial formulation by Moll et al. (1992, 133), it referenced the "historically accumulated and culturally developed bodies of knowledge and skills essential for household and individual functioning and wellbeing". Knowledge is here understood broadly as encompassing the insights, skills and languages that form part of children's socialisation and survival with peers and elders in challenging contexts (Esteban-Guitart, 2023, preface xiii). Any exclusion or devaluing of children's funds of knowledge in the formal curriculum would be particularly poignant for children living in communities suffering socio-economic precarity.

They might well be seen as 'knowledgeless'. The resulting imperative for targeted curriculum and pedagogical practices for such children is:

> to carry out activities that are pertinent to the students' social and cultural reality, with a focus on their strengths and interests rather than their limitations and alleged deficits, in such a way that they can engage in both effective and meaningful learning processes around a combination of household and academic knowledge.
> (Gaete et al., 2023)

This priority challenges the hierarchical stratification of knowledge in formal academic curriculum that tends to bracket off learning in school from lived experiences and socialisation practices outside of school. Integrating children's funds of knowledge into curriculum content would need to ensure that learning is scaffolded in what children know, is relevant and meaningful and affirms rather than denigrates or denies children's lifeworlds outside of the classroom (Zipin et al., 2012; Zipin, 2020; Esteban Guitart, 2023).

The concept of *funds of identity* (Esteban-Guitart, 2012; Esteban-Guitart and Moll, 2014a, 2014b; Hogg and Volman, 2020; Esteban-Guitart, 2021, 2023) extends the notion of funds of knowledge by drawing attention to how these and the social experiences in which they are embedded contribute to children's developing sense of themselves or their identity and self-understanding (Esteban-Guitart and Moll, 2014b; Hedges, 2015, 2021). As such, funds of identity are a source of self-expression and intrinsic to "a culturally imagined personally valued social position" (Holland and Lachicotte, 2007, 112). This concept was conceived as a corrective to the adult-centricity of funds of knowledge (Esteban-Guitart, 2021, 1) which, in some interpretations, was understood to associate knowledge production wholly with household practices, effectively underestimating the particularities of children's experiences. The latter concept therefore underscores the need for pedagogical practices to:

> take into account the learners' own voices, as well as the contexts of their lives and activities, and their own particular skills, hobbies and knowledge – independently of whether they are derived from their families' funds of knowledge or from elsewhere.
> (Esteban-Guitart, 2021)

As Zipin et al. (2012) explain:

> the aim is to engage learners from "less advantaged" regions and social-structural positions, through curricular activity that resonates with knowledge contents and ways of knowing which have meaningful use in sites of learners' lives beyond school where dispositions and identities are deeply and intimately grounded.
> (181)

Funds of knowledge and funds of identity are therefore 'mutually constitutive and interdependent' (Esteban-Guitart, 2021, 3) when addressing the educational needs of communities experiencing educational marginalisation.

There are a number of reasons why these concepts are helpful. First, they re-valorise children's knowledges and experiences as resources for learning, envisaging a creative pedagogical continuum between familiar and unfamiliar knowledge (Subero et al., 2017; Hedges, 2012). In this way, drawing on children's funds of knowledge may initiate and support their development of those forms of "powerful knowledge" associated with specialised disciplines (Young and Muller, 2013, 229).

Second, these two concepts root learning in the contexts and socialisation practices of children's lived experiences and third, they bring back the prior agency of learners, erased in the 'learning crisis' narrative. Children are recognised as having arrived at learning environments with existing knowledges and skills – they are repositioned as 'already knowers'. In effect, a curriculum that embeds children's funds of knowledge is more likely to result in participatory learning approaches in which they draw on what they know and contribute to forms of teacher-pupil talk essential to meaningful learning (Alexander, 2008). Fourth, this framing of learning notably contrasts with the pedagogical model of the teacher as the sole transmitter of knowledge in the classrooms, an approach that effectively silences pupils' knowledges, leaving them passive and non-participatory.

Finally, leveraging children's funds of knowledge reverses conventional power relationships between teachers and marginalised children and their families. This:

> dismantles the deficit thinking that exists in education by (re)conceptualising all learners as capable and valued individuals, regardless of their social, economic and cultural background.
> (Esteban-Guitart, 2021, 2)

This is achievable through developing positive relationships between families and schools and by designing culturally sensitive and contextualised curricular activities, thus 'legitimising the experiences of learners' (Esteban-Guitart, 2021, 2). The reinforcement of home-school links is particularly important here in addressing the needs of out-of-school children in sub-Saharan Africa, given the key role of parents and communities in decisions on whether children attend school or not.

The value of these two concepts in rethinking the assumptions of the 'learning crisis' is that they avoid the tendency to an individualised understanding of learners (noted as a feature of the learning crisis narrative in Part 1) by validating collective as well as individual funds of knowledge held by children and their households (Chesworth, 2016). Most importantly, the concepts of funds of knowledge and funds of identity restore an expansive understanding of learning as a situated socio-cultural practice. Hence, they enable a rethinking of what is meant by 'learner-centredness' in a meaningful and grounded rather than generic and gestural sense. As Esteban-Guitart (2023) observes "both notions invite us to consider the learner as the core of the educational activity, along with his or her multiple spaces of relationships, ranging from family to peer group" (3). So, the "curriculum can be linked to their experiences, their artefacts and the contexts of their lives".

Armed with these concepts, we describe below the emergence of CBE programme across Ghana before focusing on the distinctive challenges of educational marginalisation in the Northern region, the site of our case study.

Complementary Basic Education in Ghana in Northern Ghana

The CBE programme in Northern Ghana was set up in 2012 and has been operational ever since. Initially, it was managed and funded by the UK Department for International Development and US Aid in partnership with ten civil society organisations undertaking to implement the scheme in those rural communities with large numbers of out-of-school children. By 2018, CBE had been adopted for nationwide implementation by the Ghanaian government (Carter et al., 2023).

The programme is characterised by innovative, creative and flexible approaches to the curriculum provision associated with non-formal education programmes, and specifically oriented to the needs and lifestyles of communities marginalised from formal education systems (DeStefano et al., 2007; Longden, 2013; Sherris et al., 2014; Shinohara, 2021). It offers children aged 8–14 years who have previously been out-of-school, nine months' instruction focusing on literacy and numeracy with lesson content that is directly relevant to the social and economic lives of learners and their communities. Hence, classes are scheduled during afternoons to accommodate the farming and household demands of children's families. There are no fees. Textbooks and materials are free. Class sizes are limited to 25. Facilitators are recruited from local communities and therefore know the contexts and daily lives of the children and their families. They are given a three-week training course and encouraged to use activity-based and participatory instructional strategies. After completing nine months of CBE, children are supported to transition into the closest local public school.

As we write this, CBE is offered in 12 different community languages: Asante Twi, Brifour, Dagaree, Dagbani, Ewe, Gonja, Gurune, Kasem, Kusaal, Likpakpa, Mampruli and Sissali. The programme is implemented in 50 districts in the Northern, Upper East, Upper West, Brong Ahafo and Ashanti Regions. Between 2012 and 2018, the programme enrolled 248,556 out-of-school children, achieving a completion rate of over 95% in each year of its operation. Of significance is its very high completion rate for girls, also over 95%. The percentage of children making a transition into formal primary school rose from 84% in 2012 to 95.2% in 2017 (Government of Ghana, 2018). Explaining its decision to scale up the current CBE programme nationwide, the Ghanaian government's Education Strategic Plan 2018–30 (21) recognises that the "CBE programme is providing education in the community to thousands of out-of-school children to allow them to transition into mainstream education and so improve access to school".

The learning outcomes of the programme are also very impressive. Kwame and his colleagues' longitudinal studies of learning outcomes of 2,424 children between 2016 and 2017 tracked their progress from the start of CBE through to the end of their first year in transition schools (Akyeampong, 2018; Akyeampong et al., 2018; Carter et al., 2020). In 2016/17, only 30% of enrolled children at the beginning of the programme were able to identify letters in the local language. By the end of the programme, 57% of children were able to identify letters, an improvement of 26% points. Single number identification improved from 50% to 70% during the nine-month period. The achievements of CBE students in local language literacy, English and Mathematics at the end of their first year of transition into government schools, also compared favourably to those of non-CBE students. The evidence points, at the very least, to the successful nature of the CBE programme in re-engaging learners previously marginalised from formal educational provision, both in terms of their cognitive development and their motivation and commitment.

This evidence, however, does not mitigate the extreme educational challenges faced by out-of-school children in regions such as Northern Ghana. It is in this context, that the CBE programme had to seriously consider alternative curricular and pedagogic models.

Educational challenges in Northern Ghana

In effect, the development of the CBE programme was the result of the failure of existing formal education provision to address the needs of 'poor children' and their families in Northern Ghana. Internationally provided evidence about the out-of-school children recognised the distinctive scale of the problem in West and Sub-Saharan Africa by comparison with other regions of the world (UNESCO, 2022). The Ghanaian Ministry of Education Sector Plan (Government of Ghana, 2018, 6) noted that, whilst improvements in enrolments in basic education have been made nationally, around 450,000 children were still out-of-school in 2015, with the majority of whom coming from poor households and living in the Northern region, comprising Northern, Upper East and Upper West administrative areas. This region also had the highest illiteracy rate in Ghana, at 65%, very low performance on national educational assessments at primary level such as the Basic Education Certificate Examination, and a long history of inter-generational marginalisation from formal schooling with high rates of children dropping out-of-school (Government of Ghana, 2018). Gender disparities have also been strikingly greater here than in other regions. The Education Sector Plan (Government of Ghana, 2018) notes that:

while gender may not be the main driver of inequality at the basic level, emerging evidence indicates that adolescent girls' exclusion is reinforced when different sources of inequality – poverty, gender, geography – interact with one another.

(Government of Ghana, 2018, 6)

Failure to access the formal school system has been related to a number of supply and demand factors (Government of Ghana, 2018; Akyeampong et al., 2018), some of which are listed in Table 6.1.

Moreover, children frequently come from communities whose language may not be used as the medium of instruction in government schools, thus making early learning experiences frustrating (Carter et al., 2020). The primary and secondary school curriculum is also widely perceived to be irrelevant to children's and young people's socio-economic needs, lives and aspirations (Kwao, 2017; Okrah et al., 2020).

Historical structural, socio-economic and environmental factors have played a major part in the educational marginalisation found in Northern region of Ghana (Oteng-Ababio et al., 2017; Amagnya, 2020; Kambala, 2023). The scattered nature of community settlements and an absence of convenient school provision are linked to the low population density of the region that covers over a third of the country's land area but is home to only around 10% of its population. Harsh and unpredictable climatic conditions undermine productive farming, increasing the likelihood of food insecurity and economic shocks. Limited access to potable water, poor road conditions, lack of

Table 6.1 Supply and demand factors affecting educational provision and enrolment in Northern Ghana

Supply factors	*(a) Demand factors*
An acute shortage of trained teachers	Household poverty and families' inability to afford school fees and other indirect costs such as uniforms, transport, books and registration fees
A shortage of schools and classrooms located near the region's scattered and remote community settlements	A lack of schools for remote communities so that children have to walk long distances
Regional inequities in the national educational budget allocations that reduce funding for educational resources to the region.	The expectation that children will contribute to household survival strategies, such as subsistence farming, household chores or searching for food, rather than attending school
A lack of alignment of the school timetable to the seasonal and daily work schedules of rural communities.	Poor functionality of parent-teacher associations at the local level which means that parental support necessary to ensure pupils attend school is frequently lacking

adequate health as well as educational provision (Ghana Statistical Service, 2019) are also all legacies of long-standing state underinvestment in the region's socio-economic development (Abdulai and Hulme, 2015; Oteng-Ababio et al., 2017). Government spending on social services and infrastructure in the North is currently low compared to the rest of the country. Communities in the region consequently face endemic poverty, illiteracy as well as high rates of infant and child mortality and few economic opportunities. This makes the region an interesting case within which to study the limitations of the conventional school system in reaching underserved and deprived populations with basic education.

Family survival in such precarious circumstances means that "participation in education is often a luxury" (Akyeampong, 2004, 41). Ethnographic studies of community attitudes to learning (Hashim, 2005) in the region suggest a highly conflicted relationship with formal education. This is because of the widespread belief that it offers only limited benefits and indeed might alienate children from their necessary contribution to household survival. For these communities, child labour is recognised as a socio-economic necessity rather than being despised as an obstacle to education (Akyeampong, 2009). These structural and cultural issues throw into sharp relief the challenges faced by any intervention seeking to reintegrate out-of-school children. In this context, it is valuable to consider just how the proponents of CBE sought to confront these challenges through the timing, language and content of its educational provision. Below, using the concepts of 'funds of knowledge' and 'funds of identity', we show first how we undertook on-site research, illuminating why and how the CBE programme in this seriously deprived area oriented learning to the knowledges and experiences of children who attend.

Data Gathering: A Funds of Knowledge Approach

The analysis of funds of knowledge in CBE provision draws on data collected between 2018 and 2023 which explored its pedagogical strategies, curriculum

Table 6.2 Data gathering on the use of funds of knowledge in CBE provision

Dates	(b) Focus	(c) Methods
2018	Facilitators' instructional practices at 15 CBE centres, drawing on 40 lesson observations (Akyeampong, 2018), pedagogical practices of CBE classes and their impact on learning outcomes and experiences of CBE children	Lesson observations • Interviews with 15 facilitators (teachers)

(*Continued*)

Table 6.2 (Continued)

Dates	(b) Focus	(c) Methods
2018	a Mixed methods research into learning experiences and outcomes of children, from starting CBE to end of first year, in 15 government primary schools Learning outcomes through reading and numeracy assessments Subjective experiences of children during CBE and in transition to government schools	• Use of assessment tests in reading and numeracy at start of CBE, start of transition school and end of first year • 40 FGDs with children; parents and families; community elders; 12 teachers in government schools 12 facilitators. • 30 lesson observations of CBE graduates in formal schools (English, Mathematics) • 40 Individual interviews with CBE graduates after lessons • Role play and discussion with children
2023	Five CBE centres serving rural communities in Sene East and Tolon in Northern Ghana	• Interviews with 20 children, parents and community members, 5 facilitators • Ten lesson observations
2023	GILLBT involved in writing CBE instructional materials. CBE Co-ordinators' Managers in Ministry of Education/local NGOs implementing CBE	• Interviews with five linguists involved in preparation and production of CBE materials • Interviews with Ministry officials and representatives of local NGOs with long-standing involvement in CBE and earlier related programmes (School for Life)

content and impact on children, their transitions into government schools as well as community engagement in diverse rural contexts of Northern Ghana.[3] This is summarised in Table 6.2.

A strength of the evidence collected on the meanings and experiences of CBE provision lies in the wide range of stakeholders consulted including children, parents and guardians, facilitators, community members, linguists, teachers, writers and publishers involved in the production of instructional materials, and local implementing NGOs. Over time, our collection of data enabled a sustained, iterative dialogue with communities whose children have experienced CBE constituted a form of 'horizontal knowledge production' (Manuel-Navarrete et al., 2021). The research process was therefore recuperative, amplifying the funds of knowledge perspectives and experiences of a range of groups with long-standing familiarity with communities suffering educational marginalisation in the Northern region of Ghana. This rationale for data collection sought to rectify the evidential imbalance of EFA reports in which were missing the voices of grassroots community-based actors and those of families and children most affected by educational interventions to address marginalisation (Alexander, 2015).

It was particularly important to retrieve the perspectives and experiences of children in our research if a shift in the power asymmetries in knowledge production was to be achieved. Hence, child-friendly data-gathering methods were used. Local researchers who spoke the various mother tongue languages conducted interviews and focus group discussions (FGDs). They spent some time getting to know children and their families by visiting their homes before interviewing. These visits were analogous to teachers' quasi-ethnographic visits to the households of Mexican children in order to establish their funds of knowledge in the original iteration of this approach (Moll et al., 2006). Especially informative was the use of role play to elicit children's experiences of their learning. CBE graduates were asked to dramatise a CBE classroom and a typical class in their new school. This was followed by group discussion and reflection on their choices, and how they presented the similarities and differences between CBE and formal schooling. Subsequent FGDs enabled exploration of children's feelings and subjective experiences.

A longitudinal qualitative approach also enabled us to develop a temporal perspective on the impact of CBE provision. Interviews, FGDs and lesson observations were conducted with children during their time in CBE, and a year later after they had transitioned into government schools. This enabled us to understand the continuing impact of their experience of CBE in their imaginations and memories as well as their experiences in navigating formal educational provision. All these data-gathering methods sought to follow children as 'experts of their lives' and 'decision makers in education' (Cox and Dyer, 2010, 30).

The Embedded Funds of Knowledge in CBE

The funds of knowledge we uncovered through our research were embedded and leveraged in diverse aspects of CBE provision. Below, we outline these and discuss the implications for community engagement and on children's identity as learners over time especially during their transition to government schools. We focus first on the preparation of CBE textbooks and instructional materials and curriculum development processes, then on facilitators' pedagogical strategies, community engagement and finally on children's reflections on their experiences of learning, revealing how, when and where the recognised how their funds of knowledge came into play. The perspectives of a range of stakeholders involved in CBE ensure that the voices and experiences of those groups who are usually marginalised in discussions of the learning crisis are recentred.

Partnerships and planning

The preparation of CBE textbooks in local languages is a joint undertaking involving collaboration between Ghanaian linguists and, in particular, the Ghanaian Institute of Linguistics, Literacy and Bible Translation (GILLBT) and teachers with long-standing experience in teaching in rural communities in Northern Ghana. It also includes education specialists from local civil society organisations and NGOs with long-standing experience in offering ALPs in Northern Ghana (e.g. School for Life) as well as representatives from the local Ghana Education Service in the region's capital, Tamale. This partnership brings together diverse groups from different professional backgrounds who converge in their long-standing grassroots knowledge of communities in the Northern region. As such, they represent an innovative and localised form of educational collaboration by integrating the voices and experiences of those rarely involved in curriculum development (Alexander, 2015). Such partnerships are to be valued as a small step in reversing what has been referred to as the long-standing disabling of localised curriculum development and the privileging of outside knowledges in African contexts, dating back to the colonial era (Dunne and Adzahlie-Mensah, 2016). In this way, CBE in Ghana attests to the importance of the 'often neglected significance of civil society' in promoting educational innovations (Carter et al., 2023).

Of particular importance is the role of the GILLBT whose members provide orthographic expertise and knowledge of the sometime-complex linguistic landscape of local communities. They enable the translation of CBE instructional materials into local languages. Already involved in a process of codifying Ghana's minority languages, producing texts on farming and politics, as well as Biblical translations, GILLBT's involvement in CBE meant that it could extend its linguistic research into the field of educational provision. Its pivotal participation in CBE led to the key insights of linguists being put into the curriculum development processes. Such locally grounded linguistic knowledge, as noted in Chapter 3, is too often absent from educational planning that ignores fundamental language of instruction challenges. Explaining the vision of CBE and of the coalitions preparing instructional materials, one linguist from GILLBT commented:

> You teach a child who has just stepped into the school environment in a language that the child does not understand… I'm coming from the local environment…what I understand is the local language… I am brought up to socialise in my locality… I know things about my environment… I know things about my family and friends…I enter formal education and I am taught in English language that I don't understand in order to grab concepts…so that was where the

fundamental limitations were observed...and that was where the shift to emphasise mother tongue literacy was grounded... a child needs to learn from known to unknown ...and from the mother tongue to be able to understand the principles, concepts and values... To use that as a basis to know.

Converging around this educational mission, with experts in local languages are driven by a commitment to rooting learning in children's situated knowledges, including their languages, thereby making learning meaningful and relevant.[4]

CBE instructional materials

CBE textbooks are notable for their inclusion of images of artefacts, objects, people and the local environment that shape various aspects of the lives and experiences of children in Northern Ghana (see images 6.1 to 6.5). For example, Literacy Primer I shows beetles, pots, bicycles, acacia trees, frogs, an oil lamp and farm animals. There are also visual depictions of local farming practices – cows grazing and women and children using cutlasses to plant seeds. There is an illustration of a fisherman about to cast a net, referencing fishing which is a key source of subsistence in some parts of Northern Ghana as well as local economic activities with which children would be familiar, such as women selling goods at a local marketplace. There are images representing hygiene and health practices of households, children brushing their teeth and combing their hair, young boys cleaning the courtyard, a woman cooking food in a pot and a man drawing water from a borehole. Inter-generational socialisation practices are also referenced, notably a picture of a grandfather who sits looking pensive with a stick and another of children playing games. Individual images refer implicitly to the health challenges these communities face, such as mosquito bites.

These images concretise, make visual and reflect back to children their everyday social realities. They are also starting points for questions that invite the children to reflect on them and to share what they know – in other words, demonstrating their funds of knowledge. For example, shown in Image 6.1, are the images of shea nut and Dawadawa trees which is followed by questions that invite children to share their experiential knowledge about the important role these trees play in contributing to household subsistence and ecological safety in this region of Ghana (Hatskevich, Jenicek and Darkwah, 2011; Kent, 2018, 7; Derbile et al., 2022).

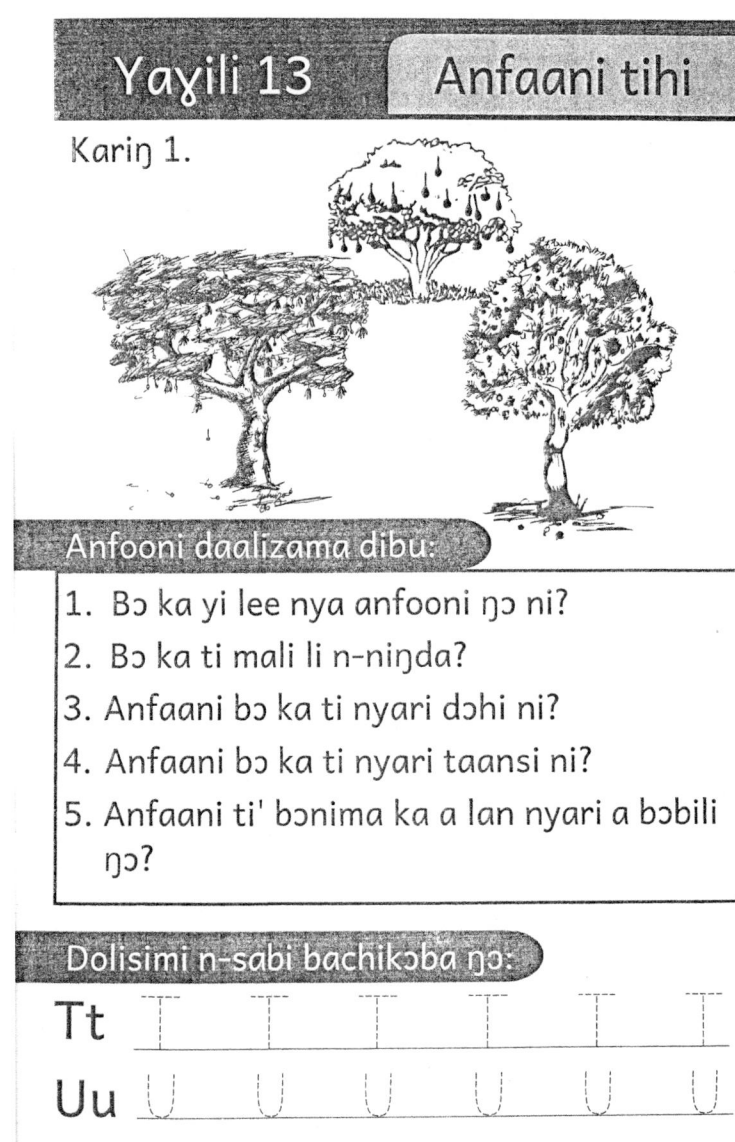

Image 6.1 Productive trees.

Picture interpretation

1 What do you see in this picture?
2 What do we use it for?

3 What benefits do we get from a Dawadawa tree?
4 What benefits do we get from shea nuts?
5 What other beneficial trees do you see in this area?

Fishing is another such reflexive activity where the image and questions invite children to comment and share their views on the purpose of the fishing net, perhaps referencing their use as substitutes for mosquito nets, which is a common practice in Northern Ghanaian communities (Image 6.2).

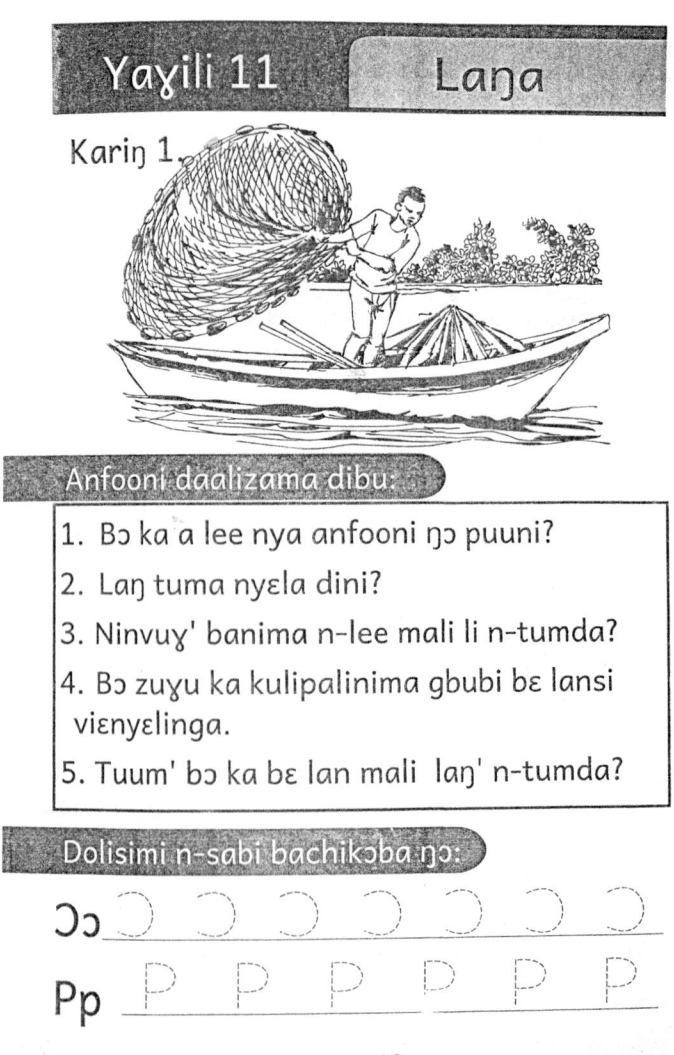

Image 6.2 Fishing.

Recognising Children's Funds of Knowledge 147

Unit 11: Fishing net

Picture interpretation

1 What do you see in this picture?
2 What do we use a fishing net for?
3 Which category of people use fishing nets?
4 Why do fishing folks hold their fishing net very well?
5 What else do they use fishing nets for?

Image 6.3 showing local animals invites children to share their experience of another mode of economic subsistence – that of domestic animal rearing – of which most have first-hand knowledge.

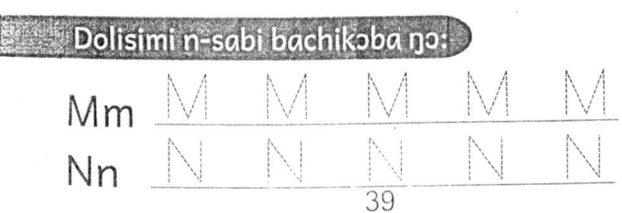

Image 6.3 Domestic animals.

148   *Reconceptualising the Learning Crisis in Africa*

Unit 10: Animals at home (cow)

Picture interpretation

1 What can you see from this picture?
2 What are the benefits of a cow to your family?
3 What do we use milk for?
4 What are we supposed to do before drinking milk?
5 What is the role of a veterinary officer towards animals?

In contrast, Image 6.4 that shows a grandfather invites children to share their experience of elders and the attitudes to them in their local community.

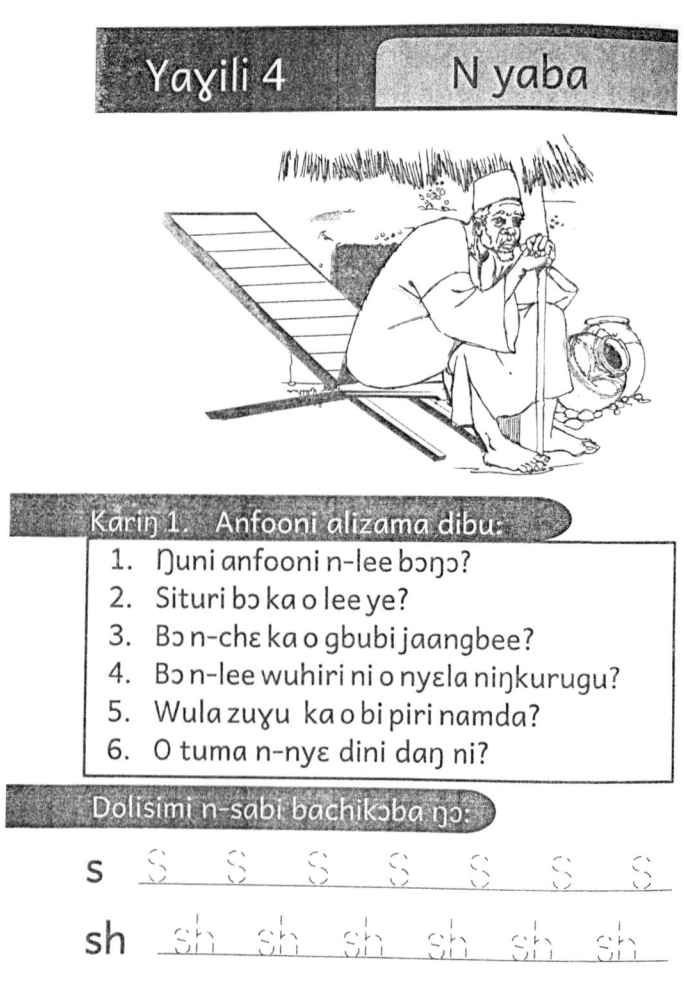

Image 6.4 Grandfather.

Unit 6.4: Grandfather

Picture interpretation

1 Whose picture is this?
2 What dress is he wearing?
3 Why is he holding a walking stick?
4 What shows he is an old man?
5 Why is he not wearing sandals?
6 What role does he play in a family?

The picture in Image 6.5 shows a boy sweeping a compound. This represents a point of departure for children to reflect on their contributions to household cleanliness.

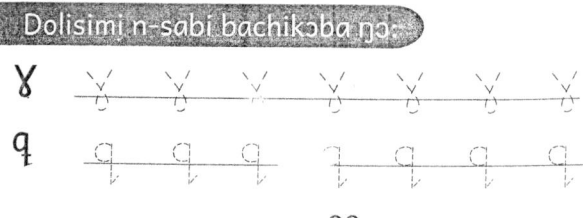

Image 6.5 Cleaning up.

Unit 6: Major roles children play

Picture interpretation

1 What can you see from this picture?
2 What are they doing?
3 What kinds of work do children perform at home?
4 What kinds of work do girls perform?
5 What kinds of work do boys perform?
6 Is it good for girls and boys?

Such visual imagery, well known as a medium to promote learning through concretising ideas, works together with the questions in CBE textbooks that trigger children's views and insights as a starting point for building literacy skills and, especially oral and written communication. By referencing the economic activities, household practices and forms of sociality that structure the children's lives the images alongside the questions orient the CBE curriculum around what Zipin (2020, 111) refers to as the 'problems that matter' approach. Together, images and words invite children to share and co-construct knowledge, positioning them as proactive and agentic as knowers. CBE instructional materials therefore shift 'power and agency' to learners (Rodriguez, 2013, 87).

Representing such familiar features of their local environment, the CBE textbooks also affirm children's funds of identity. The references to their work on farms, their contributions to household hygiene and economic survival, their relationships with peers and elders and their pleasure in playing in their local environment mirror children's multifaceted exercise of agency and the informal learning they acquire as a result. Their daily living is structured by their encounter with what is referenced in all these images (Esteban-Guitart, 2023, xiii). Such learning approaches return respect and dignity to the lives of 'poor children' and communities which are too often denied in deficit constructions of those experiencing poverty (as discussed in Chapter 2). In this context, facilitators in the CBE programme also make use of their own funds of knowledge to complement their child-focused instructional materials in their pedagogical practices.

Facilitator's pedagogical strategies

CBE facilitators are selected on the basis that they live in the communities and are able to speak the local language. They are usually chosen by the community. They are aware that their physical and social proximity is a pedagogical strength since it gives them a situated understanding of the contexts of the lives of children that they were helping. They are also familiar with the children's families and communities. For example, when asked how well he knew the community where he was facilitating the CBE, one facilitator commented: "Very well, because I live in the community, and I grew up here. Most children assist their parents in farming and fishing or even trading. That is how we are able to cater for them". The facilitators we met were also noticeably impassioned when talking about some of the hardships faced by themselves and the communities in which they taught. One pointed out that "we lack portable drinking water, the only available source of drinking water in the community is a dam which we share with animals". Sanitation challenges were recognised as a major health hazard: "the lack of toilets increases our vulnerability to infectious diseases". Facilitators were also aware of the reasons why children dropped out-of-school. One recognised that "because of lack of finance, they are made to stay home and assist us on the farm". Another noted that children were dropping out of formal schooling "because they are not able to comprehend anything in class… and then their parents decide to rather let them learn a trade".

In other contexts of schooling using a 'funds of knowledge' approach, teachers who lived outside of the local communities visited households to increase their understanding of children's experiences and knowledges so as to in help integrate them into their lessons (González et al., 2006; Esteban-Guitart, 2023, 9). The newer community-based model of CBE in Northern Ghana bypassed the need for this preparatory research by ensuring that facilitators were already familiar with children's physical and social environment.

Table 6.3 provides a selection of comments in which facilitators from five CBE programmes in Northern Ghana explained how they used children's funds of knowledge in their lessons.

Facilitators recognised the diverse pedagogical benefits of referring to children's funds of knowledge in their literacy and numeracy lessons. They pointed out that by using tangible objects and artefacts to concretise and exemplify, they were able to motivate, engage and encourage children to participate and contribute to lessons. These references enabled learning to resonate with children's exercise of agency in their own roles as contributors to farming, fishing, petty trading, environmental hygiene and protection of the local environment. Facilitators also indicated how this framing of educational provision grounded learning activities in a range of places, inside and outside the classroom. This extended to the creative use of sand, stones and fruits in the local environment (see Image 6.6). In contexts in which resources to support learning are scarce, such ingenuity enables meaningful learning to take place. Facilitators' use of these children's funds of knowledge supports the development of the disciplinary skills of literacy and numeracy as well as environmental and health education. It enables them to successfully engage with curriculum content associated with 'powerful knowledge' (Young and Muller, 2013) at the same time.

Table 6.3 Facilitators' use of the 'funds of knowledge' approach

Children's funds of knowledge	(d) Pedagogical applications
The natural environment	"I make them pick stones, sticks and local fruit and use them as counters when teaching them numeracy". (*See* Image 6.6) "In literacy lessons, I make them step out of the class and use the plain ground as their writing area to write the alphabets in Dagbani".
Use of the local environment to build literacy skills	"For literacy, when identifying the sounds and alphabets, I identify it with objects in the environment as well as in our local names. Example /a/ for 'Ati' … which is a tree in English. It helps them better understand the lesson. They participate in the lesson and add some examples".
Local stones and trees	"Yes, I use stones and trees to explain living and non-living things. The benefits that we derive from plants and the river. I use them because they are readily available, and children relate to them better for easy understanding. I use trees in the environment to teach them the names of trees and their medicinal purposes".
Mango trees	"Also, I use mango tree as an example because it is well known for its fruits, shade and beauty which is everywhere in the community. The children also enjoy eating and harvesting mangoes. The children get excited when such examples are used and share more about trees".
Farming activities	"I use trees, animals, and houses around us in my demonstrations which the children already know about. I show them houses and their local names and the reasons why people should build. I also taught animal rearing and its benefits. It helps them understand the lessons better… because we are farmers, I usually use examples relating to the farm activities to teach. For example, I ask them questions like how many seeds have you planted today?"
Petty trading	"For the learners who help their parents sell, I teach them that, someone should buy items worth 2 cedis from them and pays them with an amount of 5 cedis, they should subtract 2 from the 5 and give the change to the person. To make this understandable for them in class, I make them use counters in the form of sticks for the practical calculation. This helps them understand additions and subtractions even out of class settings".
Nutrition	"The children know it's good to eat but they do not know the essence and kinds of food that will be healthy to them. This is something I teach them that enhances what they know already".
Shea butter production	"Yes, we sometimes visit women who make kulikuli and shea butter to learn from them how they are made. I usually put the children in groups to discuss what they have learnt, and this group work has made them develop teamwork".
Local cultural practices	"I always make references to our way of life which is known to them in teaching. For examples, our festivals, songs and dance…we learn them… the 'agbaza' dance is a special dance here which I use to teach them of their culture and also to entertain the class".

Image 6.6 Numeracy lesson using local pebbles.

Community engagement

The incorporation of familiar knowledges into curriculum provision intersects with trust building with children's families (Esteban-Guitart, 2023, xiii) and with high levels of community engagement to support children's learning. This was evident in the relationships that CBE facilitators built with local communities in Northern Ghana. Facilitators spoke of their warm relationships with families, resulting from frequent visits to children's homes, and ongoing communication and contact to discuss their attendance, progress, health and well-being. One facilitator commented:

> Once I visit the parents, I tell them of the learning performance and advise them to always check the children's books when they return from school. Literate parents are told how to help their low performing children. The relationship is cordial. When the learners are late for class, I go to their various homes to entreat parents to push their children to report to class on time. They also understand and cooperate. It encourages collaboration in ensuring the children are in class on time.

Such comments attest to parental appreciation a holistic and relational approach to their children's learning. The CBE approach was recognised for its concern not just for cognitive development but also for considering how children's learning fitted into their daily lives. In turn, the facilitators appreciated the interest shown by parents in their children's learning as a result of such personal contact. One noted:

> Some members of the community visit to see what is going on in the class and encourage me to teach the children while also encouraging the children to learn hard. This really motivates me seeing the community support. The chief constantly passes by to also motivate us.

The parents we interviewed appreciated facilitators' understanding of the challenges they faced. As one parent commented: "Our facilitator was selected by us, the community members, based on the good qualities we have seen in him. So yes, we like him and appreciate the work he is doing for us in this community". Families were pleased with what they saw as the care and compassion towards their children demonstrated by the facilitator: "Our facilitator is very good; I have witnessed him teach on several occasions and I must say he is patient and always willing to assist the children to understand whatever he teaches them". There was a consensus amongst parents interviewed that facilitators' knowledge of the local community strengthened their ability to teach effectively: "it helps her to perform more in teaching the children because she is one of us".

Some parents commented on how mother tongue instruction had contributed to better peer and inter-generational communication: "my children now understand my mother tongue very well, this will help them communicate effectively with others". The impact of CBE on children's behaviour and contributions to household routines was another welcomed aspect – with a parent commenting:

> The CBE programme has made our children disciplined to learn, and this has prevented them from loitering aimlessly… they carry out their house chores diligently, keep themselves neat and practice good hygiene.

Many others pointed to the practical benefits of lesson content. One parent said that "Our children were not able to read telephone numbers but now they are able to read, write and save numbers with contact names on our phones". Another observed that "there was a time someone sent me a note in Dagbani, I couldn't read it, but my child was able to read and explain the content of the note to me".

Families also perceived CBE classes as contributing to children's exercise of agency. Parents were enthusiastic about the connections between the content of learning and their economic survival strategies. In one case, the parent reported his pleasure that "the facilitator is teaching our children best farming practices that are helpful to my farming activities". One father went so far as to say that "the children are now motivated to help us more on the farm, just so that they will be able to attend the lessons in the afternoon… this has improved my yields".

Recognising Children's Funds of Knowledge 155

Image 6.7 Facilitator taking CBE children around their local environment as part of a lesson on health and sanitation.

In addition, recognition of the contribution made by the CBE programme extended to community health and the community's cultural, environmental and socio-economic well-being (see Images 6.7 and 6.8). Hence, one parent commented:

> The CBE programme has made us increase our cleanliness and thereby improve our health. Our children have learned to keep good hygiene by covering their food. They have learned how to wash their hands first before eating and this has helped to improve their health. This has led to a reduction in sicknesses in the community.

Parental interest and enthusiasm for their children's learning were galvanised by the range of ways in which the CBE programme aligned with their daily economic, social and cultural routines, concerns and aspirations. Of particular note was their appreciation of how CBE provision encouraged children to be aware of protecting their local environment, an important element given the distinctive vulnerability of the world's poorest communities to the effects of climate change (Leichenko and Silva, 2014; Hallegatte and Rozenberg, 2017). CBE lessons encouraged children to protect their local ecology by

Image 6.8 Facilitator pointing out cow dung and explaining the dangers of spreading disease through flies.

avoiding deforestation: "the children are taught about the dangers of cutting trees and the importance of planting trees. Even in my house I had wanted to fell a tree down, but my child discouraged me". This view was complemented by the role which CBE provision played in affirming children's involvement in local cultural events – with one parent commenting: "festivals such as fire festival and Damba are occasions we celebrate with our children. They learn them from home but get the understanding at the CBE". In all of the communities reached by CBE, there was appreciation of the work done to affirm community pride, its language and ethnic identity. For example, one parent commented; "I am very happy the lessons are taught in Dagbani because this is what we are, and our language is what makes us as a people". At a practical level, the programme's synchronisation with daily work schedules of communities was also a bonus: "We are happy now we have the CBE programme class being implemented in this community. Now our children can go to the farm in the morning and the class in the afternoon".

We turn now to analyse the data that we collected from children in the villages who attended their local CBE programme using a funds of identity approach. In particular, we analyse children's reflections on their experiences of learning and its impact on their identity and agency as learners.

Children's Funds of Identity

The children in Northern Ghana whom we interviewed described the range of activities they were involved with outside of their CBE class. Thus one noted, "I prepare local drinks to sell, also do house chores and go to the bush to pick shea nuts. I sweep, wash dishes, and go and fetch water in order to help my Mom". Others emphasised their roles in contributing to their family's farming productivity:

> I take care of the farm and weed; At the farm, I plant maize, groundnut, cassava, and pepper on my grandparents' farm; we are sometimes asked to help our elder brothers who have completed school to take the cattle grazing: I weed, plant and harvest crops such as yam, maize and cassava. I also take care of animals, fowls especially by directing them to their cage when night falls.

A number spoke of their involvement in fishing, "I dive to take out wood and sand when we cast our net. Sometimes I go to the riverside to set bamboo for fishing". Such comments underline these children's multi-tasking agency in contributing to household and community survival strategies.

In this context, it was noticeable that the children whom Sean and local researchers interviewed talked positively about their CBE learning experiences. They located their learning experiences in their aspirations for their futures such as being prepared to make the transition to formal school. As one commented:

> If I am able to learn how to read and write, I will be able to become an educated person in future...the literacy skills I learn 'a, e, i, o, u' will help me to be able to read and write and further my education at the formal school.

They recognised the educational opportunity afforded by their CBE classes. For example:

> Our friends attend formal school, and the CBE classes has also given us an opportunity to also attend school......I like it because we learn a lot at the classes... how to recite alphabets in the local language such as 'a, e i, o, u and 1, 2, 3, 4, 5.

Such comments suggest a level of reflexivity about the potential benefits of their learning. In commenting on their learning and explaining why they enjoyed CBE classes; children also recognised and appreciated the practical continuum with their lives outside. Table 6.4 provides a selection of the connections they made.

By drawing upon the artefacts, objects, experiences and socio-economic and socio-cultural contexts that generated their sense of themselves, such

Table 6.4 How CBE classes connect with life outside the classroom

Child's comment	(e) Funds of identity
"I learn how to read and write in my local language…. I am now able to read numbers and alphabets in Dagbani"	Mother tongue
"I also learn addition and subtraction in selling porridge and also in class. For instance, when I'm selling and someone buys ghc20 worth of the thing and gives me ghc50, I have to give out ghc30 change. So, in class madam will write 50 and 20 under it then she will ask that when you subtract 20 from 50 what will you get? Then I respond that it's 30".	Trading
"We cook in the house, and when we come to the class then our madam will ask us that what things do we need when you want to cook? After learning in class we also do story telling which we hear about sometimes in our homes".	Cooking
"We learn about farming. The tree gives us air, fruits, provides shades. Our teacher also said the tree helps us to breathe and it also serves as food when we are hungry".	Local ecology
"Yes, I use the knowledge in making calculations to sell my local drinks and now no one can cheat me because I know how to make transactions".	Trading
"Yes. It opens my mind to understand and it's no more difficult for me to speak the local language (Ewe). My Dad is an Ada and my mom an Ewe, but I was sent to my dad's hometown, so I forgot how to speak the Ewe, but the class has helped".	Ethnic identity and language
"It is because it is my tribe, it's my language, that's why I like it".	
"Our facilitator teaches us how to farm and I help my parents farm. He teaches us how to cultivate cassava, pepper and okra".	Farming
"In my community most people like reading so if you can't read it becomes a problem. I can read the bible at my local church".	Faith practices. Status in communities

comments suggest that CBE teaching affirmed children's funds of identity (Esteban-Guitart, 2021, 2). Within these children's imaginaries, their experience of learning in CBE classes formed an important aspect of their exercise of agency throughout the day. This appeared in the purposefulness with which one girl explained her everyday life and decision-making: "I wash dishes after class, in the morning I help sell porridge, after that I go to the shop to sell water and when it's 2pm then I tell my mom it's time to go to school". Such comments attest to the impact of CBE in enabling children with a highly contingent relationship with formal education provision to integrate a positive experience of learning into their sense of themselves and as such to their self-efficacy. This positive learner identity was maintained during their navigation of their later transition into government schools.

Children's staying power in transition schools

Our observations of those children who graduated from CBE into government schools suggested high levels of participation in the latter schools' instructional processes and the presence of generally positive attitudes to learning in this new learning environment. It was particularly true of the high achievers, both boys and girls, who transitioned from CBE into formal schooling. FGDs with CBE graduates revealed how they noticed the differences between CBE and formal school provision, for example:

- the different timings and duration of lessons that made government school less convenient to attend;
- the need to wear uniforms;
- the use of corporal punishment;
- English as the language of instruction and of textbooks;
- a wider set of subjects;
- difficulties in understanding their teacher; extra costs for books and pens; and
- fewer opportunities to sing and dance.

Nevertheless, the group discussions also revealed that the CBE experience had a continuing impact on the learner identity they had developed. All CBE graduates brought to their transition a positive experience of their prior learning in CBE which, in some ways, shaped what they valued in their new environment. Some expressed appreciation of CBE for having been a vehicle of transition into formal school as one high-achieving girl observed: "the CBE is good because when you finish the CBE you can now come to formal school" (Akyeampong et al., 2018). Many expressed pride in having acquired learning skills, including reading and writing skills which had given them the tools to take pleasure in extending their knowledge. Another high-achieving girl commented that her favourite class in CBE was literacy, "because I learned the names of animals in my language that I didn't know". Many explained their sense of progress at formal school as a continuation of this process of acquiring information and mastering learning skills that they had developed during their time in CBE. A low-achieving girl revealed that she felt she was making progress because "there were things that we did not know, but now we know them". Asked if she was making progress at formal school, another replied, "yes, because I can now write". Such reflections attest to how memories of CBE underpinned their positive self-identification as learners in that they believed they had a capacity to learn and were excited about the process.

Some children, especially high achievers, also commented on their ability to repurpose particular learning attitudes and strategies that they had developed and practised in CBE. They remembered how the friendly learning environment of CBE had enabled them to ask questions if they did not understand as one girl noted: "CBE has helped me to raise my hands to answer questions in class because I was given the chance to do so at CBE". Some talked about their sense of responsibility for helping their friends to learn, an experience one high-achieving girl had valued:

> they [the friends] didn't understand it and they said I should tell them, and I did. If I see a word and they cannot pronounce, they ask me, and I pronounce it to them. I feel happy because I feel the person who knows the answer.

Of particular significance was this commitment to peer learning that the CBE students recognised had been encouraged in their classes and which they continued to invest in. As noted by Mitchell (2023), this approach to learning is missing from policy instruments in the North and signals a more collectivist approach to learning in sub-Saharan Africa, in which students tend to share responsibility for the education of their peers.

The children's recollections of CBE lessons confirm our own observations that the programme provided a generally friendly classroom environment which, given that it was free from intimidation or threats, had encouraged a high level of participation in class (Akyeampong, 2018, 7). Such experiences and the learner identity they established during those nine months evidently acted as a reference point for the CBE students.

Many higher-achieving boys and girls expressed particular enthusiasm to re-purpose the techniques they had acquired when learning their local language and apply them to their learning of English. For instance, many welcomed the fact that they had enjoyed reading in CBE and could now that a chance to repeat this experience, not only when learning local languages at formal school but also during English lessons. Explaining his success and enjoyment of reading in his formal school, one CBE graduate pointed out that "it was my experience from CBE that helped me do the reading". One higher-achieving boy noted that "I knew nothing but joining CBE made me able to read names of people and also do little reading which is the same here". CBE graduates, especially higher-achieving students, also pointed to particular processes of language learning, such as recording and spelling new words that they had already practised in their local language and were now repeating in their learning of English. One higher-achieving girl noted that

> "I was taught word and sentence formation, so when I am given an assignment here that is not easy for me, I usually recollect what I was taught in the CBE then transfer the knowledge and it will help me to do it".

Another confirmed

> "yes, I have learnt a lot especially the syllabus words; it is similar to what we did at the CBE classes; an example is the putting together of the alphabet A and B and here you combine those same alphabets".

All learners, including high and low achievers of both genders, also expressed positive attitudes and confidence in their ability to engage in mathematics lessons in formal school. This too was based on the continuities they recognised with their prior CBE experience. Thus, one lower-achieving boy noted that "Yes I do enjoy numeracy lessons, because I understand it better and it is a repetition of what was taught in the CBE classes". When asked about making progress in mathematics, another similar boy noted how he experienced formal school as a direct and meaningful extension of his prior learning. "Yes, I feel so because at the CBE we were introduced to division, subtraction, addition and multiplication but now there is the introduction of examples and many others. I do understand what the teacher teaches". Many shared the viewpoint of one higher-achieving boy who noted that "I was active in my maths class because it seemed more familiar to me, because of the numeracy classes at the CBE". Some pointed to particular activities in CBE which they believed were useful in their transition to learning mathematics, such as one lower-achieving girl who reported that "counting has helped me so much in the formal school". The emphasis of CBE on the relevance of numeracy skills was also not lost on the CBE graduates. A higher-achieving boy noted that maths was his favourite subject in formal school because 'Maybe in real life one can be given money for some transactions and this is where maths would become useful to me and so I like maths for this reason'.

Children's memories and reflections attest to the continuation of the learner identity they established by their experience of CBE. Whilst navigating the very different learning environment of formal schools in Ghana, the CBE graduates we interviewed indicated how their CBE experience has given them a sense of self-belief and self-confidence as learners that contributed to their staying power and purposefulness. Given the high rates of repeated dropping out-of-school in communities facing economic hardships, this is a particularly significant achievement of the programme.

Lessons for the 'Learning Crisis'

Figure 6.1 summarises the interconnected and multifaceted processes discussed in this chapter through which CBE provision in Northern Ghana embeds funds of knowledge in its instructional materials and pedagogical strategies and, in turn, affirms children's funds of identity in the immediate and longer terms. The analysis demonstrates the benefits of a funds of knowledge approach in leveraging a more inclusive curriculum to address educational exclusion. A recent overview of the challenges that currently undermine the SDG 4 of achieving quality education in sub-Saharan Africa has spotlighted the persistence of an inadequate curriculum at primary and secondary levels, calling for the integration of knowledge that is "socially and culturally relevant to their students", not least the inclusion of indigenous knowledge in an instructional language that children understand (Zickafoose et al., 2024). CBE does precisely this.

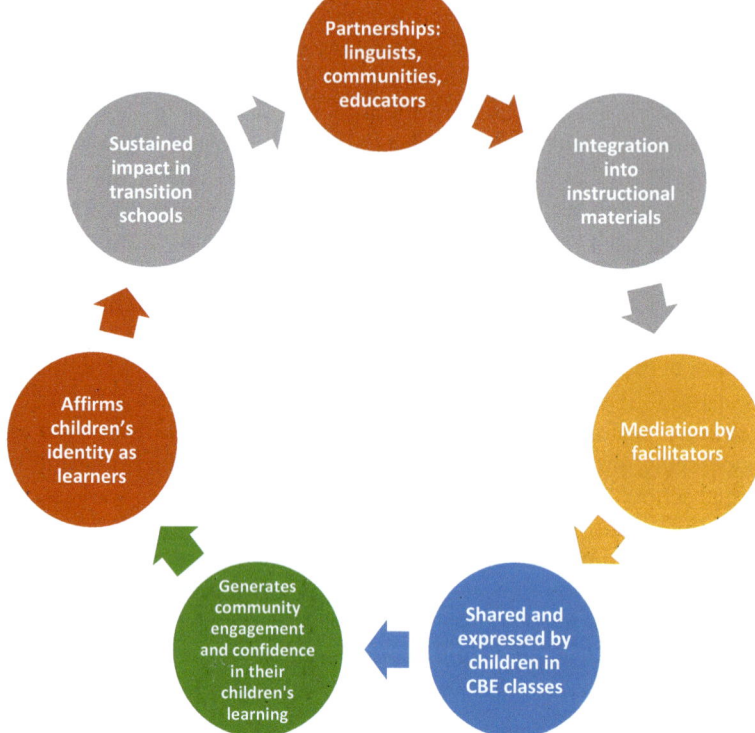

Figure 6.1 Children's funds of knowledge in CBE.

The lessons we learn from the ALP programme in Northern Ghana is the importance of building a curriculum that validates and uses the knowledges, languages and resources of the out-of-school children and their communities. The positive effects are to be found first in reversing the deficit assumptions of the crisis narrative, whilst also enabling them to achieve impressive learning outcomes. Embedding children's funds of knowledge into its curriculum content and pedagogical strategies, this ALP employs, as positive resources for learning, the multi-dimensional aspects of the agency of so-called 'poor children' discussed in Chapter 5. This approach recognises and builds directly on their feelings, social positioning and relationships with peers and their broader community, their nouse, know-how and informal learning and their contributions to household survival to create meaningful and purposeful learning opportunities. The evidence collected from Northern Ghana shows how facilitators' pedagogical approaches and strategies that are carefully thought through and planned created secure and relevant learning environments for local children, bringing along with them the support of parents and their communities. In doing so, the carefully selected facilitators demonstrate a professional agency that was rooted in their grassroots knowledge, their relationships and their reflexivity which are entirely undervalued within the deficit framings of teachers discussed in Chapter 4. The response of their students is one which not only highlights their enjoyable learning which is relevant and purposeful but also which sees them safely making the transition to a new more formal learning environment in government schools. Their identity as positive and forward-looking learners is impressive.

These successes of CBE in Northern Ghana speak back to the reductive, generic and decontextualised framings of learning within the assessment priorities of the World Bank and other aid agencies. It demonstrates the limitations of the deficit and fatalistic framings of precaritised communities that are associated by the World Bank with 'low parental investments' (2018, 9) and children who lack capability, that, in part, explains their children's failure to arrive in school ready to learn.

Instead, this ALP restores the epistemic agency of marginalised children and their communities, validating rather than devaluing their knowledges and identity to galvanise learning, bolstering their re-engagement with education provision. In this way, the CBE programme in Northern Ghana aligns with the socially transformative goals of a funds of knowledge approach (Wrigley et al., 2012; Llopart and Esteban Guitart, 2018, 151; Gaete et al., 2023) that successfully addresses, rather than reproduces, educational marginalisation. The findings of this case study underline the need for a reconceptualisation of the 'learning crisis' that promotes an expansive, situated and holistic view of educational provision.

Notes

1 Special thanks to all the Ghanaian researchers involved in data gathering and analysis for this case study, in particular Latifa Seidu, Ernest Nniakyire, Fatawu Karandey Amidu, Abdul Wahid Alhassan and Justice Agyei-Quartey (Education Development Consultant). Also to Vivien Delle, Josephine Tengan, David Haruna, Imoro Mubarak and Confidence Kpoh, Emmanuel Baapent and Elijah Yaw Danso who were involved in data gathering in 2018.
2 See studies by: Kendrick and Kakuru (2012), Joves et al. (2015), Kinney (2015), Esteban-Guitart et al. (2019), Jones and Mutumba (2019), Alvarez et al. (2021), Mashokoi (2021), Abarca et al. (2024), Veerman et al. (2023).
3 For further details on the research sites, recruitment of samples of officials, teachers/facilitators, parents and children, design of research methods and conduct of the research and analysis see: Akyeampong (2018), Higgins (2018) and Akyeampong et al. (2018).
4 In making instructional materials available to children in local languages, thereby repositioning them as active agents in learning, CBE aligns with wider pan-African initiatives such as the African Storybook Initiative (Reed and Carmo, 2016; Drew and Welch, 2017). Such publishing ventures compensate for the dire lack of appropriate instructional materials for children in Africa. In 2014, the EFA Global Monitoring Report on Teaching and Learning pointed out that: "for early grade

literacy and bilingual education to be successful, pupils need access to inclusive learning materials that are relevant to their situation and in a language they are familiar with" (UNESCO, 2014, 285). Research suggests that little has been achieved in relation to this key infrastructural support for children's learning (Piper et al., 2016).

References

Abarca, D.L., Romano, M., and Rodriguez, E., 2024. 'Latin American mothers' first-hand accounts of American statewide early intervention model: a funds of knowledge approach'. *Topics in Early Childhood Special Education*, 43(4): 306–319.

Abdulai, A.G., and Hulme, D., 2015. 'The politics of regional inequality in Ghana: state elites, donors and PRSPs'. *Development Policy Review*, 33(5): 529–553.

Akyeampong, K., 2004. 'Aid for self-help effort? A sustainable alternative route to basic education in northern Ghana'. *Journal of International Cooperation in Education*, 7(1): 41–52.

Akyeampong, K., 2009. 'Revisiting free compulsory universal basic education (FCUBE) in Ghana'. *Comparative Education*, 45(2): 175–195.

Akyeampong, K. 2018. 'An analysis of the CBE pedagogy in Ghana'. In *Evaluation of complementary basic education programme*. University of Sussex, Centre for International Education.

Akyeampong, K., Carter, E., Higgins, S., Rose, P., and Sabates, R., 2018. *Understanding complementary basic education in Ghana: investigation of the experiences and achievements of children after transitioning into public schools*. Report for DFID Ghana Office. REAL Centre, University of Cambridge.

Alexander, R., 2008. 'Culture, dialogue and learning: notes on an emerging pedagogy'. In N. Mercer and S. Hodgkinson (eds.), *Exploring talk in school*. Sage Publications, pp. 91–114.

Alexander, R., 2015. 'Teaching and learning for all?: The quality imperative revisited'. In R. Alexander (ed.), *Routledge handbook of international education and development*. Routledge, pp. 118–132.

Alvarez, A., Teeters, L.P., Hamm-Rodríguez, M., and Dimidjian, S., 2021. 'Understanding children's funds of identity as learners through multimodal self-expressions in Mexico City'. *Learning, Culture and Social Interaction*, 29: 100513.

Amagnya, M.A., 2020. 'Factors affecting education in the Builsa District of Northern Ghana'. *Africa Education Review*, 17(2): 104–121.

Carter, E., Hinton, R., Rose, P., and Sabates, R., 2023. 'Exploring the role of evidence in the government's adoption of Ghana's complementary basic education program'. *Development in Practice*, 33(8): 960–974.

Carter, E., Rose, P., Sabates, R., and Akyeampong, K., 2020. 'Trapped in low performance? Tracking the learning trajectory of disadvantaged girls and boys in the complementary basic education programme in Ghana'. *International Journal of Educational Research*, 100: 101541.

Chesworth, L., 2016. 'A funds of knowledge approach to examining play interests: listening to children's and parents' perspectives'. *International Journal of Early Years Education*, 24(3): 294–308.

Cox, S., and Dyer, C. eds., 2010. *Children as decision makers in education: sharing experiences across cultures*. A&C Black.

Derbile, E.K., Kanlisi, S.K., and Dapilah, F., 2022. 'Mapping the vulnerability of indigenous fruit trees to environmental change in the fragile savannah ecological zone of Northern Ghana'. *Heliyon*, 8(6): 1–9.

DeStefano, J., Moore, A.M.S., Balwanz, D., and Hartwell, A., 2007. *Meeting EFA: reaching the underserved through complementary models of effective schooling.* Working Paper. Academy for Educational Development. Available at: https://www.equip123.net/docs/e2-CompModelsEffectiveSchooling-Book.pdf [Accessed: 22.08.2023].

Drew, S., and Welch, T., 2017. 'Preparing to use African storybooks with children'. *African Storybook Guides*, https://www.africanstorybook.org/documents/home/Preparing_to_use_African_Storybooks_with_children.pdf

Dunne, M., and Adzahlie-Mensah, V., 2016. 'Subordinate subjects: the work of the hidden curriculum in post-colonial Ghana'. In D. Wyse, L. Hayward, and J. Pandya (eds.), *The SAGE handbook of curriculum, pedagogy and assessment.* SAGE, pp. 216–230.

Esteban-Guitart, M., 2012. 'Towards a multimethodological approach to identification of funds of identity, small stories and master narratives'. *Narrative Inquiry*, 22: 173–180.

Esteban-Guitart, M., 2021. 'Advancing the funds of identity theory: a critical and unfinished dialogue'. *Mind, Culture, and Activity*, 28(2): 169–179.

Esteban-Guitart, M. ed., 2023. *Funds of knowledge and identity pedagogies for social justice: international perspectives and Praxis from communities, classrooms, and curriculum.* Taylor and Francis.

Esteban-Guitart, M., Lalueza, J.L., Zhang-Yu, C., and Llopart, M., 2019. 'Sustaining students' cultures and identities: a qualitative study based on the funds of knowledge and identity approaches'. *Sustainability*, 11(12): 1–12.

Esteban-Guitart, M., and Moll, L., 2014a. 'Funds of identity: a new concept based on funds of knowledge approach'. *Culture and Psychology*, 20: 31–48.

Esteban-Guitart, M., and Moll, L., 2014b. 'Lived experiences, funds of identity and education'. *Culture and Psychology*, 20: 70–81.

Gaete, A., Luna, L., Silva-Peña, I., and Guerrero, P., 2023. 'The quest for justice in education: capital and funds of knowledge'. *Frontiers in Education*, 8: 1157709.

Ghana Statistical Service, 2019. *Ghana living standards survey round 7 (GLSS7)*. Main Report, pp. 1–343. Available at: https://open.africa/dataset/ghana-living-standards-survey-glss-7-2017/resource/839a1758-146c-40cd-957d-37d26aa84fb6.

González, N., Moll, L.C., and Amanti, C. eds., 2006. *Funds of knowledge: theorizing practices in households, communities, and classrooms.* Routledge.

Government of Ghana, 2018. *Education strategic plan, 2018–2030.* Available at: https://www.globalpartnership.org/content/education-strategic-plan-2018-2030-ghana [Accessed: 21.05.2024].

Hallegatte, S., and Rozenberg, J., 2017. 'Climate change through a poverty lens'. *Nature Climate Change*, 7(4): 250–256.

Hashim, I.M., 2005. *Exploring the linkages between children's independent migration and education: evidence from Ghana.* Sussex Centre for Migration Research.

Hatskevich, A., Jenicek, V., and Darkwah, S.A., 2011. 'Shea industry: a means of poverty reduction in Northern Ghana'. *Agricultura Tropica et Subtropica*, 44(4): 223–228.

Hedges, H., 2012. 'Teachers' funds of knowledge: a challenge to evidence-based practice'. *Teachers and Teaching: Theory and Practice*, 18: 7–24.

Hedges, H., 2015. 'Sophia's funds of knowledge: theoretical and pedagogical insights, possibilities and dilemmas'. *International Journal of Early Years Education*, 23: 83–96.

Hedges, H., 2021. 'The place of interests, agency and imagination in funds of identity theory'. *Mind, Culture, and Activity*, 28(2): 111–124.

Higgins, S., 2018. *Understanding complementary basic education in Ghana qualitative research report – transition experiences of CBE students in public schools.* Department for International Development in association with RTI International, Centre for International Education, University of Sussex and Research for Equitable Access and Learning, University of Cambridge.

Hogg, L., and Volman, M., 2020. 'A synthesis of funds of identity research: purposes, tools, pedagogical approaches, and outcomes'. *Review of Educational Research*, 90(6): 862–895.

Holland, D., and Lachicotte, W., 2007. 'Vygotsky, mead, and the new sociocultural studies of identity'. In D. Holland and W. Lachicotte (eds.), *The Cambridge companion to Vygotsky*. Cambridge University Press, pp. 101–135.

Ingutia, R., 2020. 'Does marginalisation in education stall the progress of sustainable development goals?' *Education 3–13*, 48(5): 495–511.

Jones, S., and Mutumba, S., 2019. 'Intersections of mother tongue-based instruction, funds of knowledge, identity, and social capital in a Ugandan pre-school classroom'. *Journal of Language, Identity and Education*, 18(4): 207–221.

Jovés, P., Siqués, C., and Esteban-Guitart, M., 2015. 'The incorporation of funds of knowledge and funds of identity of students and their families into educational practice: a case study from Catalonia, Spain'. *Teaching and Teacher Education*, 4: 68–77.

Kambala, M.I., 2023. 'Colonial origins of comparative development in Ghana'. *Journal of Development Studies*, 59(2): 188–208.

Kendrick, M., and Kakuru, D., 2012. 'Funds of knowledge in child-headed households: a Ugandan case study'. *Childhood*, 19(3): 397–413.

Kent, R., 2018. '"Helping" or "appropriating"? Gender relations in shea nut production in northern Ghana'. *Society and Natural Resources*, 31(3): 367–381.

Kinney, A., 2015. 'Compelling counternarratives to deficit discourses: an investigation into the funds of knowledge of culturally and linguistically diverse U.S. elementary students' households'. *Qualitative Research in Education*, 4(1): 1–25.

Kwao, A., 2017. 'Challenges of curriculum design and its implications on policy: the case of the Junior High School (JHS) teaching subjects in Ghana'. *Journal of Educational and Social Research*, 7(2): 93–101.

Le Fanu, G., 2013. 'Reconceptualising inclusive education in international development'. In G. Le Fanu (ed.), *Education quality and social justice in the global south: challenges for policy, practice and research*. Routledge, pp. 40–56.

Leichenko, R., and Silva, J.A., 2014. 'Climate change and poverty: vulnerability, impacts, and alleviation strategies'. *Wiley Interdisciplinary Reviews: Climate Change*, 5(4): 539–556.

Llopart, M., and Esteban-Guitart, M., 2018. 'Funds of knowledge in 21st century societies: inclusive educational practices for under-represented students: A literature review'. *Journal of Curriculum Studies*, 50(2): 145–161.

Longden, K., 2013. *Accelerated learning programmes: what can we learn from them about curriculum reform?* Background paper for *EFA Global Monitoring Report*, p. 14.

Manuel-Navarrete, D., Buzinde, C.N., and Swanson, T., 2021. 'Fostering horizontal knowledge co-production with Indigenous people by leveraging researchers' transdisciplinary intentions'. *Ecology and Society*, 26(2): 1–14.

Mitchell, R., 2023. 'Peer support in sub-Saharan Africa: a critical interpretive synthesis of school-based research'. *International Journal of Educational Development*, 96: 102686.

Moll, L., Amanti, C., Neff, D., and Gonzalez, N., 2006. 'Funds of knowledge for teaching: using a qualitative approach to connect homes and classrooms'. In *Funds of knowledge*. Routledge, pp. 71–87.

Ohanu, I.B., Salawu, I.A., and Ede, E.O., 2021. 'A critical analysis of the national curriculum for nomadic primary schools in Nigeria'. *International Review of Education*, 67(3): 363–383.

Okrah, A.K., Ampadu, E., and Yeboah, R., 2020. 'Relevance of the senior high school curriculum in Ghana in relation to contextual reality of the world of work'. *Journal of Curriculum and Teaching*, 9(1): 1–14.

Oteng-Ababio, M., Mariwah, S., and Kusi, L., 2017. 'Is the underdevelopment of northern Ghana a case of environmental determinism or governance crisis?' *Ghana Journal of Geography*, 9(2): 5–39.

Piper, B., Zuilkowski, S.S., and Ong'ele, S., 2016. Implementing mother tongue instruction in the real world: results from a medium-scale randomized controlled trial in Kenya. *Comparative Education Review*, 60(4): 776–807.

Reed, Y., and Carmo, M., 2016. 'Something new out of Africa: the African Storybook initiative as a catalyst for curriculum making'. In *International Conference on Education and New Development*. World Institute for Advanced Research and Science (WIARS), Lisbon, pp. 51–55.

Reed, Y., 2019. 'Countering linguistic imperialism with stories in the languages of Africa: The African storybook initiative as a model for enabling in and out of school literacies'. *South African Journal of Childhood Education*, 9(1): 1–8.

Rodriguez, G.M., 2013. 'Power and agency in education: exploring the pedagogical dimensions of funds of knowledge'. *Review of Research in Education*, 37(1): 87–120.

Sherris, A., Sulemana, O.S., Alhassan, A., Abudu, G., and Karim, A.R., 2014. 'School for life in Ghana: promoting literate opportunities for rural youth'. *Journal of Multilingual and Multicultural Development*, 35(7): 692–708.

Shinohara, T. 2021. 'Complementary basic education programmes for out-of-school children in Bangladesh, Ghana and Ethiopia: a comparative overview'. In J. Agebaire, A. Agema, and J. Kumari (eds.), *Education and development*. Sevhage Publishers.

Subero, D., Vujasinović, E., and Esteban-Guitart, M., 2017. 'Mobilising funds of identity in and out of school'. *Cambridge Journal of Education*, 47(2): 247–263.

Tikly, L., and Barrett, A.M., 2013. 'Education quality and social justice in the global south'. In L. Tikly (ed.), *Education quality and social justice in the global south: challenges for policy, practice and research*. Routledge, pp. 11–24.

UNESCO, 2014. *Teaching and learning: achieving quality for all*. EFA global monitoring report 2013/4. UNESCO, Paris. Available at: https://unesdoc.unesco.org/ark:/48223/pf0000225660 [Accessed: 21.07.2023].

UNESCO Institute for Statistics. 2022. *New estimation confirms out-of-school population is growing in sub-Saharan Africa*. Factsheet 62, Policy Paper 48.

Veerman, E., Karssen, M., Volman, M., and Gaikhorst, L., 2023. 'The contribution of two funds of identity interventions to well-being related student outcomes in primary education'. *Learning, Culture and Social Interaction*, 38: 100680.

World Bank, 2018. *World development report: learning to realise education's promise.* World Bank Group.

Wrigley, T., Lingard, B., and Thomson, P., 2012. 'Pedagogies of transformation: keeping hope alive in troubled times'. *Critical Studies in Education,* 53: 95–108.

Young, M., and Muller, J., 2013. 'On the powers of powerful knowledge'. *Review of Education,* 1(3): 229–250.

Zickafoose, A., Ilesanmi, O., Diaz-Manrique, M., Adeyemi, A.E., Walumbe, B., Strong, R., Wingenbach, G., Rodriguez, M.T., and Dooley, K., 2024. Barriers and challenges affecting quality education (sustainable development goal# 4) in Sub-Saharan Africa by 2030. *Sustainability,* 16(7): 2657.

Zipin, L., 2020. 'Building curriculum knowledge work around community-based "problems that matter": let's dare to imagine'. *Curriculum Perspectives,* 40(1): 111–115.

Zipin, L., Sellar, S., and Hattam, R., 2012. 'Countering and exceeding "capital": a "funds of knowledge" approach to re-imagining community'. *Discourse: Studies in the Cultural Politics of Education,* 33(2): 179–192.

7 Improving Learning Outcomes to Enable Transition

Speed Schools in Ethiopia

In the analysis and critique of the learning crisis narrative in Part 1, we noted that a core dimension of its deficit framing of children was an individualising (atomising) and decontextualised approach that focused narrowly on their achievement of cognitive learning outcomes. This framing disconnected them from the multi-dimensional aspects of their agency and experiences rooted in their relationships and environments. It thus undermined the possibility of creative and effective pedagogical practices to promote meaningful learning.

The case study in this chapter shows how an accelerated learning programme, this time in Ethiopia, used objects and materials from children's physical environments to activate collaborative and engaged learning. The approach taken by so-called Speed Schools achieves not only improved cognitive learning outcomes, as our data show, but also like CBE provides an enjoyable experience of learning that promotes confidence and successful transitions to government schools. These pedagogical strategies also validate children's engagement with their material environments experienced *in situ* at the same time as harnessing them for learning rather than dismissing them as irrelevant. The deficit framings of poor children that disconnect them from their contexts are again disrupted by alternative modalities of learning, this time posthumanist concern for how children engage the natural environment as a source of knowledge for learning.

In this chapter, the processes of learning are associated with its achieved cognitive learning gains – in other words, in children's measurable learning outcomes. The mixed methods analysis of this chapter, combining qualitative and quantitative evidence, ties together children's subjective experiences with their demonstrable cognitive gains. Our analysis therefore goes beyond any narrow concern for cognitive outcomes that are usually detached from their socio-economic conditions. The creative and innovative pedagogical processes found in this ALP precisely challenge the narrative of the 'learning crisis' and its prescriptions for Africa described in Chapter 1. For as Alexander (2015, 5) noted, such processes were precisely the 'missing ingredient' in the responses of policymakers to educational marginalisation.

DOI: 10.4324/9781003185482-10

Here, we draw upon a post-humanist approach to analyse the ways in which this ALP associates children's relationship with their physical environment, in and out-of-school, using it as a constitutive feature of their exercise of agency as learners. We describe first how this approach offers valuable conceptual tools to discard deficit notions of children, by challenging the ontological notion of human exceptionalism. We then turn to a brief discussion on how Speed School teachers operationalise the pedagogy in ways which demonstrate how their teaching builds on just such a post-humanistic approach to children's learning and their agency.

The second section sets the scene with a description of the Speed School programme in the period between 2011 and 2017 when Kwame led a team of researchers to investigate the programme using both qualitative and quantitative methods.[1] The research study drew on visual data showing children's micro-interactions to demonstrate varied ways in which the learning experiences were being offered to children. Importantly, this is complemented by an analysis of the impact of Speed Schools on children's learning outcomes based on longitudinal quantitative data covering the period 2011–2017. These data indicate that the children who experienced Speed Schools successfully transitioned into government schools and continued to achieve improved learning outcomes.

A Post-humanist Approach to Children's Learning

The reason why we turned to post-humanism to evaluate the Speed Schools in Ethiopia lies in the ability of this approach to challenge the centrality of the human in the social world and the privileging of the human individual sovereign subject as the primary locus of agency, certainty and truth. At the core of the 'learning crisis', precisely lie such assumptions that, as we have already seen, can have severe consequences when applied to non-Western collective cultures. Admittedly post-humanism is an eclectic, sometimes elusive field of theoretical reflection. It comes under a variety of names, including new materialism, relational materialism, feminist post-humanism and critical post-humanism. It draws on the work of Barad (2003) and, in relation to children's education, on the work of Murris (2016a, 2016b), De Freitas and Curinga (2015) and Taylor et al. (2012) to distance itself from human exceptionalism or, if you like, anthropocentrism. Barad (2007), for example, emphasises the idea that things – the material world or matter itself – are all dynamic and have agency along with the human. Thus, "all earth dwellers are mutually entangled and always becoming, always intra-acting with everything else" (Barad, 2007, 67). A central insight is that, always, 'matter matters' in understanding human social practices and interactions. In this reading of the social world, the agency of the human is to be understood not as separate from or superior to the non-human. Further matter is therefore construed within a post-humanist ontology as an active participant in 'the world's becoming' (Murris, 2016a, 11).

Rather than being a passive backdrop to human activity, as such, matter is 'a performative agent' (Barad, 2003, 2007). Bennett terms this vitality of the non-human, 'thing power' (Bennett, 2004, 347) indicating, therefore, that the exercise of agency is always distributed, rather than inhering only in human beings.

Various consequences result from these ontological premises for understanding the aims and goals of education and for (re)configuring childhood and conceptualising how children learn (Taylor et al., 2012; Murris, 2016a). These premises are helpful in eschewing deficit models of children's agency as learners in several ways. First, this approach to learning takes issue with notions that foreground children's ignorance. By recognising children's engagements with the natural environment as a source of knowledge and wisdom, post-humanism posits children as 'rich, resilient and resourceful' (Murris, 2016a, xiii). Hence, children are repositioned not as inferior but as equal to adults in their mutual fundamental interconnectedness with the physical world. Commonplace assumptions of a linear passage from childhood to adulthood assume the relative ignorance of the child who is thus deemed inactive in shaping processes, someone to whom knowledge is transmitted rather than engaged with. This produces 'onto-epistemic injustice':

> an ageist prejudice in which adults claim to know what true knowledge is and therefore educationally worthwhile – leaving children not listened to because being a child gives them no claim to knowledge.
> (Moss, 2016, xii)

Yet, as discussed in chapter 5, in the African context, children often share in the experiences of adulthood through the kinds of labour and community activities in which they are involved. This can sometimes blur the boundary between childhood and adulthood or make the transition less linear. It can equip children with knowledges that defy such traditional age-related understanding of their educational trajectory (Crossouard et al., 2022, 220). Revising such assumptions, a post-humanist approach recognises the child as an equal participant with adults in the intra-active processes that condition human existence. This provides the grounds for shifting traditional power relationships between teachers and pupils to affirm the knowledges and potential for the knowing of the latter.

Second, learning is not to be located only within the individual child. Rather, learning is understood as a collective process involving a 'dynamic, relational process of intra-action' (Murris, 2016a, 13) with other children and with their physical learning environments. This framing, therefore, returns attention to the contextual situated nature of learning – understood not only in terms of its social relational dimensions but also its anchoring in children's physical environments, in and out-of-school. These are what we characterised earlier in Part 1 also as components of the multi-dimensional aspects of the lives of 'poor children'.

Third, the experience of learning cannot be reducible to communicative processes that are reliant only on verbal interchange or language use. In contrast, a post-humanist approach restores the centrality of material factors in learning that operate outside of or alongside language and are themselves agentic in the process of learning (De Freitas and Curinga, 2015, 49). Post-humanism therefore shifts attention away from a concern with the teacher as the sole trigger of learning to highlight the role of the objects and material environment in which children learn as also contributing and 'agentic' in producing learning.

Such post-humanist approaches to learning have been used to explore and explain the significance of transformative learning in a variety of pedagogical approaches used in African contexts of hardship and precarity (see, for example, Murris, 2016b). However, they have not yet been applied to understand the learning processes offered to out-of-school children in ALPs. The framing of children's agency as knowers and learners entangled with their physical environments can help us understand how Speed Schools achieve successful and enjoyable learning. The language(s) with which children are familiar is significant, acting as the means through which communication and interaction with the physical and material world occur to produce meaningful and deep learning. We turn now to give a brief overview of Speed Schools' contribution to meeting the needs of out-of-school children in Ethiopia.

Speed Schools in Ethiopia

Speed Schools were introduced in 2011 in the Southern Nations, Nationalities and People's Region (SNNPR) by Geneva Global Inc., a US-based philanthropic organisation that contracted local NGOs to provide access to education for out-of-school children. The SNNPR is one of nine federal states in Ethiopia consisting of different ethnic groups and languages. The Speed School programme at its inception targeted five districts: Alaba, Boricha, Chencha, Kabena and Shebedino. Three of these have different languages, and two, in the Sidama region, share the Sidama language.

The Speed Schools Initiative later termed the Accelerated Learning for Africa programme was set up to recruit children who had missed all or part of the early years of schooling and provide an accelerated learning programme covering a condensed Grades 1-3 curriculum in a single school year. Speed Schools enrolled children aged from 9 to 14 years who had dropped out of government primary schools before they could acquire a good foundation in basic literacy and numeracy skills, and a few others who had never been to school. All these children were taken through an intensive basic literacy and numeracy programme for ten months.

Rather than being a discrete intervention, the Speed School's aim was to offer school experiences that would enable children to access and succeed within the mainstream public education system. On completing the ten-month programme of accelerated learning in the Speed School, children are then given a test, set by local education officials and government schoolteachers, to assess their attainment of the minimum competences expected at the end of Grade 3. Based on their performance, the children are then integrated into government schools, mainly entering the fourth grade and with a few others entering grades 2 or 5 depending on their performance. Since the Speed Schools work intensively in specific localities, this means that substantial numbers of students go on to particular government schools, called *Link Schools* for the purpose of the programme. Many of the Speed Schools operated near or within Link School compounds.[2]

The use of mother tongue and/or regional languages as the language of instruction in Speed Schools aligns with the Federal Mother Tongue education policy that has been in existence in Ethiopia since 1994.[3] This policy encourages mother tongue as the language of instruction throughout primary education and makes Ethiopia unique amongst African countries where 'early exit' policies drastically truncate children's opportunity to learn using the mother tongue as the medium of instruction. The Speed School programme when it started in 2011 also included a micro-financed initiative, a Self-Help Group for mothers whose children enrolled in the programme. The participating mothers were given training in running small-scale businesses with seed money to invest. Most of these mothers pooled their resources to invest in viable economic activities that had the potential to increase their incomes and cover the costs of schooling after their children had transitioned into government schools.

Using Post-humanism to Understand Children's Experiences of Learning in Speed Schools

Learning lessons from Speed Schools and what they have achieved demanded a range of different sources of data. At the heart of this research was a desire to tap the types of learning that children achieved. Given that learning is a situated inter-personal, embodied and emotionally charged activity, photographs can be a particularly useful medium (Howes and Miles, 2014) to enable scrutiny of its processes and practices. Here, we focus on the photographs of children learning in Speed Schools in diverse regions of Ethiopia (including Addis Ababa, Oromia and Amhara) that were collected as part of the various research studies (Akyeampong et al., 2012a, b; Akyeampong et al., 2016; Akyeampong et al., 2018). We also draw on the information we gathered from lesson observations when we visited the Speed Schools in action. Both the observations and photographs have been selected from an archive to help evaluate the pedagogical practices and impact of Speed Schools. They show the situated micro-level interactions of pupils at particular moments in their learning, bringing into sharp focus children's actions and emotions in response to the learning spaces and the opportunities created within Speed Schools.

Applying the insights of post-humanism to these Speed School visual data, we are able to demonstrate the various ways in which Speed Schools work with children's environments to help them learn. In particular, we focus on:

- localising the learning space;
- collaborating for learning;

174 *Reconceptualising the Learning Crisis in Africa*

- using diverse objects and activities to consolidate understanding;
- playful learning;
- recognising children's agency as learners and
- undoing gender regimes in learning processes.

Below we discuss each of these in turn.

Localising the learning space

Images 7.1–7.5 evoke the multiplicity of objects, man-made and natural, that define the space for learning in Speed Schools. That this is achieved in what is generally known as a resource-starved context of educational provision in Southern Ethiopia is remarkable.

Viewed through a post-humanist lens, these images reveal how teachers, together with children, make use of materials drawn from their local environment. There is a distinctive space for learning. The images also indicate that these materials are not a passive backdrop to the children's learning but constitutive of their learning space, inviting their actions and reactions. Objects float above the pupils from the ceiling, face them on walls and accompany them on

Image 7.1 A Speed School classroom with walls and roof space covered with learning materials made with coloured paper, including the alphabet in English and Amharic.

Improving Learning Outcomes 175

Image 7.2 Children arranging coloured pebbles for their number work.

Image 7.3 Wall showing alphabets, words and musical instruments providing visually stimulating learning environment.

Image 7.4 Locally made wood board with carved letters.

Image 7.5 Children at work surrounded by rich display of letters, words, diagrams and pots made from local clay.

the floors and tables around them. They have a performative force in defining the physical space in which children are invited to engage and to learn. In the language of post-humanism, the Speed School classroom is an 'assemblage' of heterogeneous material artefacts.

The objects are sourced from the natural and man-made local environment in which these children live. For example: bottle caps are taken from local garbage; pupils might find the stones and pebbles in the school compound or on their way to school; and clay and mud are part of the local Amhara landscape. These objects also signal the agency of children and their teachers. The bottle caps, as well as the stones and pebbles, were collected by teachers and pupils. The clay pots and wooden musical instruments were made by them. The pebbles have also been marked with numbers and coloured by them and their presence in the classroom. In addition to providing resources for learning, these artefacts recognise and valorise children's experiences in their homes, the school compound and the local landscape. The conventional division between formal teaching spaces and children's lived experiences outside the school compound is therefore resisted in the 'assemblage' of natural and man-made objects of Speed Schools. In this way, Speed Schools offer what has been defined as a 'place-based pedagogy' (Duhn, 2012).

These images confirm the evaluations of Speed School Pedagogy (Akyeampong, 2016a, 15) that describe how teachers in Speed Schools mobilised objects in a range of ways to consolidate and support learning. Hence:

> learning materials were not restricted to things that the students had constructed and displayed in the classroom but extended to handling concrete materials outside the classroom, which seemed to provide real life practical learning experiences

So, maize stems were used for counting activities. In a science lesson, "different types of soil were shown and passed around by the children so they could note their differences" (Akyeampong, 2016a, 16). Material objects were also used to support analogical reasoning to develop understanding of concepts. Thus, one teacher "took students outside to line up to explain dots, lines and angles and explain geometric shapes using the analogy of bread, moon and plate".

Collaborating for learning

Images 7.6–7.11 show the pivotal contribution of objects in initiating collaborative learning activities in Speed Schools. Figure 7.6 demonstrates how local stones promote numeracy skills through a collaborative learning process. However, what is interesting in this image is that this girl is demonstrating to the teacher and her peers who are implicated in the activity.

178 *Reconceptualising the Learning Crisis in Africa*

Image 7.6 A girl using numbered pebbles to count, a skill which she is demonstrating to her peers and rest of the class.

Image 7.7 Children using plastic bottle tops to create number signs and letters thereby doing addition together.

Improving Learning Outcomes 179

Image 7.8 Children using plastic bottle tops assisted by their teacher to carry out addition sums on a mini blackboard.

Image 7.9 Children in a group gathering around a mini blackboard learning how to write Amharic letters.

180 *Reconceptualising the Learning Crisis in Africa*

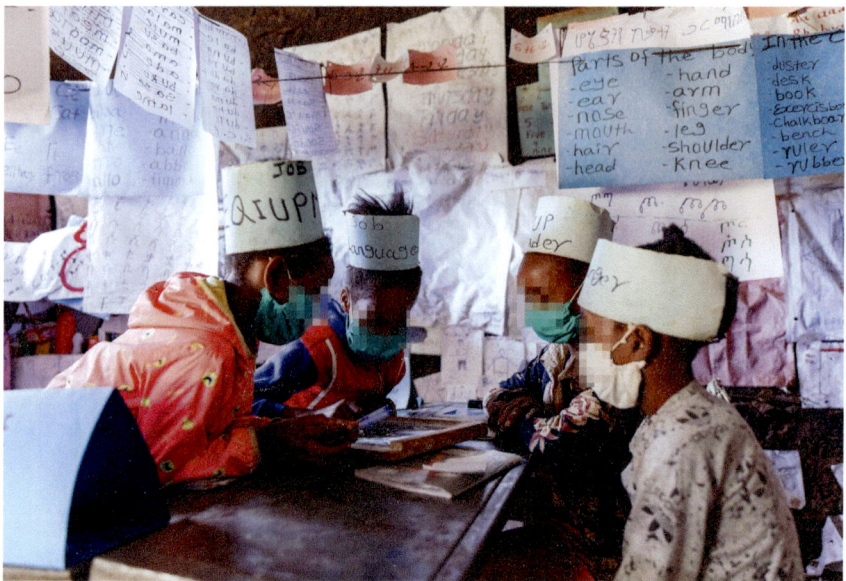

Image 7.10 Children in a group gathering around a mini blackboard learning how to write using the English alphabet.

The completed result of this activity is found in the stones that are arranged in numbers and signs on the floor (see image 7.7). Stones are also arranged in what appears to be a celebratory line underneath the numbers and signs. In these two images (see image 7.6 and 7.7), local stones and bottle tops have activated the children's collective immersion in the activity of recording their counting together, their heads down, their bodies crouching to attend to the numbers being created on the floor that register their group decisions about adding two numbers together. Here, mathematical meaning-making materialises through the children's entanglement with the stones and bottle tops with which they have become familiar from using their own creativity, and as a vital presence in their environments outside of the school. Both images therefore evoke learning emerging directly from that synergy between children and matter in the process of meaning-making that Barad (2007) characterises as the paradigmatic 'material-discursive' character of human agency.

In Images 7.8, 7.9 and 7.10, mini blackboards replaces the pebbles as the material object of engagement, attention and intra-action. Thus, all the children's attention is focused on the boy (7.9) and girl (7.10) writing on the mini blackboards.

These images capture both the embodied character of the intra-actions that constitute learning in Speed Schools as well as their strong affective and relational dimensions. Children stoop, bend, shift around and move their bodies to align with the movement not only of their discussion but also the objects they are mobilising as they develop literacy and numeracy skills. The captivated faces as well as the engaged body language of the children testify to the emotional underpinnings of their intra-actions with objects. The researchers witnessed the children's palpable joy, curiosity, excitement, concern with the objects in the process of learning. These feelings are evidently shared, as the children's engagement with objects triggers a collective, purposeful energy that flows between them and the objects.

The objects in these images, in effect, trigger a relational and collective rather than individualistic mode of learning. Understood through a posthumanist lens, this is grounded in children's simultaneous interactions with matter and with each other. This process of learning is in striking contrast to what has been noted as the 'ontologically individualistic' view of learners, and an atomistic framing of their learning experience in the discourse and practice of child centredness (Robeyns, 2003, quoted in Tikly and Barrett, 2011, 6).

Using diverse objects and activities to consolidate understanding

Images 7.11–7.13 capture a particular feature of the pedagogical processes used in Speed Schools (Akyeampong et al., 2016a). After the teacher's initial explanation of new content at the start of lessons, groups of pupils are invited to represent that content to each other in different media. So, students are encouraged to process their understanding of a new concept through a range of activities, including drama, music, storytelling and artwork.

Image 7.11 Children dramatising the process of greeting each other.

182 *Reconceptualising the Learning Crisis in Africa*

Image 7.12 Children proudly sharing their drawings of people greeting each other on coloured card.

Image 7.13 Children organising cards with words and phrases on them linked to greeting someone.

Each group of children present their re-framing of the learning content to other groups. This multi-modal pedagogical strategy encourages pupils to represent and reconceptualise what they have learned, thus consolidating their understanding. It also encourages them to develop confidence as they communicate learning to each other. So, the images show different groups of children presenting their understanding of greeting someone, through drama (7.11), drawing (7.12) and words (7.13). Describing this pedagogical process, Akyeampong et al. (2016a, 37) note that:

> students get an opportunity for elaboration that has the potential to build common understanding among them and hold them to stay engaged in the instructional process.

From a post-humanist lens, what is interesting about this process of consolidating learning is the creative use of material objects in connected learning activities that embed content in a range of activities.

Playful learning

The objects identified in the images, such as local pebbles, mud and rocks, are used by Ethiopian children to play with things that come from time outside school (Tafere, 2012; Jirata, 2019; Eriksen and Mulugeta, 2021). This is also significant in relation to the way in which, for pedagogical purposes, Speed Schools break down the often tightly defined boundaries between the space of the school and children's local environments. That the same objects are used to play as well as to learn together underpins a form of 'play-based learning' (Wang, 2018; see also Hedges and Cooper, 2018). The grounded materiality of the Speed School environment thus throws light on an important dimension of the 'joyful' learning associated with children's experiences of accelerated learning.

Recognising children's agency as learners

The learning activities shown in the images above, whether they show children recording mathematical calculations on stones or working together to process knowledge through diverse (visual, musical, verbal, dramatic) media – indicate that learners in small but nevertheless significant ways are 'knowledge producers rather than knowledge consumers' (Murris, 2016a, 146). By positioning objects and artefacts that the learners themselves have produced, and which they therefore to some extent 'own' as central to learning, Speed School classrooms thus resist the hierarchical framing of relationships between teachers and pupils found in the classroom cultures of state schooling in many contexts. Understood through a post-humanist ontology, this is achieved by a pedagogy that foregrounds the 'agency' of objects as well as children, as not lesser than that of the teacher, in the ongoing and always unresolved process of learning. The results seem to be that 'the whole experience…… appears to create learners who are not only reflexive but autonomous and resilient' (Akyeampong et al., 2016a, 8). Far from a deficit construction of children's cognitive lack or ineducability because of their long-term disconnection from formal schooling, the children in Speed Schools are recognised as already knowledgeable, resourceful and creative in and through their inter-actions with their natural environment. The 'vertical power relations' that characterise knowledge transmission in formal schooling (Dunne and Adzahlie-Mensah, 2016), with teachers as the centre of knowledge transmission, are revised such that children exercise their own power and agency in knowledge production.

Undoing gender regimes in learning processes

Finally what is also significant is that the boys and girls shown in each of the images reproduced above share the interactive space with each other and with the materials from their local natural environments. They participate collectively in learning processes triggered by them, with girls and boys exercising agency as collaborators and explorers in learning. This is a socio-emotional as well as a cognitive process as they listen to each other, express and share joy and curiosity whilst simultaneously acquiring literacy and numeracy skills. The structuring of pedagogical processes around group activities undergirds this gender-inclusive sociality of learning in Speed Schools.

Such a modality of learning sharply contrasts with the gender regimes that shape the experiences of boys and girls in primary and secondary schooling in sub-Saharan Africa. Such regimes lead to the subordination and under-achievement of girls (Bhana et al, 2011). Reporting on research into the 'hidden curriculum' of schooling in Ghana, Dunne and Adzahlie-Mensah (2016, 10) conclude that "gender was a predominant and pervasive organizing structure of a school that was active in the (re)production of sex-based segregation and hierarchies prevalent within larger society" (quoted in Crossouard and Dunne, 2021, 16). This resulted in the 'inferiorisation' and subordination of girls in a range of ways, including their location within the spaces of the classroom environment in which they were separated from boys; the allocation of responsibilities to boys as prefects rather than to girls; greater attention given to boys by teachers and a passive rather than active role for girls in lesson routines in which boys are more vocal and dominant (Dunne, 2009).

These gender dynamics are avoided in the learning environment created by Speed Schools. Their approach orients both boys' and girls' learning around materials known to them, inviting both to harness what they are familiar with in a collective process of discovery and learning. Thus, girls and boys develop self-confidence and are participatory and agentic. Whilst further research is necessary to illuminate possibilities, rooting learning in children's shared material worlds, it seems can provide opportunities to reconfigure unequal gender relations.

These findings align with research that has demonstrated that post-humanist approaches to learning open up learning activities to the 'more than human world' (Snaza and Weaver, 2015, 11). Such activities contain possibilities for undoing gender hierarchies. This forms what Snaza and Weaver (2015, 10), commenting on post-humanist approaches to learning, have termed the "radical commitment to experimentation with new, unpredictable... forms of relation". Hence, by reconfiguring learning to the 'more than human world' and harnessing children's natural environments as resources for learning, post-humanist approaches may make possible modes of relationality between boys and girls that avoid gender hierarchies and in which girls are equally agentic and participatory as boys. Osgood has noted (2014, 1), this diversification of the resources and relationships to support learning "repositions children as active agents and co-constructors in processes of developing and transgressing gendered identities". The images above, and our observations, attest to the micro-doings in Speed Schools through which this is achieved, showing how girls are active, agentic and participatory learners, rather than being subordinated as passive within learning spaces. This potentially challenges oppressive gender norms and "sex-based binary distinctions that regulate participation in learning processes" (Dunne and Adzahlie-Mensah, 2016, 225).

Accelerated learning pedagogical practices are associated with the provision of innovative forms of 'joyful' learning (Luminos Fund, 2018). The images we have shown, here, testify to the constitutive role of what could be called a post-humanist teaching approach in Speed Schools in Ethiopia in contributing to this ethos. Such an approach is also associated with the learning gains and successful transition into government schools that we discuss after the next section.

Learning to Teach as a Speed School Teacher

Despite, or perhaps because of, the low resourcing of Speed Schools, teachers working in such schools were able to promote more holistic and post-humanist approaches to learning. To ensure alignment with how Speed School students were expected to learn in their reconfigured classrooms, Speed School teachers training had to reflect this anticipated change in their role as teachers. The way in which they were trained mattered. Kwame, together with University of Sussex and Ethiopian researchers (Akyeampong et al., 2016a, 2018) observed their training to understand how their professional roles and identity were meant to change to support an alternative model of teaching and learning for out-of-school children.

Speed School teachers are all recruited on the basis of their fluency in the local language. The content of training focused on the practical with an emphasis on getting the trainees to *think, devise* and *share* activities that could be used typically in the classroom, modelling what is the Speed School approach to activity lessons. Trainees worked in groups mirroring how Speed School students are, on occasion, grouped in class. The groups we observed which were named: *Handicraft, Games, Storytelling,* and *Music* were used as the main modes for facilitating learning and encouraging students to use their funds of knowledge to (re)present subject content. For each curriculum topic, teacher trainees described potential activities and their mode of presentation, before volunteering to demonstrate their ideas to the training class. These activities could, for example, involve telling a comic tale or using cards to teach numbers or stones for counting in a game, or singing a song. The training emphasised that there are many ways to address the same content and that it was up to trainees to find them. The importance of accepting students' funds of knowledge as legitimate and important sources was emphasised, as well as the straitened circumstances students found themselves in. In the training, whole class discussion centred on giving a rationale for each part of a lesson, articulated as *'revealing the learning'* so that what was being learnt and how was overtly signalled by the trainees. The 'activity' or 'doing' part of the lesson was used to model how Speed School students would be expected to *'re-teach and re-test'* the content of a lesson and concepts to the whole class through songs, cards, stories or games. This rehearsal of content by different groups of learners in tandem with using simple local resources meant that students 'saying again' in the teacher trainees' own words, or their actions, or by using artefacts became part of the lesson content. In this way, their students could appropriate and own the lesson.

Overall, the training involved a pedagogic approach that trainees were unlikely to have experienced as students themselves, or even as trainee teachers if they had already gone through a government teacher training programme (Abebe and Woldehanna, 2013). The training sought quite explicitly to differentiate the Speed School approach from what happens in government schools and change how teachers view learning and their own professional identity in the Speed School classroom. Rather than teach them to follow pre-determined instructions or teach using a prescribed script they were expected to use pedagogical principles to engage the content of the government textbook, emphasising the importance of teacher agency and professionalism.

How Speed School teachers exercise agency to promote holistic learning

The observations of four Speed School teachers' teaching revealed that, although there were differences in how they managed the varied circumstances of their classes with different levels of expertise and success, their pedagogies had much in common. Their classroom practices revealed seven common characteristics in which they and their students' exercised agency:

1 Students' engagement in discussion and collaboration over common activities in group work was central. This involved re-enacting content knowledge through multimodal means and performing this knowledge reciprocally to and with the rest of the class.
2 Within a framework set by the teacher, in group work and reporting back, students took some control over the selection, sequencing, pacing and evaluation of their work.
3 A range of teaching and learning materials and activities within and outside the classroom were used, and modelled by teachers, with students making many of the resources to show or represent the content.

4 Lesson planning was flexible as it involved teachers in devising or selecting activities and materials rather than implementing prescribed activities.
5 The teachers were responsive to students and encouraged individual and group thinking, sharing and verbalisation of knowledge in the mother tongue.
6 All the students were involved in class, group and individual activities.
7 The activities specified and the social relations generated by the pedagogy ensured that students engaged in a very wide range of learning talk which they used to develop their ideas with the teacher and with peers, in groups and to the whole class. (Akyeampong et al., 2016a, 2018)

Speed School teachers' instructional practice not only encouraged students to develop confidence in their ability to think and make sense of what had gone on before but also encouraged them to reflect on the day's lesson as it progressed. Students were allowed to repeat and remember most of what they learned the last time. By revising new concepts as lessons advanced, students could easily catch up with what was being taught, ensuring that most students progressed together as a group.

The core elements of the Speed School pedagogy fell into three categories:

Activity-based learning through group work – this emphasised learning through group activity and process skills wherein pupils re-enact pedagogic content knowledge through multimodal means.
Flexible lesson planning and delivery – there was an emphasis on using a wide range of learning resources and activities within and outside the classroom that kept lessons lively and engaging.
Reflexive student thinking and verbalisation of knowledge – all teachers encouraged individual or group student thinking, sharing and verbalisation of understanding.
(Akyeampong et al., 2018)

Speed School teachers recruited locally come with a better understanding of meanings attached to local languages. Arguably this allowed them to connect better with the micro-level educational experiences of students and utilise shared funds of knowledge as an important resource to tackle gaps in students' basic skills, whilst ensuring their education has a broad purpose. What strikes an observer of these Speed School classes in Ethiopia is the industry of activity in which teachers and learners are equally and passionately invested. The most important aspect of the pedagogy is how it is collaborative and promotes close social relations between teachers and students.

Alexander (2008, 112) claims that one of the most important dimensions of pedagogical practices to promote meaningful learning is the provision of opportunities for children to engage in different kinds of learning 'talk'. This includes opportunities for them to, for example, narrate, explain and instruct; ask different kinds of question; receive, act and build upon answers; analyse and solve problems; speculate and imagine; explore and evaluate ideas; and discuss, argue, reason, justify and negotiate. Most of these learning opportunities were promoted by the Speed School teachers, triggered in this case by the constitutive role of children's material environments in their learning.

Improving Learning Outcomes and Transition

The discursive framing of the 'learning crisis' focuses its concerns on the persistent under-achievement of African children in Foundational Literacy and Numeracy (FLN) tests. The approach to addressing this problem is often to introduce methods such as structured pedagogy or scripted lesson plans (see Chapter 4) in order to close the FLN skills gaps of the under-achieving child. The issue here, as we have already argued, is that this 'solution' focuses narrowly on learning as simply acquiring cognitive skills based on a deficit characterisation of children and teachers. It sustains the one-dimensional discourse of derision and erasure of agency that we challenged in Chapter 5. This discourse stands in sharp contrast to the modus operandi of teachers trained to teach in Speed Schools. A critical question for any ALP is whether it produces a more holistic learning experience that improves children's FLNs and is a sustainable route back into government schools for out-of-school children. Beyond the provision of accelerated learning, limited evidence has been provided thus far on whether children who benefit from it have also been able to improve their FLN skills, and successfully complete a basic education after transition.

From 2011, Kwame and his team of researchers from the University of Sussex, UCL Institute of Education and Hawassa University in Ethiopia (see Akyeampong et al., 2012a, 2012b, 2018) started to address this question through a series of studies that compared Speed School students' performance against a matched sample of students in government schools.[4] In their first study (Akyeampong et al., 2012b), they looked at what Speed School students were able to achieve after ten months on the programme. They followed this with a study that tracked students' progress after transitioning into those government public schools that are labelled 'Link Schools'. For the purposes of these research projects, Link Schools were re-labelled 'Improved Schools' because many Speed Schools operated in their compounds and so were visible to these public school teachers. The close proximity was also to ensure the government Link schools would improve as their teachers interacted with and observed Speed School teacher's instructional approaches, and that this would improve learning for students in their classes whether or not they had attended Speed Schools.[5]

The research studies also included a group of government schools that were used as a 'control group' to compare with the Speed and 'Improved' schools. We were also interested in comparing the achievement of Speed School students with non-Speed School students (students in government 'controlled' and 'Improved' schools), before completing either their primary or lower secondary education, the dropout rates after transition and their completion rates.

We included dropouts in the analysis so as to ascertain whether even after Speed school students had transitioned to government schools and dropped out, they still retained more of their learning than students from the other schools who had also dropped out. The study, in effect, evaluated the impact of the Speed Schools on students' trajectories and their achievement levels. The results of this evaluation are described below.

Speed School students' performance after ten-months

In Kwame and his colleagues' first study, a quasi-experimental design was used to sample a total of 1,875 students – 625 students in each of three groups (the Speed School group, a government school group as the 'control' and an Improved school group); they were matched based on age, gender and poverty status. Children from government 'Improved' schools and the government school group were selected from Grades 1–4 of primary school as these were the grades of the first cycle of primary education, which all the out-of-school students had dropped out of. Teachers and head teachers helped to identify children who were not attending regularly or were underperforming academically relative to other children in the same grade. This selection process meant that many government 'Improved' schools and government 'control' school students were overage for their grades (although the age and grade of children were already factors considered in the selection of children). Overage, low attainment and irregular attendance have been identified as precursors to dropping out-of-school (Lewin, 2007; Hunt, 2008). Thus, they shared a similar academic and school experience profile as the Speed School students.

Children enrolled in the Speed Schools were not more likely to attend pre-school than children enrolled in government 'Improved' schools or government 'control' schools (see Table 7.1). Similarly, no differences with respect to the average age at which children started school were found, as the average age of first enrolment between children enrolled in Speed Schools

Table 7.1 Descriptive statistics for children's school history

Variables	Speed school	Improved school	Government school	Statistic	Significance
% children attended pre-school	9.6	5.3	7.5	Cramer's V	No
Age when children started school	7.7	8.4	8.6	t-test	No
% children repeated a grade	43.5	24.8	19.6	Cramer's V	Yes
% children absenteeism previous year	77.0	61.4	56.1	Cramer's V	Yes
% children who dropped out	97.9	49.8	20.1	Cramer's V	Yes

Source: Speed School Project Survey (2011). Wave 1. Akyeampong et al. (2012a).

(7.7 years) was not statistically significantly different from children enrolled in 'Improved' schools (8.4 years) or in government schools (8.6 years).

After 10 months of the Speed School programme, students were tested in language and mathematics abilities, following the same test format as the one they completed at baseline. The pre- and post-intervention tests were designed to measure improvements in their abilities in these two subjects. The basic assumption was that children should be able to complete a higher proportion of the test as a result of an effective learning experience during the school year. If there had not been improvements then children would attain a similar percentage of correct responses to the test during baseline and endline surveys.

Literacy test results

In the literacy test, students were asked to respond to six literacy tasks that included letter recognition (Task 1), reading single words (Task 2), reading short and simple sentences (Task 3), reading a paragraph (Task 4), comprehension about the paragraph that was read (Task 5) and a writing test, the ability to write name, words and sentences (Task 6). The tasks progressed from low to moderately high difficulty. The maximum score on the test was 45 points (Akyeampong et al., 2012b).

Figure 7.1 summarises the results and shows the cumulative change in literacy scores for students according to the type of school attended. On average, Speed School students increased their score by 0.4 points in the first task of literacy and 2.8 points based on tasks 1 and 2. In effect, Speed School students

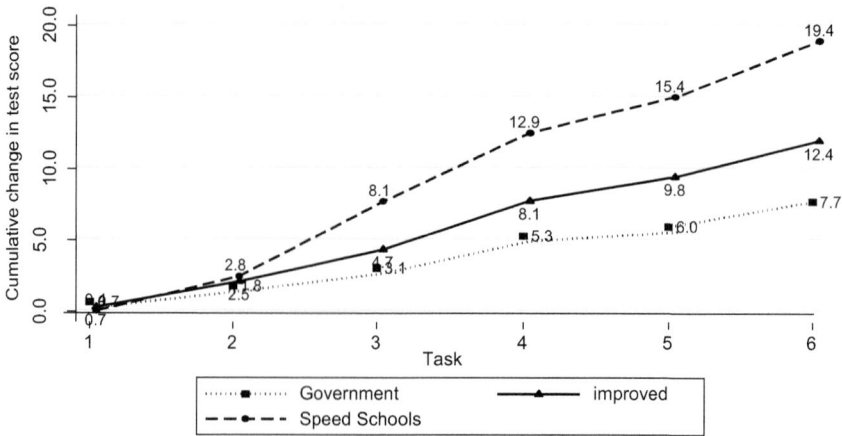

Figure 7.1 Cumulative change in score for literacy test.
Source: Akyeampong et al. (2012b, 15).

responded correctly to almost 3 more questions of the two tasks together between the baseline and the endline period. Students in the 'Improved' government schools increased their scores in tasks 1 and 2 by 2.5 points whereas those in government schools used as the control group increased their score by about 1.8 change in points. The results also showed that Speed School students achieved 19 cumulative scores (out of a total of 45 points) between the baseline and the endline. Students in the 'Improved' schools achieved 12 cumulative in scores and those in government 'control' schools 7.7 cumulative in scores.

The cumulative score for students in Speed Schools up to task 2 was 34.9 points in the baseline and 41.6 in the endline, making an improvement of 6.7 points. Overall, for the 6 tasks, the cumulative change over time for students in Speed Schools was 11 points. On average, Speed School students achieved 10.8 more points during the second test (endline), conditional on the first test results, compared with students enrolled in government 'control' schools. They showed an improvement of around 11.5 points in reading scores compared with students in government 'control' schools (Akyeampong et al., 2012b, 13–15).

Numeracy test results

The numeracy test covered knowledge, concept and applications in the areas of number recognition, basic summation, subtraction and multiplication, number sequencing, problem-solving, fractions, extracting information from figures. The test was based on the Early Grade Mathematics Assessment developed by United States Agency for International Development (USAID) and used widely in East Africa. Individual items assessed single rather than multiple skills. Items for the test were selected to ensure that they corresponded to learning goals of the Ethiopian primary mathematics curriculum.

Cumulative change in scores (Figure 7.2) shows a cumulative improvement in the numeracy test with the greatest improvement achieved by students in the Speed Schools (11 points), compared with government schools (7.5 points) and Improved Schools (5.1 points). For the final task, there was a negative change over time for all children, meaning children were less able to respond to the exercise in the endline than during the baseline, but with Improved schools doing rather poorly.

Improvement in test scores for children enrolled in Speed Schools was about 8.9 points. This was nearly 9 points higher in the second test, conditional on the first test results, compared with children enrolled in government schools. Overall, the test results for literacy and numeracy showed that Speed School children improved and outperformed children already attending government schools after receiving a second chance programme lasting 10 months.

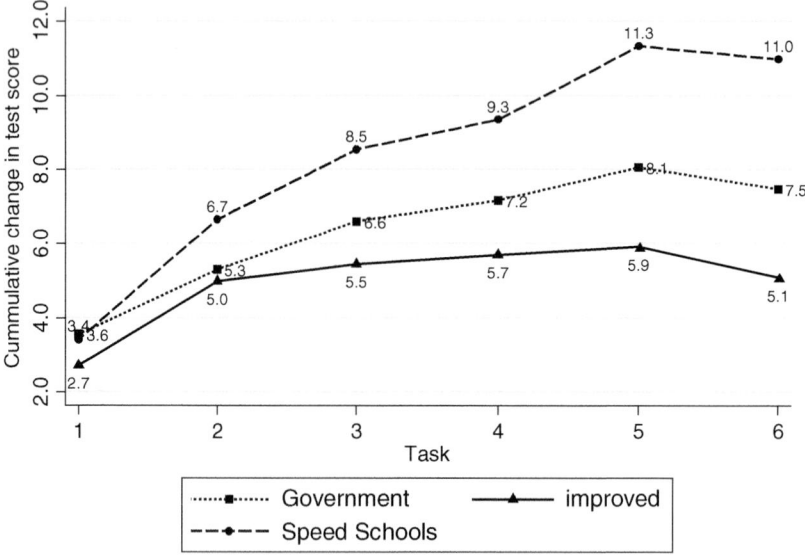

Figure 7.2 Cumulative change in score for numeracy test.
Source: Akyeampong et al. (2012b, 19).

Progress after transition: completion and repetition

In the longitudinal tracking study, we used a similar sampling approach to track progress in terms of who completed primary or secondary school and who dropped out (Akyeampong et al., 2018). This time we used a *propensity score matching method* to assess the comparability of the samples.[6] Completion rates measured as the proportion of students who successfully completed primary education were nearly twice as high for Speed School students than it was for government 'control' school students. In addition, relatively poor Speed School students achieved a higher completion rate than children in government 'control' schools and 'Improved' schools. The ratio of completion rates between the 'richest' and 'poorest' students was only 1.32 for Speed School students with the ratio much higher for students who attended government 'control' schools, indicating that Speed School students had a better chance of completing primary education (at Grade 6) than students who had attended a government or 'Improved' school of any wealth quartile (Table 7.2).

Gender and wealth were found to be key drivers of inequality in relation to completion (see Table 7.2) especially after considering the effect of factors such as child work, early marriage and pregnancy. Both male and female Speed School students had a higher chance of completing their education (59% and 52% respectively) than students in government school or 'Improved' schools. However, for Speed School students, the likelihood of completing secondary

Table 7.2 Primary completion by wealth and gender

	Speed	Government 'control'	Improved
Panel A – Wealth			
Q1	0.49	0.18	0.11
Q2	0.49	0.28	0.23
Q3	0.63	0.36	0.24
Q4	0.65	0.47	0.37
Ratio – Q4/Q1	1.32	2.63	3.25
Panel B – Gender			
Male	0.59	0.30	0.28
Female	0.52	0.32	0.24
Ratio – Male/female	1.12	0.93	1.17
Mean	0.56	0.31	0.26

Source: Akyeampong et al. (2018, 26).

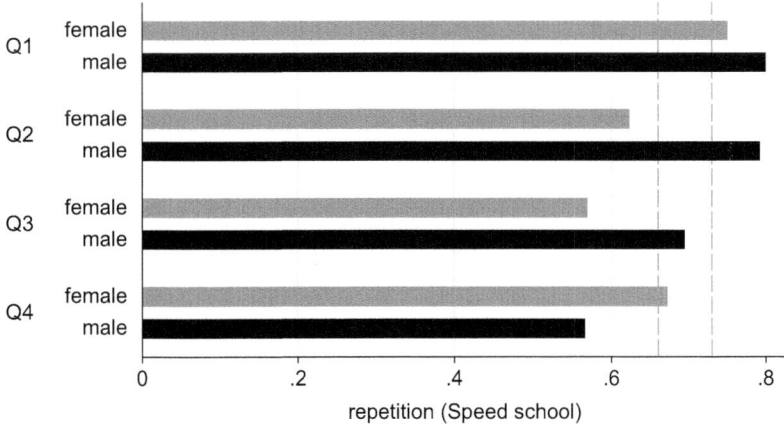

Figure 7.3 Repetition by wealth for Speed School students.

schooling was higher for a male than it was for a female student (about 12% higher) (see Table 7.2).

Speed School students were more likely to repeat a class though after transition – about 69% – higher for boys (73%) than for girls (66%) (see Figure 7.3). This could be attributed to the challenges of adjusting to their new learning environment, where the experience of large class size, didactic instruction and loss of opportunity to learn in groups may have unsettled many (Akyeampong et al., 2018; Humphreys et al., 2017). Transitioning from a highly participatory and, collaborative learning environment with 25 students in a class, to a teacher-centred instructional environment with 60 students or more, posed initial challenges for many Speed School students. Humphreys et al. (2017) found that Speed School students who had repeated a class reported difficulties in adjusting to the rigid instructional environment in government schools. Family poverty continued to be a key factor constraining their engagement with schooling. This was related to their capacity to withstand shocks such as death and sickness in the family, or environmental shocks such as drought' (75). Figure 7.3 shows that the poorest male Speed School students were more likely to repeat a grade than their poorest female counterparts (Quintiles 1, 2 and 3). Surprisingly, the trend reverses with the relatively 'richest' students where girls are more likely than boys to repeat.

Learning outcomes

Using an analysis that involved item response test (IRT)[7] continuous scores to assess learning outcomes showed that former Speed School students at the end of their basic education performed better than students in the other types of schools (Figure 7.4 – the vertical lines are further to the right). But the results also showed that the IRT only works for maths (unimodal distribution) and not for Sidama (mother tongue) and English scores where the graph for former Speed School students has two distinct modes (or bumps). A raw percentage of correct answers or tercile distributions produced a robust analysis of learning gains (see Tables 7.3 and 7.4). On average, the performance

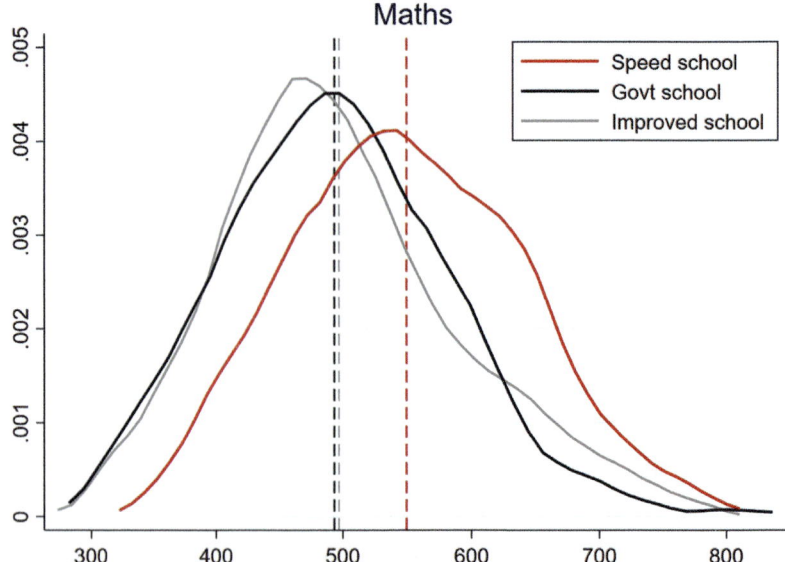

Figure 7.4 Learning scores distributions based on IRT (2PL).
Source: Akyeampong et al. (2018, 30).

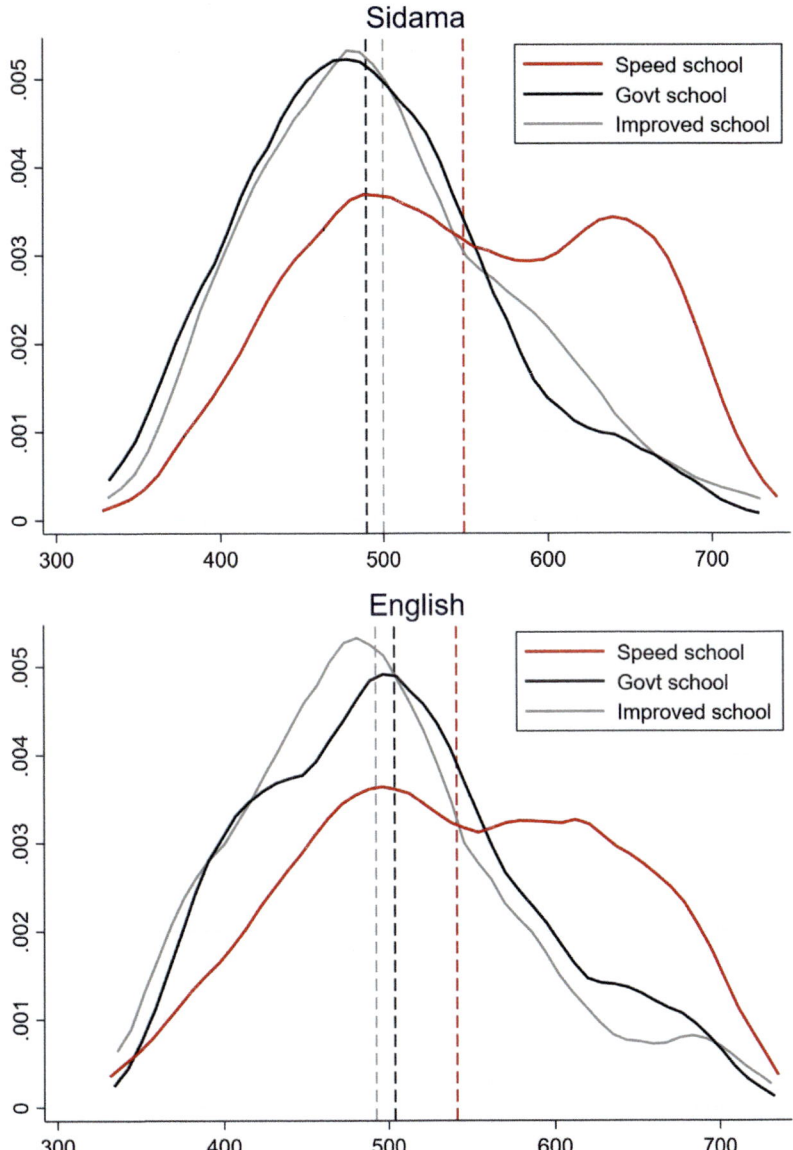

Figure 7.4 (Continued).

of former Speed School students was consistently better than government and 'Improved' school students for all three subjects. Speed School students scored more points than students in the government school sample –10.4% more in maths, 13.5% more in Sidama and 7.4% more in English. All the differences were statistically significant. Also, Speed School students were able

Table 7.3 Percentage of correct answers

School type	Maths	Sidama	English
Speed	47.6	46.4	42.6
Government	37.2	32.9	35.1
Improved	38.5	35.7	33.5

Source: Akyeampong et al. (2018, 30).

Table 7.4 Percentage of correct answers by primary completion

School type	Maths		Sidama		English	
	Did not complete	Complete	Did not complete	Complete	Did not complete	Complete
	(1)	(2)	(3)	(4)	(5)	(6)
Speed	43.0	51.3	40.7	50.9	36.2	47.7
Government	34.4	43.4	30.9	37.3	32.1	42.0
Improved	35.9	45.8	34.4	39.5	31.7	38.7

Source: Akyeampong et al. (2018, 31).

to answer correctly between around 0.9-2.1 (or one and two) more questions correctly than students who attended government 'control' schools for all the test items. This ability was statistically significant at the 1% level (see Table 7.3).

All students who had completed primary school generally achieved higher scores in Maths, Sidama and English, than those who dropped out before they could complete. Interestingly, both Speed School completers and non-completers scored higher than their government 'control' and Improved school counterparts (Table 7.4).

For maths, only 22.4% of former Speed School students were in the low achievers' category[8] compared to 42% and 43% of children in government sand Improved schools, respectively (see Figure 7.5). About 45% of Speed School students had moved into the top achiever's category (top tercile – T3), by the end of primary education as compared to only 24.8% and 25.8% of students in government and Link schools who reached the top level. Similar patterns emerged for Sidama and English (see Figure 7.5).

On the percentage of correct answers for maths, Sidama and English using students from government schools as a reference group, Speed School students performed better in the three subjects compared to government school students even after controls were included in the analysis. Speed School students, tested at the end of primary school, scored about nine times better than children in government schools. In English, they scored six times better and for Sidama about 12 times better. Overall Speed School students were getting nearly twice as many correct answers as children in government schools and doing much better in Sidama and maths, and English by the end of their primary education (Akyeampong et al., 2018).

Improving Learning Outcomes 197

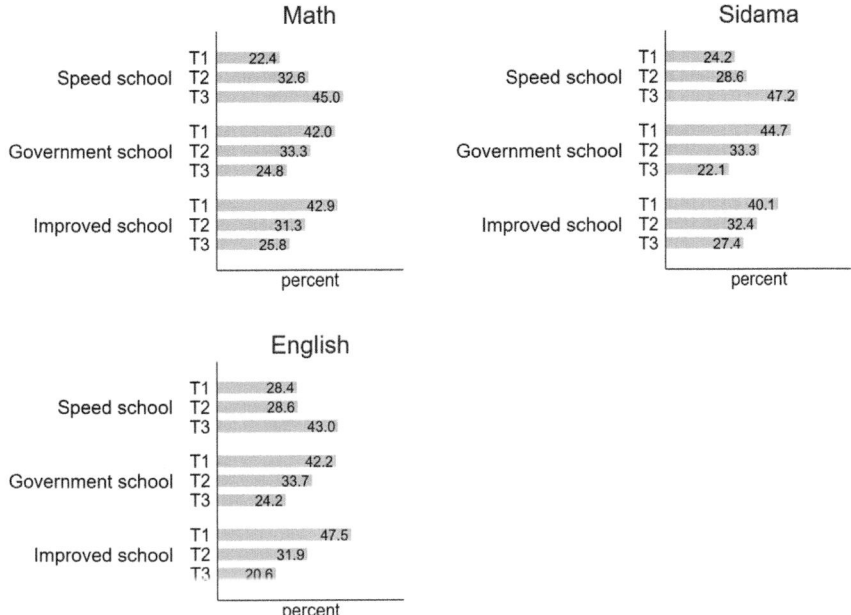

Figure 7.5 In attendance performance: Terciles of learning score distributions by school type for those currently attending.
Source: Akyeampong et al. (2018, 37).

Speed School students who dropped out *before* completing primary education also performed better than government and Improved school students who had also dropped out at similar points (see Figure 7.6). About 28.1% of Speed School dropouts performed at the top tercile (T3) in the maths test compared to 17.4% and 18.7% of government and Improved school students who dropped out respectively (see Figure 7.6). For the Sidama test, the non-completers (dropouts) from the Speed School group outperformed those from the other groups still attending (Akyeampong et al., 2018). Learning in the local language appears to have a lasting effect in terms of performance in Sidama, for Speed School students who dropped out compared with other students still in school.

The results showed that "about 28.1% of former Speed School children who had dropped out, scored at the top tercile level in maths, whereas for government and 'Improved' school students *still attending*, about 24.8% and 25.8% scored at the top tercile level in maths (see Figure 7.4). These differences were all statistically significant at the 1% level" (Akyeampong et al., 2018, 37, 39). In explaining these results, we argued that:

> Speed School students received a solid foundation in their basic skills, *in addition to* greater learning skills and motivation … that even if the instruction they receive in government schools is of a lower quality, they

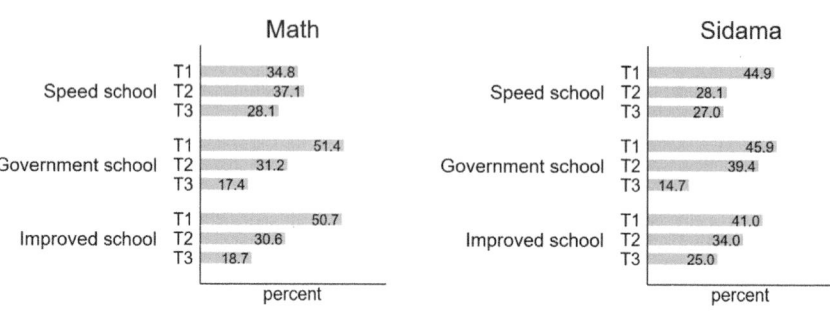
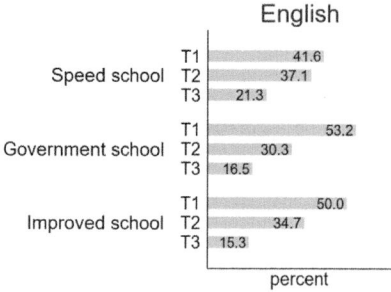

Figure 7.6 Drop out performance - Terciles learning score distributions by school type for those who had dropout.

Source: Akyeampong et al. (2018, 39).

are still better able and more motivated to learn on their own and with classmates ... Classroom observations in 'Improved' Schools revealed that though the pedagogy is not as participatory as the Speed School pedagogy, nevertheless, Speed School students are able to make the most of opportunities to learn because of the confidence it instilled in them to engage and contribute to classroom activity.

(Akyeampong et al., 2018, 33)

Neither age nor living with parents or caregivers was found to be correlated to learning (Table 7.5). Female students did not perform as well as male students in math, but gender estimates were found to be marginally significant for Sidama and English. In offering an explanation, the researchers argued that "domestic tasks are clearly a barrier for girls' learning and farm tasks for boys ... and, as before, educational aspirations are very strong determinant of learning levels – Speed School students appear to have this in abundance" (see Table 7.5; Akyeampong et al., 2018, 33).

A striking insight from the from longitudinal study is that students in 'Improved' Schools generally performed better than students in government schools. Speed School students who had transitioned into 'Improved' schools did even better. The programme's hypothesis was that children attending

Table 7.5 OLS⁹ estimates for percentage of correct answers

	Math			Sidama			English		
	(1)	(2)	(3)	(4)	(5)	(6)	(7)	(8)	(9)
	M0	M1	M2	M0	M1	M2	M0	M1	M2
Improved school	1.249	−0.483	−0.241	2.670*	1.973**	2.299***	−1.785**	−2.632***	−2.319**
Speed school	10.335***	9.816***	8.626***	13.295***	13.158***	12.560***	7.282***	6.840***	5.594***
age		0.021	−0.004		−0.114	−0.092		0.106	0.160
# children (higher than 3)		0.844	0.664		−0.116	0.045		−0.329	−0.287
live with parents		5.011***	0.251		4.884*	3.930		2.787	−1.373
wealth Q2		0.711	0.425		−0.498	−0.464		−0.914	−1.158
wealth Q3		5.922***	4.715***		2.161**	1.495		1.281	0.119
wealth Q4		6.878***	4.807***		2.476*	1.247		2.639*	0.451
responsibility care – high		−0.913	−0.703		−1.410	−1.208		−2.264	−2.203
responsibility care – high x female		−7.717***	−7.072***		−4.086*	−3.271		−3.806**	−2.755*
responsibility domestic task high		3.642	2.999		3.612	2.967		4.379*	3.690
responsibility domestic task high x female		0.562	1.420		0.346	1.053		1.733	2.710*
responsibility farm task high		−4.249***	−4.155***		−1.911	−2.143		−5.511***	−5.538***
responsibility farm task high x female		−2.276	−1.514		0.195	0.646		−0.463	0.510
responsibility farm task high x female		6.453***	5.813***		1.340	0.712		3.673***	2.520**
Education aspirations – high			6.411***			4.778***			7.298***
Woreda, Shebedino	1.366	−0.621	−0.927	3.045**	1.993*	2.018**	2.449*	1.766	1.324
Observations	1,589	1,576	1,535	1,589	1,576	1,535	1,589	1,576	1,535
R-squared	0.069	0.129	0.150	0.094	0.109	0.123	0.048	0.067	0.098

Source: Akyeampong et al. (2018, 32).

Speed Schools would do well in 'Improved' schools if their teachers key elements of the Speed School pedagogy 'Improved' school teachers were able to leverage Speed School students' funds of knowledge and agentic learning behaviour to enrich the teaching and learning experience of all (Akyeampong et al., 2016b). In effect, 'Improved' school teachers interaction with Speed School students was also providing benefits for non-Speed School students in their class.

For Speed School students, although the pedagogy encountered in 'Improved' Schools was different, the participatory pedagogy of the Speed School had enabled them to master the basic concepts of the first three grades of primary education, which meant the difficulties they experienced was 'short-lived' (Humphreys et al., 2017, viii). The boost they receive from the Speed Schools not only brings them up to the standard of their peers but also gives them an advantage over the majority. "Paradoxically, the one year in a Speed School is a better preparation for success in the later grades of the 'Improved' schools than three years in their earlier grades" (Akyeampong et al., 2016b).

Lessons for the 'Learning Crisis'

Using the insights of post-humanist framings of learning, this chapter has made visible the creative pedagogical practices of Speed Schools in Ethiopia in which students' engagement with their material worlds generates joyful and purposeful learning that affirms their agency as learners, as individuals and in their collective interactions. That such innovative holistic and materially based approaches to learning are yielding concrete benefits in terms of their learning outcomes has also been demonstrated through the analysis of quantitative data tracking students' progress. Evidently, making learning enjoyable in a grounded way that recognises, validates and uses objects, artefacts, as well as local environmental knowledge has a wide range of learning gains. Learning also become enjoyable when fully participatory in these schools, galvanising students' self-confidence as learners and empowering many of them to make a successful transition into government schools.

There are valuable, important lessons to be learnt therefore from Speed Schools in Ethiopia. This chapter has outlined only some of them, but these have demonstrated, even at a minimum level, ways to improve the learning experiences of African children. The elements described here mean returning attention to creative pedagogical processes that address learners *in situ,* as part of a relational and physical world outside of school. Also, these processes need to value the opportunities offered by recruiting teachers with local knowledges and languages who are trained to celebrate and not pathologise the children they serve. In the Speed Schools, there are no 'failures' as such, only rich and situated resources that can benefit their learning.

Notes

1 We wish to acknowledge the members of the research who contributed to the studies including from Sussex, John Pryor, Sara Humphreys, Jo Westbrook, Benjamin Zeitlyn, Marcos Delprato, Ricardo Sabates, from Institute of Education UCL Zoe James, and from Hawassa University, Abinet Mensite, Rahel Abraham, Solomon Wolde and Teketel Adane. Asmelash Haile Tsegay led a team of local researchers to track the 2011 baseline students and assisted in the translation and piloting of test items for the study.
2 See in particular Akyeampong et al. (2012, 2016a, 2016b, 2018).
3 See studies by Alemayehu (2022), Seid (2016), Aschale (2013).
4 Thanks to members of the research team including from Sussex, John Pryor, Sara Humphreys, Jo Westbrook, Benjamin Zeitlyn, Marcos Delprato, Ricardo Sabates, and UCL's Zoe James, and from Hawassa University, Asmelash Haile Tsegay, Abinet Mensite, Rahel Abraham, Solomon Wolde and Teketel Adane.
5 The hypothesis was that these so called 'Linked' schools might have offered government teachers a chance to learn about a new pedagogy by observation. Many government school teachers visited Speed School classrooms to observe how teaching and learning was being organised, and that they would adopt elements of the Speed School pedagogy to minimise learning disruption of Speed School students after transition and by extension improve learning for their other students.
6 With the propensity score matching, a number of other important variables are used to compute the probability that a student who is enrolled in a Speed School shares similar characteristics with a student from the government schools. This probability is based on observed characteristics, such as household level of poverty and number of children living in the household. The propensity score – a number between 0 and 1 – enabled researchers to match students from the Speed Schools who had a close propensity score to students from the government schools, in effect turning the matched children in the Link and government schools into a comparison group. In total 625 Speed Schools children were matched with 625 children from Link Schools and 625 children from other Government Schools, making a total of 1,875 children who were tracked for the study.
7 Item Response Theory Model (IRT) is used for modelling the relationship between the latent abilities of a group of subjects and the examination items used for measuring their abilities. In the Speed School study IRT analysis calculated the probability with which children are able to answer a specific test question (for maths, English and Sidama separately) correctly. The probability is based on two factors: (i) the difficulty of the test question (given by the number of children who answer it correctly); and (ii) the child's overall test scores (how many questions the child was able to answer). To obtain the continuous score a two-parameter logistic model (2PL model) was used, where item responses are typically of the form yes or no, correct or incorrect, etc. Items are assumed to vary in discrimination and difficulty.
8 We grouped the achievers by terciles (i.e. ordered distribution in three groups) with the lowest achievers in the bottom third and the highest achievers in the top third.
9 OLS stands for Ordinary Least Squares regression (OLS) and is a common technique statistical technique for estimating coefficients of linear regression equations.

References

Abebe, W. and Woldehanna, T., 2013. *Teacher training and development in Ethiopia: Improving education quality by developing teacher skills, attitudes and work conditions.* Young Lives. Working Paper 103 published by Young Lives.

Akyeampong, K., Amado, Y., Sabates, R., and Zeitlyn, B., 2012a. *Evaluation of speed school project – baseline report*. Research Report Centre for International Education, University of Sussex, UK.

Akyeampong, K., Amado, Y., Sabates, R., and Zeitlyn, B., 2012b. *Evaluation of speed school project – impact report*. Research Report Centre for International Education, University of Sussex, UK.

Akyeampong, K., Delprato, M., Sabates, R., James, Z., Pryor, J., Westbrook, J., Humphreys, S., et al., 2018. *Tracking the progress of speed school students 2011–2017*. Research Report Centre for International Education, University of Sussex, UK.

Akyeampong, K., Pryor, J., Westbrook, J., Abraham, R., Adane, T., and Wolde, S., 2016a. *Research into the speed school curriculum and pedagogy in Ethiopia*. Research Monograph 1. Centre for International Education, University of Sussex.

Akyeampong, K., Pryor, J., Westbrook, J., Abraham, R., Adane, T., and Wolde, S., 2016b. *Pedagogy in link schools attended by graduates of speed schools*. Research Monograph 2. Centre for International Education, University of Sussex.

Alemayehu, E., 2022. 'Ethiopia's mother tongue instructional language policy: a methodological discourse'. *International Journal of Research in Academic World*, 1(8): 20–27.

Alexander, R., 2008. *Education for all, the quality imperative and the problem of pedagogy*. CREATE Pathways to Access Research Monograph No. 16. University of Sussex.

Alexander, R., 2015. 'Teaching and learning for all? The quality imperative revisited'. In R. Alexander (ed.), *Routledge handbook of international education and development*. Routledge, pp. 118–132.

Aschale, A., 2013. *Language policy and practices in Ethiopia from Post 1991*. Foreign Languages and Literature, Addis Ababa University.

Barad, K., 2003. 'Post humanist performativity: toward an understanding of how matter comes to matter'. *Signs: Journal of Women in Culture and Society*, 28(3): 801–831.

Barad, K., 2007. *Meeting the universe halfway: quantum physics and the entanglement of matter and meaning*. Duke University Press.

Bennett, J., 2004. 'The force of things: steps toward an ecology of matter'. *Political Theory*, 32(3): 347–372.

Bhana, D., Nzimakwe, T., and Nzimakwe, P., 2011. 'Gender in the early years: boys and girls in an African working class primary school'. *International Journal of Educational Development*, 31(5): 443–448.

Blaikie, F., Daigle, C., and Vasseur, L., 2020. *New pathways for teaching and learning: the post humanist approach*. Canadian Commission for UNESCO, Ottawa, Canada.

Burman, E., 2018. 'Towards a posthuman developmental psychology of child, families and communities.' In *International handbook of early childhood education*. Springer Nature, pp. 1599–1620.

Crossouard, B., and Dunne, M., 2021. *Gender and education in postcolonial contexts*. Oxford research encyclopaedia of education.

Crossouard, B., Dunne, M., Szyp, C., Madu, T., and Teeken, B., 2022. 'Rural youth in southern Nigeria: fractured lives and ambitious futures'. *Journal of Sociology*, 58(2): 218–235.

De Freitas, E., and Curinga, M.X., 2015. 'New materialist approaches to the study of language and identity: assembling the posthuman subject'. *Curriculum Inquiry*, 45(3): 249–265.

Duhn, I., 2012. 'Places for pedagogies, pedagogies for places'. *Contemporary Issues in Early Childhood*, 13(2): 99–107.
Dunne, M., 2009. 'Gender as an entry point for addressing social exclusion and multiple disparities in education'. In *Technical paper: UNGEI global advisory committee technical meeting* (Vol. 27). New York United Nations Girls Initiative.
Dunne, M., and Adzahlie-Mensah, V., 2016. 'Subordinate subjects: the work of the hidden curriculum in post-colonial Ghana'. In D. Wyse, L. Hayward, and J. Pandya (eds.), *The SAGE handbook of curriculum, pedagogy and assessment*. Sage Publications, pp. 216–230.
Eriksen, S.H., and Mulugeta, E., 2021. 'Leisure time of working children in Addis Ababa'. *Childhood*, 28(3): 395–408.
Ferrante, A., and Sartori, D., 2016. 'From anthropocentrism to post-humanism in the educational debate'. *Relations. Beyond Anthropocentrism*, 4: 175.
Hedges, H., and Cooper, M., 2018. 'Relational play-based pedagogy: theorising a core practice in early childhood education'. *Teachers and Teaching*, 24(4): 369–383.
Howes, A.J. and Miles, S., 2021. 'The contact zone: photography and social justice in educational research'. *International Journal of Qualitative Studies in Education*, 34(5): 464–479.
Humphreys, S. Mengiste, A., Getachew, S., Akyeampong, K., and Semela, T., 2017. Research into self-help groups and speed school graduates' experiences of schooling. Research Monograph 3, Centre for International Education, University of Sussex.
Hunt, F., 2008. *Dropping out from school: a cross-country review of literature*. CREATE Pathway to Access Research Monograph No. 20. Centre for International Education, University of Sussex: CREATE.
Jirata, T.J., 2019. 'The cultural spaces of young children: care, play and learning patterns in early childhood among the Guji people of Ethiopia'. *Global Studies of Childhood*, 9(1): 42–55.
Lewin, K.M., 2007. *Improving access, equity and transitions in education: creating a research agenda*. CREATE Pathways to Access Series, No. 1. Brighton: University of Sussex.
Luminos Fund, 2018. *Annual report*. Available at: https://luminosfund.org/wp-content/uploads/2021/10/Luminos_Annual_Report_2018_spreads.pdf
Moss, P., 2016. 'Introduction'. In K. Murris (ed.), *The posthuman child: educational transformation through philosophy with picture books*. Routledge.
Murris, K., 2016a. *The posthuman child: educational transformation through philosophy with picture books*. Routledge.
Murris, K., 2016b. 'Philosophy with children as part of the solution to the early literacy education crisis in South Africa'. *European Early Childhood Education Research Journal*, 24(5): 652–667.
Murris, K. (2018). 'Posthuman child and the diffractive teacher: decolonizing the nature/culture binary'. In A. Cutter-Mackenzie-Knowles, K. Malone, and E.B. Hacking (eds.), *Research handbook on childhood nature*. Springer.
Osgood, J., 2014. 'Playing with gender: making space for post-human childhood(s)'. In J. Moyles, J. Payler, and J. Georgeson (eds.), *Early years foundations: Critical issues* Open University Press, pp. 191–202.
Robeyns, I., 2003. 'Sen's capability approach and gender inequality: selecting relevant capabilities'. *Feminist Economics*, 9(2–3): 61–92.
Seid, Y., 2016. 'Does learning in mother tongue matter? Evidence from a natural experiment in Ethiopia'. *Economics of Education Review*, 55: 21–38.

Snaza, N., and Weaver, J.A. eds., 2015. *Posthumanism and educational research* (Vol. 35). Routledge.

Tafere, Y., 2012. 'Children's experiences and perceptions of poverty in Ethiopia'. *Young Lives*.

Taylor, A., Pacinini-Ketchabaw, V., and Blaise, M., 2012. 'Children's relations to the more-than-human world'. *Contemporary Issues in Early Childhood*, 13(2): 81–85.

Tikly, L., and Barrett, A.M., 2011. 'Social justice, capabilities and the quality of education in low income countries'. *International Journal of Educational Development*, 31(1): 3–14.

Wang, L., 2018. 'All work, all play: harnessing play-based learning in Ethiopia and Liberia to create lifelong learners'. *Childhood Education*, 94(5): 4–13.

8 Engaging Parents, Extended Families and Communities

Second Chance Programmes in Conflict-affected Liberia

We noted in Part 1 that deficit framings of 'poor children' also extend to their guardians, families and wider communities who experience long-term inter-generational educational marginalisation in contexts of multiple forms of hardship. Hence, they too are constructed as passive and lacking in agency, within top-down and judgemental framings made in educational interventions that all too frequently bypass the pivotal role of community engagement. Yet, when Benavot (2016) critiques the 'educational reforms' associated with the Education for All agenda, that "rest on technical solutions alone" he has noted that: "strategies for learning are most effective when they develop strong links with existing community priorities" (5).

This chapter focuses on how another accelerated learning programme (ALP), this time called *Second Chance* that is based in conflict-affected Liberia, offers a contrasting way of engaging with rural impoverished communities[1] Several studies have shown the effectiveness of ALPs in addressing long-term disengagement from educational provision not only in impoverished but also in conflict-affected contexts where the majority of the world's out-of-school children (OOSC) live and where marginality intersects with wider socio-economic drivers of conflict and peace[2] This chapter builds on those studies by spotlighting here the contribution that innovative modes of community engagement in Second Chance's approach make to addressing systemic educational exclusion in Liberia.

We start by outlining the theoretical lenses we use to understand and explain the strengths of the Second Chance approach. For this case study, we draw on Butler's ontology of the agency of precaritised communities as emergent from, and rooted in, their experience of vulnerability (Butler, 2016). This framing of the experiences of communities suffering precarity enables us to rethink the modalities of engagement with communities who suffer educational marginalisation, outside of assumptions of their passivity and lack of agency.

We then describe the issues at stake in this case study, first by showing how decentralisation initiatives in Africa have reproduced deficit assumptions about educationally marginalised communities. We explain the conflict-affected context of Liberia and its distinctive challenges in ensuring access to education provision for its rural, impoverished communities – challenges that intersect

DOI: 10.4324/9781003185482-11

with the historical socio-economic and political drivers of conflict and also with current perceptions of peacebuilding processes in that country. In the rest of this chapter, we describe how the Second Chance ALP seeks to address these challenges, in particular focusing on the Parental Engagement Groups (PEGs) through which the programme builds relationships with the families and communities of children who attend. We report the data collected using novel data-gathering methods that help us understand the perceptions and experiences of a group of parents who are usually ignored within the poverty-education alleviation models discussed in Part 1.

Informed by Butler's conceptual lens about the co-existence of vulnerability and resistance to precarity, our analysis shows how the PEGs demonstrate a grounded, context-responsive modality of engagement. This connects with and builds on, rather than bypasses or pathologises, the exercise of agency by communities experiencing educational marginalisation – part of their broader navigation of multiple forms of socio-economic hardship. In doing so, the PEGs open up the possibility of sustained parental support for their children's re-engagement with educational provision. The conclusions drawn from Second Chance ALP provide lessons about how to reconfigure community outreach beyond the assumptions characterising the 'learning crisis' narrative.

Rethinking Community Engagement: Vulnerability and Resistance

Butler's theorisation of the vulnerability as well as the resistance of communities experiencing precarity offers a powerful conceptual apparatus to rethink top-down and dismissive approaches. Butler's starting point is a critique of the influential dichotomy within social theory and popular discourse drawn between vulnerability and resistance (Butler et al., 2016; Polychroniou, 2022) and the assumptions that flow from this division. The notion of vulnerability refers not only to "subjective dispositions but...exposure to power relations" that produce socio-economic precarity differentially experienced by some populations (Butler et al., 2016, 3). The notion has a twofold reference (Polychroniou, 2022). First, it refers to the context-specific experience of forms of precarity including homelessness, unemployment, illiteracy and lack of access to education. These result from socio-historical conditions and asymmetrical power relationships in particular contexts. The experiences of conflict-affected communities in Liberia discussed later in this chapter attest to precisely this condition. Second, it refers to a universal ontological condition of being human that is embodied, affective and inter-relational. Butler counter-poses this framing of the human against individualistic conceptions of agency which are problematised as symptomatic of 'capitalist concepts of self-interest and masculinist fantasies of sovereign mastery' (2016, 3).

Importantly for our purposes, Butler critiques the tendency to use external interventions to overcome the experiences of vulnerability suffered by precaritised populations where it is conceived as a problem that can be corrected and solved. Hence:

> vulnerability requires and implies the need for protection and the strengthening of paternalistic forms of power at the expense of collective forms of resistance and social transformation.
>
> (2016, 1)

This results in "the idea that paternalism is the site of agency and vulnerability, understood only as victimisation and passivity, invariably the site of inaction" (2016, 1).

Such logics are evident in the approaches to educationally marginalised communities such as those in Liberia. Hence, as discussed in Part 1, bypassing meaningful community engagement, any improvement of assessment systems and the measurement of learning outcomes – prescriptions modelled by Western global aid institutions – have been advocated as panaceas for the learning challenges in Africa. This assumes that these communities are inherently problematic and in need of interventions by outsiders that purport to be redemptive and transformative, but which offer only externally led, frequently doctrinaire prescriptions and guidance. These responses to educational marginality reiterate assumptions embedded in global development and humanitarian agendas that reify certain populations including the 'poor' as 'vulnerable' and therefore in need of protection (Butler, 2016, 5; Cornwall and Fujita, 2012; McWhorter, 2016).

All these framings amount to a form of paternalism and judgementalism that forecloses responses which prioritise meaningful engagement with the affected communities themselves. Such responses would seek to understand their knowledges and experiences, their exposure to power relationships that have produced their 'vulnerability' and therefore the need to respect, recognise and build on their prior exercise of agency in challenging circumstances. Without such responses, policymakers are most likely to bypass the possibility that the very experience of vulnerability itself may be mobilised in the process of challenging and ameliorating the conditions that produce those experiences, in modes of resistance. As Butler argues, the experience of vulnerability may be simultaneously 'perilous and enabling' (Butler et al., 2016, 1) and thus a locus not of passivity but also of agency.

Butler's rethinking of the connections and continuum between vulnerability and resistance can be used to critique and re-envision framings and experiences of a range of precaritised groups (Butler et al., 2016). However, it is also productive as an analytical and explanatory resource to rethink actual engagement with communities who experience educational marginality, such as those with whom the Second Chance programme engages in Liberia. First, Butler's theory returns attention to what is too frequently bypassed, the need for meaningful consultation and dialogue to understand the intersecting experiences of socio-economic marginality in which their children's failure to access education provision is embedded. Engagement needs to shift the power relationships that, as discussed above, result in tokenistic approaches to community participation in which the voices, knowledges and experiences of those suffering from educational marginality are suppressed or ignored. Second, the processes of engagement need to re-establish and recognise community agency not just in navigating circumstances of precarity in their daily lives, but also in the acts of resistance to their educational marginality. Such approaches would recognise communities as precarious but also agentic, inviting forms of community engagement that recognise their daily navigation of intersecting hardships. Third, locating educational marginality as a form of vulnerability counteracts the view that reduces the learning challenge to a question of improving cognitive outcomes in literacy and numeracy. Understanding the vulnerability of communities whose relationship with formal educational provision has been tenuous necessitates an expansive understanding that recognises the intersection of this form of marginality with other forms of precarity – social, economic and political. Finally, in highlighting the essential inter-dependent and relational character of the experience of vulnerability, Judith Butler's thinking opens up a critique of the individualistic framings of learning and educational success associated narrowly with performance in assessment regimes.

With this agenda in mind, we start by showing how deficit assumptions about communities experiencing educational marginalisation are repeated by decentralisation initiatives in the African context.

Deficit views of communities experiencing educational marginalisation

Studies of decentralisation initiatives in sub-Saharan Africa that aim to involve communities in their children's schooling paradoxically have found that negative assumptions about parents held by teachers and education authority figures undermine the forms of communication and consultation with which they seek to achieve these goals.[3] We know that the dominance of negative and judgemental views of parents, in particular, can lead to a disjunction between 'policy intention and policy implementation' (Khanal, 2013, 235). Parent Teacher Associations and School Management Councils are often established as institutional mechanisms to amplify parents' voices. Yet, studies of their operation in the micro-spaces of meetings have shown how parents' experiences and knowledges are frequently disparaged within judgemental and regulatory approaches by teachers and educational officials. They are seen as 'willing but unable' (Beasley and Huillery, 2017, 531) or as 'ignorant' and in need of 'sensitisation' (Humphreys et al., 2015, 142). Such views have resulted in 'punitive attitudes' that are characterised by a tendency to 'talk down to parents' who were 'castigated and regulated', and 'called to order' (Humphreys et al., 2015, 142). An ethnographic study in North Eastern Nigeria of school-community relations in six primary schools found that, during PTA meetings, teachers would offer "corrective advice to parents about pupil late coming, absenteeism, dropout or enrolment" (Dunne et al., 2021, 854). This resulted in 'agonistic relations' and 'social tensions', with some parents afraid to 'talk back' for fear that their child would be 'victimised'. Importantly, a study of school community relations in sub-Saharan Africa, Dunne et al. (2007, 25) point out that "parents may internalise deficit constructions of themselves in relation to schooling, which may negatively affect their children's participation in school".

These approaches appear either to blame parents for their children's disengagement from learning or frame them as uninterested in their children's schooling. For instance, Unterhalter et al.'s (2012) study of attitudes of Kenyan education officials to parents experiencing poverty found that "national and provincial officials describe poor parents not in terms of hardship or the struggle to survive but in terms of educational, economic or cultural deficits" (224). Such judgementalism forecloses more grounded, empathetic engagements that could have recognised the complex socio-economic structural circumstances that shape parents' attitude towards educational provision for their children (Yamada, 2014, 166; Akyeampong and Adzahlie-Mensah, 2018).

Such asymmetrical power relationships between parents (suffering intergenerational exclusion from education) and education's official representatives and managers such as teachers and administrators may 'subjugate parental views' (Bulgrin, 2022). Power asymmetries within communities undermine inclusive participation in which all parents are listened to and respected. In the Ghanaian context, Essuman and Akyeampong (2011, 513) found that:

> in poor rural contexts it is often the local elite and relatively more educated members of the community who become the new brokers of decision making and, through their actions, close up the spaces for representation and participation by community members in the affairs of the schools.

The lack of meaningful, inclusive and equitable consultation with parents means that deep-rooted and systemic challenges that negatively affect school-community relationships remain unaddressed. Schooling may therefore remain 'an unknown' to communities with long-term experience of never attending school (Dunne et al., 2007, 26). For instance, Pryor (2005, 193) observed that "for community members to participate in the school world, engagement with it and the recognition of its importance are preconditions for it to be perceived as a meaningful world" (quoted in Yamada, 2014, 167). Studies that have highlighted a lack of trust between parents and educational providers managing processes of decentralisation (Teise and Barnett, 2021; Bulgrin and Semedeton, 2022) point to the need for meaningful and non-judgemental collaborative partnerships to support children's learning. Also, as Yamada (2014) argues, the tendency for men and male elders to dominate school-community interactions means that consultation with parents has to find ways to privilege the voices and experience of women.

All these findings underscore not just the significance but the potential of engagement with communities to address the social, economic, material, affective challenges leading to educational marginalisation. The goal is to collectively navigate across schools, teachers, parents and the wider community. We now turn to characterise the nature of the challenges faced in conflict-affected Liberia.

Conflict, Education and 'Liberal Peace Building' in Liberia

Liberia suffered a brutal and protracted civil conflict between 1989 and 2003 that decimated the already fragile social infrastructure, including education and health services. It resulted in the killing of over 500,000 people and large-scale displacement and involved abuses of human rights including the conscription of women and children into sometimes drug-induced violence. The conflict crushed already weak democratic institutions and put a stop to commercial and agricultural activity. Commentators have reported on the traumatic legacy of the conflict, in particular the fracturing of trust and social cohesion amongst communities across the country (TRC, 2009).

The drivers of grievance and conflict still remain 20 years after the Peace Agreement[4] These include massive rural-urban inequalities and inequitable access to health and education provision (Svoronos et al., 2015; Gabani and Guinness, 2019; World Bank, 2023) and the exclusionary processes of associated with political representation and weak state-society relations (Funaki and Glencorse, 2017). There is also an ongoing monopoly of economic resources and opportunities by elites and dominant ethnic groups (Gadkari, 2022). For example, land concessions are given to international corporate companies to export the country's rich natural resources with the result that local communities are displaced and remain impoverished (Vinck et al., 2011; Mitman, 2021). Consequently, social tensions over land rights and tenure (Kepeh and Suah, 2021) undermine the capacity in rural areas to diversify agricultural production beyond subsistence farming, thereby creating food shortages (Moore and Harder, 2015).

These drivers of conflict were rooted in the foundation of the modern Liberian state in 1842 by the American Colonisation Society that privileged incoming Americo-Liberians over indigenous communities. The resulting and continuing precarity of much of the population, especially in rural areas, has led many commentators to classify Liberia as having attained what has been called a 'negative peace' (Galtung, 1969) in which the structural factors creating conflict remain unaddressed. Liberia is positioned 175 out of 189 countries in the UNDP Human Development Index (UNDP, 2020).

The majority of the population still lacks access to basic utilities and facilities, including water supplies, sanitation and electricity (Kanagasabai et al., 2021; Amoak et al., 2023; Innis and van Asche, 2023). Food security is very low; some 32% of children under five are stunted and malnourishment is pervasive (Kumeh et al., 2020). High under-five and maternal mortality rates result from limited access to health services (Brault et al., 2018).

Shepler and Williams (2017, 424) refer to Liberia as facing a 'crisis of youth' because of non-existent economic opportunities and extreme poverty. Given that 58% of Liberia's population are under 25 (Cunningham et al., 2023), this is a major national challenge (McMullin, 2022; US Aid, 2019). Widespread drug abuse amongst youth is linked to poverty, homelessness and being out-of-school as well as lack of employment prospects (Petruzzi et al., 2018). The horrific violence and human rights abuses during the conflict continue to fracture the psycho-social health of children and youth (Yoder et al., 2016; Borba et al., 2016; Levey et al., 2016) undermining community well-being (Sharma et al., 2023).

Meanwhile, patriarchal attitudes result in various forms of inequality and gender-based violence that remains pervasive (Coker et al., 2023). Women have less access to public services and lack socio-economic power and decision-making authority at local and national levels (Gizelis and Cao, 2021; Cunningham et al., 2023; Karra et al., 2023). The country was rated 156 out of 162 countries in 2019 in the Gender Inequality Index (UNDP, 2020, 5).

Recent protests to draw attention to such economic hardship (Toweh, 2022) as well as the ongoing threat of violence during elections (Pruett et al., 2024) attest to the continued existence of these multiple drivers of conflict. It goes without saying that the education system has been affected.

'Liberal peacebuilding' and formal education

The experience of 'negative peace' by the majority of Liberians in its various social, political and economic dimensions intersects with their negative experiences of educational provision (Santos and Novelli, 2017). The education system was destroyed during the conflict and the work of reconstruction continues. Today, there is a continuing shortage of schools, qualified teachers and instructional materials. Moreover, the state has faced the additional challenge of reintegrating demobilised child soldiers and internally displaced children (Boayue, 2014).

The massive surge in student enrolments in the years immediately after the Peace Agreement in 2003 (Catholic Relief Services, 2016) indicated the high societal expectations of education as a benefit of the peace. However, Liberia still has one of the highest proportions of out-of-school children (OOSC) in the world (Luminos Fund, 2018, 2020, 8; UNICEF, 2023) with 31.4% of school children at primary level for the year 2020 being out-of-school (UNESCO Institute of Statistics, UIS, 2024). The Education Sector Plan for 2022–2027 notes that:

> in Liberia too many children still remain out of school, especially the poorest girls and boys in underserved areas with their rights to a quality education unrealised and their potential unfulfilled.
>
> (UNESCO, 2022, 21)

Hence, "the critical task ... is therefore to bring more children, especially those from poorer, underserved areas, into the education system at the right age" (UNESCO, 2022, 22).

The low level of participation in formal education provision results mainly from nationwide poverty, with parents unable to afford school fees as well as indirect costs such as school uniforms, shoes, transportation or school supplies. Family decisions to take children out-of-school to help with subsistence farming or household chores also contribute to low enrolment, as do children's hunger, malnutrition and illness (Dago and Yogo, 2022; UNESCO, 2022, Education Sector Plan, 2022–2027). Girls are also more likely to drop out as a result of social norms privileging the education of boys and traditional gender roles, early marriage and teenage pregnancy, unequal division of domestic labour and low numbers of women teachers to act as role models (Stromquist et al., 2013). Spotlighting the social practices within schools that compound these barriers, the Truth and Reconciliation (TRC) report (2009, 258) noted that "the educational system has not succeeded so far in creating an environment where girls would feel welcome at school and where their needs are met". That teachers are unable to communicate with marginalised communities in their local languages also undermines the possibility of building trusting and collaborative relationships likely to support children's and particularly girls' sustained engagement with formal schooling. This compounds a pre-existing cynicism about the benefits of formal education amongst rural impoverished communities that stems from long-term inter-generational disengagement and a sense of being abandoned by the state (Svoronos et al., 2015; Vinck et al., 2011).

As in other conflict-affected contexts, the challenge of ensuring equitable educational provision in Liberia is inextricably bound up with broader societal concern to address the drivers of conflict and achieve sustainable peace (Barrios-Tao et al., 2017; Novelli et al., 2014). Improving access to educational provision, addressing rural-urban inequalities and reducing out-of-school rates and increasing retention and completion rates for girls are recognised as key contributors to national peacebuilding in Liberia's Poverty Reduction and Growth Strategy (International Monetary Fund IMF, 2021, xiii). Nationwide consultations with rural communities across Liberia (Vinck et al., 2011) report that access to education and health services were their key priorities for peacebuilding, alongside improving employment opportunities and land rights. The pivotal contribution of education to peacebuilding in the country was also recognised in the *Liberian Strategic Road Map for National Healing, Reconciliation and Peacebuilding* (Government of Liberia, 2017). This report envisaged education provision as catalysing a holistic process of post-war national development. This would entail, for example: achieving economic transformation and addressing poverty and social inequalities; decentralising political power to communities outside Monrovia; remedying the exclusion of youth from national life and the dearth of education and employment opportunities available to them (Government of Liberia, 2017, 12); and achieving the equal participation of women and men across political and socio-economic spheres (Government of Liberia, 2017, 13) as well as equality of access to social services.

Of particular relevance to the concerns of this chapter is the importance that the country's Education Sector plans attach to effective community engagement, stating that "community involvement will be key to promoting the schooling of out of school children" (UNESCO, 2022, 86) – a strategy which will "require a multifaceted, inter-sectoral response" (UNESCO, 2022, 86). Such explicit recognition of the significance of community engagement underscores the inadequacy of the responses envisioned in the conventional narrative of the 'learning crisis' in which community voices and experiences remain invisible or belittled.

Liberia's conflict-affected rural communities are, within Butler's terms, a precaritised population, differentially exposed to power relations that have rendered them vulnerable to a range of socio-economic and political hardships, of which educational marginalisation is but one component. The next section highlights a tendency within international peacebuilding missions working within Liberia to ignore the grassroots agency of local communities and their ability to navigating such harsh conditions.

Top-down state-centric approaches to educational challenges

Liberia's educational challenges call for a grounded approach that is attentive to the experiences of the affected communities. Yet, 'liberal peacebuilding' interventions by the international community tended to offer a top-down, state-centric approach that ignores and disavows the experiences and agency of local communities (Shepler and Williams, 2017; Richmond, 2011). Investment in social services such as education and health has taken second place to a focus on security and economic liberalisation (Amin, 2023; Fearon et al., 2009) and is presented as a peace dividend, despite the fact that education is often a core demand of communities affected by conflict. Also, education interventions in Liberia and other conflict-affected contexts have followed decontextualised global policy prescriptions. These offer a generic menu of programmes (including peace education and learner-centred pedagogy) that ignore the needs and experiences of conflict-affected communities (Novelli et al., 2014, 4).

The reduction of peacebuilding to processes of securitisation or marketisation led by international actors has tended to see local people within highly negative terms as lacking in capacity or construed within a form of judgementalism that "juxtaposes western liberalism against others who are identified as 'barbaric' against the liberal norm" (Richmond, 2011, 60; see also McGinty and Richmond, 2013). The proliferation of peace education programmes insisting on attitudinal and behavioural change in conflict-affected populations is a case in point (Higgins and Novelli, 2020). Within such interventions, the locus of agency remains with international agents and actors whilst conflict-affected and impoverished communities are blamed for their alleged personality traits such as a predisposition to violent conflict or inability to solve conflict peacefully (Higgins and Novelli, 2020, 18). Hence, curriculum interventions "may serve a regulatory and disciplinarian agenda that blames them for moral failure" (Higgins and Novelli, 2018, 48). Such approaches to communities experiencing poverty and conflict reproduce what has come to be known as 'Afro-pessimism' (Abrahamsen, 2005) that stereotypes African states and their societies as threats to global security requiring regulation and pacification.

Privatisation initiatives in Liberia to provide fee-paying schools for the poor led by international corporate agencies have been found to demonstrate this approach in recent studies (Hook 2023). In this case, they align with the operation of global extractive capitalism. Thus, Hook argues that the failure to consult the communities targeted and the use of generic scripted lessons for teachers that characterises the Liberian Educational Advancement Programme "perpetuates plantation logics that label communities and geographies in Africa as 'in crisis' or 'without' and therefore in need of technopolitical institutions". (89).

We now turn to look at the overall strategy of the Second Chance programme before focusing attention on its form of community engagement through PEGs.

The Second Chance Programme and Accelerated Learning in Liberia

The Liberian state and its Ministry of Education recognise ALPs, such as Second Chance, as an important part of its strategy to address educational marginalisation (UNESCO, 2022). The "accelerated" nature of the learning provided condenses the national curriculum to fit the equivalent of three years in a much shorter period (usually nine months) and prioritises literacy and numeracy skills. This is deemed especially relevant in a context, where catching up on lost learning because of protracted conflict remains an urgent priority for thousands of children and their families (USAID, 2017).

However, the ALPs' great success in Ethiopia is widely attributed to their broader community-oriented focus (Boayue, 2014; USAID, 2017). Here, community patterns of daily and seasonal work, especially involving subsistence agriculture or petty trading, inform decisions about the timing of accelerated learning classes. As in Northern Ghana and in Ethiopia, facilitators are recruited from local communities and thus know the backgrounds and contexts of precarity faced by the children they teach. Classrooms are also open to parents and family members to visit. Classes are free and do not involve further payments for instructional materials whilst uniforms are not required.

This community rootedness yields significant benefits in terms of motivating parents and guardians to support their children's attendance and to take an interest and celebrate their learning (Boayue, 2014). As a result, the TRC report for Liberia (2009) notes that:

> accelerated learning programs and supplementary adult literacy and numeracy classes for children or young adults who missed out on education

during the war have had a positive impact and need to be continued and expanded for all children and young adults to be able to catch up on the many years of education they lost.

(258)

Such is the success of the ALP in re-integrating OOSC that the National Education Sector Plan (2022–2027) promises to "dramatically scale up accelerated learning programmes by establishing ALP classes in existing lower basic schools and providing top-up incentives for lower basic teachers working on ALPs after class hours" (22).

The Second Chance programme is managed by the Luminos Fund in partnership with four national NGOs (Westbrook and Higgins, 2019). It provides accelerated learning for ten months to children aged 7–11 who have not accessed formal educational provision, through 66 classes in Bomi and Montserrado counties *Second Chance* offers a condensed and highly structured curriculum, with an emphasis on developing literacy, using a phonics approach, and numeracy. Class parents are responsible for cooking food for the children who receive a cooked lunch each day. By 2022, Second Chance had reached 5,010 children (Luminos Fund, 2022).

Facilitators for the programme are recruited from the massive numbers of rural unemployed youth. Most have graduated from high school and have received low passes in English and Maths. Whilst they lack teaching experience and are usually educated only to West African Secondary School Certificate or senior secondary level, they are trained intensively and supported to use activity-based teaching using phonics. They are predominantly male, but special efforts are made to recruit women from local communities, given their chronic under-representation in the country's teaching profession (Stromquist et al., 2013, 2017).

Evaluations of the Second Chance programme have demonstrated its success in achieving impressive cognitive learning outcomes. A recent randomised control trial conducted by IDinsight (2023) compared OOSC in 50 treatment communities where the programme was offered in the 2022–2023 school year, with 50 control communities where the programme was not offered. The trial assessed 1,502 OOSC at baseline and endline on literacy (using the Early Grade Reading Assessment or EGRA) and numeracy (using the Early Grade Mathematics Assessment or EGMA). The evaluation (IDinsight, 2023, 4) noted that "the results show large, significant learning gains on all tasks in literacy and numeracy in the treatment communities compared to the control communities". Hence, on average, "treatment OOSC were able to read 29 words per minute compared to 7 words per minute for control OOSC at endline". Moreover, "OOSC correctly answered twice as many addition questions and twice as many subtraction questions than control OOSC". The report concludes that

> compared with government schoolchildren in the same communities, children in the Luminos Programme started the year with much lower

literacy and numeracy scores but ended the school year with similar numeracy scores and substantially higher literacy scores than their peers in school.

These impressive learning outcomes are complemented by the programme's positive impact on children's attitudes to learning. Drawing on classroom observations and interviews with children, a report on the quality of teaching and learning in the Second Chance programme (Westbrook and Higgins, 2019) noted the pride and self-belief which learners, both boys and girls, developed as a result of their experiences, qualities which equipped them to make a successful and sustained transition into government schools.

Parental engagement groups (PEGs)

Whilst such achievements are attributable to the programme's curriculum and its innovative pedagogical strategies, its community outreach through the PEGs is a significant component in explaining its success. Monthly meetings are held between Project Managers and parents, extended families and the wider communities whose children participate in Second Chance. Facilitators teaching in the programme as well as children also attend.

During these meetings:

> parents identify the barriers to education within their community—including social norms, economic constraints, and safety concerns—and organically devise solutions to those barriers. Financial support through self-help groups further facilitates the transition of these students into government schools.
> (Wang, 2018, 8)

PEGs have been characterised as 'building a community in which parents participate in their children's education by mobilising immediate and long-term support for keeping children in school and succeeding' (Wang, 2018, 8). As such, they form an important dimension of the 'holistic approach to the challenge of out of school children' (7) adopted in the Second Chance programmes. That PEGs are gatherings that include not only children's parents but also their extended families and wider community is important in recognising the inclusive nature of African kinship systems (Makiwane and Kaunda, 2018). The main purpose, however, is to demonstrate to parents the learning activities undertaken by their children.

Listening to the Experiences of Parental Engagement Groups (PEGs)

The approach of our research team can be described as broadly interpretative and phenomenological. We were concerned with how the participating families perceived, experienced and responded to PEGs and the meanings they attached to them (Nizza et al., 2021). The research on which this analysis is based took place between December 2018 and June 2019 (see Higgins and Westbrook, 2019 for further details). The methods of data collection included: participant observations of PEG meetings at three sites serving communities in Montserrado and Bomi counties; photographs of the meetings; three focus group discussions with attendees (including women and men, parents and extended families of children attending Second Chance programmes) about their relevance and usefulness, as well as extended interviews with the facilitators and programme managers who organised the meetings. Generating visual as well as verbal evidence, these diverse methods complemented each other in yielding insights into what was said at the meetings, the social, emotional and inter-personal dynamics of interaction during them, as well as the meanings and significance attributed to the PEGs by all those attending.

Our data collecting methods sought to 'recentre' southern experiences of education through innovative research practices that reveal and retrieve the voices and feelings of those ignored in hegemonic policy discourses (see Swartz et al., 2024). Our aim was to achieve 'thick description' (De Certeau, 1984) of micro-social events in the lives of the Second Chance communities, and how PEG was experienced. Our approach aligned with methodological insights from the sociology of everyday life in which small-scale 'events' become objects worthy of investigation as part of a broader 'science of the ordinary' (Ghisleni, 2017, 530). For example, when seeking to explore how parents understood and experienced the PEG meetings, the research operationalised an expansive notion of meaning-making. This includes attention to their emotional responses, not understood as possessions of individuals but in their inter-personal circulation following affect theory. As summarised by Wetherell (2012, 2), the "turn to affect is mainly a stimulus to expand the scope of social investigation… to attempts to understand how people are moved". Our research, in effect, sought precisely to understand how those attending the PEGs were 'moved'.

Above all, in zooming in on, and bearing witness to, these meetings, our research methods attempted to remedy the injustice in which these constituencies are ignored or problematised in policy responses. They aligned with 'emancipatory' research methods that advocate for a "wider range of experiences as constitutive of the human condition" (Cooper et al., 2019, 29). In the following analysis, quotes are provided from parents and others who attended PEGs, with the aim of recuperating and valorising their voices (speaking in Liberian Kreyol which was the language spoken at the PEGs).

Vulnerability and Resistance in PEGs

Drawing on Butler's conceptual prism, we show below how the PEGs create a meeting space in which parents, carers and guardians of children who attend the Second Chance ALP are able to express their viewpoints, feelings and perspectives on the vulnerabilities shaping and constraining their engagement

218　*Reconceptualising the Learning Crisis in Africa*

with formal educational provision as well as the forms that their resistance takes. As we shall see PEGs, in effect, created space for celebrating, for example: learning as a social event; promoting girls' agency as learners; catalysing collective joy and hope; creating a democratic and inclusive space of dialogue and consultation; providing opportunities to strategise in response to poverty, food insecurity and malnutrition and promoting peace and mobilising youth agency. We describe each of these in turn.

Celebrating learning as a social event

The photographs we took at the Second Chance classes show parents, guardians and extended families as well as elders, watching the facilitator together with their children demonstrating a typical lesson. This is the central event of the PEGs that aim to showcase learning activities experienced by those children who attend the programme.

Images 8.1 and 8.4 evoke the rapt attention of parents as they watch the facilitators teaching their children. Image 8.2 shows children at their desks enthusiastically raising their hands in answer to the facilitator's question. Image 8.3 shows a girl on the blackboard demonstrating her understanding of the sounds that make up particular words. Image 8.4 shows children demonstrating their ability to read a passage aloud with the support of their facilitator, whilst parents and village elders look on. They all show the makeshift spaces, usually

Image 8.1 Parents and extended family members watching the facilitator and children.

Image 8.2 Children responding enthusiastically to a question from the facilitator.

dilapidated buildings, some partially destroyed during the conflict and still not repaired, in which the PEG meetings take place. The presence of the blackboard, as well as instructional materials on the walls, indicate how these spaces have been temporarily transformed for the educational purposes of the PEGs.

All these images indicate how the PEGs make learning a social event. Children's experiences of learning are at the centre of collective interest and watching. Showing adults preoccupied by the learning activities taking place and children participating with enthusiasm, they capture the social and affective intensity of the exchange meeting. Also, by rendering learning a sociable event open to impoverished rural communities, the space created in the PEG meetings interrupts the rigid demarcations between spaces of education and community spaces that characterise the exclusionary nature of educational provision in Liberia. As such, the PEGs may be understood as an 'experimental community' (Tavares, 2016, 84) – as something unfamiliar and outside of the norms of conventional educational engagement.

Image 8.3 A girl demonstrating understanding of sounds and words.

Comments in focus group discussions capture the significance of this event for parents. A key theme for participants was the way in which their children's learning, previously something mysterious and unknown to them, was rendered visible. One mother said:

> I am very happy for here today for what I observed from the meeting actually since I wake up, I have not seen any school to do such a thing like this. They called the students to demonstrate in a meeting like this they want to inform the parents. It just tells the parents what they are really learning in school that my first time seeing it and it is from Luminos Fund. They are doing well even the facilitators, trying to prove to us that what they are teaching the children the children do the practice right in front of us here. I am very happy for that ... No academic school had ever carry on such a program. They call meeting and see children performing.

Engaging Parents, Extended Families and Communities 221

Image 8.4 Parents, extended families and community elders watching and listening to children reading.

Parents recognised the PEGs as enabling a form of sociality in which their children's learning could not only be witnessed but also celebrated. A mother said: "she is my daughter. I am so grateful that she can stand before one or two persons and demonstrate". A father said, "I was so happy because my son do it, everybody was clapping for him". A mother said:

> Yeah, I am very happy because my little son was not used to write, but now he can write. He can spell his name. Sometime when they give him lesson, he can come say mama, I pass oh, I can say thank you. I can be happy. So, I tell LIPACE thank you.

For some, watching the individual achievements of their children inspired competitive expectations for their success after transitioning into government schools and the effects on the community. Hence, one mother noted:

> God will bless them. My brother's daughter, big girl about 11 years old, she was not in school but since she started coming here, she can challenge the 4th graders them. They can take it in spelling. Any small thing y'all want make palaver, she can say let's catch it in copybook and pencil… And she will beat them in spelling…. so, I believe that when

they go in any other school they will really do well. They will compete with that particular class. They will be in the front page school.

Other parents recognised how individual children's knowledge acquisition contributed to broader community well-being:

What I observe today from the meeting our children learning improve. Because some of them enter this place they don't even know how to write A. But from today what I saw the Second Chance program doing well for them and the community as a whole. Because the people from in the community make up the community. So, they are giving a lift to our children. Their performances tell us that the facilitators are really teaching them.

A mother summed up the impact of watching their children's learning: "It is a big pride to the community and tears want to run down my eyes".

These comments indicate the role of the PEGs in galvanising parents' and guardians' interest and support for their children's learning. The distinctive sociality of the space of the PEGs reverses the rigid spatial demarcation between schooling and the lives of communities which, as noted earlier, has proved a key challenge in addressing educational marginalisation. But the PEG event also creates a space of resistance to their experience of vulnerability as communities engage, celebrate and take ownership of their children's learning for the first time. Out of this process of witnessing learning emerges their recognition of its transformational impact on their children, on their relationships with them and the wider community. Rather than confirming assumptions that parents are lazy, uninterested or in need of capacity building, the PEGs create a space in which parents can demonstrate their interest and enthusiasm and in which their children's learning is a source of communal celebration. That parents and guardians thereby gain understanding of what learning means for their children also reverses the power relationships which, within Liberia's exclusionary education system, have foreclosed such forms of engagement. Hence, some parents put the PEGs' showcasing of their children's learning activities in a wider historical perspective as a form of reparation for their own experience of marginality. One father said: "The thing they are learning... some of us during our days as we said we did not come across it but for them now they are on the bridge trying to cross it".

Promoting girls' agency as learners

Parents also emphasised how the PEGs provided a space in which girls' agency as learners was celebrated and promoted. Image 8.5 shows a girl demonstrating how to decode words into sounds using phonic boxes.

It shows a girl-friendly learning environment, in which the showcasing of learning encouraged girls' active participation in learning and hence was validated by all those present. As one mother commented:

Engaging Parents, Extended Families and Communities 223

Image 8.5 A girl demonstrating her learning to the PEG.

> I think the girls it give them confidence because myself tell me right here. When they called the first person (a girl) to say a word it make me proud, because I feel fine because it good to send your daughter to school.... So, I feel that the girls them they are confident because no man speak for me to hear it but that the women speak, I hear their voice. So, I feel to myself the girl is confident.

Such collective validation of girls exercising agency as learners was understood as counter-cultural in that it challenged pervasive patriarchal attitudes to girls' education. One mother observed: "they are saying that in our setting Liberia here we can say I ain't want send woman to school because they will not be learning". Another said,

> But even here, like my very self that here, I got, I have 11 brothers, every one of them my father sent them to school, with 12 girls, can you just imagine, 12 girls - none of us go to school.

PEGs therefore create a space of resistance to gender regimes that render girls vulnerable to social norms and power relationships that constrain their agency as learners (Crossouard and Dunne, 2021). The PEGs were construed by the women and men present as sites within which to rethink the gender norms and expectations that acted as barriers to girls accessing learning. Far from being positioned on the periphery of learning spaces in a classroom with conventional gender seating arrangements (Dunne et al., 2007, 45; see also Dunne, 2009), here, girls and their learning are centralised and celebrated. Recognising girls' learning achievements in this way confounded the tendency amongst teachers and parents to have lower expectations of girls, a major contributory factor in their under-achievement (Dunne, 2009, 6). Such micro-interactions between a facilitator/teacher and a girl within a community space interrupts some of the gender norms (Dunne, 2009, 7) that constrain girls' engagement in schooling. That a male teacher models respect for this girl's learning within a community space is also important in challenging the pervasive under-valuation of girls as learners (see Images 8.3 and 8.5) below and also 8.3).

The celebration of girls' learning within a gathering of local community members that includes parents, guardians, elders, extended family members, men as well as women also leverages the wider African kinship systems (Makiwane and Kaunda, 2018) to resist oppressive gender regimes. Going beyond including more girls in formal schooling as measured through quantitative indicators (Dunne, 2019; Holmarsdottir, 2013), Speed Schools in Liberia with their PEGs thus actively interrupt the gender norms that as associated with female educational exclusion.

Catalysing collective joy and hope

The showcasing of children's learning in the PEGs generated intense emotional reactions amongst all present. The rapt faces in the images above capture the emotional charge of the PEG meetings. Parents described how the experience of seeing their children learn generated hope for their children's and their own futures. One mother said:

> ..we thought children were just having fun but now we see in the PEG how much they are learning.….my child will pick up in the government school because they are doing well in Second Chance.

Another said: "I always want she must always be the dux in the school". Many expressed the 'dream' that through education their children would 'be someone tomorrow'. They believed that their children would participate in Liberia's national development: 'they can be future for tomorrow'. Seeing their children learning activated hope for their own future security. One mother said:

> my dream for my children, I want them to be, some of them to be a medical doctor, or even a representative or president. That tomorrow

when I'm old as soon as I call them one time, they will be running to me. I will not suffer in my old age.

Some parents framed their hope as an expression of securing inter-generational well-being. One father said:

I am very, very happy, I am standing here because I was thinking how my son will know, to put my name down for his name, tomorrow when am old and go to my grave tomorrow. But I can see him, when he come sometimes, I can say bring your grade sheet, I can take some paper from him. He drawing flag, Liberia flag doing this one. I can, sometimes I can go in the room I cry, I say yeah. Let our children them learn. Our own of time almost finish and we can't sit down and die.

Parents also commented on the joy with which their children participated in the innovative, phonics based, learning opportunities to support reading offered by Second Chance. One father said:

..sometime when they doing it, you can hear them, just like they singing. Ehn, you know, you can hear them, when you go near the school, they can be singing, (singing), Laughing... O, U, I, O, U.

Image 8.2 shows children demonstrating their joy in learning at the PEGs with their hands raised in anticipation of answering the facilitator's question, and some leaning forward to focus carefully on what their facilitator is saying.

In contexts such as Liberia, where the experience of educational marginality is connected with despair about the prospects of engaging with or benefiting from schooling, these expressions of positive emotion towards the process of learning are poignant. They align with the association of education provision with cultivating hope in challenging conflict-affected contexts (Wrigley et al., 2012; Burde and King, 2023; Nordström, 2024). The community engagement offered by the PEGs created a space in which parents' feelings about their children's learning could be expressed and acknowledged and, in so doing, catalysed a collective celebration of hope and joy in learning – or, within a Butlerian frame – a shift from vulnerability to resistance.

Creating a democratic and inclusive space of dialogue and consultation

Whilst focused largely on the educational needs of their children, many parents at the PEG meetings recognised the wider significance of PEGs as open, democratic and inclusive spaces of discussion that promoted cohesion and community togetherness. A mother said that PEGs provided an opportunity in which:

we can put our differences. We can't talk about that other fightin' now, we can talk about how the children they knowing book now. Then we can just leave the palaver now... we come together. So, the meeting make us self to come together because when we see the children now, … that book business we can be talking now.

Such comments indicate how converging around 'book business' was simultaneously a means of trust building (Bulgrin and Semedeton, 2022) and social healing following the conflict and its continuing legacy. Signalling the rehabilitation of such inter-personal relationships, the inclusive and democratic modality of consultation opened up by the PEGs offers a striking contrast, both to the troubled spaces noted by Dunne et al. (2021), and to the tendency for parents of out-of-school children to experience rudeness and disparaging remarks in PTA meetings noted above. The open discussions offered a model of 'genuine' rather than 'pseudo' participation (Rose, 2003) where parents and guardians of children attending the Second Chance programmes felt able to bring their concerns and challenges without any particular pre-conceived agenda.

Albeit in connection with education provision, the PEGs were meaningful in relation to what has been termed the ongoing but 'elusive quest for democracy' (Quaynor, 2015, 24) in a country in which historically rooted traditions of political authoritarianism continue to drive conflict. Recent commentators have argued that the breakdown of democracy that was key conflict driver in the country's civil wars remains unresolved (Kieh, 2018; Spatz and Thaler, 2018). The result, for much of the Liberian youth, is captured by Quaynor's quote from one of them who expressed fear about talking about issues of human rights linked to citizenship education: "I do not have the means to speak" (2015, 24). This lack of democratic spaces or channels of representation illustrates community members' continuing vulnerability to the power asymmetries established during the foundation of the Liberian state that undermined the majority indigenous population's ability to participate in the public political sphere.

Commentary on post-conflict national reconciliation processes has emphasised the need for locally owned, inclusive arenas for discussion and decision-making so as to address the social divisions and tensions of exclusionary political and social systems dominated by elites (Richmond, 2011). Nationwide consultations on strategies for peace promotion emphasise the need for spaces to represent the voices of the indigenous rural poor in decision-making at all levels of politics (Vinck et al., 2011; Gadkari, 2022). The meanings attributed to the PEGs quoted above indicate that, whilst their overriding purpose was to reach out to communities experiencing educational marginality, in effect their vulnerability to systemic democratic deficits and their resistance to such experiences are being catalysed and appreciated.

The perception of mothers of children attending Second Chance classes, many of them illiterate, that they had a voice and could contribute to decision-making is significant in relation to the equity imperative of women's activism to promote peace in Liberia (Shulika, 2022). PEGs were recognised as a forum in which women's participation was actively respected and encouraged. For instance, one mother noted that 'women can talk more'. Another recognised that "sometime when we come to the meeting, the people can make us to express ourselves". A key goal of many initiatives, including the Women in Peace Building Network, the Women in Peace and Security Network and the inter-religious Liberian Mass Action for Peace, has been to challenge patriarchal norms that have silenced women's voices (Gbowee and Mithers, 2011, 168; Shin, 2020) and excluded them from deliberations about Peace Agreements and peace processes (Cunningham et al., 2023, 7). Shin (2020) notes that these initiatives allowed the "unheard voices of ordinary women" (2020, 12) who were not well educated or belonging to the middle or upper classes, in other words "ordinary mothers' wisdom" (2020, 5), were heard. The PEGs facilitate a similar micro-scale transformation in relation to female educational marginality, from the vulnerability of voicelessness to the resistance of active participation in their children's learning.

Providing opportunities to strategise in response to poverty, food insecurity and malnutrition

In the focus group discussions held after the PEG meetings, parents recounted how watching their children's learning had motivated them to find ways of raising money to be able to support children's transition into government schools. One said:

> I make a little garden so that when I get money to buy the uniform and whatsoever needed for the next year. I will not let my children to sit down because I am happy today for the level of improvement.

This sense of a newfound resourcefulness and agency in relation to improving their economic livelihoods is also shown in one father's observation:

> the children only perform to encourage you… You should put on your garment now, put on strong shoe to tell your children to go forward in school…. their performances make us strong for the children to go forward in education.

Such comments directly led parents to describe the diverse material challenges they worried about, in particular paying school and PTA fees and uniform costs. One father explained: "once you are not working as the father, you want to do the job, you want send your children to school but you do not get the money". This comment typifies just how contingent is the relationship with formal education because of the economic uncertainty that characterises the daily lives of families in rural Liberia as in many parts of Africa. (Cooper and Pratten, 2014).

However, the PEGs potentially offered a forum in which mothers and parents could discuss ways of increasing their incomes, beyond the limited and unpredictable sales of charcoal, cassava or palm wine. Their discussions highlighted the structural challenges they faced in ensuring their economic survival, especially as a result of lack of access to land and land ownership, as one parent said, "We decided really to do something, but for here, we wanted to do, to do garden, agriculture, but we don't have land here". Whilst the PEG discussions did not result in any concrete or quick solutions to what appears to be an intractable problem, at the meeting parents collectively resolved to write to elders in the community to press their cause. There were also promising discussions of the entrepreneurial possibilities of soap making. At one PEG meeting, representatives from another PEG shared their success with soap making and selling as a successful means of improving community livelihoods. They brought to the meeting a bar of soap (Image 8.6) and provided details of costs of bags of caustic and oil.

One parent summed up appreciation of their exchange: Okay now, we have many people say there is no challenge, the parents from Gbarde's town had a challenge but the soap making helped them now they are generating income.[5] Coming out of discussions within the PEGs, parents who had publicly discussed their anxieties about their ability to support their children's schooling had now been told of a solution. As one father movingly remarked:

Image 8.6 A bar of soap produced by a PEG.

Then I come to this Parental Engagement Meeting, then I hear oh, I don't have money and am thinking how to get money. Then Gbarde's town PTA meeting and I am living in Gbarde's town. And I hear say the chairman say oh, parents who don't have money, you can do this to get money. How can I get money? You can make soap. Oh, I can make soap. Okay so I learn, I know how to make soap. Now, I am more serious about my child education. I don't go on the farm again. I am home. 2 O' Clock, John are you, you not going for class? You understand. That meeting changed me. That meeting changed me.

The PEGs we observed whilst not solving all issues, nevertheless, provided an important space for parents' vulnerability to be recognised as an existential predicament, involving experiences of anxiety, fear and uncertainty. In doing so, PEGs enabled their exercise of individual and collective agency.

A similar topic of discussion at the PEGs that addressed families' precarity was the provision of a cooked meal for the children who attend the Second Chance classes. Local NGOs provided rice and beans whilst parents were expected to find firewood and utensils to cook with and elect a class parent and other volunteers to cook the food each day. This system of food provision was greatly appreciated by parents. One mother commented: "there are some children they don't even have food for them to eat at their houses coming to this school and making them to have something at least something to eat". Another said: "they helping the children because food is life. If you are not alive you will not learn". Liberia, with 41% of its population evaluated as food insecure, has one of the lowest rates of food security in the world, alongside high levels of child malnourishment (World Food Programme, 2022). Sub-Saharan Africa is the only region in the world where rates of child malnutrition are rising (Ingutia et al., 2020, 2). That attendance during the Second Chance programme is high and near 100% confirms the proliferating evidence in other contexts of sub-Saharan Africa that providing free meals raises enrolment and promotes regular attendance, as well as improving educational outcomes and children's overall health.[6]

Promoting peace and mobilising youth agency

Parents at the PEGs and in focus group discussions even spoke of the Second Chance programme as contributing to peace, whether it was reducing conflict in the country or promoting national peace or giving parents' peace of mind or modelling peaceful behaviour and relationships. These themes were framed in a variety of ways. The very existence of the programme to enable previously OOSC to access learning was understood as a demonstrable sign of peace in Liberia. "They are going to school, they are moving, that's peace", said one mother. That there were no fees and no insistence on school uniforms in second chance classes also represented the removal of barriers to their children's learning, which amounted to peace promotion. One said:

> Second Chance, they don't care whether you, y'all they care for uniform business. All you know is you make your child clean, bring them to school. Actually, and they are not asking us for money. That actually helps us…….it is actually a big peace for us.

For many parents, by removing the financial barriers the Second Chance programme enabled children not only to learn but also to socialise together. One mother said:

> So, it is one of the most important thing in our country to bring free education. So we really support that it will help us in the peace building process. So, this school now bringing children together from different, different communities, different houses and to know one another how to play together, how to love one another and be serious to learn. So, it is one of the peace building there.

The Second Chance programme's focus on teaching reading through phonics was seen as contributing to post-conflict national development. One parent said: "the Phonetics pronunciation of the child, when the child learns it from the foundation and they get up there, it becomes very easy for them to read. And Liberia's problem is reading in this country". Moreover, Second Chance facilitators' friendly and supportive relationships with the children that the parents witnessed in the PEGs were also associated with the promotion of national peace. One explained; "because of the way the boy takes care of the children. The way he talks to the children the way he teach them. yeah... it's very peaceful. Yes, because he teach them how to talk to their friends". Another commented on the facilitator's pastoral concern for the children attending the classes, in particular their commitment to following up if children did not attend or were ill. One parent said:

> ..even the day when this teacher them not see the children they get them from house to house. You wah not want go to school we begging y'all, y'all go to school. So, we call that one peace. Your children not go to school even when the children them be sick all the children will follow to speak to the children. To see the person that is sick. They will tell the child sorry, but we beg you, you want come to school yea. They see the child two or three days they will go find them. So, I take that to be peace.

Parents also identified the friendly nature of the relationships between children cultivated during Second Chance classes as modelling a form of sociality that was conducive to their exercise of peaceful behaviours in their wider relationships in their households and communities:

> That child will take it in so that the peace that the children are building in between there, because they are going to school peacefully, they come

home they meet their parents they are peacefully, so ... they are taking the role of peace around them.

These comments all underscore how educational provision offered by the Second Chance ALP was valued for promoting children's learning in an expansive sense, as a form of community-rooted peace. As such PEGs align with what Richmond (2011) termed the often missed significance of 'local peacebuilding' within conditions of pervasive material hardship and chronic insecurity. When parents and extended families suffering educational marginalisation exercise agency in the long aftermath of conflict in these spaces, they demonstrate what has been termed the 'creativity and resolution finding ability of local actors' (Bräuchler and Naucke, 2017, 429). In doing so, they indicate how the Second Chance programme recognises the experience of vulnerability faced by communities suffering the legacies of conflict as well as the importance of a forum for generating resistance through actively promoting a collective peace.

Facilitators also engaged with this peace promoting activism. They reported valuing the Second Chance programme because it provided an opportunity for youth in Liberia to contribute to national peacebuilding. One said: "being a facilitator is like preparing a group of people for a better nation'. Another said: 'If I am teaching those children, I am building peace". This meant a commitment to breaking the cycle of inter-generational precarity and disengagement from learning. As one put it: "to help these children find a way out... I have a passion for the youth and that of the country... so I decided to impart knowledge in them". Facilitators were indeed motivated by the hope discussed earlier, to contribute to the nation's future:

> the children are future leaders for tomorrow. You don't know who that child will be. Sometimes that child will be doctor, president, nurse, teacher... most of our relatives and friends are on the streets there doing nothing.

Echoing parental perceptions, they were also aware of how their approach to teaching in Second Chance classes helped develop children's behavioural and inter-personal skills that contributed more broadly to societal peace promotion. As one pointed out:

> yes, if I am teaching those children, I am building peace... because you are teaching them how to have good morals... how to become good service for the nation.

This wider understanding of agency in relation to the Second Chance programme confirms other evidence into teachers' perceptions of their role in conflict-affected contexts (Sayed and Novelli, 2016). In Liberia, Adebayo (2019, 8) found that teachers see themselves and also are seen by communities, as "second parents, humanitarians, 'town criers,' role models, guardians, parents, counsellors, unifiers, agents of peace, 'Hercules,' and psychologists".

This diversified view of teacher agency, integrating learning with a range of contributions to social healing, is informed by teachers/facilitators' recognition of the multiple challenges children and their parents face in a country in which the legacy of conflict continues across social, cultural and political dimensions.

Some facilitators pointed out that young people were less likely to be drawn into violence as a result of their involvement in the Second Chance programme. One said:

> the programme is really doing well for the youth because 95 or 99% of the facilitators - they are youth and once you are keeping the youth busy, I think I don't think you will just see some like maybe this kind of violence.

Such comments confirm the findings of a nationwide consultation of Catholic Relief Services (2016) on perceptions of how peace may best be promoted. These noted an overwhelming desire for peace amongst rural communities in Liberia, not least amongst the nation's large youth constituency. Against a background of the vulnerability of youth to the frustrations and despair of unemployment noted earlier, the Second Chance programme's recruitment of facilitators from the same communities gives them the chance to support the national drive to address educational marginality in communities with which they are familiar. This ambition aligns with aspirations to involve youth in peace promotion and social transformation and promote their self-efficacy, as well as offering them hope for their own and their communities' future (priorities set out in the state's Peacebuilding Plan (Government of Liberia, 2017)). This peace promotion also runs in parallel with the mobilisation of youth during the Ebola crisis to disseminate health messages and provide guidance to communities (Santos and Novelli, 2017, 7). The framing of youth as a national resource who can contribute to Liberia's social transformation strikingly contrasts with the tendency in many conflict-affected contexts to problematise youth as security risks (Lopes Cardozo et al., 2016). For youth involved in the Second Chance programme, therefore, their experience of vulnerability as educational agents in a conflict-affected context was both 'perilous' but also 'enabling' (Butler et al., 2016, 1).

Lessons for the 'Learning Crisis'

These findings are not intended to romanticise or idealise the agency of communities when "exercised from positions of structural marginalisation" (Lister, 2021, 123). Despite the success of the PEGs at the personal level, these communities continue to suffer and experience vulnerability. As Butler (2016, 13) has cautioned, "resistance never vanquishes the experience of vulnerability" that is an ongoing predicament for some communities, including those targeted by the Second Chance programme. Eschewing the short-termism of a problem-solving approach, the PEGs are repeated events in which the process of community engagement is ongoing and sustained over time.

Having said that, PEGs in Liberia demonstrate a modality of community engagement that contrasts sharply with the deficit, pejorative and top-down approaches, seen in the responses of international organisations to the learning challenge in the global South. Using Butler's theoretical framework, the analysis of the data collected has demonstrated how the PEGs recognise and valorise the agency of communities in resisting their vulnerability in a conflict-affected context. The Second Chance programme offers an expansive understanding of how education provision can address marginality through ongoing engagement with affected communities and their children. First, the PEGs create an unprecedented arena that encourages meaningful, responsive engagements well beyond tokenistic or judgmental forms of interchange. Such engagements elicit, hear and recognise the positionality of parents in situations of educational marginalisation. Second, by showcasing children's learning activities for parents, they render what has previously been mysterious, unknown or in some cases irrelevant, visible and open to collective ownership and celebration. In doing this, they connect with and respond to their experience of vulnerability to asymmetrical power relations that has rendered that very activity unknown and unfamiliar through years of inter-generational educational marginalisation resulting from elite monopoly of provision in a conflict-affected context. This has important implications for generating community-rooted support for girls' agency as learners and also for catalysing parents' positive, affective orientations to their children's learning. Third, PEGs create opportunities for parent-led discussion of the diverse dimensions of precarity that combine to exclude their children from education and offer opportunities for community-rooted responses to the challenges of gender norms, poverty, health concerns and youth frustrations. In doing so, they open up possibilities for parents' sustained support for their children's learning.

The modality of community engagement made possible by the PEGs underscores how education provision in these local micro-settings acquires meaning and significance. Such provision recognises and connects with their vulnerability and resistance as they navigate multiple broader societal processes of peacebuilding in a conflict-affected setting and importantly, it challenges top-down, state-centric interventions premised on deficit modelling of the poor, conflict-affected and marginalised.

Perhaps most important, by developing a relationship of solidarity and trust with parents, extended family networks and communities, the Second Chance programme in Liberia, in addition to providing accelerated learning to their children, recognise the relational and multi-dimensional character of children's lives in a conflict-affected setting. There is much to learn from this innovative ALP.

Notes

1 This chapter draws on data collected and analysed by Sean Higgins and Jo Westbrook (University of Sussex Centre for International Education) who wrote the subsequent *Report on the Evaluation of the Quality of the Teaching and Learning in*

the Second Chance Program for Out of School Children in Liberia, July 2019. Thanks also go to the Luminos Fund team in Liberia, Abba Karnga Jr and Alphanso Menyon as well as Nikita Khosla (LF programme manager in Liberia), Alpha Simpson, CEO of Q & A, Inc, in Liberia and local researchers H. Kulu Blanyon, Clara P. Merchant, Joe Thomas and Joanna N. D. Welwean.
2 See studies by Nicolson (2007), Burde et al. (2015), Menendez et al. (2016), Billagher and Kaushik (2020), Higgins et al. (2022), Mfum-Mensah and Friedson-Ridenour (2014); Baraket et al., 2013.
3 See studies by Rose (2003), De Grauwe et al. (2005), Dunne et al. (2007), Khanal (2013), Yamada (2014), Dunne et al. (2021), Bulgrin (2022).
4 See Truth and Reconciliation Commission of Liberia, TRC Report (2009), Drew and Ramsbotham (2012), Catholic Relief Services (2016).
5 Small scale soap making enterprises (see studies by Wrigely Asante, 2008; Jaiyeola et al., 2019; Shimba et al., 2019; Kiluvia, 2021) have offered a means of improving household livelihoods, and in particular supporting women's entrepreneurship, in other African contexts. See also Wrigley-Asante, 2008.
6 See studies by Jomaa et al. (2011), Adekunle and Christiana (2016), Drake et al. (2017), Aurino et al. (2019), Dago and Yogo (2022).

References

Abrahamsen, R., 2005. 'Blair's Africa: the politics of securitisation and fear'. *Alternatives*, 30(1): 55–80.

Adebayo, S.B., 2019. 'Emerging perspectives of teacher agency in a post-conflict setting: the case of Liberia'. *Teaching and Teacher Education*, 86: 102928.

Adekunle, D.T., and Christiana, O.O., 2016. 'The effects of school feeding programme on enrolment and performance of public elementary school pupils in Osun State, Nigeria'. *World Journal of Education*, 6(3): 39–47.

Akyeampong, K., and Adzahlie-Mensah, V., 2018. 'Recent trends in school social control in Sub-Saharan Africa'. In K. Akyeampong and V. Adzahlie-Mensah (eds.), *The Palgrave international handbook of school discipline, surveillance, and social control*. Palgrave Macmillan, pp. 191–211.

Amin, N.A., 2023. *Pathways to post-liberal peacebuilding: a reconceptualization through comparative analysis* (Master's thesis, The American University in Cairo (Egypt)).

Amoak, D., Bruser, G., Antabe, R., Sano, Y., and Luignaah, I., 2023. 'Unequal access to improved water and sanitation in a post-conflict context of Liberia: evidence from the demographic and health survey'. *PLOS Water*, 2(4): e0000050.

Aurino, E., Jean-Pierre, T., Diallo, A., and Gelli, A., 2019. 'School feeding or general food distribution? Quasi-experimental evidence on the educational impacts of emergency food assistance during the conflict in Mali'. *Journal of Development Studies*, 55(1): 7–28.

Barakat, S., Connolly, D., Hardman, F., and Sundaram, V., 2013. 'The role of basic education in post-conflict recovery'. *Comparative Education*, 49(2): 124–142.

Barrios-Tao, H., Siciliani-Barraza, J.M., and Bonilla-Barrios, B., 2017. 'Education programs in post-conflict environments: a review from Liberia, Sierra Leone, and South Africa'. *Revista Electrónica Educare*, 21(1): 1–22.

Beasley, E., and Huillery, E., 2017. 'Willing but unable? Short-term experimental evidence on parent empowerment and school quality'. *The World Bank Economic Review*, 31(2): 531–552.

Benavot, A., 2016. 'Assuring quality education and learning: lessons from education for all'. *Prospects*, 46: 5–14.

Boayue, N.M., 2014. *An exploration of the challenges of access and retention: reintegrating former refugee and internally displaced girls into secondary school in post-conflict Liberia* (Master's thesis, Oslo and Akershus University College). Semantic Scholar [Accessed: 15.11.2023] https://oda.oslomet.no/oda-xmlui/handle/10642/2146].

Borba, C.P., Ng, L.C., Stevenson, A., Vesga-Lopez, O., Harris, B.L., Parnarouskis, L., Gray, D.A., Carney, J.R., Domínguez, S., Wang, E.K., and Boxill, R., 2016. 'A mental health needs assessment of children and adolescents in post-conflict Liberia: results from a quantitative key-informant survey'. *International Journal of Culture and Mental Health*, 9(1): 56–70.

Bräuchler, B., and Naucke, P., 2017. 'Peacebuilding and conceptualisations of the local'. *Social Anthropology/Anthropologie Sociale*, 25(4): 422–436.

Brault, M.A., Kennedy, S.B., Haley, C.A., Clarke, A.T., Duworko, M.C., Habimana, P., Vermund, S.H., Kipp, A.M., and Mwinga, K., 2018. 'Factors influencing rapid progress in child health in post-conflict Liberia: a mixed methods country case study on progress in child survival, 2000–2013'. *BMJ Open*, 8(10): e021879.

Bulgrin, E., 2022. 'Inclusion and exclusion in local governance: a post-development and spatial perspective on a field study from Benin'. In E. Bulgrin (ed.), *Reading inclusion divergently* (International Perspectives on Inclusive Education, Vol. 19). Emerald Publishing Limited, pp. 93–108.

Bulgrin, E., and Semedeton, S.V., 2024. 'The importance of trust in education decentralisation in West Africa'. *Compare: A Journal of Comparative and International Education*, 54(6): 914–932.

Burde, D., Guven, O., Kelcey, J., Lahmann, H., and Al-Abbadi, K., 2015. 'What works to promote children's educational access, quality of learning, and wellbeing in crisis-affected contexts'. In *Education rigorous literature review*. Department for International Development, pp. 1–93.

Burde, D., and King, E., 2023. 'An agenda for hope: how education cultivates and dashes hope among youth in Nairobi and Karachi'. *Comparative Education Review*, 67(3): 465–485.

Butler, J., 2016. 'Rethinking vulnerability and resistance'. In J. Butler, Z. Gambetti, and L. Sabsay (eds.), *Vulnerability in resistance*. Duke University Press, pp. 12–27.

Cardozo, M.T.L, Higgins, S., and Le Mat, M.L., 2016. *Youth agency and peacebuilding: an analysis of the role of formal and non-formal education: synthesis report on findings from Myanmar, Pakistan, South Africa and Uganda*. UNICEF.

Catholic Relief Services, 2016. *State of peace, reconciliation and conflict in Liberia*. Bishops Conference of Liberia's Justice and Peace Commission, Catholic Relief Services.

Coker, G.C., Akua, M., and Twum, A., 2023. 'Gender-based violence tops women's-rights issues in Liberia; citizens say it is a criminal matter'. *Afrobarometer Dispatch no. 695*.

Cooper, E., and Pratten, D. eds., 2014. *Ethnographies of uncertainty in Africa*. Springer.

Cooper, A., Swartz, S., and Mahali, A., 2019. 'Disentangled, decentred and democratised: youth studies for the global South'. *Journal of Youth Studies*, 22(1): 29–45.

Cornwall, A., and Fujita, M., 2012. 'Ventriloquising "the poor"? Of voices, choices and the politics of "participatory" knowledge production'. *Third World Quarterly*, 33(9): 1751–1765.

Crossouard, B., and Dunne, M., 2021. *Gender and education in postcolonial contexts*. Oxford research encyclopaedia of education.

Cunningham, W., Gupta, S., and Johansson de Silva, S., 2023. *An assessment of gender gaps in Liberia through a women's empowerment lens*. World Bank.

Dago, D., and Yogo, T., 2022. 'Do school feeding programmes reduce child labour? Evidence from Liberia'. *Journal of Development Studies*, 58(11): 2222–2236.

de Certeau, M. 1984. *The practice of everyday life*. University of California Press.

De Grauwe, A., Lugaz, C., Baldé, D., Diakhaté, C., Dougnon, D., Moustapha, M., and Odushina, D., 2005. 'Does decentralisation lead to school improvement? Findings and lessons from research in West Africa'. *Journal of Education for International Development*, 1(1): 1–15.

Drake, L., Fernandes, M., Aurino, E., Kiamba, J., Giyose, B., Burbano, C., Alderman, H., Mai, L., Mitchell, A., and Gelli, A., 2017. *School feeding programs in middle childhood and adolescence* (3rd edn). The International Bank for Reconstruction and Development / The World Bank.

Drew, E., and Ramsbotham, A., 2012. 'Consolidating peace: Liberia and Sierra Leone'. *Accord series* (23).

Dunne, M., 2009. 'Gender as an entry point for addressing social exclusion and multiple disparities in education'. In *UNGEI Global Advisory Committee Technical Meeting* (Vol. 27). United Nations Girls' Education Initiative.

Dunne, M., 2019. 'Gender docility: the power of technology and technologies of power in low income countries'. In A. Chronaki (ed.), *Mathematics, technologies, education: the gender perspective*. Thessaly University Press, pp. 45–56.

Dunne, M., Akyeampong, K., and Humphreys, S., 2007. *School processes, local governance and community participation: understanding access. Create pathways to access*. Research Monograph No. 6. Department for International Development, https://www.gov.uk/research-for-development-outputs/school-processes-local-governance-and-community-participation-understanding-access.

Dunne, M., Humphreys, S., and Bakari, S., 2021. 'Troubled spaces: negotiating school–community boundaries in northern Nigeria'. *Journal of Education Policy*, 36(6): 843–864.

Essuman, A., and Akyeampong, K., 2011. 'Decentralisation policy and practice in Ghana: the promise and reality of community participation in education in rural communities'. *Journal of Education Policy*, 26(4): 513–527.

Fearon, J.D., Humphreys, M. and Weinstein, J.M., 2009. 'Can development aid contribute to social cohesion after civil war? Evidence from a field experiment in post-conflict Liberia'. *American Economic* Review, 99(2): 287–291.

Funaki, Y., and Glencorse, B., 2017. 'Anti-corruption or accountability? International efforts in post-conflict Liberia'. In L. Jonas, and O. Camilla (eds.), *Corruption in the aftermath of war*. Routledge, pp. 114–132.

Gabani, J., and Guinness, L., 2019. 'Households forgoing healthcare as a measure of financial risk protection: an application to Liberia'. *International Journal for Equity in Health*, 18: 1–12.

Gadkari, A.M., 2022. 'Peacebuilding as a new form of colonialism: a case study of Liberia and Sierra Leone'. *Lentera Hukum*, 9: 333.

Galtung, J., 1969. 'Violence, peace, and peace research'. *Journal of Peace Research*, 6(3): 167–191.

Gbowee, L., and Mithers, C., 2011. *Mighty be our powers: how sisterhood, prayer, and sex changed a nation at war*. Beast Books.

Ghisleni, M., 2017. 'The sociology of everyday life: a research program on contemporary sociality'. *Social Science Information*, 56(4): 526–543.

Gizelis, T.I., and Cao, X., 2021. 'A security dividend: peacekeeping and maternal health outcomes and access'. *Journal of Peace Research*, 58(2): 263–278.

Government of Liberia, 2017. *Sustaining peace and securing development: Liberia peacebuilding plan.*

Higgins, S., Daoust, G., Kutan, B., and Novelli, M., 2022. *Strengthening rapid education responses in acute emergencies.* Synthesis Report Centre for International Education, University of Sussex.

Higgins, S., and Novelli, M., 2020. 'Rethinking peace education: a cultural political economy approach'. *Comparative Education Review*, 64(1): 1–20.

Higgins, S. and Novelli, M., 2018. 'The potential and pitfalls of peace education: a cultural political economy analysis of the emerging issues teacher education curriculum in Sierra Leone'. *Asian Journal of Peacebuilding*, 6(1): 29–53.

Higgins, S., and Westbrook, J., 2019. *Report on the evaluation of the quality of the teaching and learning in the second chance program for out of school children in Liberia carried out by the University of Sussex.* Luminos Fund.

Holmarsdottir, H., 2013. 'Moving beyond the numbers: what does gender equality really mean?' In H. Holmarsdottir, V. Nomlomo, A. Farag, and Z. Desai (eds.), *Gendered voices: reflections on gender and education in South Africa and Sudan.* Sense Publishers, pp. 9–24.

Hook, T., 2023. 'Schooling as plantation: Racial capitalism and plantation legacies in corporatized education reform in Liberia'. *Comparative Education Review*, 67(S1): S89–S109.

Humphreys, S., Moses, D., Kaibo, J., and Dunne, M., 2015. 'Counted in and being out: fluctuations in primary school and classroom attendance in northern Nigeria'. *International Journal of Educational Development*, 44: 134–143.

IDinsight, 2023. *Luminos programme impact evaluation.* Available at: https://www.idinsight.org/publication/luminos-program-impact-evaluation/ [Accessed: 30.05.2024].

IMF, 2021. *Liberia poverty reduction and growth strategy.* Available at: imf.org [Accessed: 10.11.2023].

Ingutia, R., Rezitis, A.N., and Sumelius, J., 2020. 'Child poverty, status of rural women and education in sub Saharan Africa'. *Children and Youth Services Review*, 111: 104869.

Innis, P.G., and van Assche, K., 2023. 'Permanent incompleteness: slow electricity roll-out, infrastructure practices and strategy formation in Monrovia, Liberia'. *Energy Research and Social Science*, 99: 103056.

Jaiyeola, R.A., Akinyele, S.T., and Akinyele, E.F., 2019. 'Entrepreneurial skills acquisition in soap making production among small scale enterprise (SSES) performance in Abeokuta, Nigeria'. *Journal of Management Sciences and Entrepreneurship*, 19(7): 247–269.

Jomaa, L.H., McDonnell, E., and Probart, C., 2011. 'School feeding programs in developing countries: impacts on children's health and educational outcomes'. *Nutrition Reviews*, 69(2): 83–98.

Kanagasabai, U., Enriquez, K., Gelting, R., Malpiedi, P., Zayzay, C., Kendor, J., Fahnbulleh, S., Cooper, C., Gibson, W., Brown, R., and Nador, N., 2021. 'The impact of Water Sanitation and Hygiene (WASH) improvements on hand hygiene at two Liberian hospitals during the recovery phase of an Ebola epidemic'. *International Journal of Environmental Research and Public Health*, 18(7): 3409.

Karra, M., Del Bono, M., Wilde, J., Cunningham, W., and Gupta, S., 2023. *Liberian women count: evidence from a macrosimulation of the gender dividend.* World Bank Policy Research Working Paper 10425.

Kepeh, T., and Suah, N., 2021. 'Land and fragility of peace in postwar Liberia: concessions and conflicts in the midst of poverty'. *Journal of Peacebuilding and Development*, 16(3): 377–381.

Khanal, P., 2013. 'Community participation in schooling in Nepal: a disjunction between policy intention and policy implementation?' *Asia Pacific Journal of Education*, 33(3): 235–248.

Kieh, G.K., 2018. 'State collapse and democratic construction: prospects for Liberia'. In G.K. Kieh (ed.), *Multiparty democracy and political change.* Routledge, pp. 151–170.

Kiluvia, V.O., 2021. *Establishment of liquid soap making project to improve income of Jithamini Group in Gongolamboto Ward in Ilala Municipality, Dar es Salaam.* Doctoral dissertation, The Open University of Tanzania.

Kumeh, O.W., Fallah, M.P., Desai, I.K., Gilbert, H.N., Silverstein, J.B., Beste, S., Beste, J., Mukherjee, J.S., and Richardson, E.T., 2020. 'Literacy is power: structural drivers of child malnutrition in rural Liberia'. *BMJ Nutrition, Prevention and Health*, 3(2): 295.

Levey, E.J., Oppenheim, C.E., Lange, B.C., Plasky, N.S., Harris, B.L., Lekpeh, G.G., Kekulah, I., Henderson, D.C., and Borba, C.P., 2016. 'A qualitative analysis of factors impacting resilience among youth in post-conflict Liberia'. *Child and Adolescent Psychiatry and Mental Health*, 10(1): 1–11.

Lister, R., 2021. *Poverty.* John Wiley & Sons.

Lopes Cardozo, M.T., Higgins, S., and Le Mat, M.L., 2016. *Youth agency and peacebuilding: an analysis of the role of formal and non-formal education: Synthesis report on findings from Myanmar, Pakistan, South Africa and Uganda.* UNICEF.

Luminos Fund, 2018. *Annual report.* https://luminosfund.org/wp-content/uploads/2021/10/Luminos_Annual_Report_2018_spreads.pdf.

Luminos Fund, 2020. *Annual report.* https://luminosfund.org/wp-content/uploads/2021/07/2020-Annual-Report_The-Luminos-Fund_digital_spreads.pdf.

Luminos Fund, 2022. *Annual report.* https://luminosfund.org/wp-content/uploads/2023/05/Luminos-Fund_2022-Annual-Report.pdf.

Mac Ginty, R., and Richmond, O.P., 2013. 'The local turn in peace building: a critical agenda for peace'. *Third World Quarterly*, 34(5): 763–783.

Makiwane, M., and Kaunda, C., 2018. *Families and inclusive societies in Africa.* Human Sciences Research Council, South Africa.

McMullin, J.R., 2022. 'Hustling, cycling, peacebuilding: narrating postwar reintegration through livelihood in Liberia'. *Review of International Studies*, 48(1): 67–90.

McWhorter, L., 2016. 'Review of *Vulnerability in resistance*: Judith Butler, Zeynep Gambetti, and Leticia Sabsay (eds)'. *Contemporary Political Theory*, 17: 119–122.

Menendez, A.S., Ramesh, A., Baxter, P., and North, L., 2016. *Accelerated education programs in crisis and conflict.* The Pearson Institute.

Mfum-Mensah, O., and Friedson-Ridenour, S., 2014. 'Whose voices are being heard? Mechanisms for community participation in education in northern Ghana'. *Prospects*, 44: 351–365.

Mitman, G., 2021. *Empire of rubber: firestone's scramble for land and power in Liberia.* The New Press.

Moore, A., and Harder, A., 2015. 'Capacities of extension personnel within the pluralistic system of post-conflict Liberia'. *Journal of International Agricultural and Extension Education*, 22(3): 7–19.

Nicholson, S. 2007. 'Accelerated learning in post conflict settings: a discussion paper'. Save the Children US. INEE. Available at: https://inee.org/fr/node/7088 [Accessed: 15.11.2023].

Nizza, I.E., Farr, J. and Smith, J.A., 2021. 'Achieving excellence in interpretative phenomenological analysis (IPA): Four markers of high quality'. *Qualitative Research in Psychology*, 18(3): 369–386.

Nordström, A., 2024. 'Reimagining joy as a performative force in early childhood education'. *Contemporary Issues in Early Childhood*, 25(1): 80–92.

Novelli, M., Higgins, S., Ugur, M., and Valiente, O., 2014. *The political economy of education systems in conflict-affected contexts: a rigorous literature review*. Project Report, DfID.

Petruzzi, L.J., Pullen, S.J., Lange, B.C., Parnarouskis, L., Dominguez, S., Harris, B., Quiterio, N., Lekpeh, G., Manobah, B., Henderson, D.C., and Borba, C.P., 2018. 'Contributing risk factors for substance use among youth in postconflict Liberia'. *Qualitative Health Research*, 28(12): 1827–1838.

Polychroniou, A., 2022. 'Towards a radical feminist resignification of vulnerability: a critical juxtaposition of Judith Butler's post-structuralist philosophy and Martha Fineman's legal theory'. *Redescriptions: Political Thought, Conceptual History and Feminist Theory*, 25(2):113–136.

Pruett, L., Dyzenhaus, A., Karim, S., and Freeman, D., 2024. 'Election violence prevention during democratic transitions: a field experiment with youth and police in Liberia'. *Journal of Peace Research*, 20(10): 1–16.

Pryor, J., 2005. 'Can community participation mobilise social capital for improvement of rural schooling? A case study from Ghana'. *Compare: A Journal of Comparative and International Education*, 35(2): 193–203.

Quaynor, L., 2015. '"I do not have the means to speak": educating youth for citizenship in post-conflict Liberia.' *Journal of Peace Education*, 12(1): 15–36.

Richmond, O.P., 2011. 'Becoming liberal, unbecoming liberalism: Liberal–local hybridity via the everyday as a response to the paradoxes of liberal peacebuilding'. In *Rethinking the liberal peace*. Routledge, pp. 37–56.

Rose, P., 2003. 'Community participation in school policy and practice in Malawi: balancing local knowledge, national policies and international agency priorities'. *Compare: A Journal of Comparative and International Education*, 33(1): 47–64.

Santos, R., and Novelli, M., 2017. *The effect of the Ebola crisis on the education system's contribution to post-conflict sustainable peacebuilding in Liberia*. Centre for International Education, University of Sussex.

Sayed, Y., and Novelli, M., 2016. 'The role of teachers in peacebuilding and social cohesion'. In *The research consortium on education and peacebuilding*. Universities of Amsterdam, Sussex and Ulster, pp. 1–100.

Sharma, M., Backman, A., Vesga-Lopez, O., Zayas, L., Harris, B., Henderson, D.C., Koenen, K.C., Williams, D.R., and Borba, C.P., 2023. 'Trauma, risk, and resilience: a qualitative study of mental health in post-conflict Liberia'. *Transcultural Psychiatry*, 61(4): 652–667.

Shepler, S., and Williams, J.H., 2017. 'Understanding Sierra Leonean and Liberian teachers' views on discussing past wars in their classrooms'. *Comparative Education*, 53(3): 418–441.

Shimba, C., Luvinga, K., and Kilasara, S.A., 2019. 'Assessment of women food vending and local soap making micro enterprises in Temeke Municipal: a costs benefit analysis approach'. *Advances in Social Sciences Research Journal*, 6(6): 11–21.

Shin, W., 2020. '"Mama, keep walking for peace and justice": gender violence and Liberian mothers' interreligious peace movement'. *Religions*, 11(7): 323.

Shulika, L.S., 2022. 'Women's agency for peace in conflict times: case study of Liberian women organisations'. In *Critical perspectives on governance, religion and humanitarian aid in Africa*, pp. 100–124. Alternation African Scholarship Book Series (AASBS) CSSALL Publishers, South Africa.

Spatz, B.J., and Thaler, K.M., 2018. 'Has Liberia turned a corner?' *Journal of Democracy*, 29(3): 156–170.

Stromquist, N.P., Lin, J., Corneilse, C., Klees, S.J., Choti, T., and Haugen, C.S., 2013. 'Women teachers in Liberia: social and institutional forces accounting for their underrepresentation'. *International Journal of Educational Development*, 33(5): 521–530.

Stromquist, N.P., Lin, J., Corneilse, C., Klees, S.J., Choti, T., and Haugen, C.S., 2017. *Women teachers in Liberia: social forces accounting for professional underrepresentation*. Women Teachers in Africa, pp. 41–63.

Svoronos, T., Macauley, R.J., and Kruk, M.E., 2015. 'Can the health system deliver? Determinants of rural Liberians' confidence in health care'. *Health Policy and Planning*, 30(7): 823–829.

Swartz, S., Singal, N., and Arnot, M., 2024. 'Recentring, reframing and reimagining the canons of educational research'. In *Educational research practice in southern contexts*. Routledge.

Tavares, H.M., 2016. *Pedagogies of the image: photo-archives, cultural histories, and postfoundational inquiry*. Springer.

Teise, K., and Barnett, E., 2021. 'Is decentralisation a suitable response to improve South African rural education?' *International Journal of Learning, Teaching and Educational Research*, 20(6): 211–224.

Toweh, A., 2022. 'Liberians protest over economic hardship and president's absence'. *Reuters*, Available at: https://www.reuters.com/world/africa/liberians-protest-over-economic-hardship-presidents-absence-2022-12 [Accessed: 15.12.2023].

Truth and Reconciliation Commission, 2009. *Final report of the truth and reconciliation commission of Liberia (TRC) volume 1: Findings and determinations*. Available at: https://hmcwordpress.humanities.mcmaster.ca/Truthcommissions/wp-content/uploads/2018/10/Liberia.TRC_.Report-FULL.pdf.

UNDP, 2020. *Briefing notes for countries on the 2020 human development report*. Available at: https://www.rodra.co.za/images/countries/ethiopia/country_reports/Human%20Development%20Report%202020.pdf.

UNESCO, 2022. *Republic of Liberia Ministry of Education: Education sector plan 2022/23–2026/7*. Available at: liberia_esp_2022.pdf (unesco.org) [Accessed: 12.12.2023].

UNESCO Institute of Statistics (UIS), 2024. *SDG 4*. February 2024 release https://sdg4-data.uis.unesco.org/ [Accessed: 05.04.24].

UNICEF, 2023. *Liberia country office education fact sheet 2023–2024*. Available at: https://www.dropbox.com/scl/fi/u4dbi2kbh63p0siqec97a/UNICEF-LCO-Education-Fact-Sheet.pdf?rlkey=tl4ftcrr2i4uqaafdciwtzld7anddl=0

Unterhalter, E., Yates, C., Makinda, H., and North, A., 2012. 'Blaming the poor: constructions of marginality and poverty in the Kenyan education sector'. *Compare: A Journal of Comparative and International Education*, 42(2): 213–233.

USAID, 2017. *Accelerated quality education for Liberian children*. Available at: https://pdf.usaid.gov/pdf_docs/PA00SSBV.pdf.

USAID, 2019. *Liberia youth situational analysis*. Available at: https://www.youthpower.org/sites/default/files/YouthPower/files/resources/Liberia%20Youth%20Assessment%20Situational%20Analysis%20Report_0.pdf.

Vinck, P., Pham, P., and Kreutzer, T., 2011. *Talking peace: a population-based survey on attitudes about security, dispute resolution, and post-conflict reconstruction in Liberia*. University of California Press.

Wang, L., 2018. 'All work, all play: harnessing play-based learning in Ethiopia and Liberia to create lifelong learners'. *Childhood Education*, 94(5): 4–13.

Westbrook, J., and Higgins, S. 2019. *Report on the evaluation of the quality of teaching and learning in the second chance programme for out of school children in Liberia*. Centre for International Education, University of Sussex.

Wetherell, M., 2012. *Affect and emotion: a new social science understanding*. Sage.

World Bank, 2023. *Liberia poverty assessment towards a more inclusive Liberia*. World Bank, DC. https://documents.worldbank.org/curated/en/099032124150035378/P17739418373d30c419ffb1cd3dd5dfb684

World Food Programme, 2022. *Liberia*. https://www.wfp.org/countries/liberia

Wrigley, T., Lingard, B., and Thomson, P., 2012. 'Pedagogies of transformation: keeping hope alive in troubled times'. *Critical Studies in Education*, 53(1): 95–108.

Wrigley-Asante, C., 2008. 'Men are poor but women are poorer: gendered poverty and survival strategies in the Dangme West District of Ghana'. *Norsk Geografisk Tidsskrift / Norwegian Journal of Geography*, 62(3): 161–170.

Yamada, S., 2014. 'Determinants of "community participation": the tradition of local initiatives and the institutionalisation of school management committees in Oromia Region, Ethiopia'. *Compare: A Journal of Comparative and International Education*, 44(2): 162–185.

Yoder, H.N., Tol, W.A., Reis, R., and de Jong, J.T., 2016. 'Child mental health in Sierra Leone: a survey and exploratory qualitative study'. *International Journal of Mental Health Systems*, 10(1): 1–13.

9 Accelerated Learning and the Power of African Values

The goal of this chapter is to establish the cultural responsiveness of accelerated learning programmes (ALPs) in the African context by synthesising the findings of the three case studies discussed in chapters 6 to 8. By illuminating their embodiment of an African value system, this chapter adds a further layer of understanding of the diverse ways in which ALPs represent a reconceptualisation and alternative response to educational marginalisation in Africa and, even more significantly, to the almost universal ways in which international agencies have addressed such marginalisation. This chapter extends understanding of what can be achieved in terms of rethinking educational provision, the role of the teacher and their pedagogy for out-of-school children. By locating ALPs culturally, we can illuminate their strengths beyond a 'what works' framing of effectiveness in educational interventions (Tikly, 2015) that tends to disregard their location within context-specific cultural norms. ALP's reframing of the African child in this way takes us far beyond deficit categorisations and projections.

Centring Ubuntu in Education and Development

Originating in South Africa and finding resonance in the beliefs, values, norms and practices of different African societies, *Ubuntu* is founded on the isiXhosa proverb '*umuntu ngumuntu ngabantu*' that translates as 'I am therefore you are' (Letseka, 2012, 48). This encapsulates its key ontological insight that all of us come into our being as humans through our interdependence with others. As Waghid (2018, 56) has noted, within the ubuntu value system, "a human being cannot lay claim to his or her humanity without engaging with other humans". In this sense, ubuntu frames the human subject as emergent from relational, inter-personal social processes. And this foregrounding of the inextricably relational dimension of human existence also extends to the non-human and the natural environment (Le Grange, 2018).

Ubuntu has various names in different African contexts and languages (Van Norren, 2017; Takyi-Amoako and Assié-Lumumba, 2018, 10). Hence it is called 'unhu' amongst the Shoa people of Zimbabwe; 'ubuntu' among the Nguni speakers of Southern Africa; 'utu' amongst the Swahili speakers of East Africa; and 'bumuntu' in Tanzania (Mawere and Mubaya, 2016, 98). Scholars have also noted how ubuntu is an emergent form of African oral *sagesse*, a type of wisdom passed down orally across generations (Mawere and Mubaya, 2016, 99; Brás, 2024, 64). However, whilst observing its localised expressions in diverse African contexts, scholars have noted its resonance as a cultural worldview pervasive across Africa. Hence scholars have recognised its status as "simultaneously the foundation and the edifice of African philosophy, (Ramose, 1999, 9), 'Africa's moral compass' (Mawere and Mubaya, 2016, 104) and a 'continent wide value system" (Van Norren, 2022, 2793).

This uniquely African value system represents a critique of individualistic notions of human subjects through its ethical virtues of care, concern and responsibility for the other and a shared common humanity (Tutu, 2000). Broodryk (2002, 13) describes it as a "comprehensive ancient African worldview based on the values of intense humaneness, caring, sharing, respect, compassion and associated values". Within indigenous African thought, ubuntu can be said to "articulate our communal interconnectedness, our common humanity, our interdependence, and our common membership to a community" (Letseka, 2013, 339) – a social ethic celebrated as Africa's distinctive contribution to the world (Mawere and Mubaya, 2016, 95), the "great gift from Africa" (Metz, 2021).

The values and insights of ubuntu have been drawn on to critique and re-envision assumptions and practices of dominant agendas in the field of education and development.[1] Van Norren (2022, 2791), for example, explains that whilst the Sustainable Development Goals (SDGs) were "multilaterally negotiated and claim universality", they are "underpinned by assumptions associated with European modernism (individuality, growth, separation of nature and humans etc)". Hence, "to be truly inclusive of Africa, they can do more justice to ubuntu" (2022). This failure to draw on an African value system arguably demonstrates a disconnect between their conceptualisation of development and the cultural norms and worldviews or 'cosmovisions' (Van Norren, 2020, 434) in diverse global contexts, including ubuntu, but also, for example, the native American idea of *Buen Vivir* (Van Norren, 2020). Despite adopting a rhetoric of inclusivity of a range of cultural world views, the SDGs arguably commit what de Sousa Santos (2014) has termed epistemic violence, that results "when we do not take the ontological and epistemological positions of differing life worlds" into account (92).

Piper (2016) has argued that "Ubuntu is an African philosophy of human kindness: applying it in the Global South would fundamentally alter the design of the education sector" (1). Its 'educational potential' (Abdi, 2018, 58) has been recognised in supplying ethical insights into the nature of the human and social life through which to analyse, critique and re-envision educational practice in diverse African contexts.[2] Ubuntu values have been drawn on, for example, in:

- studies of the higher education curriculum (Le Grange, 2014; Hlatshwayo and Shawa, 2020; Maditsi and Bhuda, 2023);
- peace education (Murithi, 2009);

- adult and vocational education (Tran and Wall, 2018); environmental education (Frempong and Kadam, 2022);
- global citizenship education (Waghid and Hungwe, 2023);
- language of instruction and assessment (Brock-Utne, 2016; Beets and Le Grange, 2005);
- school leadership (Setlhodi, 2019);
- early childhood education (Koen et al., 2021);
- the provision of culturally relevant pedagogy (Biraimah, 2016; Waghid et al, 2018);
- educational responses to student mothers (Chinkondenji, 2022);
- disability (Berghs, 2017; Ramose 2021) and
- critiques of the failure of the 'sub-Saharan Africa school curriculum to incorporate indigenous knowledges' (Shizha, 2013) or indigenous forms of play in primary schools (Nxumalo and Mncube, 2018).

All these studies are driven by a concern to show how "education can be brought closer into line with ubuntu values" (Biraimah, 2016, 62) that offer a means of renewing African educational provision (Assié-Lumumba, 2016, 11). Such studies seek to rehabilitate what is regarded as an indigenous knowledge and value system within a decolonising imperative to ensure epistemic justice (Le Grange, 2020; Gumbo et al., 2022; Brás, 2024) in the curriculum content at all levels of the education system. This repurposing of ubuntu for educational transformation is a key dimension of the process of "reclaiming indigenous cultures in sub-Saharan African education" (Shizha, 2015, 301), correcting what is perceived to be the enduring legacy and dominance of Western-centric knowledge within African education provision. As Ndlovu-Gatsheni (2021, 887) writes, drawing on ubuntu values:

> speaks to the failures in the domain of knowledge to recognise the different ways of knowing by which diverse peoples across the human globe make sense of the world and provide meaning for their existence.

Takyi-Amaoko and Assié-Lumumba (2018, 5) argue that "global engagement with stated goals of addressing Africa's educational shortcomings repeatedly miss their targets in great part because the problems are inadequately analysed, and the solutions are ill conceived". Hence, there is a need to "fundamentally re-envision educational provision in Africa to suit its philosophical, historical and cultural context by employing the ubuntu framework". These authors explain well this impulse to Africanise:

> the ubuntu philosophy and ideals must be made central to Africa's education policy processes, systems and agents' actions and must be evoked for an effective re-envisioning of Africa's education. This is because currently the philosophy and its ideals, which constitute the essence of Africa and its people as well as their indigenous knowledges and history,

are lacking in the educational policies and systems of the continent. This absence has culminated in an incongruent link between who Africans are as a people and the educational systems that are meant to help unlock and develop their talents and potential for socio-economic development.
(Takyi-Amoako and Assié-Lumumba, 2018, 10)

Of particular relevance to the concerns of this book is Frempong and Kadam's (2022) underscoring of the benefits to children's experiences of learning such that "an ubuntu mindset offers unique possibilities of bringing learners close to their social realities and helping them to learn together better, the Africentric way" (1). However, the values of ubuntu have yet to be mobilised in relation to analysis and understanding of the characteristics, impact and success of ALPs in African contexts when engaging children suffering educational marginalisation. This is the goal of the next section that reflects on the findings of the case studies in Chapters 6–8.

Ubuntu, Learning and the Dignity of the African Child

As noted, the foundational principle of ubuntu is the interconnectedness of all human beings. This stress on interdependence challenges the individualism of Western-centric systems of thought deriving from the European enlightenment. Le Grange (2018) has written that ubuntu therefore "catalyses a shift from the arrogant I (of Western individualism) to the humble I, to the I that is embedded, extended and enacted" (41). Ubuntu as a relational concept of being human is based on the idea of continually 'being coming into being' (Brás, 2024, 63) through our encounters with others and in that process, it foregrounds inter-relationships with others as the basis of everyone's humanity (Le Grange, 2018).

Extended to education, this ontological insight insists on a framing of African children as always relational and situated, deriving dignity from their interconnections with others in their families and communities – something as we have seen the ALPs are particularly focused on (Brás, 2024, 65). Le Grange (2018, 41), seeking to show how ubuntu is relevant to inclusive forms of pedagogical practices, notes that "the idea of the human as an atomised and autonomous individual… should be jettisoned". Hence, ubuntu-inspired analysis of education provision critiques the dominance of atomising and individualising models of learners to be found in the modes of learning and assessment that conflate individual learning outcomes in generic tests with their educational achievements. As noted in Part 1, this approach reduces complex pedagogical processes to 'inputs' and 'outputs', ignoring what is 'in between'. Foregrounding only the individuals' learning outcomes, such approaches construe educational practices as analogous to the competitive individualism of the marketplace (Abdi, 2018; Takyi-Amoako and Assié-Lumumba, 2018; Klees, 2020). Moreover, as discussed earlier in this book, framings of children influenced by human capital theory align children's agency and development to an abstract economistic trajectory of national economic growth.

An ubuntu-inspired framing of children as learners offers an alternative to such economistic and disembedded accounts of their agency. This framing re-dignifies their intrinsic humanity, outside of economistic approaches that present them as potential carriers of capital. Hence, "in this world of neoliberal globalisation, ubuntu emerges as an ecopolitical alternative. It is a form of knowledge that makes us more humane" (Brás, 2024, 61; see also Swanson, 2010). Ubuntu encourages "education *qua* education" rather than as an "extension of the overall radical economisation of life" (Abdi, 2018, 26), thereby foregrounding children's relationships with their communities, peers and environment as an intrinsic aspect of their exercise of agency as children and as learners as well as with the material environment in which they live.

The curriculum content and pedagogical practices of ALPs in Ghana, Ethiopia and Liberia revealed in the case studies in Chapters 6–8 are all aligned with, and enact in diverse ways, this relational framing of the dignity of the African child. As we have seen in Chapter 6, the complementary basic education (CBE) programme in Northern Ghana, through leveraging children's funds of knowledge, mirrors back to children living in rural contexts of educational marginalisation, their multiple relationships as valued resources for learning. CBE textbooks reference children's relationships with families and elders. They reference their farming practices, their contributions to household survival as well as their games with local materials. They refer to their local landscape as well as its need to be protected.

As we saw in Chapter 7, Speed Schools in Ethiopia use local materials familiar to children from their environment and are often used outside of school to encourage play and enjoyable learning. The use of traditional stories in local languages as instructional materials also aligns with ubuntu's understanding of our humanity in relation not only to those we interact with in the present but also to the departed (Ramose, 1999, 62). By making learning relevant and resonant with children's lives, the curriculum and instructional materials of ALPs operationalise the vision of African educationists such as Nkrumah who insisted that school content should offer them an "African view based in concrete studies of the problems of the tropical world" (Akyeampong, 2010, 2). Through such a context-responsive curriculum, ALPs generate collective processes of learning in which children participate based on their shared experiences and knowledges of the environment and relationships they are all familiar with.

The analysis of the role of Parental Engagement Groups (PEGs) in Chapter 8 also shows how ALPs install at the heart of their educational vision a relational framing of children within the broader kinship networks that support and sustain them. Ngubane and Makua (2021, 6) note that "Ubuntu pedagogy.... asserts learners as significant others who bring unique backgrounds, experiences and prior knowledge for teachers to build on towards the development of new knowledge". African children's sociality and its potential to promote group learning and knowledge acquisition are dignified, rather than devalued or ignored in the classrooms of the three ALP programmes we studied.

By valuing the informal, community/environment-rooted learning that children gained through their socialisation practices outside of the formal learning space, these ALP classrooms install children's *relationality* as a source of, and a resource for, their learning.

The Implications for Pedagogical Practices

In showing how ALPs align with and use, in effect, ubuntu values, we gain a deeper sense of their significance in reconfiguring the African child within a value system that is culturally resonant. In each of the following subsections, we spotlight those aspects of the educational provision of the three ALPs that, on the one hand, challenge any deficit model of the marginalised, in this case the out-of-school child, their supposed learning problems and their parents' inadequacies in relation to education of their children. On the other hand, these ALPs proffer a different pedagogy that is suited to the vision of a child who is capable of learning, who does learn and whose learning is grounded in all aspects of their lives. The fundamental logic behind this alternative pedagogy is one that is recognisably related to ubuntu. We discuss in turn: the language of instruction; peer learning; community engagement; learning from the natural world; a pedagogy of care and compassion and modalities of learning that go beyond the cognitive.

The language of instruction

As Chapter 3 put so strongly, one of the key factors that has negatively affected children's learning in Africa is the language of instruction, producing a systemic form of epistemic and in turn social exclusion. We saw in Chapter 5 how addressing the language challenge is an essential component of a multi-dimensional approach to addressing educational marginalisation, especially for those children living in rural poverty. When the values of ubuntu are applied to schooling, this leads to a re-envisioning of the language of instruction policies and practices. As Brock-Utne (2016) has argued, recognising the rich linguistic resources in which African children exercise agency in relationships with others within language of instruction practices is a pedagogical extension of ubuntu's central insight, the fundamental interconnectedness of our being in the world (see also Makalela, 2016; Le Grange, 2018; Mkosi et al., 2023). This approach operates within what has been termed the 'humanity logic' of the 'I x We' (Makalela, 2018, 490) within its basic tenet: '*I am because you are; you are because I am*'. Ubuntu's foregrounding of relationality as a key feature of the human underlines a view of languages as social practices that enable that inter-relationality to be achieved. Drawing on multiple linguistic resources thus becomes a means of bridging the intersection between the 'I' and the 'we'. Thus, Makalela argues that "fluid African multilingualism is an African cultural competence, rooted in the value system of ubuntu: 'I am because you are'" (Makalela, 2016, 194).

The concept of 'ubuntu translanguaging' (Makalela, 2015) shows how the values of ubuntu apply to language of instruction practices. This "denotes that no one language is complete without the other since they are involved in infinite relations of dependency" (Brock-Utne, 2018, 731). This recognises the realities of linguistic exchange in African contexts where interpersonal communication often draws on more than one language. Ubuntu underscores the benefits to learners of bilingual pedagogical practices that draw upon local as well as colonial languages.

Chapter 6 described the centralisation of children's funds of knowledge in the CBE programme in Ghana that used local languages as the medium of instruction and in the textbooks used. Instructional materials are developed with the assistance of local communities who offer their expertise in local language usage. The revaluing of African children's linguistic repertoires within a situated understanding of their learning needs and the choice of the medium of instruction aligns with the respect for African linguistic realities and forms of communication associated with ubuntu's framing of human interdependence. Valuing children's home languages as resources for learning also enables teachers to draw on their situated learning and constructions of meaning outside formal learning environments. This recognises them as relational members of families and communities, and as such, negotiators and navigators of meaning in multiple spaces. All these elements contribute to the child's learning, combining cognitive and social development. In mobilising African children's rich communicative resources, in all their linguistic interdependence, such pedagogical practices exemplify the ubuntu principle of openness to the other.

Moreover, the case study on CBE in Northern Ghana showed how the use of such languages of instruction in the nine months of the ALPs contributes to, rather than undermines, the later acquisition of English by children who transitioned to government schools where they repurpose skills used in local language literacy in developing English competence. This continuum between competence in local languages and competence in English demonstrates the need to avoid binarising either as "sealed entities capable of being placed in boxes" (Makalela, 2015, 200) for the purposes of effective pedagogical practice and children's intellectual development. Children previously marginalised from educational provision developed pride and self-confidence as learners through learning in their local languages, a self-belief that contributed to their staying power in government schools, as also illustrated in the Ethiopia Second Chance case study in Chapter 7. Interpreted through the lens of ubuntu ontology, this sustained impact on their agency as learners may be understood as an effect of, at least partial, recognition of the linguistic conditions of their shared humanity when learning with their facilitator and their peers in the ALP classes.

There are many further opportunities to build on the local language learning approaches demonstrated in ALPs through some of the translanguaging strategies discussed in Chapter 5, which further recognise children's complex and dynamic linguistic repertoires and align with "an 'ubuntu' lens of viewing the world" (Makalela, 2018, 24). This would open up, in appropriate contexts, the possibilities of code switching that harnessed children's entire language repertoire and familiarity with more than one local language to support their learning. This would maximise the opportunities for children to engage in exploratory talk.

Peer learning

Ubuntu's fundamental insight into human interdependence and mutuality is also associated with pedagogical practices that promote collaborative learning or peer support in the process of learning. For Oviawe (2016) "rediscovering the ubuntu paradigm in education" involves restoring processes of mutual meaning-making at the heart of learning "within a collective approach as opposed to an individualistic one" (3). As Waghid (2018) has noted, "when humans engage in an encounter they encourage and stimulate one another to develop a sense of self-worth and dignity" (57). When they come together to learn, children are:

> not merely an aggregation of individuals but are intricately engaged in some form of social practice which allows them to become associated with one another through the understandings and ways of seeing the world.
>
> (58)

Yet Mitchell (2023) notes that peer learning has received limited attention in official education discourse. This neglect may be attributed to the "dominance of research from the global north in knowledge production" (1) which has had the effect of "establishing European and North American countries as 'reference societies' or models for emulation" (1). Such approaches foreclose recognition of the intersection between education provision and Afrocentric cultural values. Whilst acknowledging a need to be wary of essentialising narratives across a socio-economically diverse region such as sub-Saharan Africa, Mitchell (2016, 1) notes that the

> basic distinction between more individualistically oriented Euro-American societies and more collectively oriented African ones has been widely observed and is supported by research in the field of cultural psychology.

Ugandan theorist Sylvia Tamale (2020) evokes the cultural resonance and rootedness of this collective orientation, noting that:

> the shared values of communal life and group solidarity, embedded in the philosophical concept of ubuntu... differentiate African people from modern Euro-American societies... even as individualism has penetrated the market driven societies of neoliberal Africa, many fundamental

aspects of African lives remain anchored in collective relationships and efficacy, where individuals are part of a unity that is interdependent and mutually beneficial.

(12, quoted in Mitchell, 2016, 1)

The images of children happily learning together in Speed Schools in Ethiopia (Chapter 7) demonstrate how mutually supportive peer learning at the core of the programme's pedagogical strategies enables them to achieve high learning outcomes. As we saw earlier, encouraging children to learn together and to learn from each other by constructing knowledge together is a key strength of the pedagogical practices in Speed Schools in Ethiopia. The evaluation report found that this involved investing trust in children to process knowledge through group activities inviting them to represent a concept or information to each other in different media, whether through art, music, drama, storytelling or games (Akyeampong et al, 2020). It found that "this 'relearning' or rehearsal of content by different groups (of children) in tandem with simple teaching and learning resources is at the heart of the Speed School pedagogic approach" (University of Sussex, 2015, 9). Such activities enable pupils' collaborative processing of content, catalysing their "active engagement with all the senses" (University of Sussex, 2015, 9). Here, peer learning structures participatory pedagogical practices, enabling the "saying again" in the pupils' own words, so that they appropriate and own the learning (University of Sussex, 2015, 9). Peer learning experienced in this way is enjoyable, with a "positive effect on the learning experiences of pupils" (University of Sussex, 2015, 9) – it is interactive and sociable.

As we have seen, peer learning also formed part of a broader concern by facilitators to create a positive enabling environment for their pupils and one in which pupils 'were responsible for one another's well-being and learning' (10) with facilitators reinforcing the idea that 'learning was a collective responsibility' (10). Peer learning in Speed Schools was part of their inclusive pedagogy that recognises that 'effective learning involves collaborative effort, which requires every child to participate' (Akyeampong et al., 2020, 37). Through centralising peer learning, ALPs therefore enact a culturally responsive pedagogy.

Community engagement

The Second Chance ALP in Liberia discussed in Chapter 8 shows how the ubuntu ontology of the human orientation to the communal is evident in its outreach to communities suffering educational marginality in a conflict-affected context. Van Norren (2022, 2794) argues that, within ubuntu, "community and (extended) family-centred thinking is important since 'man [sic] is defined by reference to the environing community'" (quoted from Menkiti, 1984, 171) and personhood is something that has to be achieved in the context of participation in the community.

All the case studies in this book display the innovative approaches through which ALPs engage the families and communities of children experiencing educational marginalisation. This is achieved in multiple ways. For example, timings of classes are scheduled to synchronise with the situated temporal rhythms of rural agricultural labour. Curriculum and textbook content connect directly with and valorise the funds of knowledge and language children acquire from socialising in their communities as well as mirroring their situated lived experiences. As Chapter 6 describes, the development of textbooks in local languages for CBE draws directly on the linguistic and knowledge resources of those members of rural communities invited to participate, recognising the positive agency of constituencies. The PEGs in Liberia, discussed in Chapter 8, celebrate children's learning as a communal and community-based event, worthy of collective celebration and pride. Bringing together the extended family networks in which children are cared for, these PEGs recognise that the "inclusive framework upon which African family life is grounded" (Makiwane and Kaunda, 2018, 6) is a valued social resource that can support learning. Such groups palpably epitomise the communal spirit of ubuntu – they recognise through their practice that 'it takes a village to raise a child' (Mabovula, 2011). Such engagement with communities with large numbers of out-of-school children avoids the patronising and pathologising assumptions about the rural poor found in educational decentralisation initiatives discussed in Chapter 8. All these features of ALPs shift the asymmetrical power relationships in policy and programming that are meant to address educational marginalisation. They aim to recognise the agency, knowledge, voices and concerns of communities affected and their children. In doing so, their explicit and multi-faceted orientation to the communities, as well as the children living with vulnerability and precarity, installs at the core of the vision of learning offered in ALPs – the communal values of ubuntu (Mabovula, 2011).

Learning and the natural environment

Ubuntu emphasis on the human's reciprocity with nature and the natural environment offers a 'cosmovision' that has "an inherent biocentric value orientation" (Van Norren, 2020, 431). It extends "the same respect to nature as to people" (Van Norren, 2020). As such, it critiques extractivist approaches to the natural world seeing these as a departure from the need for "development as service to one another and to the Earth" (Van Norren, 2020). Ubuntu's framing of the relationship of humans to the Earth is especially relevant in the context of ALPs given the fact that climate change and food insecurities resulting from environmental degradation affect the poor disproportionately (Tamasiga et al., 2023). Extended to education, an ubuntu approach underscores the importance of integrating awareness of, and respect for, the environment into curriculum content and pedagogical strategies, not least as a matter of environmental protection and socio-economic well-being.

Aligning with such logics, the ALPs discussed in this book all make children's environments integral to pedagogical activities and curriculum content in diverse ways. The case studies of CBE in Ghana (Chapter 6) and Speed Schools in Ethiopia (Chapter 7) demonstrated their use of local materials such as stones and sand as resources for learning. Through referencing the environment in activities in textbooks – its trees, water supplies, agricultural land, contaminated land – children were invited to draw on their knowledge and experiences in discussing a range of issues, whether hygiene, land use or environmental safety and protection. Facilitators also took children outside to use the local landscape as a resource for learning.

In all these ways, learning within the classroom is not sealed off from this wider dimension of their lives but becomes a porous space that refers to their experiences outside as a positive resource for meaningful and context-responsive pedagogical practices. Textbooks recognise the particular relationships that children living in poor rural contexts have with their natural environment, whether as a place to play, to work, to experience joy, or as land to be protected, respected and nurtured, and worked according to the seasons. These relationships are used to catalyse learning, whilst recognising children's exercise of agency in this environment. In this way, they embody an ecological framing of children that reproduces ubuntu's vision of the human.

The timing of learning, in the ALPs discussed in this book, is also aligned with the seasonal cycles and changes that impact agricultural work and productivity. Multi-season research with poor children has revealed how children's lives in rural contexts of precarity in Ethiopia, Nigeria and Zambia are shaped by the need to respond to labour demands generated by changing agricultural conditions (Humphreys et al., 2015, 139; Phiri and Abebe, 2016). Thus, in certain periods of the year such as the planting and harvesting seasons, there is greater pressure on families to get their children to contribute to their household's socio-economic survival (Humphreys et al., 2015). The need for children to work on farms or household chores early in the morning, or to support their families during market days, in turn puts pressure on their ability to attend schooling at the appropriate times.

Tracking fluctuations in primary school and classroom attendance in northern Nigeria, Humphrey et al.'s (2015, 139) study found that misalignments between pupils' lives and school administrative structures, in particular annual, weekly and daily school timetables, contributed to "low or non-attendance of pupils officially enrolled in schools". Hence the importance, as a means of fostering their re-engagement, of synchronising the timings and scheduling of schooling with the temporal rhythms of the lives of those children living in rural poverty. Orienting the timing of learning to children's situated experiences of time facilitates children's attendance and encourages their positive disposition to the prospect of learning that fits into their routines. Applying an ubuntu lens we can go further. By timing classes to accommodate children's quotidien realities, ALPs reconfigure educational provision within a relational approach to time which is associated with ubuntu values. This valorises the socially rooted experiences of time within African rural communities and challenges the dominance of wholly linear framings of time within educational provision shaped by colonialist and Western temporal frameworks (Hunfeld, 2022).

A pedagogy of care and compassion

Perhaps, the most significant aspect of the ubuntu social ethic for educational practices is its emphasis on the humane virtues of concern and compassion for others. The proverb 'I am therefore you are' has been interpreted as providing the basis for the integration into pedagogical relationships of an 'ethic of care' (Waghid and Smeyers, 2012, 6; Ukpokodu, 2016; Koen et al., 2021). This forms part of a vision of teaching and learning as a profoundly ethical practice rooted in cultivating caring relationships between teachers and learners and also between learners. In this way, an ubuntu approach serves to 'humanise pedagogies' (Maditsi and Bhuda, 2023, 282).

The title of Omiunota Ukpokodu's book (2016), *You Can't Teach Us If You Don't Know Us and Care about Us: Becoming an Ubuntu, Responsive and Responsible Urban Teacher*, encapsulates this caring dimension. She writes that:

> teaching with the spirit of ubuntu allows a teacher to be open, to be fully available to his/her students, their families and community and to be invested in them in ways that they can't fail them.

For Waghid (2018, 58) mobilising ubuntu values in relation to education foregrounds its "hospitality dimension which can be enacted on the grounds that ubuntu relates to caring, trust, respect and compassion – all virtues that constitute hospitality". However, these values tend to be effaced within economistic framings of educational goals and outcomes that ignore the profoundly relational nature of pedagogical processes. This insistence on the sociality of educational practices is all the more relevant in contexts in which children's relationship with learning is highly contingent.

In contrast, the case studies in this book demonstrate how ALPs demonstrate just such an 'ethic of care' in alignment with the values of ubuntu. Hence, the facilitators in the CBE programme in Northern Ghana are praised by parents for visiting their homes, getting to know their circumstances, following up in the case of absences and showing their children kindness. One boy attending the *Second Chance* programme in Liberia said of his facilitator:

> If I na [/don't/] bring money and I go ask him he can give me it. If I na [/don't/] pay I say brother Abraham I [/am/] hungry…he can take out thirty dollar he say go buy kala [/deep fried yeast buns/].

As a result of their knowledge of facilitators' caring behaviour, family members expressed trust and confidence in the learning opportunities which ALPs opened up. Moreover, parents appreciated how facilitators, as a result of living in their communities, were aware of the challenges they faced in sending their children to school. Likewise, the outreach to parents in the *Second Chance* programme in Liberia was positive (Chapter 8), with parents appreciating how the parental engagement groups gave them a space in which their concerns and challenges were recognised with compassion. The provision of a meal for children attending ALP class, a vital addition in a context of food insecurity and child malnutrition, was also recognised as caring. As one mother said, 'they are helping the children because food is life, if you are not alive you will not learn'.

Modalities of learning that go beyond the cognitive

As explained in Chapters 6–8, all of the case studies of ALPs achieved success in generating excellent learning outcomes, and in this way, they succeed when measured against narrow preoccupations with the development of cognitive skills as sole indicators of educational success. However, the case studies also root their cognitive successes within an approach to learning that goes beyond the narrowly cognitive. All of the alignments between ALPs and ubuntu discussed above converge in an expansive view of education provision, in which the development of children's cognitive skills is grounded in and acquires meaning and purpose in the relational and therefore social nature of their learning. All of the above strategies promote children's participation, confidence and agency as learners. They nurture their positive emotional dispositions to the activity of learning. These impacts are sustained over time, in particular during children's transition into government schools. Learning is here a social and situated practice. In our research (Akyeampong et al., 2018), we noted that ALPs provide learning environments where the development of social and emotional competences becomes an integral part of the learning experience: (35). This in turn unlocks the learning and creative potential of children who have been marginalised from formal schooling. In this way, ALPs capitalise on the benefits of social and emotional learning – benefits that have been thrown into relief particularly by the experiences of children and families unable to access educational provision during the Covid-19 epidemic (Yorke et al., 2021). The social and emotional competencies of children are not 'add-ons' to the promotion of cognitive skills but integrated into their approach to learning as a humane, ethical enterprise, one that nurtures their agency as learners.

Some forms of social and emotional learning, for instance in socio-emotional literacy programmes, have been critiqued (Messina-Albarenque et al., 2024) for their tendency to focus on the acquisition of generic behaviours by individual children as an addition to their development of cognitive skills. This approach is again based on "individualist models of self" (Hoffman, 2009, 533) that contrast sharply with the vision of children and of the human offered in ubuntu. Such an individualising approach amounts to a form of social regulation rather than contributing to children's wellbeing *in situ*. It decontextualises children's social and emotional development from the specific contexts and relationships in which it is shaped and nurtured. When carved out and delivered in a separate area of the curriculum, such approaches ignore what has been evident in the discussion of ALPs throughout this chapter, that the social and emotional dimensions of children's lives, emergent from particular contexts, are intrinsic to learning. Barry (2022, 69) explains that Western models of educational provision, especially those dominated by testing regimes,

> tend to separate the different aspects of schooling into teaching, content, subject knowledge, learners learning and study each of these in relative isolation. In doing this.... We often overlook the wonderful bond of interconnectedness from which all meaningful learning springs.
>
> (2022)

Through offering educational provision that constantly interconnects the content and processes of children's learning with their situated experiences, grounded in their circles of relationships, accelerated learning provision aligns with this vision of learning and marks a decisive shift away from any deficit image of the individual 'out-of-school' child, their parents and community, and an equally decisive shift away from understanding learning in narrowly cognitive terms.

Conclusions: Accelerated Learning Programmes and Ubuntu

In connecting ALPs to the African values of ubuntu, our analysis recognises that pedagogy, as Alexander (2009, 930) has explained, is always a value-laden activity, combining "the act of teaching" with the "ideas, values and beliefs by which the act of teaching is informed and justified". The key strengths of ALPs made visible in the previous case studies all align with and mediate the Afrocentric value system of ubuntu and as such are a direct challenge to the Western-centric logics underlying the narrative of the 'learning crisis'. Consequently, they offer a model of educational provision that valorises the knowledge, agency and languages of African children and their communities, at the same time as they gain credibility in the African context because of their cultural resonance. Applying an ubuntu lens has demonstrated how ALPs, whilst noted for their role in speeding up learning processes, and delivering successful learning outcomes, as shown in all the case studies, also make the learning process deeper and more culturally responsive in its timings, content, pedagogical values and recognition of African children, their families and communities. This adds a further crucial dimension to our understanding of their significance in offering alternative, culturally grounded solutions to learning challenges in Africa.

Notes

1 The SDGs have been critiqued for their failure to reference ubuntu's biocentric concerns with the reciprocity between human and planetary well-being; and the

responsibility therefore to challenge extractive capitalist exploitation of the earth's resources driven by the individualistic pursuit of profit (Van Norren, 2017, 2020, 2022; Komatsu et al., 2021; Frempong and Kadam, 2022).

2 See studies by Oviawe (2016), Assié-Lumumba (2016), Takyi-Amoako and Assié-Lumumba (2018), Diarra (2018), Elonga Mboyo (2019). The ethical values associated with ubuntu have also been mobilised to critique and rethink a range of social practices in African contexts, including social work (Ross, 2018; Tamburro, 2013); provision for the disabled (Falola and Hamel, 2021; Berghs, 2023); and national reconciliation and healing after conflict (Hapanyengwi-Chemhuru and Shizha 2012; Tutu, 2000).

References

Abdi, A.A., 2018. 'The humanist African philosophy of Ubuntu: anti-colonial historical and educational analyses'. In A.A. Abdi (ed.), *Re-visioning education in Africa: Ubuntu-inspired education for humanity*. Palgrave Macmillan Cham, pp. 19–34.

Akyeampong, K., 2010. *Educational expansion in Ghana: a review of 50 years of challenge and progress*. Consortium for Research on Educational Access, Transitions and Equity.

Akyeampong, K., Carter, E., Higgins, S., Rose, P., Sabates, R., 2018. Understanding Complementary Basic Education in Ghana: Investigation of the experiences and achievements of children after transitioning into public schools. *Report for DFID Ghana Office* (November 2018). REAL Centre, University of Cambridge. https://doi.org/10.5281/zenodo.2582955

Akyeampong, K., Pryor, J., and Ampiah, J.G., 2006. 'A vision of successful schooling: Ghanaian teachers' understandings of learning, teaching and assessment'. *Comparative Education*, 42(2): 155–176.

Akyeampong, K., Westbrook, J., and Pryor, J., 2020. 'The speed school pedagogy and how it unlocks the creative and learning potential of disadvantaged children in Ethiopia'. In *NISSEM global briefs*. University of Sussex, pp. 34–53. https://hdl.handle.net/10779/uos.23478908.v2 Published by NISSEM.

Alexander, R., 2009. 'Towards a comparative pedagogy'. In R. Alexander (ed.), *International handbook of comparative education*. Springer Netherlands, pp. 923–939.

Assié-Lumumba, N.D.T., 2016. 'Evolving African attitudes to European education: resistance, pervert effects of the single system paradox, and the Ubuntu framework for renewal'. *International Review of Education*, 62: 11–27.

Barry, G.C., 2022. 'Ubuntu in education: the narratives of emotional intelligence in education'. *Cuidado mutuo: corporeidad, cultivo de sí y ética del cuidado. Foro por la vida XI*, 5: 57–73. https://repository.ucatolica.edu.co/server/api/core/bitstreams/9b94480a-8fe0-4440-a8eb-90ad09e6b56c/content

Beets, P., and Le Grange, L., 2005. 'Africanising assessment practices: does the notion of Ubuntu hold any promise?' *South African Journal of Higher Education*, 19(1): 1197–1207.

Berghs, M., 2017. 'Practices and discourses of Ubuntu: implications for an African model of disability?' *African Journal of Disability*, 6(1): 1–8.

Biraimah, K.L., 2016. 'Moving beyond a destructive past to a decolonised and inclusive future: the role of Ubuntu-style education in providing culturally relevant pedagogy for Namibia'. *International Review of Education*, 62: 45–62.

Brás, J.G.V., 2024. 'For an epistemic decolonisation of education from the Ubuntu philosophy'. *Pedagogy, Culture and Society*, 32(1): 61–76.
Brock-Utne, B., 2016. 'The Ubuntu paradigm in curriculum work, language of instruction and assessment'. *International Review of Education*, 62: 29–44.
Brock-Utne, B., 2018. 'Researching language and culture in Africa using an auto ethnographic approach'. *International Review of Education*, 64: 713–735.
Broodryk, J., 2002. *Ubuntu: life lessons from Africa*. Ubuntu School of Philosophy.
Chinkondenji, P., 2022. 'Schoolgirl pregnancy, dropout or pushout?: An Ubuntucentric re-construction of the education for student mothers in Malawi'. *Gender and Education*, 34(6): 738–753.
Diarra, M.C., 2018. 'Ubuntu as humanistic education: challenges and perspectives for Africa?' In M.C. Diarra (ed.), *Re-Visioning education in Africa: Ubuntu-inspired education for humanity*. Palgrave Macmillan Cham, pp. 119–134.
Elonga Mboyo, J.P., 2019. 'Reimagining Ubuntu in schools: a perspective from two primary school leaders in the Democratic Republic of Congo'. *Educational Management Administration and Leadership*, 47(2): 206–223.
Falola, T., and Hamel, N. eds., 2021. *Disability in Africa: inclusion, care, and the ethics of humanity* (Vol. 91). Boydell and Brewer.
Frempong, G., and Kadam, R., 2022. 'Educational paradigm with Ubuntu mindset: implications for sustainable development goals in education'. In G. Frempong and R. Kadam (eds.), *Active learning-research and practice for STEAM and social sciences education*. IntechOpen.
Gumbo, M.T., Gasa, V., and Knaus, C.B., 2022. 'Centring African knowledges to decolonise higher education'. In *Decolonising African higher education*. Routledge, pp. 21–36.
Hapanyengwi-Chemhuru, O., and Shizha, E., 2012. 'Unhu/Ubuntu and education for reconciliation in Zimbabwe'. *Journal of Contemporary Issues in Education*, 7(2): 16–27.
Hoffman, D.M., 2009. 'Reflecting on social emotional learning: a critical perspective on trends in the United States'. *Review of Educational Research*, 79(2): 533–556.
Hlatshwayo, M.N., and Shawa, L.B., 2020. 'Towards a critical re-conceptualization of the purpose of higher education: the role of Ubuntu-Currere in re-imagining teaching and learning in South African higher education'. *Higher Education Research and Development*, 39(1): 26–38.
Humphreys, S., Moses, D., Kaibo, J., and Dunne, M., 2015. 'Counted in and being out: fluctuations in primary school and classroom attendance in northern Nigeria'. *International Journal of Educational Development*, 44: 134–143.
Hunfeld, K., 2022. 'The coloniality of time in the global justice debate: de-centring Western linear temporality'. *Journal of Global Ethics*, 18(1): 100–117.
Klees, S.J., 2020. 'Beyond neoliberalism: reflections on capitalism and education'. *Policy Futures in Education*, 18(1): 9–29.
Koen, M., Neethling, M., and Taylor, B., 2021. 'The impact of COVID-19 on the holistic development of young South African at-risk children in three early childhood care and education centres in a rural area'. *Perspectives in Education*, 39(1): 138–156.
Komatsu, H., Rappleye, J., and Silova, I., 2021. 'Student-centered learning and sustainability: solution or problem?' *Comparative Education Review*, 65(1): 6–33.
Le Grange, L., 2014. 'Currere's active force and the Africanisation of the university curriculum'. *South African Journal of Higher Education*, 28(4): 1283–1294.

Le Grange, L., 2018. 'The notion of Ubuntu and the (post) humanist condition'. In L. Le Grange (ed.). *Indigenous philosophies of education around the world*. Routledge, pp. 40–60.

Le Grange, L., 2020. 'Decolonising the university curriculum: the what, why and how'. In *Transnational education and curriculum studies*. Routledge, pp. 216–233.

Letseka, M., 2012. 'In defence of Ubuntu'. *Studies in Philosophy and Education*, 31(1): 47–60.

Letseka, M., 2013. 'Educating for Ubuntu/botho: lessons from Basotho indigenous education'. *Open Journal of Philosophy*, 3(2): 337–344.

Mabovula, N., 2011. 'The erosion of African communal values: a reappraisal of the African Ubuntu philosophy'. *Inkanyiso: Journal of Humanities and Social Sciences*, 3(1): 38–47.

Maditsi, M.E., and Bhuda, M.T., 2023. 'Decolonising and humanising pedagogies in South African postgraduate education: lessons from indigenous knowledge systems'. In M.E. Maditsi and M.T. Bhuda (eds.), *Digital preservation and documentation of global indigenous knowledge systems*. IGI Global, pp. 282–302.

Makalela, L., 2015. 'Moving out of linguistic boxes: the effects of translanguaging strategies for multilingual classrooms'. *Language and Education*, 29(3): 200–217.

Makalela, L., 2016. 'Ubuntu translanguaging: an alternative framework for complex multilingual encounters'. *Southern African Linguistics and Applied Language Studies*, 34(3): 187–196.

Makalela, L., 2018. 'Multilanguaging and infinite relations of dependency: re-theorizing reading literacy from Ubuntu'. In L. Makalela (ed.), *Theoretical models and processes of literacy*. Routledge, pp. 485–496.

Makiwane, M., and Kaunda, C., 2018. *Families and inclusive societies in Africa*. Human Sciences Research Council, South Africa.

Mawere, M., and Mubaya, T.R., 2016. *African philosophy and thought systems: a search for a culture and philosophy of belonging*. African Books Collective.

Menkiti, I.A., 1984. 'Person and community in African traditional thought'. In R. Wright (ed.), *African philosophy, an introduction* (3rd edn). University Press of America, pp. 171–182.

Messina-Albarenque, C., de Andrés-Viloria, C., de Pablo-González, G., and Benito-Ambrona, T., 2024. 'Emotional education: a critical review of the voices against its implementation in schools'. *Environment and Social Psychology*, 9(3): 1–13.

Metz, T., 2021. *A relational moral theory: African ethics in and beyond the continent*. Oxford University Press.

Mitchell, R., 2023. 'Peer support in sub-Saharan Africa: a critical interpretive synthesis of school-based research'. *International Journal of Educational Development*, 96: 1–9.

Mkosi, N.N., Mavuso, M.P., and Olawumi, K.B., 2023. 'Using Ubuntu values in integrating African indigenous knowledge into teaching and learning: a review of literature'. *International Journal of Learning, Teaching and Educational Research*, 22(5): 140–159.

Murithi, T., 2009. 'An African perspective on peace education: Ubuntu lessons in reconciliation'. *International Review of Education*, 55(2–3): 221–233.

Ndlovu-Gatsheni, S.J., 2021. 'The cognitive empire, politics of knowledge and African intellectual productions: reflections on struggles for epistemic freedom and resurgence of decolonisation in the twenty-first century'. *Third World Quarterly*, 42(5): 882–901.

Ngubane, N., and Makua, M., 2021. 'Ubuntu pedagogy – transforming educational practices in South Africa through an African philosophy: from theory to practice'. *Inkanyiso: Journal of Humanities and Social Sciences*, 13(1): 1–12.

Nxumalo, S.A., and Mncube, D.W., 2018. 'Using indigenous games and knowledge to decolonise the school curriculum: Ubuntu perspectives'. *Perspectives in Education*, 36(2): 103–118.

Oviawe, J.O., 2016. 'How to rediscover the Ubuntu paradigm in education'. *International Review of Education*, 62: 1–10.

Phiri, D.T., and Abebe, T., 2016. 'Suffering and thriving: children's perspectives and interpretations of poverty and well-being in rural Zambia'. *Childhood*, 23(3): 378–393.

Piper, B., 2016. 'International education is a broken field: Can ubuntu education bring solutions?'. *International Review of Education*, 62: 101–111.

Ramose, M.B. 1999. *African philosophy through Ubuntu*. Mond Books.

Ramose, M.B., 2021. 'Ethical responsibility for the other arrested by epistemic blindness, deafness, and muteness: an Ubuntu perspective'. In *The Palgrave handbook of positive peace*. Springer, pp. 909–933.

Ross, E., 2018. 'Reimagining the South African social work curriculum: aligning African and Western cosmologies'. *Southern African Journal of Social Work and Social Development*, 30(1): 1–16.

Santos, B.D.S. 2014. *Epistemologies of the south: justice against epistemicide*. Routledge.

Setlhodi, I.I., 2019. 'Ubuntu leadership: an African panacea for improving school performance'. *Africa Education Review*, 16(2): 126–142.

Shizha, E., 2013. 'Reclaiming our indigenous voices: the problem with postcolonial Sub-Saharan African school curriculum'. *Journal of Indigenous Social Development*, 2(1): 1–18.

Shizha, E., 2015. 'Reclaiming indigenous cultures in sub-Saharan African education.' In *Indigenous education: language, culture and identity*, pp. 301–317. Springer.

Takyi-Amoako, E.J., and Assié-Lumumba, N.D.T., 2018. 'Introduction: re-visioning education in Africa—Ubuntu-inspired education for humanity'. In *Re-visioning education in Africa: Ubuntu-inspired education for humanity*, pp. 1–17. Palgrave Macmillan.

Tamale, S. and Knowles, C., 2021. 'Decolonization and Afro-Feminism'. *Journal of Contemporary African Studies*, 39(4): 644–657.

Tamasiga, P., Onyeaka, H., Akinsemolu, A., and Bakwena, M., 2023. 'The interrelationship between climate change, inequality, poverty and food security in Africa: a bibliometric review and content analysis approach'. *Sustainability*, 15(7): 1–35.

Tamburro, A. (2013). 'Including decolonization in social work education and practice'. *Journal of Indigenous Social Development*, 2(1): 1–16.

Tikly, L., 2015. 'What works, for whom, and in what circumstances? Towards a critical realist understanding of learning in international and comparative education'. *International Journal of Educational Development*, 40: 237–249.

Tran, L.T., and Wall, T., 2018. 'Ubuntu in adult vocational education: theoretical discussion and implications for teaching international students'. *International Review of Education*, 65(4): 557–578.

Tutu, D., 2000. *No future without forgiveness: a personal overview of South Africa's truth and reconciliation commission*. Rider; https://repository.ucatolica.edu.co/entities/publication/deaf5a7c-3971-4a95-8ac9-d67436ac2cd6utu -Rider no future

Ukpokodu, O.N., 2016. *You can't teach us if you don't know us and care about us: becoming an Ubuntu, responsive and responsible urban teacher*. Peter Lang International Academic Publishers.

University of Sussex, 2015. *Learning the speed school way; analysis of speed school pedagogy in Ethiopia*. Luminos Fund and Hawassa University.

Van Norren, D.E, 2017. *Development as service: a happiness, Ubuntu and buen vivir interdisciplinary view of the sustainable development goals* (PhD Thesis, Tilburg University).

Van Norren, D.E, 2020. 'The sustainable development goals viewed through gross national happiness, Ubuntu, and Buen Vivir'. *International Environmental Agreements: Politics, Law and Economics*, 20(3): 431–458.

Van Norren, D.E, 2022. 'African Ubuntu and sustainable development goals: seeking human mutual relations and service in development'. *Third World Quarterly*, 43(12): 2791–2810.

Waghid, Y., 2018. 'On the educational potential of Ubuntu'. In Y. Waghid (ed.), *Re-visioning education in Africa: Ubuntu-inspired education for humanity*. Palgrave Macmillan Cham, pp. 55–65.

Waghid, Y. and Hungwe, J.P., 2023. "'Globalizing'ubuntu for global citizenship education: A decolonial perspective'. *Citizenship Teaching & Learning*, 18(2): 215–227.

Waghid, Y., and Smeyers, P., 2012. 'Reconsidering Ubuntu: on the educational potential of a particular ethic of care'. *Educational Philosophy and Theory*, 44: 6–20.

Waghid, Y., Waghid, F., and Waghid, Z., 2018. *Rupturing African philosophy on teaching and learning: Ubuntu justice and education*. Springer, pp. 1–44.

Yorke, L., Rose, P., Bayley, S., Wole, D., and Ramchandani, P., 2021. 'The importance of students' socio-emotional learning, mental health and wellbeing in the time of COVID-19'. *Rise Insights*, 25: 1–11.

10 Beyond the 'Learning Crisis'
The Implications for Policy to Improve Basic Education in Sub-Saharan Africa

In this book, we have argued that education policy in sub-Saharan Africa (SSA) has tended to be top-down, offering technocratic solutions and approaches that are based on seriously problematic assumptions about the learning needs of the African child. The insights from the three ALPs we studied, force a rethink of education policy. They suggest revisiting the meaning and purposes of basic education such that African children's basic education is transformed, and they become confident and successful learners from the start. Any such re-envisioning of education policy would have to replace the image of African school children as passive learners and the image of their teachers as incapable of responding to, and producing, effective pedagogical responses to children's learning needs. It also means shifting basic education's emphasis from economistic imperatives with their reductionist framings of learning to the multidimensionality which has already been demonstrated by African ALPs to widen the range of skills that children develop in becoming successful learners.

The challenge to achieving this goal is that it demands that global education policies, which exert strong influence on national basic education policies, reconsider their assumptions, strategies and interventions. Such policies offer solutions which tend to be uniform, decontextualised and converging on a few 'globally tested approaches'. – They are driven by narrow definitions of learning around the improvement of foundational literacy and numeracy (FLN) skills (see Chapters 1 and 2). The post-colonial history of basic education reforms in SSA suggest that such a narrow strategy to improve learning has not led to deep systemic changes to the prevailing teaching and learning culture in public schools nor in any substantial reduction of inequality between rich and poor, male and female students and rural and urban communities. For over four decades, Western-inspired pedagogic reforms such as 'learner-centred instruction' have been promoted in African education systems with the promise that it would enhance students' learning experiences and improve learning outcomes at scale. These expectations have not materialised. Tabulawa (1997) offers an example that might explain why this fails in the Botswana classroom context. He adopts the use of a medical metaphor – 'tissue rejection' – to explain that this rejection is because such Western pedagogical interventions adopt a "technicist approach to problems of pedagogical change (and) is faulty in that it treats pedagogical innovations as value-neutral" (189). Interventions that assume a 'learning crisis' using social constructions of learning and pedagogy outside the African context are likely to face rejection by their very nature. The global instrumental solutions offered are incongruent with the local pedagogical culture of the African classroom and hence at best will have only a short-term impact. The issue is that the so-called 'best pedagogic practices' to address the 'learning crisis' are already based on the assumption that African classrooms are value neutral and can therefore accept unproblematically globalised pedagogical innovations without any re-contextualisation and re-construction in line with the African social and cultural values that already mediate how pedagogical processes are shaped, received and succeed.

Another argument we have put forward is that global and globally influenced basic education policies present the educational challenge in one-sided deficit terms – emphasising what is lacking in current schooling provision and failing to recognise the potential of existing knowledge resources of teachers, students and their communities to overcome learning challenges. Instead, the focus is often on infrastructural challenges rather than the collective potential *within* SSA communities, families and children. Also, as Mkumbo (2017) points out in the case of Tanzania, such strategies fail to note the critical obstacles to improving learning in:

> the deterioration of school infrastructure and inputs, shortage of teachers, poor integration of information and communication technology in teaching and learning ... outdated curriculum that does not match with ongoing economic and social development reforms.
> (Mkumbo's, 2017, 353–355)

Whilst it is important to address these infrastructural problems, the instructional solutions to the 'learning crisis' generate false hope that they will necessarily improve learning. In reality, such policies also require fundamental changes to the pedagogical culture to maximise improvements in learning. The policy responses to the many educational challenges in Africa use an inputs and outputs analysis with little emphasis on what happens in between. ALPs teach us, as we have seen, that basic education policy in the African context needs to elevate bottom-up pedagogical approaches that reflect African social constructions of learning, community interactions and values as well as receive financial and other support to roll out such a programme.

Towards an Afrocentric Policy Response

This book has argued that deficit projections and the assumptions of the 'learning crisis' narrative restrict the development of meaningful approaches to improving the learning needs of marginalised children in communities experiencing multi-dimensional poverty and resulting in low quality, arguably unsuccessful, basic education provision. The evidence shows that such children either do not attend, drop out or fail to progress. We have argued that the so-called crisis, as it were, does not lie in African children, teachers or communities but rather in the failure to recognise the importance of privileging localised ideas and processes that can better respond to local challenges. Our concern is that the 'learning crisis' narrative with its neo-liberal political development agenda standardises learning and promotes accountability regimes that, in turn, stifles or ignores bottom-up pedagogical innovations such as we have found in ALP instructional environments.

Many of the children who had benefitted from the ALPs we discussed in Part 2 had attended public basic education schools but had dropped out as a result of poor learning experiences and outcomes. Public basic schools failed them. But in the ALP classes, we found that these same children were not lacking in cognitive ability – what transformed their learning and produced impressive gains was the dismantling of the learning barriers that their early education had erected. Policy reforms in African basic education need to prioritise the inequalities of access to productive learning, the gender and socio-economic inequalities amongst children and the pedagogic transition from basic to secondary education. Such reforms need to centre children's academic potential and African teachers' capabilities within educational innovation and pedagogical practice. Doing so would produce transformative learning experiences for the African child, as the ALPs are doing, and offer an alternative modality of engagement. Programmatically, for such policy reforms to succeed, the five key elements we outline below need addressing.

First, we need to reconceptualise the basic education *curriculum*, placing greater emphasis on the pedagogical processes that can translate its goals into productive learning experiences. The curricula of the three ALPs we researched are specifically designed to promote a holistic view of learning such that local funds of knowledge, linguistic and cultural identities, and children's experiences are valued and used to achieve their goals. Children are engaged throughout as active contributors of learning and not regurgitators of pre-ordained knowledge. The ALPs' curricula come to life in the classroom when children and teachers interact authentically co-creating knowledge, using thoughtfully chosen learning resources, and where children can vocalise their learning to a range of audiences including their communities.

Second, the *language of instruction* used by ALPs enables children to express their learning in ways which are meaningful to them. We find it surprising that the 'learning crisis' discourse gives this dimension minimal attention, especially in the early years of schooling. The language of instruction can act as a gateway to communal engagement in learning, allowing children to bring what they know and experience into the classroom learning environment. In contrast, if children encounter formal schooling in a language they do not know or struggle to understand, it produces a sense of alienation from learning and consequently it is hardly surprising that many teachers resort to rote teaching which in turn produces rote learning. In contrast, as we have seen, using children's first languages as the medium of instruction unlocks the familiarity of their world, shows them their potential to succeed and produces, in turn, deep and meaningful learning.

A third important issue is to employ *pedagogical approaches* that support holistic forms of learning such that they dignify the agency and identity of the African child and their cultural and material environments. As we pointed out, the global analysis of the 'learning crisis' and responses to it bypass the critical role of pedagogical processes and cast teachers as only needing training to implement externally derived pre-packaged instructional approaches or use formal assessment tools to improve childrens' learning which is narrowly defined as foundational literacy and numeracy (FLN) skills. This results in the erosion of confidence in, and deskilling of, the African basic education teacher and the de-professionalisation of teaching in the African context. Our studies of three ALPs offer a vision of how we can reinstall teachers' agentic and responsive instructional behaviour. Within ALP classrooms, the teachers we observed identified what worked for the children they needed to engage. They drew on, for example, their local knowledge and deeper understanding of how learning can be encouraged in rural poor communities; strategies that responded to the time and space of local contexts; and, the ontological and ethical concerns of the distinctively collective African value system of Ubuntu. What such teachers teach us is the importance of installing pedagogy which respects and promotes the dignity, agency, material and cultural worlds, and relationality of the African child.

A fourth key point is the need to promote *community engagement* that avoids top-down approaches by connecting to the real-life experiences, the vulnerabilities but also the power of community agency. In the name of their children, community engagement needs to contribute actively to their children's schooling and be active in promoting it through joy in its potential to make a difference in their lives. The ALPs demonstrate that poor communities can contribute to the curriculum by providing stories, local histories and descriptions of cultural and social events that children can relate and use to articulate what they are learning and its meanings. This enables the curriculum to be contextually grounded in the social and cultural realities of children and their material world. It shifts the gaze of communities to the power and potential of childrens' learning journeys and the hope it inspires for the future – particularly exemplified in the Liberia and Ghana cases.

Fifth, promoting *African-centred values* in a re-envisioned curriculum for African children is imperative. ALP curriculum content, teaching and learning processes privilege narratives and stories which reflect strong African social values of community and solidarity. Singing, storytelling and Afrocentric play-based activities are not treated as peripheral to learning but integral to the development of deep learning. African traditional education places emphasis on holistic development, communal values and the interconnectedness of learners with their environment. At an ontological level, the African child only exists 'in relation'. The spiritual, moral and emotional development of the African child is always in evidence and meets a diversity of needs through a communal approach to learning – the progress of one is the progress and responsibility of all. African culture is vibrant, expressive and colourful allowing all senses to be engaged in social interaction and the production of learning. Such a distinctive ontological culture of being in which children's voices, body movements and social interactions are privileged is currently missing in formal education and is even less likely to be included or celebrated in the individualisation and the cultural silence that is promoted, celebrated and reinforced by performance hierarchies.

Through the evidence in our case studies, we have shown how attention to all these dimensions inter-connects in ALPs to disrupt gender regimes that undermine or exclude the agency of girls as learners. In framing gender identity as a verb rather than as a noun (Unterhalter, 2017), as relational and contingent, we have demonstrated their significance in creating learning environments whose pedagogical processes and forms of community engagement reposition girls outside of deficit stereotypes and assumptions. Moreover, our analysis goes beyond the reductive and misleading association of gender justice with statistical metrics of the number of girls and boys able to access educational provision (Crossouard and Dunne, 2021).

On teachers, it is vitally important for their professional identities to align with the principles and practices promoted by schooling. As we have seen in ALP classrooms, teachers need to commit to the goals and classroom strategies that work for local children. If they are to succeed in promoting confidence amongst such children and their parents in the project of schooling, they need to acquire the ability to employ imaginative and innovative pedagogic practice. They also need to have the skills to develop a post-humanistic and materially grounded community-centred learning around children's education. And at the heart of the curriculum in teacher education should be strong positive beliefs about African children's funds of knowledge and identity and their capacity to have agency but also resistance. Such a curriculum should envision:

> children who are poor ... and speakers of languages other than English, as learners who already know a great deal and who have experiences, concepts and languages that can be built upon on and expanded to learn even more ... see their roles as *adding* to help them learn even more ... *add*ing to rather than replacing what students bring to learning ... convinced that all students are capable learners who bring a wealth of knowledge and experiences to school.
> (Villegas and Lucas, 2002, 23, emphasis added)

Doing all of the above clearly requires national policymakers actively to develop new local partnerships which reinstate the voices and experiences of children, teachers and communities. It means preventing asymmetrical power hierarchies and policy prescriptions encouraged by the imposition of a global menu to narrowly construe local education provision and instrumentalise it in reductive ways. Such prescriptions treat symptoms rather than causes and underlying factors. This means more than nuancing a doctrinaire global education al agenda. It means starting afresh with an Africa-centred approach that can build upwards from the funds of language, culture and knowledge in local communities and their children, the rural economies in which children participate, the ubuntu principles embedded in collectivity and relationality. It means connecting with the vulnerability and the resistance of communities who are navigating challenging contexts of poverty and conflict rather than problematising them as in need of redemptive external interventions that bypass their exercise of agency.

At a deep level, this means that the reshaping of the global educational agenda has to address fundamental ontological and epistemological issues of the purpose of education in the African context. In essence, we are calling for a paradigm shift in the Education for All (EFA) agenda such that it *challenges and finds new valued and valuable forms of education for* children in SSA and for political recognition of African voices, values, innovations and scholarship in international policy-making circles. As this book has shown, African scholars have already provided a rich thread of research into schooling in disadvantaged marginalised communities. If this book has done one thing, we hope that it has brought their research to the fore.

ALPs provide us with a looking glass into how we might see Afrocentric values, processes and practices which appear to respond that much better to the learning needs of African children, many of whom are living in poverty and experiencing precarity and educational marginalisation. Basically, this book's argument is that the required approach to successfully promoting EFA in SSA needs directly to address the theoretical and empirical concerns about the ways in which the 'learning crisis' has been conceptualised and addressed, the implications for African education of its assumptions and strategies, and to be prepared to learn from the innovations of the ALPs revealed in this book.

A Renewed Postcolonial Agenda for EFA

Our journey in addressing this key educational issue in Africa has led us to identify 12 key principles that are essential if we are to re-envision the goals and purposes of basic education in the African continent. These principles are focused especially, but not uniquely, on benefitting educational children experiencing educational marginalisation, many of whom are out-of-school, or have dropped out or failed to progress to or in secondary schools. Of course, these principles need to be carefully concretised in specific contexts by the voices and experiences of affected communities and children themselves but there are some universal strategies that could be used to link principles to practice:

1 (Re)recognise the agency and knowledges of African children and their families in their relational worlds in planning curriculum and pedagogical strategies to re-engage them in learning, within a multi-dimensional approach to their agency as learners.

2 Ensure curriculum and pedagogical practices are relevant, meaningful and integrate the lived experiences, funds of knowledge and identity that children bring to them as a result of their socialisation in families, extended families and the wider community.
3 Replace deficit and essentialising approaches with framings that dignify and valorise the African child's agency in navigating circumstances of hardship as well as that of their communities and in contributing to those communities through their responsibilities and labour.
4 Address the language of instruction as a central issue in educational underachievement that currently reproduces educational exclusion and marginality, as evidenced by research over the past 50 years; in particular, by ensuring that children can learn for longer in their local languages.
5 Prior to any interventions, do linguistic mapping to ensure that curriculum and pedagogy are responsive to communities' linguistic practices.
6 Replace preoccupation with cognitive learning outcomes as the key measure of success with a holistic framing of children's learning needs and the pedagogical and socio-cultural processes needed to provide an expansive view of education.
7 Ensure meaningful learning engagements with communities that avoid pathologising the poor and blaming them for their condition and by encouraging them to share positive actions and see future value in children's formal education.
8 Prioritise pedagogical practices and processes in any framing of educational responses to educational challenge particularly as it relates to children's learning.
9 Select and valorise the key pedagogical roles of locally based teachers, drawing on their experiences and language capabilities, and their ability to leverage their knowledge of the environment in which children live.
10 Reject the deficit view of teachers and refashion teacher education so that teachers are understood to be knowledgeable agents in improving children's learning capable of developing appropriate innovative capabilities in working with marginalised communities.
11 Recentralise teaching and learning as social, situated and ethical practices grounded in the collective/relational value system of care and compassion promoted in ubuntu.
12 Centralise the role of teachers, and all those involved in responding to educational marginality, in challenging gendered stereotypes in social practices that may produce gendered binaries in teaching that undermine the potential of both boys and girls.

Installing these principles in policy-making means a radical departure from the assumptions, content and priorities of the narrative of the 'learning crisis', whose failure, in sub-Saharan Africa, to connect with rural poverty, on the one hand, and educational marginalisation, on the other, repeats the erasures associated with the global educational policy agendas (Verger et al., 2018). Doing so would open up possibilities for an urgently needed transformation rather than a continuation of the status quo which has evidently failed such educationally excluded communities of children. They empower African governments to own and develop further effective innovative educational strategies to reduce social inequalities in access and transitions to secondary education appropriate to their own cultural context and values.

These principles are also based on this book's key concern to widen the epistemic base informing discussion of the challenges and possibilities of EFA beyond narrowly economistic lenses. Throughout we have sought to show how the insights from a range of disciplines outside of education and of the conceptual frames of diverse social theorists may enrich and enhance understanding of African children's learning experiences. Hence our ongoing commitment to the synergy between theory and practice and our concern to challenge artificial demarcations between researchers and practitioners, especially when the well-being of millions of children is at stake.

We are offering these principles in a spirit of humility, aiming to open up a horizon of possibilities to improve public basic education systems, especially in the early years. Essentially, what we are arguing for is to recognise the work which countries like Ghana, Liberia and Ethiopia are developing in their accelerated learning programmes. Our intention is not to offer ALPs as another set of fixes, prescriptions or panaceas. This would be to reproduce the totalising and universalising certainties of the 'learning crisis' narrative which have demonstrably failed. The evidence we have marshalled in this book suggests that there is a need for further research on situated modalities of learning provision. Ours is a call, first of all, for a research agenda that prioritises an expansive view of learning.

Yet international and national policymakers in SSA have much to learn from ALPs such as those described in this book, as do policymakers in other regions in the global South. Such programmes, in essence, are a critically important post-colonial response to the imposition of externally framed educational agendas. They represent contemporary culturally relevant strategies for promoting greater social inclusion and learning for all. If scaled up, they offer unique opportunities to address the inequalities of access to formal schooling, improve the transition from basic to secondary education, challenge gender and socio-economic inequalities amongst children in supporting their academic potential and place African teachers knowledges and experiences at the centre, not the periphery of educational progress. Post-colonial opportunities lie in the insights these programmes offer – they point the way to a much more optimistic future about the power of education in national development.

So, we end with a message of hope. We hope that the message of this book will resonate with teachers, policymakers, national and international aid organisations, researchers and scholars, all of whom all too often are working separately and in relative isolation. It is our hope that all these professional and epistemic communities may converge in thinking through how to move beyond the assumptions of the learning crisis in a way that places African values and strategies at the heart of addressing educational marginalisation.

References

Crossouard, B., and Dunne, M. (2021, June 28). *Gender and education in postcolonial contexts*. Oxford Research Encyclopedia of Education. Available at: https://oxfordre.com/education/view/10.1093/acrefore/9780190264093.001.0001/acrefore-9780190264093-e-1583 [Accessed: 13.10.2024]..

Mkumbo, K., 2017. 'The effectiveness of the new education and training policy in addressing the learning crisis in Tanzania'. *International Journal of Management in Education*, 11(3): 347–366.

Tabulawa, R., 1997. 'Pedagogical classroom practice and the social context: the case of Botswana'. *International Journal of Educational Development*, 17(2): 189–204.

Verger, A., Novelli, M., and Altinyelken, H.K., 2018. 'Global education policy and international development: a revisited introduction'. In A. Verger, M. Novelli, and H.K. Altinyelken (eds.), *Global education policy and international development: new agendas, issues and policies* (2nd edn). Bloomsbury, pp. 1–34.

Villegas, A.M., and Lucas, T. (2002). 'Preparing culturally responsive teachers – rethinking the curriculum'. *Journal of Teacher Education*, 53(1): 20–32.

Unterhalter, E., 2017. 'Thinking about gender in comparative education'. In E. Unterhalter (ed.), *Fifty years of comparative education*. Routledge, pp. 122–136.

Index

Note: **Bold** page numbers refer to tables; *italic* page numbers refer to figures and page numbers followed by "n" denote endnotes.

Abebe, T. 36, 40, 104, 106, 110, 114–115
Accelerated Education Working Group (AEWG) 13, 14, 17; aspirations of 20
Accelerated Learning Programmes (ALPs) 11–17, 133, 205, 242; for Africa programme 172; children's experiences of 183; community engagement 250–251; illuminating ALPs through social theory 14–17; language of instruction 247–249; learning and dignity of African child 245–247; learning and natural environment 251–253; in Liberia 214–216; modalities of learning that go beyond the cognitive 254–255; pedagogical practices 185, 247–255; pedagogy of care and compassion 253–254; peer learning 249–250; and power of African values 242–256; re-envisioning through 11–14; re-envisioning through diverse evidence 17–19; in the Speed School 172; and Ubuntu 245–247, 255; Ubuntu in education/development 242–245
accountability regimes and practices 90–91
activity-based learning 187
Adamson, L. 67, 72–73
Adebayo, S. B. 231
Adzahlie-Mensah, V. 68, 71, 143, 184, 185, 209
Africa: -centred values 264; communities experiencing educational marginalisation 208–210; kinship systems 216, 224; learner-centred instruction in 84–85; multilingualism 63, 115, 247; and oral culture 84–85
African authors: Abebe 36, 40, 104, 110, 122n1; Adebayo 231; Adejunmobi 63, 68; Adzahlie-Mensah 68, 71, 143, 184, 185, 209; Akyeampong 8, 13, 82–84, 86, 87, 92–95, 119, 120, 138–140, 159, 160, 163n3, 173, 177, 181, 183–185, 187, 188, 191–193, 196–198, 200, 201n2, 209, 246, 250, 254; Alidou 62, 64, 65, 71; Ananga 9, 51; Asie-Lumumba 242, 244, 245, 256n2; Bamgbose 65, 118; Kaunda 216, 224, 251; Le Fanu 133; Letseka 242, 243; Makalela 69, 116, 247–249; Makiwane 216, 224, 251; Makua 246; Mbembe 64; Mfum-Mensah 13, 114, 115, 234n2; Muriithi 111; Ndlovu-Gatsheni 244; Ngubane 246; Obanya 67, 71; Ofosu-Kusi 52, 101–104, 107; Ohanu 133; Okonkwo 71; Oviawe 249, 256n2; Phiri 36, 40, 101, 102, 104–106, 110, 113–115, 122n1, 252; Sefa Dei 64, 66; Speciale 72; Sylvia Tamale 249; Tafere 102, 105, 107, 113, 183; Takyi-Amoako 242, 244, 245, 256n2; Ukpokodue 253; Waghid 242, 244, 249, 253; Wrigley-Asante 52, 163, 225
African Development Bank 48
African educationists 71, 246
African multilingualism 63, 115, 247
African teachers: accountability regimes and practices

90–91; deficit characterisation of 80–95; deficit framings of 91–95; de-professionalisation through structured lesson plans 88–90; imperfect measurements 85–88; learner-centred instruction 84–85; oral culture 84–85; symbols of teaching quality 85–88; teacher education reforms 91–95
African values 242–255
Afrocentric African values and accelerated learning 242–255; cultural values 249; learner-centred instruction 84; pedagogy 94; play-based activities 264; policy response 262–266; power of 242–255; values 266; values of education 93; value system of Ubuntu 255
Afro-pessimism 52, 64, 74, 214
Alexander, R. 51, 73, 83, 169, 187, 255
American Colonisation Society 210
Ansell, N. 38
Anyon, J. 15
Assié-Lumumba, N. D. T. 244
Association for the Development of Education in Africa (ADEA) 65, 71

Balagopalan, S. 50–51
Banerjee, A. V. 107
Bangladesh Rural Advancement Community 11
Barad, K. 170, 180
Barry, G. C. 255
basic education 2, 63, 66, 194; African 81, 85–86, 88, 92, 264, 266; Afrocentric policy response 262–266; alternative 11; complementary 11, 20, 133–164, 246; curriculum 263; free 5; language of instruction in 19; policy to improve 261–268; renewed postcolonial agenda for EFA 266–268; in Rwanda 72; in Sub-Saharan Africa 261–268; teachers in sub-Sahara Africa 20, 80, 86, 261–268
Benavot, A. 205
Benjamin, Walter 109
Bennell, P. 82, 86
Benson, C.J. 116, 118
Bessel, S. 32
Biesta, G. 16
Bonal, X. 43
Bourdillon, M. 109

Boyden, J. 36, 47, 102, 105, 112
Bray, R. 35
Brock-Utne, B. 65, 68, 70, 115, 117, 247
Broodryk, J. 243
Bunyi, G. 65
Burman, E. 52
Butler, J. 206–208, 217, 232; critique of paternalism and judgementalism 207; theorisation of vulnerability and resistance 206–208; usefulness for re-thinking approaches to marginalized communities 206–208

Caillods, F. 35, 37
Carnoy, M. 41
Catholic Relief Services 232, 234n4
Chant, S. 44
Charamba, E. 117
child-centred pedagogy 85
childhood studies 32, 46
children: as agents of modernisation 42–43; children's social positioning in 114–115; deficit views of 208–210; feelings 111–114; foundational learning and numeracy (FLN) 81, 120, 188; friendship groups 114–115; funds of knowledge in CBE 133–163; informal learning/knowledge-building in social practices 106–108; intellectual formation 42; learning and dignity of African 245–247; linguistic agency for learning 115–118; negative experiences of learning 70–73; out-of-school 4, 11, 13–15, 18–19, 49, 63, 122, 133, 136–138, 140, 162, 172, 185, 188, 197, 211, 216, 251; Pande, M: child carers 104; play as vehicle for learning 108–110; as potential economic capital 41–42; reciprocal obligations 115; social positioning in friendship groups/family networks/communities 114–115; staying power in transition schools 159–161; temporalities and spatialities of lives 110–111; viewpoints and perspectives 101–103
children's agency 179–180: in anti-child labour campaigns 105; children's agency as learners 64, 156, 170, 171, 174, 183–184, 254; children's linguistic agency for learning

115–118; children's social positioning 114; and contribution to household survival 103–106; and development 245; epistemic agency of children 163; as knowers 172; as learners 171, 183–184; loss/absence of 51–52; multi-dimensional framing of 99–118, *100*; and redemptive interventions 51–52
Clegg, J. 73
communities 205–233; educational marginalisation 208–210; pathologization of 8
community engagement 20–21, 31, 46, 141, 142, 153–156, 205, 213–214, 225, 232–233, 247, 264–265; ALPs 250–251; community agency 208; power of community agency 264; resistance 206–210; Second Chance programmes 206–210; vulnerability 206–210
compartmentalization of interventions 32
complementary basic education (CBE) 11, 20, 133, 246; embedded funds of knowledge in 142–156; *vs.* formal schooling 142; funds of identity 134–137; funds of knowledge 134–137, *162*; instructional materials 144–150, *145–149*; in Northern Ghana 134, 137–140, 163, 246; provision use of funds of knowledge in 140–141
conflict-affected rural communities 213
Connell, R. 87
Cornwall, A. 39, 45
Covid-19 pandemic 13, 18, 34, 50
crisis of learning 4, 5, 51
Croft, A. 84–85
Crossouard, B. 110
culture/cultural: of deprivation 43, 114; oral 84–85
Cummins, J. 118
Curinga, M. X. 170
curriculum: curriculum development 20, 114, 142–143; curricular inclusion 133

Dale, R. 104
Daniel, M. 106
decontextualised framings of learning 163; deficit framings of communities 8, 10, 16, 20, 136–137, 163, 169, 205–206, 208, 222, 232, 251, 265; of the 'poor child' 40–47; teacher education reforms 91–95; of teachers 91–95
deficit framings: in educational thought and practice 53
De Freitas, E. 170
de Sousa Santo: ecology of knowledges 16
developing world 8, 43
development, and Ubuntu 242–245
DFID 11
disadvantaged communities 8, 12, 119
dominant groups 53, 91
Dubeck, M. M. 88–89
Dunne, M. 22, 46, 110, 184

Early Grade Mathematics Assessment 191, 215
economic capital 41–42
education: basic 261–268; centring Ubuntu in 242–245; challenges in Northern Ghana 138–140; economic growth black box 41; formal 211–213; in Liberia 210–214; top-down state-centric approaches to challenges in 213–214
educational marginalisation 5–8, 15–21, 31, 37–38, 47, 49, 52, 62, 66, 73, 89, 110, 121, 136, 141, 163, 169, 251, 266–267; damaging impact of 5; deficit views of communities experiencing 208–210; distinctive challenges of 134, 137; found in Northern region of Ghana 139; long-standing inter-generational 11, 205, 233; in sub-Saharan Africa (SSA) 4, 62, 242; teachers and communities experiencing 14
educational provision 32–39
educational quality 13, 66, 85–88
Education for All (EFA) 5, 13, 16, 31, 49, 66, 68, 82, 266–268; *Education for All Global Monitoring Report* 68; educationism 18; educationist approaches 121; Education Sector Plan 138, 211, 213; EFA Global Monitoring Report for Teaching and Learning (UNESCO) 13
Educative Curriculum Materials 89
edu-workscape 110
Edwards, J. 45
embedded funds of knowledge: in CBE 142–156; CBE instructional materials

144–150, *145–149*; community engagement 153–156; facilitator's pedagogical strategies 150–151, **152**, *153*; partnerships and planning 143–144
empowerment 8, 44–45, 49, 73
epistemic exclusion 19, 63, 72
Erling, E. J. 66
Escobar, A. 40
Essuman, A. 209
Esteban-Guitart, M. 137
Ethiopia 11–12, 14, 21; ethnographic research in 109; rural 114; Speed Schools in 169–201; urban 114
evidence-based approaches, promising 73

Fafunwa, A. B. 117
families: extended families 205–233, family networks 114–115; parents 205–233; parent-teacher associations 208
Farrell, J.P. 14, 22n1
Fassin, D. 51–52
Federal Mother Tongue education policy 173
Feeny, T. 36, 47, 102, 105, 112
Fixing the Broken Promise of Education for All 13, 16, 49, 50
flexible lesson planning and delivery 187
food insecurity: in Liberia 227–229; providing opportunities to strategise in response to 227–229
Foreign and Commonwealth Development Office 11
formal education 9, 13, 35, 37, 42, 45, 49, 63, 73, 112, 134, 137, 138, 140, 142, 143, 158, 208, 211–213, 265
foundational literacy and numeracy (FLN) 92; skills 81, 94, 261; tests 188
Frempong, G. 245
Fujita, M. 39
funds of identity 20, 133–137, 140, 150, 157–161
funds of knowledge 15, 20, 70, 133–137, **140–141**, 140–142, **152**; embedded in CBE curriculum 133; partnerships and planning 143–144

Geduld, D. 92
gender: binary between girlhood 44; disparities 4, 138; gendered experiences of poverty 43–46; gendered experiences of schooling 45; justice 45, 265; operation of gender norms 44; parity 45; production of girls as deficit 43–46; undoing gender regimes in learning processes 184–185
Geneva Global Inc. 172
Ghanaian Institute of Linguistics, Literacy and Bible Translation (GILLBT) 143
Ghanaian Ministry of Education Sector Plan 138
girling of development 34; smart economics 43, 44
girls: challenging patriarchal norms 21; girls empowerment 44; inferiorisation of 184; 'poor girls' 43–44; production of girls as deficit 43–46; promoting girl's agency 222–224; social positioning in the community 45
global cognitive justice 16
global educational culture 41
global educational policy: geopolitical power relationships of 19; historical framings of 39; resistance to change 66–67; silences in 65–67; silences in global educational policy 65–67
Global Initiative on Out of School Children 13, 49, 63
Global South 7, 9, 34, 38, 43, 44, 46, 51, 64, 81, 101, 102, 113, 120, 233, 243, 268

Hallak, J. 35, 37
Hartwell, A. 14
hegemonic link 33; hegemonic status of empiricism 15
Heugh, K. 73
historicizing deficit framings of the "poor child" 40–47
Hook, T. 90
Hopkins, L. 46
horizontal knowledge production 141
household survival: and children's agency 103–106; contribution to 103–106
human capital theory 41, 245
humanitarian reason 51
Humphreys, S. 37, 46, 110, 194, 252

indigenous communities 9, 64–65, 210
informal learning in social practices 106–108

Ingutia, R. 133
Inter-Agency Network for Education in Emergencies (INEE) 13
inter-generational educational marginalisation 11, 138
International Convention on the Rights of the Child (ICRC) 74n1
international development community of scholars 5
International Monetary Fund (IMF) 33, 82
Item Response Theory Model (IRT) 194, *194*, 201n7

Jackson, A.Y. 16
Jomtien Conference 1990 5
Jones, S. 117, 122n2, 163n2
joyful learning 11, 13, 15–16, 183, 185

Kabeer, N. 44
Kakuru, D. 134
Katz, C. 51, 107, 109
Kendrick, M. 134
Kennedy, M. M. 81, 83, 87
Khoja-Moolji, S. 34, 52
Klees, S.J. 6, 7, 45, 51, 65
knowledge: -building in social practices 106–108; networks 52; reflexive student thinking and verbalisation of 187
Kyomuhendo, G. B. 113

language: and children's identities 62–74; cultural knowledge 118; and culture 71, 116; and girls education 72; and learning 62–74; and mathematics abilities 190; and multilingual education 66; untapped communicative resources 69
language of instruction 8, 19, 62–74, 115–116, 118, 121, 143, 173, 247–249, 263; African multilingualism 63, 115, 247; children's negative experiences of learning 70–73; as instructional materials 246; instruction policies, language of 64–65; languages as resources for learning 116; language code-switching practices 116; largely technical activity 51, 65; in the 'learning crisis' 62–65; linguistic boxes 116; as medium of instruction 248; monoglossic orientations 69; mother-tongue–based bilingual programmes 116; mother-tongue language 51, 67, 142; policies 68–70; resistance to change 66; as social practice 243; stupidification 72; and teachers' pedagogical choices 68–70; verbalisation of knowledge 187; vertical power relations 184
learner-centred instruction 38, 84–85, 194, 261
learner-centred pedagogy 38, 108, 213; ontologically individualistic 181; student-centred pedagogy 91
learning: accelerated 214–216; activity-based 187; children's linguistic agency for 115–118; children's negative experiences of 70–73; children's play as vehicle for 108–110; cognitive achievement 40; cognitive and skills development 108; cognitive justice 16, 108; collaborating for learning 177–181, *178–180*, collective joy and hope 224–225; and dignity of African child 245–247; holistic learning 186–188; informal 106–108; learning space *174–176*, 174–177; learning talk 187; modalities of 254–255; narrow framings of 37–39; and natural environment 251–253; oral culture 84–85; peer 249–250; play-based learning 183, 187; playful 183; playful learning 183; problem solving 8; reflexive student thinking 187; as situated sociocultural activity 6–7, 15; social event, learning as 218–222; in social practices 106–108; socio-emotional skills 40; to teach as Speed School teacher 185–188
'learning crisis' 5, 8, 18; critique of the 'learning crisis' narrative 5–11; global 'learning crisis' 4–22; implications for rethinking 52–53; language of instruction in 62–65; learning loss 5, 13, 88; lessons for 73–74; mission civilisatrice 42; neo-colonialism 8, 10, 42, 90; reframing 120–122; techno-rationalist approach 45
learning outcomes 7, 9, 13, 15, 17–18, 20–21, 34, 51, 64, 80–81, 84, 91, 95, 105, 133, 138, 162, 169–201, 207, 215, 245, 254, 261
Learning to Realise Education's Promise (World Bank) 4, 50

Le Fanu, G. 133
Le Grange, L. 245
liberal peacebuilding in Liberia 211–213
Liberia: accelerated learning in 214–216; collective joy and hope 224–225; communities experiencing educational marginalisation 208–210; conflict in 210–214; democratic/inclusive space of dialogue/consultation 225–227; education in 210–214; food insecurity in 227–229; formal education 211–213; learning as social event 218–222; 'liberal peace building' in 210–214; Liberia conflict in 210–214; Liberian Educational Advancement Programme 214; *Liberian Strategic Road Map for National Healing, Reconciliation and Peacebuilding* (Government of Liberia) 212; malnutrition in 227–229; negative peace 210–211; parental engagement groups 216; Peace Agreement 210–211, 227; peace and mobilising youth agency 229–232; poverty in 227–229; promoting girls' agency as learners 222–224, *223*; Second Chance programmes in 205–233; top-down state-centric approaches to educational challenges 213–214; Truth and Reconciliation (TRC) 212, 214
Lister, R. 39, 99, 122
literacy and numeracy skills 6, 15, 47, 172, 180, 184, 214
Low-fee private education 90
Luminos Fund 13, 215, 220

MacGillivray, L. 90–91
MacLure, M. 16; value of theory 16
macro-social perspective 9, 51
Makua, M. 246
malnutrition: in Liberia 227–229; opportunities to strategise in response to 227–229
Mason, M. 39
Mazzei, L.A. 16
McKinney, C. 68–69
Mexican immigrants Funds of Knowledge 134
Millennium Development Goals (MDGs) 5, 19; different goals 67; history of 5
Milligan, L.O. 72–73
Mitchell, R. 14, 160, 249
Mkumbo, K. 262

modernisation: children as agents of 42–43; modernization theory 42, 46
Moll, L. 134
Moriarty, K. 42
multi-dimensional framing: relational dimension 100, 114, 171, 180, 242
Muriithi, A. G. 111
Murris, Karen 15, 170
MUSTER project 93
Mutumba, S. 117

National Education Sector Plan 215
Ndlovu-Gatsheni, S. J. 244
Ngubane, N. 246
Ngutuku, E. 36
Nieuwenhuys, O. 32, 46
Nike Foundation 43
Northern Ghana: ALPs in 20, 143, 162; communities 146, 153; data gathering **140–141**, 140–142; educational challenges in 138–140; educational provision/enrolment in **139**; embedded funds of knowledge in CBE 142–156; enrolment in **139**; families and communities in 11; families of children in 114; funds of identity 134–137, 157–161; funds of knowledge 133–163, **140–141**; lessons for 'learning crisis' 161–163; out-of-school children in 14, 133
Norwegian Refugee Council 11
Novelli, M. 19

Obanya, P. 67, 71
Ofosu-Kusi, Y. 104
Opoku-Amankwa, K. 69, 70
Optimising Learning and Education in Africa: The Language Factor (ADEA report) 71
Ordinary Least Squares regression (OLS) 201n9
Osgood, J. 185
out-of-school children 9, 11, 13–15, 18–19, 49, 63, 122, 133, 136–138, 140, 162, 172, 185, 188, 197, 211, 216, 251
Oviawe, J. O. 249

pandemic 5; and climate change 34; Parental Engagement Groups (PEGs) 206, 214, 216–233, 246, 251, 254; resistance: community engagement 206–210; in PEGs 217–232 pedagogical: approaches 13, 21, 116, 162, 172, 262, 264; facilitators' pedagogical strategies 150–151; processes 7, 10–11, 37, 46, 69, 82, 85, 169, 181, 184, 200, 245, 253, 262–265; strategies 150–151, **152**, 153

pedagogy: Afrocentric 94; of care and compassion 253–254; child-centred 85; critical pedagogy 40; culturally responsive pedagogy 250; inclusive pedagogy 250; learner-centred 38, 108, 213; multi-dimensional pedagogy 99–122; pedagogical strategies 20, 21, 39, 62, 69, 70, 115, 134, 140, 142, 150, 162, 169, 216, 250, 251, 266; place-based pedagogy 177; scripted lesson plans (SLPs) 90–91, 188; structured pedagogy 86, 88, 188; structured lesson plans (SLPs) 86–87; student-centred pedagogy 91

peer learning sub-Saharan Africa 249–250

Pesambili, J. C. 83

Phiri, D.T. 36, 40, 106, 110, 114–115

Piper, B. 88–89, 243

plantation-style education monologue 90

'poor child': children as agents of modernisation 42–43; children as economic capital 41–42; cultural politics of 46–47; decontextualised 47–51; deficit models of children's agency 171; gendered experiences of poverty 43–46; historicising deficit framings of 40–47; loss/absence of children's agency 51–52; poverty alleviation/educational provision 32–39; production as deficit 31–53; production of girls as deficit 43–46; redemptive interventions 51–52; rethinking 'learning crisis' 52–53

post-colonial theory 21, 46, 67, 268; renewed postcolonial agenda for EFA 266–268

post-humanism 173–185; natural environment 107, 169, 171, 184–185, 242, 251–253; post-humanist theorisations 15

post-humanist theorisations 15

poverty: alleviation 19, 31–39, 41, 43–44, 102; anti-poverty agents 43; economic framings of poverty 99; gendered experiences of 43–46; in Liberia 227–229; multi-dimensional approach 19–20, 32, 99–122; multi-dimensional framing of 99–118, *100*; narrow framings of 35–36; *Poverty and Shared Prosperity, Reversals of Fortune* (World Bank) 50; Poverty Reduction and Growth Strategy (IMF) 212; Poverty Reduction Strategy Papers and education 33, 35, 43; poverty-shame nexus 112; providing opportunities to strategise in response to 227–229; symbolic dimension 100, 112; utopian rhetoric of 121; ventriloquizing the poor 73

precaritised communities and educational marginalisation 163, 205; socio-economic hardship 5, 10, 206; socio-economic precarity 8, 134, 206; socio-economic survival 107, 252

primary education 13, 19, 49, 117, 173, 189, 196, 200

Pryor, J. 94, 209

Rai, S. M. 103

Reaching the Marginalised (UNESCO) 47

Redmond, G. 112

Report on the Evaluation of the Quality of the Teaching and Learning in the Second Chance Program for Out of School Children in Liberia 233n1–234n1

research methods: focus group discussions (FGDs) 142, 159; funds of knowledge approach 140–142, 151, **152**, 161–163; group work 187; interpretative 216; observation 85, 173, 217; participatory research 103; photographs 17, 173, 218; propensity score matching method 192; qualitative 17, 83, 85, 100, 103, 142, 169–170; quantitative 9, 17, 20, 37, 80, 83, 170, 200, 224; surveys 82, 190; voices of children 10, 14, 101–103

Resnik, J. 41

Richmond, O. P. 231

Robertson, S. L. 80, 82, 86, 104

Roy, A. 18

Sachs, W. 40

Sathorar, H. 92

Sayed, Y. 42

Schon, D. A. 89, 92
School Management Councils 208
Schweisfurth, M. 37
Second Chance programmes 215–216, 222, 226, 229–233, 253–254; and accelerated learning in Liberia 214–216; community engagement 206–210; conflict 210–214; in conflict-affected Liberia 205–233; data gathering 216–217; education 210–214; lessons for 'learning crisis' 232–233; 'liberal peace building' 210–214; listening to experiences of PEGs 216–217; vulnerability and resistance 206–210, 217–232
Second World War 19, 40
Shalem, Y. 89
shame: experienced by children navigating poverty 112, 113
Shin, W. 227
Silova, I. 8, 11
social theory 14–17, 206; hegemonic status of empiricism 15; modernization theory 42; role of in explanation 39; social imaginaries 31, 39; theory into practice 16–17; as vehicle for illuminating pedagogical practices and ALPS 14–17; vulnerability and resistance 16, 206–210, 218–232
Sousa Santos, B. de 16, 108
Southern Nations, Nationalities and People's Region (SNNPR) 172
Speed Schools: children's agency as learners 183–184; collaborating for learning 177–181, *178–180*; in Ethiopia 169–201; gender regimes in learning processes 184–185; improving learning outcomes and transition 188–200; learning to teach as Speed School teacher 185–188; lessons for 'learning crisis' 200; localising the learning space *174–176*, 174–177; objects and activities in understanding 181–183, *182*; playful learning 183; post-humanism 173–185; post-humanist approach to learning 170–172; students' performance 189–194; teachers promoting holistic learning 186–188
Sriprakash, A. 6–7, 46, 53n1

structural adjustment programmes 51, 82, 86
sub-Saharan Africa 261–268
Sustainable Development Goals (SDGs) 5, 7, 19, 33, 35, 41, 50, 63, 91, 103, 119, 161, 255n1
Sweetman, C. 44

Tabulawa, R. 261
Tafere, Y. 102, 105, 113
Takyi-Amoako, E. J. 244
Tamale, S. 249
Taylor, A. 170
teachers: accountability 81; African 80–95; deficit characterisation of 80–95; deficit framings of 91–95; deficit framings of marginalised communities 212; de-professionalisation through structured lesson plans (SLPs) 88–90; education reforms 91–95; and language of instruction policies 68–70; as multi-dimensional agents 118–120; pedagogical choices 68–70; pre-service teacher education 88, 91–93, 120; relatability of 119; Speed School 185–188; *Teach Observer Manual* 83; training 92, 119, 186; *see also* African teachers
Thiong'o, Ngugi wa 64
Tikly, L. 15, 38, 66
top-down state-centric approaches to education 213–214
Twum-Danso, A. 115

Ubuntu 16, 21, 242; and ALPs 255; centring in education and development 242–245; community engagement and Ubuntu 247, 250; critiques of 244; implications for pedagogical practices 247–255; learning and dignity of the African child 245–247; translanguaging 248
Ukpokodu, O.N. 253
UNDP Human Development Index (UNDP) 210
UNESCO Institute of Statistics (UIS) 4, 33, 38, 49
United Nations Educational, Scientific and Cultural Organization (UNESCO) 11, 47, 48, 64, 116; Global Initiative 63; Global Monitoring Report 47

United Nations International Children's Emergency Fund (UNICEF) 11, 38, 47
United States Agency for International Development (USAID) 191
Unterhalter, E. 45, 209
The Use of Vernacular Languages in Education 63

Van Norren, D. E. 243, 250
vulnerability 16, 34, 88, 111, 151, 205, 207; community engagement 206–210; in PEGs 217–232; and resistance 16, 206–210, 217–232

Waghid, Y. 242, 249, 253
Westbrook, J. 201n1, 201n4, 233n1

Western education models: western-centric stereotypes 31; western-derived assessment practices 73
Wetherell, M. 217
Wheelahan, L. 41
World Bank 7, 11, 14, 33, 35, 37, 38, 40, 41, 43, 45, 48, 65, 80
World Education Forum 5
Wulff, A. 38

Yamada, S. 209, 234n3
Yeboah, S.A. 106
Yunus, R. 33

Zancajo, A. 43
Zipin, L. 135, 150
Zuilkowski, S. S. 86, 91

For Product Safety Concerns and Information please contact our EU representative GPSR@taylorandfrancis.com Taylor & Francis Verlag GmbH, Kaufingerstraße 24, 80331 München, Germany